Eighth Edition

Keys to Success

Carol Carter

Sarah Lyman Kravits

Peter J. Maurin

VICE PRESIDENT, EDITORIAL: Anne Williams
ACQUISITIONS EDITOR: Mark Grzeskowiak
MARKETING MANAGER: Michelle Bish
CONTENT MANAGER: John Polanszky
PROJECT MANAGER: Kimberley Blakey
CONTENT DEVELOPER: Jennifer Murray
MEDIA EDITOR: John Polanszky
MEDIA DEVELOPER: Olga Avdyeyeva
PRODUCTION SERVICES: Cenveo® Publisher Services

PHOTO PERMISSIONS RESEARCH: Integra Publishing Services, Inc.
PERMISSIONS PROJECT MANAGEMENT: Integra Publishing Services, Inc.
INTERIOR DESIGNER: Cenveo Publisher Services
COVER DESIGNER: Cenveo Publisher Services
COVER IMAGE: Key: In-Finity/Shutterstock; Phone: Maksim Kabakou/Shutterstock
VICE-PRESIDENT, CROSS MEDIA AND PUBLISHING SERVICES: Gary Bennett

Pearson Canada Inc., 26 Prince Andrew Place, North York, Ontario M3C 2H4.

9780134456607

6 2020

Library and Archives Canada Cataloguing in Publication

Carter, Carol, author
    Keys to success. Building analytical, creative and practical skills / Carol Carter, Sarah Lyman Kravits, Peter J. Maurin.—Eighth Canadian edition.

ISBN 978-0-13-445660-7

    1. College student orientation—Canada—Handbooks, manuals, etc.
2. Study skills--Handbooks, manuals, etc. 3. College students—Canada—
Life skills guides. I. Kravits, Sarah Lyman, author II. Maurin, Peter,
author III. Title. IV. Title: Building analytical, creative and practical
skills.

LB2343.34.C3C37 2017   378.1'980971   C2017-905767-7

This book is dedicated to the memory
of my parents, Peter and Blanka Maurin.
—*Peter J. Maurin*

Carol Carter has spent her entire career in the business world, where she has a track record of success in corporate America, entrepreneurship, and non-profit. Her student success work is driven by first-hand knowledge of what employers expect and demand from today's graduates. As President of LifeBound, an academic and career coaching company, she drives the company's goal to help middle school and high school students become competitive in today's world, and she teaches study, interpersonal, and career skills to students as well as training and certifying adults in academic coaching skills. Carol speaks on educational topics nationally and internationally and is an expert blogger for the Huffington Post under "Impact," "College," and "Business." Carol is a co-author on many books for Pearson including the *Keys to Success* series as well as *Keys to Business Communication* and the *Career Tool Kit*. She has also published a series of books for K-12 students through LifeBound, including *Dollars and Sense: How To Be Smart About Money* and *Majoring In the Rest of Your Life: Career Secrets for College Students*.

Sarah Kravits teaches student success at Montclair State University and has been researching and writing about student success for over 15 years. As a parent of three children (ages 14, 12, and 8), a collaborator, a co-author, and an instructor, she lives the strategies for success she writes about, striving daily for goal achievement, productive teamwork, and integrity. Sarah is a co-author on the *Keys to Success* series, including *Keys to College Success, Keys to Community College Success, Keys to College Success Compact, Keys to Effective Learning, Keys to Online Learning,* and *Keys to Success Quick*. Sarah presents workshops and trainings on student success topics such as critical thinking, risk and reward, and time management at schools all over the country. Having attended the University of Virginia as a Jefferson Scholar, she continues to manifest the Jefferson Scholars Program goals of leadership, scholarship, and citizenship with her efforts to empower college students to succeed in school and in all aspects of their lives.

Peter J. Maurin received his Masters Degree in Sociology from McMaster University in 1992, his Honours BA from Brock University in 1989, and his Diploma in Radio and Television Arts from Niagara College. He has taught at Mohawk College since 1990. He has also been an instructor at Brock University, Niagara College, and Seneca College. He is a strong advocate of blended learning and online collaboration. In 2013, Peter was honoured to receive both the Mohawk College President's Award for Excellence and the Mohawk College Award for Excellence.

Peter has been an author for Pearson Canada since 1996, co-authoring Canadian editions of both *The Media of Mass Communication* and *Keys to Success*.

In addition to his work as a freelance writer, Peter is also a broadcaster, logging over 35 years on the air for several radio stations in Ontario. He is currently the host of "Oldies Without Borders" on 101.5 The Hawk in Hamilton. It is an eclectic mix of music from all genres and interviews with singer/songwriters.

Finally, and most importantly, Peter been together since 1981 with his soul mate Kim. Together, they have two amazing children: Sonja and Josh.

BRIEF CONTENTS

CONTENTS

CHAPTER 4 ## Personality and Learning Preferences 79

Who Are You and What Makes You Unique?

CHAPTER 5   **Critical, Creative, and Practical Thinking   105**

How Can You Maximize Brain Power?

CHAPTER 8   Test Taking 195

How Can You Show What You Know?

PREFACE

IT'S NOT JUST WHAT YOU KNOW
it's what you know how to do

Keys sets the standard for connecting academic success to success beyond school, showing students how to apply strategies within post-secondary, career, and life. *Keys* retains its tried-and-true emphasis on thinking skills and problem solving, re-imagined with two goals in mind: one, a **risk and reward** framework that reflects the demands today's students face, and two, a focus on student experience specific to **institution** with a more extensive research base. The material helps students take ownership, develop academic and transferable skills, and show the results of commitment and action so they are well equipped with the concentration, commitment, focus, and persistence necessary to succeed.

NEW TO THIS
edition

Post-Secondary Connection to Career and Life Goals: infused with **risk and reward**.

- **NEW! Risk and Reward Theme.** To be rewarded with goal achievement in the fast-paced information age, students must take calculated, productive risks. The benefit of risks small (putting in the work your courses require) and large (aiming for a degree in a tough major, working toward a challenging career) is learning transferable skill building, persistence, and confidence. (Ex.—In every chapter, and in features such as the opening and closing to each chapter's case study.)
- **NEW! Inspiring, motivating case studies focused on risk and reward.** Students derive motivation from reading about how others have taken risks, gotten through struggles, overcome challenges, and earned rewards. Each chapter begins with a case study focusing on a personal challenge and details the risk taken to face and surmount it. The closing section at the end of each chapter finishes the story and shows the reward earned at that time and the rewards that the person has subsequently gained from continued risk and effort. This section also relates the story to the reader's life and challenges them to think expansively about how to make personal improvements related to the chapter. (Ex.—Beginning and end of each chapter.)

Thinking Skills Coverage:

- **NEW! Brain-based learning and metacognition.** Cites research on building intelligence, the science of learning, the changes in the brain that happen when you remember, the cost of switch-tasking, brain development in adolescence and early adulthood, and more. This information builds student metacognition. (Ex.—Throughout the book as applicable, i.e., Chapter 1 (introduction), Chapter 5 (thinking), Chapter 7 (memory).)
- **REVISED! Successful Intelligence Framework.** Builds a comprehensive set of analytical, creative, practical thinking skills to empower students to strengthen their command of the problem-solving process and take practical action. (Ex.—Introduced in Chapter 1; expounded upon in thinking chapter (Chapter 5); in-chapter exercises (*Get Analytical, Get Creative, Get Practical*).

- **REVISED! In-chapter exercises focused on analytical, creative, and practical thinking, and financial literacy.** These exercises give readers a chance to apply a chapter idea or skill to their personal needs and situations in a particular type of thinking. For example, in Chapter 2:
  - *Get Analytical* builds analytical thinking skill
  - *Get Creative* builds creative thinking skill
  - *Get Practical* builds practical thinking skill
  - Get *$mart* builds financial literacy
- **REVISED! End-of-chapter exercises, each with a distinctive practical goal,** have been re-titled and revised, targeted to develop a particular skill to have readers perform a chapter-related task that has specific personal value. For example, in Chapter 4:
  - *Know It* builds critical thinking skill
  - *Write It* builds emotional intelligence and practical writing skill
  - *Work It* builds career readiness
- **REVISED! Updated Canadian information on rewards of post-secondary education.**
  - Revised Canadian material on stress, depression, substance abuse, and anxiety among Canadian students
  - Updated section on Canadian student debt
  - Revised material on the multicultural make up of Canada
  - Several new Canadian student profiles
- **NEW! Chapter on Post-Secondary Life and Resources.** This chapter includes creating a "well-rounded" experience, accessing supportive resources, topics for students living on campus, and details about different ways to get involved and connected to campus. Coverage of teamwork and study groups is included here.

One last note: Many of our best suggestions come from you. Please contact your Pearson representative with questions or requests for resources or materials. Send suggestions for ways to improve *Keys to Success* to Carol Carter at caroljcarter@lifebound.com, Sarah Kravits at kravitss@mail.montclair.edu, or Peter J. Maurin at maurin@bell.net. We look forward to hearing from you!

STUDENT
resources
MyLab Student Success

NEW! Personalized Learning with MyLab Student Success: MyLab Student Success (www.pearson.com/mylab) is a Learning Outcomes based technology that promotes student engagement through:

- Full Course Learning Path that delivers individualized results for students to practise and master key topics and build critical thinking skills and problem-solving abilities.
- Learning Path includes the Conley Readiness Index (CRI). CRI is the only readiness inventory based on more than a decade of research analyzing the content of entry-level college courses and the opinions of thousands of secondary and postsecondary students and instructors about what it takes to succeed in college.

INSTRUCTOR
resources

Instructor's Manual This manual provides a framework of ideas and suggestions for activities, journal writing, thought-provoking situations, and online implementation including MyLab Student Success recommendations.

PowerPoint Presentation This comprehensive set of PowerPoint slides can be used by instructors for class presentations and also by students for lecture preview or review. The PowerPoint presentation includes summary slides with overview information for each chapter. These slides help students understand and review concepts within each chapter.

ACKNOWLEDGMENTS

The efforts of many have combined to make this Eighth Canadian edition, Keys to Success, more than the sum of its parts.

We would like to thank all those students across the country who helped us (and their fellow students) by providing student profiles:

Patrick Belliveau, Sheridan College
Kayla Brogan, Nova Scotia Community College
Peyton Campbell, Fleming College
Olivia Daub, University of Waterloo
Humaira Falak, Columbia College
Christian Gaumont, Sprott-Shaw Community College
Mina Huang, Wilfred Laurier University
Katie Hudgins, CDI College
Kelcy McNally, University of Prince Edward Island
Tia Nguyen, Ryerson University
Dion Redgun, CDI College
James Shields, University of King's College
Hongman Xu, Seneca College

Thanks also to our reviewers, whose comments and suggestions have helped us in the preparation of this eighth Canadian edition:

Brenda Bogardis, Georgian College
Adele Caruso, Niagara College
Shauna Longmuir, Fleming College
Tara Gauld, Confederation College
Brian Hucker, St. Clair College
Sarah Hunter, Georgian College
Alaina Roach O'Keefe, University of PEI
Angela Peterson, Algonquin College
and others who chose to remain anonymous.

Thanks to the staff at Pearson Canada:

Kimberley Veevers, executive acquisitions editor
John Polanszky, senior content manager
Jennifer Murray, content developer
Kimberley Blakey, project manager
Vastavikta Sharma, vendor project manager
and Ruth Chernia, copyeditor.

Although I am the Canadian author for this eighth Canadian edition of *Keys to Success*, the contents of this book are really the product of years of teaching (and learning) at several institutions. Thanks to my current and former students at Mohawk College and to the many former students at Brock University and Niagara College. Whether I was teaching Communications, Media Law, Career Planning, Sociology, or Popular Music and Society sociology, you always taught me something in the process. Learning is indeed a lifelong process.

I'd also like to thank all my colleagues at Mohawk College in Hamilton. We are an amazing team whose passion for teaching is second to none.

Finally, to my gifted crew at home—Kim, Sonja, and Josh: You are my "keys to success." Thanks for your love, patience, and understanding. Always remember that "I love you more."

Peter J. Maurin, M.A.

QUICK START TO POST-SECONDARY LIFE

Helpful Information and Advice As You Begin

This section contains information about what your school expects of you, to help you feel more in control as you start your journey toward the achievement of an education. When you clarify expectations right at the start, you can minimize surprises that could present obstacles later on. As you read, consult your school's handbook and/or website to learn about the specific resources, policies, and procedures of your school. Since expectations differ from school to school, use the material that follows as general guidelines.

FOLLOW PROCEDURES
and fulfill requirements

Understanding and following college procedures will smooth your path to success.

Registration

Registration most likely takes place through your school's computer network or via an automated phone system, although occasionally a school will still hold an in-person registration in a large venue such as an athletic facility or student union. Scan the school's website and consider these factors as you make your selections:

- Core/general requirements for graduation
- Your major or minor or courses in departments you are considering
- Electives that sound interesting, even if they are out of your field

Once you choose courses, but before you register, create a schedule that shows daily class times to see if the schedule will work out. Meet with your advisor for comments and approval. Some schools put a "hold" on your registration that is only lifted after you see your advisor.

Graduation and Curriculum Requirements

Every school has degree requirements stated in the catalog and website. Make sure you understand those that apply to you. Among the requirements you may encounter are:

- Number of credits needed to graduate, including credits in major and minor fields
- Curriculum requirements, including specific course requirements
- Departmental major requirements

School Procedures

Your college or university has rules and regulations, found in the school's handbook and on the website, for all students to follow. Among the most common procedures are:

Adding or dropping a class. This should be done within the first few days of the term if you find that a course is not right for you or that there are better choices for your schedule. The sooner you make adjustments, the easier it will be to catch up with any new courses you add as you finalize your schedule. Withdrawals after a predetermined date, other than those approved for special cases, receive a failing grade.

Taking an incomplete. If you can't finish your work due to circumstances beyond your control—an illness or injury, for example, or a death in the family—many colleges allow you to take a grade of Incomplete. The school will require approval from your instructor and you will have to make up the work later, usually by a predetermined date.

Transferring schools. Research the requirements of other schools and submit transfer applications. If you intend to transfer to a particular school, take the courses required for admission to that school. In addition, be sure all your credits are transferable, which means they will be counted toward your diploma or degree at the new school.

UNDERSTAND YOUR
school's grading system

When you receive grades, remember that they reflect your work, not your self-worth. Most schools use grading systems with numerical grades or equivalent letter grades (see Key QS.1). Generally, the highest course grade is an A, or 4.0, and the lowest is an F, or 0.0.

In every course, you earn a certain number of credits, called *hours*. For example, Accounting 101 may be worth three hours. These numbers generally refer to the number of hours the course meets per week. When you multiply each numerical course grade by the number of hours the course is worth, take the average of all these numbers, and divide by the total number of credit hours you are taking, you obtain your grade point average, or GPA.

Learn the minimum GPA needed to remain in good standing and to be accepted and continue in your major. Key QS.2 shows you how to calculate your GPA. You can also use web resources such as http://www.back2college.com/gpa.htm to calculate your GPA electronically.

GRADE POINT AVERAGE (GPA)

A measure of academic achievement computed by dividing the total number of grade points received by the total number of credits or hours of course work taken.

KEY QS 1 Understand letter grades and equivalent numerical grades per semester hour.

Letter grade	A	A–	B+	B	B–	C+	C	C–	D+	D	F
Numerical grade	4.0	3.7	3.3	3.0	2.7	2.3	2.0	1.7	1.3	1.0	0.0

COURSE	SEMESTER HOURS	GRADE	POINTS EARNED FOR THIS COURSE
Chemistry I	4	C (2.0 points)	4 credits × 2.0 points = 8
Communications	3	B+ (3.3 points)	3 credits × 3.3 points = 9.9
Philosophy	3	B– (2.7 points)	3 credits × 2.7 points = 8.1
Introduction to Statistics	3	C+ (2.3 points)	3 credits × 2.3 points = 6.9
Social Justice	2	A– (3.7 points)	2 credits × 3.7 points = 7.4
Total semester hours **Total grade points for semester**	**15**		**40.3**

GPA for semester (total grade points divided by semester hours): 40.3 divided by 15 = 2.69
Letter equivalent grade: C+/B–

MAKE THE MOST OF YOUR
school's computer system

A large part of post-secondary communication and work involves the computer. In a given day you might access a syllabus online, email a student, use the Internet to tap into a library database, write a draft of an assignment on a computer, and send an essay draft to an instructor electronically. Most dorm rooms are wired for computers, and an increasing number of campuses have wireless networks. Some schools are even moving to a "paperless" system where all student notifications are sent via email, requiring every student to activate an email account and check it regularly. Here are some suggestions for using your computer effectively:

- *Get started right away.* Register for an email account and connect to your school's network. In addition, register your cell phone number with the school so you can get emergency alerts.
- *Use the system.* Communicate with instructors and fellow students using email. Browse the school's LMS (Learning Management System). Search databases at the college library.
- *Save and protect your work.* Save electronic work periodically onto a hard drive, CD, flash drive, or location in the cloud. Use antivirus software if your system needs it.

One of the most important directives for students communicating via computer is to follow guidelines when contacting instructors via email. When you submit assignments, take exams, or ask questions electronically, rules of etiquette promote civility and respect. Try these suggestions the next time you email an instructor:

- *Use your college or university account.* Instructors are likely to delete unfamiliar emails from their overloaded email inboxes. "Helen_Miller@yourschool.edu" will get read, but "disastergirl@yahoo.com" may not.
- *Don't ask for information you can find on your own or bother your instructor with minor problems.* Flooding your instructor with unnecessary emails may work against you when you really need help.
- *Write a clear subject line.* State exactly what the email is about.
- *Address the instructor by name and use his or her title.* "Hello Professor Smith" or "Hi Dr. Reynolds" is better than "Hey."

- *Be clear and comprehensive.* First, state your question or problem and what you want to achieve. For example, "In my essay, I believe I covered the key points. I would like to meet to discuss your critique." Next, if necessary, support your position, using bullet points if you have a number of support statements. Finally, end by thanking the instructor and typing your full name.
- *Avoid abbreviations and acronyms.* Write as though you were crafting a business letter, not a social email to a friend.
- *Use complete sentences, correct punctuation, and capitalization.* Be sure to reread your email before sending, so that you have a chance to correct any mistakes.
- *Give the instructor time to respond.* Don't expect a reply within two hours. If you hear nothing after a couple of days, send a follow-up note that contains the full text of your first message. A note that simply says "Did you get my last email?" won't be helpful if for any reason your instructor didn't receive or read the first one.

READ AND USE
your syllabi

You will receive a syllabus for each of your courses, either online or in person at the first class meeting (or both). Each syllabus is a super-resource for that course, providing information including:

> SYLLABUS
> A comprehensive outline of course topics and assignments.

- Focus and goals of the course
- Required and optional reading, with a schedule of when that reading is covered
- Dates of quizzes and exams and due dates for assignments
- The instructor's grading system and components of your final grade
- Your instructor's policy regarding latecomers and missed class meetings
- How and when to connect with your instructor in person, by phone, or online
- Important college-wide policies such as the academic integrity policy

You might consider each syllabus as a "contract" between you and your instructor, outlining what your instructor expects of you (readings, assignments, class participation) as well as what you can expect from your instructor (availability, schedule of topics, clarification of grading system). Key QS.3 shows a portion of an actual syllabus with important items noted.

Put this super-resource to use by reading syllabi thoroughly and referring to them throughout the term. When you have a question, look for an answer in your syllabus first before you contact your instructor. Marking up your syllabus will remind you of responsibilities, as will "backdating"—noting in your written or electronic planner the interim goals to achieve by particular dates in order to complete assignments. For example, if you have a 15-page paper due on October 12, you would enter dates in September and October for goals such as choosing a topic, first draft, and final draft.

You are beginning the journey of your post-secondary education and lifelong learning. The work you do in this course will help you achieve your goals in your studies, your personal life, and your career. Psychologist Robert J. Sternberg, the originator of the successful intelligence concept discussed in *Keys to Success*, said that those who achieve success "create their own opportunities rather than let their opportunities be limited by the circumstances in which they happen to find themselves."[1] Let this book and this course help you create new and fulfilling opportunities on your path to success.

ENG 122 Spring 2007

Instructor: Jennifer Gessner
Office Hours: Tue & Thur 12:30–1:30 (or by appointment) in DC 305
Phone: 303-555-2222
E-mail: jg@abc.xyz

How to connect with the instructor

Required Texts: *Good Reasons with Contemporary Arguments,* Faigley and Selzer
A Writer's Reference, 5th ed., Diana Hacker

Required Materials:
- a notebook with lots of paper
- a folder for keeping everything from this class
- an active imagination and critical thinking

Books and materials to get ASAP

Course Description: This course focuses on argumentative writing and the researched paper. Students will practise the rhetorical art of argumentation and will gain experience in finding and incorporating researched materials into an extended paper.

Writer's Notebook: All students will keep, and bring to class, a notebook with blank paper. Throughout the semester, you will be given writing assignments to complete in this book. You must bring to class and be prepared to share any notebook assignment. Notebook assignments will be collected frequently, though sometimes randomly, and graded only for their completeness, not for spelling, etc.

Course coverage, expectations, responsibilities

Grading:
- Major Writing Assignments worth 100 points each.
- Final Research Project worth 300 points.
- Additional exercises and assignments range from 10 to 50 points each.
- Class participation: Based on the degree to which you complete the homework and present this in a thoughtful, meaningful manner in class.
- Attendance: Attendance is taken daily and students may miss up to three days of class without penalty, but will lose 5 points for each day missed thereafter.
- Late work: All work will lose 10% of earned points per class day late. No work will be accepted after five class days or the last class meeting.

How grades are determined for this course

Final Grade: The average of the total points possible (points earned divided by the total possible points). 100–90% = A; 89–80% = B; 79–70% = C (any grade below 70% is not passing for this class).

Academic Integrity: Students must credit any material used in their papers that is not their own (including direct quotes, paraphrases, figures, etc.). Failure to do so constitutes plagiarism, which is illegal, unethical, <u>always recognizable</u>, and a guaranteed way to fail a paper. The definition of plagiarism is "to steal and use (the writings or ideas of another) as one's own."

Reflects school's academic integrity policy

Week 4
2/1   The Concise Opinion.
                HW: Complete paper #1 Rough Draft (5–7 pages double-spaced)

                How Professionals Argue
                HW: Read Jenkins Essay (p 501 of *Good Reasons) and* Rafferty Essay (p 525); compare argumentative style, assess and explain efficacy of arguments.

Week 5
2/15   Developing an Argument
                Essay Quiz on Jenkins and Rafferty Essays
                HW: Chap 5 of *Good Reasons;* based on components of a definition of argument, write a brief explanation of how your argument might fit into this type.

2/17   Library Workday: Meet in Room 292
                — PAPER #1 DUE

Topic of that day's class meeting

Notice of due date for paper draft

Notice of reading assignments to complete

Notice of quiz

Notice of final due date for paper

Source: Jennifer Gessner, Community College of Denver.

Keys to Success

Courtesy of John Diaz

Approach your post-secondary journey as an optimistic learner with a growth mindset, willing to risk effort, dedication, and focus for the extraordinary rewards that education can provide.

The Rewards of Post-Secondary Education

WHAT ARE YOU WILLING TO RISK TO REACH YOUR GOALS?

What Would You Risk? *John Diaz*

THINK ABOUT THIS SITUATION AS YOU READ, AND CONSIDER WHAT ACTION YOU WOULD TAKE. THIS CHAPTER JUMP-STARTS YOUR TRANSITION WITH INFORMATION ON WHAT POST-SECONDARY EDUCATION HAS TO OFFER AND WHAT IT TAKES TO SUCCEED.

A brother to three sisters and the only son of divorced parents, John Diaz went to university aiming for a career in broadcast journalism. He started working at the school newspaper and campus radio station. He knew this didn't guarantee career success, but he felt confident in his prospects. He thrived in the close-knit environment where the professors were so engaged with the students. "It really was the right fit for me," John says.

Back then, John had low-risk ambitions—he didn't crave a wealthy lifestyle or imagine crusading for global causes through journalism. However, the reality of the job market stalled even his reasonable career goals. First of all, in the late 1970s, the Watergate scandal had boosted interest in journalism, creating, as John puts it, "a glutted market" of journalists looking for work. Second, John worked at a local truck stop to help cover expenses, so he wasn't available for internships that could have improved his job prospects.

Although discouraged by the fact that the number of journalism students exceeded the total jobs in the industry, John was ready to take a risk. He polished his résumé, created demo tapes, and sent out hundreds of job inquiries. His initial reward was exactly one positive response that turned out to be a dead end. Two months after graduating, he was working in a shoe store, wondering if any reward would come from his effort in university. "I was hoping lightning would strike," John recalls.

To be continued . . .

IN THIS TEXT, YOU WILL MEET PEOPLE LIKE JOHN WHO HAVE TAKEN RISKS THAT HELPED THEM ACHIEVE IMPORTANT GOALS. WHETHER OR NOT YOU HAVE SOMETHING IN COMMON WITH THESE PEOPLE, THEY WILL EXPAND YOUR PERSPECTIVE AND INSPIRE YOU TO MOVE AHEAD ON YOUR OWN PATH. YOU'LL LEARN MORE ABOUT JOHN, AND THE REWARD RESULTING FROM HIS ACTIONS, WITHIN THIS CHAPTER.

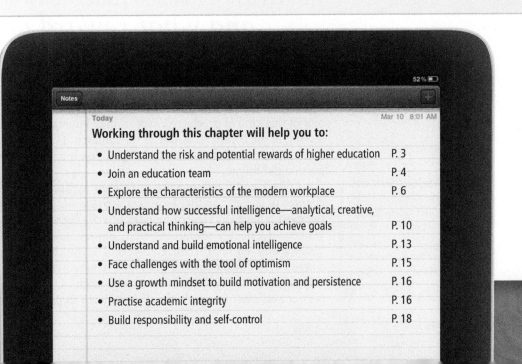

Today   Mar 10 8:01 AM

Working through this chapter will help you to:

- Understand the risk and potential rewards of higher education   P. 3
- Join an education team   P. 4
- Explore the characteristics of the modern workplace   P. 6
- Understand how successful intelligence—analytical, creative, and practical thinking—can help you achieve goals   P. 10
- Understand and build emotional intelligence   P. 13
- Face challenges with the tool of optimism   P. 15
- Use a growth mindset to build motivation and persistence   P. 16
- Practise academic integrity   P. 16
- Build responsibility and self-control   P. 18

status CHECK

Left to Right: Luis Santos/Shutterstock; Antonio Guillem/Shutterstock; antoniodiaz/Shutterstock; mimagephotography/Shutterstock; Djomas/Shutterstock; WAYHOME studio/Shutterstock

How Ready Are You to Risk Effort for the Rewards of Post-Secondary Education?

For each statement, fill in the number that best describes how often it applies to you.

1 = never   2 = seldom   3 = sometimes   4 = often   5 = always

1. I look forward to challenging tasks and situations.	① ② ③ ④ ⑤
2. I feel ready to handle post-secondary–level work.	① ② ③ ④ ⑤
3. I am prepared to work hard in classes both within and outside my major.	① ② ③ ④ ⑤
4. I am willing to seek help and cooperate with others as I pursue my degree.	① ② ③ ④ ⑤
5. I am aware of what it takes to succeed in today's technology-driven, ever-changing workplace.	① ② ③ ④ ⑤
6. I believe my intelligence can increase as a result of my efforts.	① ② ③ ④ ⑤
7. I am willing to believe that effort and focus are more essential to success than ability or talent.	① ② ③ ④ ⑤
8. I am able to accurately perceive my own emotions, as well as those of others.	① ② ③ ④ ⑤
9. I can explain the reward of acting with academic integrity.	① ② ③ ④ ⑤
10. I am able to disconnect from electronic distractions to focus on coursework.	① ② ③ ④ ⑤

Each of the topics in these statements is covered in this chapter. Note those statements for which you filled in a 3 or lower. Skim the chapter to see where those topics appear, and pay special attention to them as you read, learn, and apply new strategies.

REMEMBER: NO MATTER HOW PREPARED YOU ARE TO SUCCEED IN UNIVERSITY OR COLLEGE, YOU CAN IMPROVE WITH EFFORT AND PRACTICE.

WHY IS POST-SECONDARY EDUCATION A RISK,
and what reward does it offer?

MyLab Student Success
(www.mystudentsuccesslab.com) is an online solution designed to help you "Start Strong, Finish Stronger" by building skills for ongoing personal and professional development.

Think about the word *risk*. What, specifically, comes to mind? There are two different ways to think about risk. One involves risky behaviour—impulsive decisions made with little or no forethought—such as substance abuse, unsafe sex, or breaking the law. The other concept is one of deliberate risk calculated to bring reward. Examples of this kind of productive risk include buying shares of stock in a new company or serving in the combat division of the military. This is the concept of risk that will take focus in this text—the one that will give you the power to achieve the rewards that are meaningful to you.

College and university are often seen as risk-free, safe choices that increase your chances of career stability. However, striving for a degree in higher education is one of the most potentially rewarding risks of your lifetime. To follow this path, you will risk your most valuable resources—time, money, and yourself. You will dedicate time to learning and self-improvement. You, and anyone helping to finance your education, will commit a significant amount of money. You will sign up for years of responsibilities and challenges to both your mind and your body. Obtaining your degree or diploma is a perfect example of a targeted risk, calculated to produce reward down the line.

Well then, why take calculated risks? Why not save your money, time, and effort? Because only with productive risk-taking (not risky behaviour) come the rewards essential to your success. Skills, intelligence, motivation, employment, growth, and advancement can be yours, but only as a result of hard work, dedication, and focus.

The Value of Risk in the Modern World

You are beginning your post-secondary experience in a time marked by rapid change that presents both opportunity and crisis. For example:

- Many formerly domestic jobs have moved overseas.
- Graduates now compete with and work with people who live in different time zones, speak different languages, and have different perspectives.
- Civic unrest is growing around the world. With the "Occupy" movement of late 2011, for example, people pushed back against a tough economic climate.
- Global media, communication technology, and transportation methods enable exposure to different people, places, values, cultures, beliefs, and perspectives.
- Technological development continues at an ever-faster pace, demanding constant learning and training.

Even as university or college are risks, they offer you the training, habit of learning, and comfort with risk-taking that you need to survive in this environment. Post-secondary education also improves your earning power. Post-secondary graduates still earn more than those with just a high school diploma. Money isn't everything, but that amount can make a significant difference in your ability to pay loans, manage costs, and provide stability. Increased income is just one reward that makes post-secondary education worth the risk. There are many more.

The Rewards of Higher Education

You are aware of the risk you face. What rewards await you? As one of over two million Canadian college and university students, you are an investor who has purchased three to four years of citizenship in a post-secondary community, with access to everything it has to offer. As such, you seek a rewarding return on the risk of that investment. Think about the following rewards as you choose how to spend your valuable time and energy. Your college or university website, student handbook, and course catalog will have specifics appropriate to your school.

Skills specific to academic subjects, career paths, or nonacademic areas

Nearly all students choose a major and take a series of courses focused on areas relevant to that major. For some professions (medical doctors, lawyers), further graduate study is required. For other career areas, graduate-level study may or may not be beneficial. For example, some economics majors may want to continue on and obtain a Master of Business Administration (MBA), while others may go directly into the workforce. Some students dive into their careers even before graduating by volunteering or getting internships.

Higher education also gives you a chance to build skills outside of your academic pursuits, as John did when he worked with the newspaper and radio station. Are you a performer? You may be able to audition for plays or find opportunities to sing. Are you into politics? Political clubs, as well as school government, may give you a chance to shine and to grow.

A liberal arts education

Going back to the earliest days of education in this country, one of the focuses of post-secondary education has been to give students a liberal arts education. In fact, the concept of a liberal arts education has its roots far in the past. Educators during the

LIBERAL ARTS EDUCATION
Comprehensive instruction in a variety of areas essential to being a well-rounded citizen.

3

Roman Empire in the fifth century c.e. defined the liberal arts as those areas in which a "free" person (as opposed to a slave) needed to develop. Thus the term *liberal*, which comes from the Latin *liber,* meaning free.

Opportunities to grow as a social being

Effective human interaction is an essential life skill. In school, at work, or in your personal life, you connect with people in some way every day. If you do it well, you will be able to accomplish your most important goals more easily. If you don't, your progress may be limited.

You are building social skills and self-knowledge as you negotiate with a roommate over storage space, get to know new friends and stay connected with old ones, develop relationships with instructors and advisors, play collegiate or intramural sports, hang out between classes, and go to formal or impromptu social events. Later in this chapter, you will read more about how your emotional intelligence will help you handle social situations effectively.

Support in your times of academic, physical, or emotional need

While a wonderful opportunity, college or university is also a time of challenge and stress for most students. A 2011 study found that just over 50% of students labelled their emotional health as "above average," down from 55.3% in 2009 and 63.6% in 1985. Much of this drop can be attributed to high levels of stress.[1]

When you are struggling physically or emotionally, you may experience difficulty thinking and managing your studies. Knowing this, schools provide support services to help students manage their health and find a balance. Take advantage of services that support physical wellness (athletic facilities and clubs), physical and emotional health (student health and counselling services), and academic progress (tutors and academic centres).

Chances to expand your horizons

As a citizen of a global community, your ability to interact productively with people demands an understanding of other cultures and perspectives. A post-secondary education can help you expand your horizons.

GLOBAL COMMUNITY People and other living things in all nations worldwide, dependent on one another and connected through modern electronic communication systems.[2]

Most colleges and universities offer opportunities to study abroad for a full term, or a shorter period of time, at schools in other countries where they have partnerships. Some schools sponsor travel opportunities for students either over holiday breaks or in conjunction with specific courses. Universities and colleges also provide less costly ways to "travel" through clubs and programs that introduce you to people, arts, and food from cultures other than your own.

Opportunities to give back to those around you

One of the best ways to develop valuable skills, both transferable and task specific, is through giving to others. See if your college or university has an office that coordinates volunteer opportunities. It might also offer particular courses with a service-learning component—courses that have specific service to an organization built into the curriculum that is required as part of the course. In this type of course, the curriculum is designed to prepare students for the service project, and the service project aims to improve the students' understanding and mastery of the course material.

The reward you earn depends on the risk you take. If you engage fully with your educational team and actively pursue opportunities, you are likely to find that you can make the most out of your money and time—perhaps more than you ever imagined.

You Have Joined an Education Team

No student faces the risk of post-secondary education alone. You lead a team with a single, focused goal: producing a graduate ready to contribute in the workplace and make the most of life. Everyone on the team has responsibilities. For example, your school and instructors are responsible for providing learning opportunities, guidance, and resources. As the student, you are responsible for taking advantage of those opportunities, choosing and using resources, and working hard.

Following are some essential strategies for effective teamwork. They are as necessary now, for working with others in school, as they will be in your career.

Defined responsibilities. The tasks necessary to move your team ahead are divided among team members. Key 1.1 lists responsibilities involved in graduating successfully.

Agreement on a goal and a plan. All team members need to be aware of the goal and plan, and they must be ready to adjust if goals or plans change. For example, you may have a goal of majoring in engineering, but you could end up

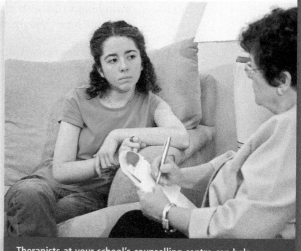

Therapists at your school's counselling centre can help you manage a variety of personal challenges.

KEY 1.1   Everyone on your educational team has responsibilities.

TEAM MEMBERS	RESPONSIBILITIES
You, the student  Lightpoet/Fotolia	• Define personal academic goals • With guidance, plan out coursework and major • Attend class on time, consistently, and with necessary supplies • Complete readings, assignments, and projects • Independently manage your time and schedule • Interact respectfully with peers and faculty • Pay bills (tuition, room, board) on time
Instructors Lisa F. Young/Fotolia	• Provide a detailed syllabus to students • Teach material as outlined on the syllabus • Be on time and prepared for class meetings • Be available to consult with students • Evaluate students fairly and respectfully • Motivate students to learn
Advisors Alexander Raths/Fotolia	• Meet with students regularly (usually once per term at minimum) • Assist students in mapping out a plan for majoring and coursework • Help students who want to change majors • Assist with student conflicts and issues
School (administration and employees) Cfarmer/Fotolia	• Maintain safe, clean, and functional school buildings and property • Provide needed coursework and skilled instructors • Provide for nonacademic student needs (physical and mental health services, social opportunities, career counselling, and so on)
Family Xixinxing/Fotolia	• Emotional support • Often, financial support

switching majors, or changing schools due to an emergency. It is your responsibility to keep the team informed, updated, and involved.

Communication. Communicate with team members regularly. Every syllabus will have your instructor's available office hours and contact information. Take advantage of those hours to ask specific questions about coursework or just to get to know your instructors better. Contact your advisor more than just once a term. Set up a communication plan with your family so you feel supported but not overwhelmed by texts and emails. Contact your dean or other administrators if there is a problem they can help you solve.

Collaboration. No student ever gets to the finish line alone. Although you will be the one holding the diploma or degree, many team members will be able to share in your victory. Your instructors, advisors, and administrators really want you to succeed—especially in a climate in which many post-secondary students won't graduate on time.

Conflict management. Issues may arise with other students, an instructor, or others with whom you interact regularly. Don't let your educational team fall apart over a conflict. Address the conflict directly or bring in another team member—an advisor, dean, or resident advisor (RA)—to help. Get the problem on the table and work through it so you can refocus your energy on your goals.

No matter your path—becoming a journalist like John Diaz, starting a nonprofit, joining a traditional for-profit company, or any other professional or personal quest—you can use your post-secondary experience to shape a productive and satisfying life. The spirit of risk with which you approach education, learn from others, and honour and develop your personal qualities will reward you with a full life in this rich, diverse, and often challenging world.

WHAT DOES THE
workplace demand of you?

You will be entering (or may have already entered) the workplace during a time of great economic challenge. As of June 2016, the Canadian unemployment rate was 6.8%, with 1.3 million unemployed workers. As indicated in Key 1.2, statistics show that completing some level of post-secondary education increases your chances of finding and

KEY 1.2 Education and income.

Statistics Canada compared the annual incomes of high school grads with college and university grads between 1991 and 2010. Their study, "An Investment of a Lifetime? The Long-Term Labour Market Premiums Associated with a Postsecondary Education," suggests that the more education you have, the more likely you are to make more money. For example, during that 20-year time frame:

- Men with a high school diploma: $975,000
- Men with a college diploma: $1,222,000
- Men with a university degree: $1,707,000

Meanwhile:

- Women with a high school diploma: $525,000
- Women with a college diploma: $704,000
- Women with a university degree: $973,000

In addition to better income, the study also says that individuals with post-secondary education were also less likely to be laid off.

Source: Statistics Canada, The Long Term Labour Market Premiums Associated with a Postsecondary Education. Reproduced and distributed on an "as is" basis with the permission of Statistics Canada.

keeping a highly skilled, well-paying job. According to Human Resources and Skills Development Canada, "the benefits of learning and higher education levels include higher earnings and lower unemployment risks, both of which contribute to individuals' and families' financial security."[3] In simple terms, this means not only more money per week, but also the ability to save more money and generate more retirement income.

Statistics Canada compared the annual incomes of high school grads with college and university grads between 1991 and 2010. Their study, "An Investment of a Lifetime? The Long-Term Labour Market Premiums Associated with a Postsecondary Education," suggests that the more education you have, the more likely you are to make more money. In addition to better income, the Statistics Canada study also says individuals with post-secondary education were also less likely to be laid off.[4] Education is linked with many benefits in Canada.

Although this is likely one of your first courses, it can lay the foundation for career exploration and workplace skill development. You will learn to distinguish yourself in a global marketplace, in which North American workers often compete with workers from other countries. Thomas Friedman, author of *The World Is Flat*, explains how the digital revolution has transformed the working environment you will enter after your post-secondary education:

DIGITAL REVOLUTION
The change in how people communicate brought on by developments in computer systems.

> It is now possible for more people than ever to collaborate and compete in real time with more other people on more different kinds of work from more different corners of the planet and on a more equal footing than in any previous time in the history of the world—using computers, email, networks, teleconferencing, and dynamic new software.[5]

What Jobs and Employers Require

As industry has given way to technology, more and more jobs demand knowledge work. Today's employers also report that transferable skills—skills applicable to any work or life situation—are what they need most in their employees. Workers who change jobs frequently may find that transferable skills are more important for employability than job-specific skills.

KNOWLEDGE WORK
Work that is primarily concerned with information rather than manual labour.

Taking a careful look at what the current workplace demands of workers and what it rewards, education and business leaders have founded an organization called the Partnership for 21st Century Skills. Together, these leaders developed the Framework for 21st Century Learning shown in Key 1.3, delineating the categories of knowledge and skills that successful workers need to acquire.

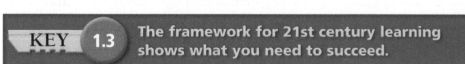

KEY 1.3   The framework for 21st century learning shows what you need to succeed.

CORE SUBJECTS AND 21ST CENTURY THEMES	LEARNING AND INNOVATION SKILLS
• Global Awareness • Financial, Economic, Business, and Entrepreneurial Literacy • Civic Literacy—Community Service • Health Literacy	• Creativity and Innovation • Critical Thinking and Problem Solving • Communication and Collaboration
INFORMATION, MEDIA, AND TECHNOLOGY SKILLS	**LIFE AND CAREER SKILLS**
• Information Literacy • Media Literacy • ICT (Information, Communications, and Technology) Literacy	• Flexibility and Adaptability • Initiative and Self-Direction • Social and Cross-Cultural Skills • Productivity and Accountability • Leadership and Responsibility

Source: Adapted from Partnership for 21st Century Skills Framework, www.p21.org/index.php?option=comcontent&task=view&id=254&Itemid=120.

get $mart

ORGANIZE YOUR FINANCES

Creativenv/Shutterstock

Avoid that situation when, buried in mid-term work, you realize that you haven't touched that stack of bills, statements, and receipts in a couple of months. Set yourself up to stay aware and in control of your day-to-day financial activities. Perform the following actions:

1. Find a place to store financial paperwork, perhaps a file drawer or filing box, and set up folders for each category (bank statements, tuition/financial aid, paid bills, and so on).
2. If you want to pay some or all of your bills online, set up online payments with those accounts. If you have the ability to choose due dates, cluster your due dates together at the same time of the month so you can pay bills all at once.
3. Make sure that you are set up to stay on top of tuition payments and financial aid responsibilities. Note payment or financial aid filing deadlines in your planner, phone calendar, or online calendar. Consider setting smartphone reminders and alarms.

Looking at this framework, you will see that success in today's workplace requires more than just knowing skills specific to an academic area or job. Author Daniel Pink argues that the ability to create, interact interpersonally, generate ideas, and lead diverse teams—skills all found in the Framework for 21st Century Learning—will be more and more important in the workplace. Because coursework traditionally focuses more on logical and analytical skills, building your interpersonal and creative skill set will require personal initiative from you. Often, these skills can be developed through in-class collaboration and teamwork as well as volunteer work, internships, and jobs.[6]

This text will frequently refer to the Employability Skills 2000+ Profile developed by The Conference Board of Canada. It is a research organization whose members include Canadian corporations and the government. "Employability Skills" are defined as "the skills you need to enter, stay in and progress in the world of work—whether you want to work on your own or as part of a team."[7]

Many Canadian companies helped to determine which skills were essential. These were broken down into three categories: fundamental skills, personal management skills, and teamwork skills (see Table 1.1). This text will put skills learned in the classroom into the broader context of developing your employability skills.

These themes are also reflected by the CMEC (Council of Ministers of Education, Canada), a think tank of ministers of education from Canada's provinces and territories. In *Learn Canada 2020*, it states that there is a "direct link between a well-educated population and . . . a vibrant, knowledge-based economy in the 21st century, . . . a socially progressive, sustainable society, and . . . enhanced personal growth opportunities for all Canadians."[8]

College and University Build Your Transferable Skills

Graduating with a well-rounded educational base, in addition to your major concentration, will build your employability. If you put effort into your studies, you can develop transferable skills in every course you take. You can solve problems in math as well as in sociology; build a strong work ethic in a Spanish course as well as in

TABLE 1.1 Employability Skills 2000+

The skills you need to enter, stay in, and progress in the world of work—whether you work on your own or as a part of a team.

These skills can also be applied and used beyond the workplace in a range of daily activities.

Fundamental Skills	Personal Management Skills	Teamwork Skills
The skills needed as a base for further development	The personal skills, attitudes, and behaviours that drive one's potential for growth	The skills and attributes needed to contribute productively

You will be better prepared to progress in the world of work when you can:

Communicate
- read and understand information presented in a variety of forms (e. g., words, graphs, charts, diagrams)
- write and speak so others pay attention and understand
- listen and ask questions to understand and appreciate the points of view of others
- share information using a range of information and communications technologies (e. g., voice, email, computers)
- use relevant scientific, technological, and mathematical knowledge and skills to explain or clarify ideas

Manage Information
- locate, gather, and organize information using appropriate technology and information systems
- access, analyze, and apply knowledge and skills from various disciplines (e. g., the arts, languages, science, technology, mathematics, social sciences, and the humanities)

Use Numbers
- decide what needs to be measured or calculated
- observe and record data using appropriate methods, tools, and technology
- make estimates and verify calculations

Think & Solve Problems
- assess situations and identify problems
- seek different points of view and evaluate them based on facts
- recognize the human, interpersonal, technical, scientific, and mathematical dimensions of a problem
- identify the root cause of a problem
- be creative and innovative in exploring possible solutions
- readily use science, technology, and mathematics as ways to think, gain, and share knowledge; solve problems; and make decisions
- evaluate solutions to make recommendations or decisions
- implement solutions
- check to see if a solution works, and act on opportunities for improvement

You will be able to offer yourself greater possibilities for achievement when you can:

Demonstrate Positive Attitudes & Behaviours
- feel good about yourself and be confident
- deal with people, problems, and situations with honesty, integrity, and personal ethics
- recognize your own and other people's good efforts
- take care of your personal health
- show interest, initiative, and effort

Be Responsible
- set goals and priorities balancing work and personal life
- plan and manage time, money, and other resources to achieve goals
- assess, weigh, and manage risk
- be accountable for your actions and the actions of your group
- be socially responsible and contribute to your community

Be Adaptable
- work independently or as a part of a team
- carry out multiple tasks or projects
- be innovative and resourceful: identify and suggest alternative ways to achieve goals and get the job done
- be open and respond constructively to change
- learn from your mistakes and accept feedback
- cope with uncertainty

Learn Continuously
- be willing to learn and grow continuously
- assess personal strengths and areas for development
- set your own learning goals
- identify and access learning sources and opportunities
- plan for and achieve your learning goals

Work Safely
- be aware of personal and group health and safety practices and procedures, and act in accordance with these

You will be better prepared to add value to the outcomes of a task, project, or team when you can:

Work with Others
- understand and work within the dynamics of a group
- ensure that a team's purpose and objectives are clear
- be flexible: respect and be open to and supportive of the thoughts, opinions, and contributions of others in a group
- recognize and respect people's diversity, individual differences, and perspectives
- accept and provide feedback in a constructive and considerate manner
- contribute to a team by sharing information and expertise
- lead or support when appropriate, motivating a group for high performance
- understand the role of conflict in a group to reach solutions
- manage and resolve conflict when appropriate

Participate in Projects & Tasks
- plan, design, or carry out a project or task from start to finish with well-defined objectives and outcomes
- develop a plan, seek feedback, test, revise, and implement
- work to agreed quality standards and specifications
- select and use appropriate tools and technology for a task or project
- adapt to changing requirements and information
- continuously monitor the success of a project or task and identify ways to improve

255 Smyth Road, Ottawa
ON K1H 8M7 Canada
Tel. (613) 526-3280
Fax (613) 526-4857
Internet: www.conferenceboard.ca/nbec

Source: Conference Board of Canada, Employability Skills 2000+, in www.conferenceboard.ca/education/learning-tools/esp2000.pdf.

The Rewards of Post-Secondary Education

biochemistry; develop verbal communication skills by speaking up in accounting class as well as in any of your electives. Even your leisure time can be productive. If you take the risk to participate in activities, you will build communication, teamwork, and problem-solving skills, just to name a few.

While you're a post-secondary student, you can also prepare to seek and secure full-time employment. According to a 2011 study of post-secondary graduates, many graduates specifically indicated they wished they had started their job search earlier (26%), spent more time networking (29%), and applied for more jobs prior to graduation (26%).[9] To earn greater rewards and have fewer regrets, take these three risks during your post-secondary school years.

Challenging times have occurred in the past and there will be additional challenging times in the future. The more willing you are to grow and to put yourself on the line in these times, the greater your chances of finding reliable work, staying employed, and earning a living.

Now consider a set of thinking skills that will be your essential risk-taking tools as you build on your abilities and talents in your quest for employability and personal satisfaction.

HOW CAN SUCCESSFUL INTELLIGENCE
help you achieve your goals?

For centuries, thinkers and educators have tangled with questions about human achievement: What helps a person succeed? Why do some people succeed while others fail? What helps a person overcome a failure and persist? Not so long ago, the prevailing wisdom centred on the idea that people are born with a fixed level of intelligence that is measurable with an intelligence quotient (IQ) test. This theory didn't do much to promote motivation; after all, why work hard if you cannot override the destiny set by your IQ?

Cutting-edge researchers have effectively challenged this theory.[10] When test anxiety caused Robert Sternberg (a psychologist known for his work on intelligence and creativity) to score poorly on IQ and other standardized tests during elementary school, he delivered what was expected of him—very little. However, his fourth-grade teacher turned his life around when she expected more. Sternberg has conducted extensive

Courtesy of John Diaz

talk risk and reward . . .

Risk asking tough questions to be rewarded with new insights. Use the following questions to inspire discussion with classmates, either in person or online.

- When you are faced with a challenge, what is your *modus operandi*—your habitual reaction to it? Do you risk dealing with it, run in the other direction, ignore it and hope it goes away? What tends to result from your action (or inaction)?

- What do you think about the "double whammy" of the high cost of post-secondary education and the difficult job market? In your opinion, what actions and/or resources should students use to handle the situation?

CONSIDER THE CASE: Right after graduation, John Diaz wasn't sure that university had given him what he needed to succeed in the workplace. What reward do you need from your years in post-secondary education? As a student, what risks are you willing to take to become more employable?

research showing that traditional intelligence measurements lock people into poor performance and often do not reflect their potential.[11]

Researching how children cope with failure, Stanford psychologist Carol Dweck gave elementary school students a set of puzzles that grew increasingly difficult. To her surprise, certain students welcomed failure as an opportunity. "They knew that human qualities, such as intellectual skills, could be cultivated through effort. . . . Not only weren't they discouraged by failure, they didn't even think they were failing. They thought they were learning."[12] Dweck's research since then has focused on the idea that mindset sets the stage for intellectual growth.

Sternberg's, Dweck's, and others' research suggests that intelligence is *not* fixed; people have the capacity to increase intelligence. In other words, the risk of effort and focus can produce the reward of greater brain power. Studies in neuroscience show that a learning brain can develop throughout life. Recent research shows that when you learn, your brain and nerve cells (neurons) form new connections (synapses) among one another by growing new branches (dendrites).[13] These increased connections then enable the brain to do and learn more.

The Three Thinking Skills

How can you take productive risks that move you toward your important goals in college or university, work, and life? According to Sternberg, it takes three types of thinking: analytical (critical), creative, and practical. Together, he calls them *successful intelligence*,[14] a concept that he illustrates with a story of a book-smart boy and a street-smart boy running from a bear in the forest. While the book-smart boy is figuring out the exact amount of time they have before being attacked, the street-smart boy puts on his running shoes and dashes off, having realized that he only needed to outrun the first boy in order to survive.[15]

This story shows that successful goal achievement and problem solving require more than book smarts. When confronted with a problem, using *only* analytical thinking put the first boy at a disadvantage. On the other hand, the second boy *analyzed* the situation, *created* options, and took practical *action*. He took the wisest risk and earned his reward: living to tell the tale.

Stephen Coburn/Fotolia

How Thinking Skills Move You toward Your Goals

Sternberg explains that although those who score well on tests display strong recall and analytical skills, they are not necessarily able to put their knowledge to work.[16] No matter how high you score on a library science test, for example, as a librarian you will also need to devise useful keyword searches (creative thinking) and communicate with patrons (practical thinking). Of course, having only practical "street smarts" isn't enough either. Neither boy in the bear story, if rushed to the hospital with injuries sustained in a showdown with the bear, would want to be treated by medical personnel lacking in analytical skills.

What does each of the three thinking skills contribute to goal achievement?

- Commonly known as *critical thinking*, analytical thinking starts with engaging with information through asking questions and then involves analyzing and evaluating information, often to work through a problem or decision. It often involves comparing, contrasting, and cause-and-effect thinking.
- Creative thinking involves generating new and different ideas and approaches to solving problems, and, often, viewing the world in ways that disregard convention. It can involve imagining and considering different perspectives. Creative thinking also means taking information that you already know and thinking about it in a new way.

get analytical

Darren Baker/
Shutterstock

DEFINE YOUR "POST-SECONDARY SELF"

Dario Sabljak/Shutterstock

Complete the following on paper or in digital format.

When you understand who you are as a student, you will be more able to seek out the support that will propel you toward your goals. Using the following questions as a starting point, analyze and describe your "post-secondary self." Write and save your description to revisit later in the course.

■ What is your student status—traditional or returning, full- or part-time, resident or commuter?

■ How long are you planning to be at your current school? Have you transferred in, or is it likely that you will transfer in the future?

■ What goals or rewards do you aim to achieve by attending post-secondary school?

■ What family and work obligations do you have?

■ What is your culture, ethnicity, gender, age, lifestyle?

■ What are your biggest fears right now, and how do they affect your willingness to take risks?

■ What challenges (physical or learning disabilities, emotional issues, language struggles) do you face?

■ Has your family attended post-secondary school for generations, or are you a first-generation student?

■ What do you like to study, and why does it interest you?

■ Practical thinking refers to putting what you've learned into action to solve a problem or make a decision. Practical thinking often means learning from experience and emotional intelligence (explained later in the chapter), enabling you to work effectively with others and to accomplish goals despite obstacles.

Together, these abilities move you toward a goal, as Sternberg explains:

> Analytical thinking is required to solve problems and to judge the quality of ideas. Creative intelligence is required to formulate good problems and ideas in the first place. Practical intelligence is needed to use the ideas and their analysis in an effective way in everyday life.[17]

The following example illustrates how this works.

How the thinking skills of John Diaz helped him move toward a personal goal.

■ He *analyzed* his abilities and ambitions, taking a challenging workplace situation into account as he determined what he was willing to risk and what reward he sought.

■ He *created* an effective résumé and demo tape, as well as a plan to implement an extensive job search strategy.

■ He took *practical action* and risked sending his materials to hundreds of employers.

Why is developing successful intelligence so important to your success?

1. *It improves understanding and achievement, increasing your value in school and on the job.* People with critical, creative, and practical thinking skills are in demand because they can apply what they know to new situations, be innovative, and accomplish their goals.

2. *It boosts your motivation.* Because it helps you understand how learning propels you toward goals and gives you ways to move toward those goals, it increases your willingness to risk.

3. *It shows you where you can grow.* Students who have trouble with analytical skills can see the role that creative and practical thinking play. Students who test well but have trouble innovating or taking action can improve creative and practical skills.

WHY DO YOU NEED *emotional intelligence?*

Success in a diverse world depends on relationships, and effective relationships demand emotional intelligence. Psychologists John Mayer, Peter Salovey, and David Caruso define *emotional intelligence* (EI) as the ability to understand "one's own and others' emotions and the ability to use this information as a guide to thinking and behavior."[18] An emotionally intelligent person uses an understanding of emotions to make choices about how to think and how to act.

Modern neuroscience holds that thought and emotion function together in the brain and depend on one another. One particular research project showed that brain-injured patients who cannot perceive their own feelings experience severe difficulty in thinking, highlighting the importance of emotion.[19] "Emotions influence both what we think about and how we think," says Caruso. "We cannot check our emotions at the door because emotions and thought are linked—they cannot, and should not, be separated."[20]

Emotions also connect you to other people. Research has demonstrated that the brain and nervous system have cells called (mirror neurons). When a friend of yours is happy, sad, or fearful, you may experience similar feelings out of concern or friendship. An MRI brain scan would show that the same area of your friend's brain that lit up during this emotional experience lit up in your brain as well.[21]

MIRROR NEURONS Specialized brain cells that fire both when a person performs an action and when that person watches someone else perform an action.

How Emotional Intelligence Benefits You

Two short stories illustrate the power of emotional intelligence.

1. Two applicants are competing for a job at your office. The first has every skill the job requires, but doesn't respond well to cues when you interview him. He answers questions indirectly and keeps going back to what he wants to say. The second isn't as skilled, but you feel during the interview as though you are talking with a friend. He listens carefully, picks up on emotional cues, and communicates a strong willingness to learn on the job. Whom would you hire?

2. Two students are part of your group for a project. One always gets her share of the job done but has no patience for anyone who misses a deadline. She is quick to criticize group members. The other is sometimes prepared, sometimes not, but responds thoughtfully to what is going on with the group. She makes up for it when she hasn't gotten everything done, and when she is on top of her tasks she helps others. Whom would you work with again?

To be clear: Skills are crucial. However, emotional intelligence in communication and relationships is a necessary component of success along with job-specific skills.

PORTRAIT IMAGES ASIA BY NONWARIT/Shutterstock

Emotional intelligence helps you build positive and productive relationships in and out of school.

get practical

Diego Cervo/Shutterstock

USE EMOTIONAL INTELLIGENCE TO GET INVOLVED

binkski/123RF

Complete the following on paper or in digital format.

First, look in your student handbook at the resources and organizations your school offers. These may include some or all of the following:

Academic centres (reading, writing, and so on)

Academic organizations	Religious organizations
Adult education centre	School publications
Arts clubs (music, drama, dance, and so on)	School TV/radio stations
Fraternities/Sororities	Sports clubs
Groups for students with disabilities	Student associations
International student groups	Student government
Minority student groups	Volunteer groups
On-campus work opportunities	

As you read the list, take note of how different organizations or activities make you feel. What interests you right away? What makes you turn the page? What scares you? What thoughts do your feelings raise—for example, why do you think you like or fear a particular activity? Is a positive outcome possible from trying something that scares you at first?

After thinking about this emotional intelligence feedback as well as your self-analysis from other exercises, risk trying some new experiences. List three offices or organizations you plan to explore this term. Then, using school publications or online resources, find and record the following information for each:

- Location
- Hours, or times of meetings
- What it offers
- Phone number, website, or email

Finally, when you have made contact, note what happened and whether you are considering getting involved.

Research using an assessment measuring emotional intelligence (MSCEIT) shows how strongly it predicts work and life success:[22]

- Emotionally intelligent people are more competent in social situations.
- Managers in the workplace with high emotional intelligence have more productive working relationships.
- Employees scoring high in emotional intelligence were more likely to receive positive ratings and raises.

The bottom line is that more emotional intelligence means stronger relationships and better goal achievement.

The Abilities of Emotional Intelligence

Emotional intelligence is a set of skills, or abilities, that can be described as *reasoning with emotion* (an idea illustrating how thought and emotion work together). Key 1.4 shows how you move through these skills when you reason with emotion.

KEY 1.4 Take an emotionally intelligent approach.

PERCEIVING EMOTIONS

Recognizing how you and others feel

THINKING ABOUT EMOTIONS

Seeing what thoughts arise from the feelings you perceive, and how they affect your mindset

UNDERSTANDING EMOTIONS

Determining what the emotions involved in a situation tell you, and considering how you can adjust your mindset or direct thinking in a productive way

MANAGING EMOTIONS

Using what you learn from your emotions and those of others to choose behaviour and actions that move you toward positive outcomes

Source: Adapted from Mayer, John D., Peter Salovey, and David R. Caruso, "Emotional Intelligence: New Ability or Eclectic Traits?" *American Psychologist,* vol. 63, no. 6, pp. 505–507. September 2008.

As you encounter references to emotional intelligence in this course and elsewhere, think of it as thinking skills applied to relationships. Putting emotional intelligence to work means taking in and analyzing how you and others feel, seeing the ideas those feelings create, and taking action in response—all with the purpose of achieving a goal.

WHAT CHARACTERISTICS
promote success?

Several particular characteristics have been connected to success. As one example, a *New York Times* article entitled "What If the Secret to Success Is Failure?" details the experience of David Levin, the head of KIPP, a middle school filled with students who have scored high on achievement tests. After 10 years of following students' progress, Levin found that only 33 percent went on to graduate from four-year institutions. A closer examination of these most successful students showed that they demonstrated characteristics such as optimism, persistence, and self-control.[23]

Put the following characteristics to work now. They will help you take productive risks that have more chance to reward you with success than any test score or transcript grade.

Learned Optimism

Psychology professor Dr. Martin Seligman developed the theory of *learned optimism,* which evolved from his study of how individuals react to adversity—the inevitable setbacks and failures that everyone experiences in life. His research illustrates how optimistic and pessimistic world views affect the ability to persist and succeed:[24]

- Reactions to bad things follow the ABCs: **A**dversity happens, and your thoughts about it create **B**eliefs, which give rise to **C**onsequences—what you feel and do as a result.

- People with a pessimistic world view believe that bad things are permanent (everlasting), personal (caused by their own action or inaction), and pervasive (affecting all corners of their lives). As a result, they feel helpless and unwilling to take risks.

- People with an optimistic world view believe that bad things are temporary (will eventually end), external (caused by something outside of themselves), and specific (only affecting one corner of their lives). As a result, they feel empowered and ready to take risks.

Research has demonstrated that optimism leads to greater achievement and persistence. John Diaz benefited from an optimistic world view when he headed into a challenging job market after graduation. So, what if you have a pessimistic world view? Seligman argues that anyone can use optimism as a tool. He names *disputation* as a key strategy to building optimism. Three ways to dispute, or argue with, a negative belief are as follows:

- *Evidence to the contrary.* Name evidence that contradicts your belief.
- *Alternatives.* Think about less negative or destructive possible causes of the situation.
- *Usefulness.* Consider whether your belief is useful or damaging.

Key 1.5 presents examples of how to dispute belief productively.

Growth Mindset

All individuals have their own unique set of **motivators.** Motivators can be positive or negative, such as personal achievement, financial gain, fear of parental disapproval, the threat of failure, a desire to impress someone, and much more. Motivators can also be external or internal. If you are motivated by external factors (your parents, circumstances, luck, grades, instructors' feedback, and so on), you have an external locus of control. If you are motivated by internal factors (values and attitudes), you have an internal locus of control.

MOTIVATORS
Ideas or goals that move a person to action.

Most people experience external and internal factors in combination. However, if you are more often motivated by internal factors, Carol Dweck's research indicates that you are likely to experience greater success. Why? Because you cannot control the external factors. The only things you can control are the internal factors, such as your attitude or mindset. Through her work, Dweck developed the idea of a *growth mindset—* the perception that talent and intelligence can develop with effort—and she established that this mindset promotes persistence toward goals as well as successful goal achievement. "This view creates a love of learning and resilience that is essential for great accomplishment," says Dweck.[25]

According to Dweck, people demonstrating a *fixed mindset* believe that they were born with an unchangeable level of talent and intelligence. Because of this view, they tend to work and risk less. Like Seligman, Dweck is focused on the ability to adjust attitude. As she puts it, "You have a choice. . . . Mindsets are just beliefs. They're powerful beliefs, but they're just something in your mind, and you can change your mind."[26] Combine her work with Seligman's, and you have a solid case for the value of effort, optimism, and persistence.

ACADEMIC INTEGRITY
Following a code of moral values in all aspects of academic life, such as classes, assignments, tests, papers, projects, and relationships with students and faculty.

Academic Integrity

Each action you take in school has an effect that shapes your immediate experience and perhaps your life. Having **academic integrity** means taking actions based on ethics

KEY 1.5	Increase optimism by building an argument against negative beliefs.	
	ADVERSITY: RECEIVING A D ON A MID-TERM	**ADVERSITY: LOSING TOUCH WITH SOMEONE**
Negative belief	Tests are a disaster for me.	I am a horrible friend.
Evidence to the contrary	I did fine on my other mid-terms. I did okay on the first test for this course.	I have many other friends. I talk to them, see them, and help them out however I can.
Alternatives	Perhaps I didn't prioritize this mid-term over others. Maybe I need better study techniques.	Maybe she is just overwhelmed and busy. Perhaps she lost my cell phone number.
Usefulness	Not useful—it may dissuade me from putting in my best effort with future tests.	Not useful—it may lead me to shut myself off from friends.

(your sense of what is right to do) and the value of hard work. The International Center for Academic Integrity (ICAI) defines academic integrity as a commitment to five fundamental values:[27]

- *Honesty*. Honesty defines the pursuit of knowledge and implies a search for truth in your classwork, papers, lab reports, and your teamwork with other students.
- *Trust*. Trust means being true to your word. Mutual trust—between instructor and student, as well as among students—makes the exchange of ideas possible.
- *Fairness*. Instructors must create a fair academic environment where students are judged against clear standards and in which procedures are well defined.
- *Respect*. In a respectful academic environment, both students and instructors accept and honour a wide range of opinions, even if the opinions are contrary to core beliefs.
- *Responsibility*. You are responsible for making choices that will provide you with the best education—choices that reflect fairness and honesty.

Students are not the only ones who need to act with integrity. Bill Taylor, emeritus professor of political science at Oakton Community College, wrote a letter to his students explaining that academic integrity makes requirements of both students and instructors. For example, while students need to come to class on time and prepared to contribute, instructors need to arrive on time prepared to teach; while students need to hand in their own work, instructors need to give relevant assignments and grade fairly.[28]

Violations of academic integrity include turning in previously submitted work, using unauthorized devices during an exam, providing unethical aid to another student, and downloading passages or papers from the internet. Consequences of violations vary from school to school and include academic integrity seminars, grade reduction or course failure, suspension, or expulsion.

When you enrolled, you agreed to abide by your school's academic integrity policy. Find it in your student handbook, school website, or syllabus, and read it thoroughly so you know exactly what it asks of you. Measure the consequences of violating the policy against the risk of working hard to complete your degree with integrity. Which reward would you choose?

It may seem that a slip here and there is no big deal. However, as Professor Taylor states in his letter, "Personal integrity is . . . a quality of character we need to nurture, and this requires practice in both meanings of that word (as in practice the piano and practice a profession). We can only be a person of integrity if we practice it every day."[29] Finally, know that a growth mindset can help. Because academic integrity comes naturally to students who see struggle and failure as opportunities to learn, maintaining a growth mindset promotes academic integrity and makes its rewards more obvious (see Key 1.6).

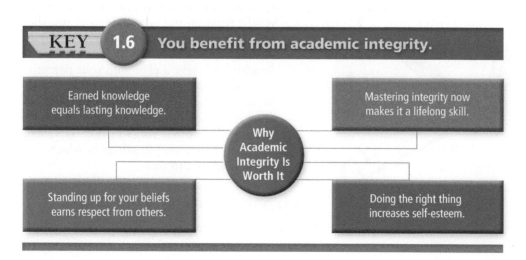

KEY 1.6 You benefit from academic integrity.

Earned knowledge equals lasting knowledge.

Mastering integrity now makes it a lifelong skill.

Why Academic Integrity Is Worth It

Standing up for your beliefs earns respect from others.

Doing the right thing increases self-esteem.

get creative

ARGUE YOUR WAY TO OPTIMISM

Complete the following on paper or in digital format.

Name two bad things, major or minor, that have happened to you recently and produced negative beliefs. With Key 1.5 as your guide, note the following for each of the two adversities:

- Negative belief produced
- Evidence to the contrary
- Alternatives
- Usefulness of the belief

Finally, describe whether any changes in your beliefs took place as a result of thinking through the situations in this way.

Self-Sufficiency

Many students have a "helicopter parent" (one who hovers over and monitors a child) or a "Velcro parent" (one who is constantly calling, texting, or emailing, unable to unhook). Despite loving intentions, both types of interaction can hamper a child's ability to function independently. This can have negative repercussions for adult life, where children need to make their own way through the minefield of life's challenges and adversities.

Starting your post-secondary studies is an ideal time to learn how to advocate for yourself in pursuit of the reward of independence and confidence. When you are tired, overwhelmed, struggling with coursework or a personal relationship, butting heads with an instructor, or forgetting due dates for tests or assignments, you are now your own first line of defence.

When a problem appears, take the risk and ask an instructor, advisor, counsellor, dean, RA, or friend for help. The reward is the ability to benefit from resources around you, one that you will use throughout your life as you encounter workplace and personal problems. In addition, make a plan with your parent(s) or guardian(s) that allows you to build independence, learn from your mistakes, and feel deserved pride in your accomplishments. Consider how often you will text, talk, and email, and define the situations in which you will you reach out to them.

Responsibility and Planning

Research shows that today's students put in an average of less than 15 hours of study time a week, compared

Dbarby/Fotolia

student PROFILE

Humaira Falak

COLUMBIA COLLEGE
CALGARY, ALBERTA

About me:

I am currently doing a diploma in human services. I have always been a passionate person in everything I do. I could never choose a career that is incompatible with my personality and interests. I have my degree in English literature from Lahore, Pakistan. When I came to Canada destiny brought me into contact with social workers and non-profit organizations. It was after they helped us that I suddenly realized that this is what I really want to do. It was only in the worst circumstances of my life that I discovered my best possible self.

What I focus on:

Despite being a single parent, I motivate myself to do best. I am obsessively passionate about my career and kids. I try to complete all my tasks on time and stay focused. Despite all the obstacles, I have a positive outlook toward life and I am fully determined to make the best out of everything. I strongly make use of my personality to keep me going against all odds and to help me adjust in a different working environment. As I want to become a human-rights activist in the future, I have developed a well-planned strategy to achieve my goals. The strategy helps in keeping me focused and move systematically toward attaining my goal within the set timeframe.

What will help me in the work place?

I guess my passion and dedication will help me in the future. Since I have chosen a career based on my strengths and interests, I am hopeful that I would be able to work to the best of my abilities and enjoy it as well. I strongly believe that the job never becomes boring or monotonous if we choose to do what we actually love doing.

The Rewards of Post-Secondary Education

to the nearly 25 hours of studying per week by students in 1961. This drop of more than 10 hours is likely a factor behind faltering graduation rates, as well as reason for the growing ranks of students taking more time to complete their degrees than they would like.[30]

There is simply no shortcut to learning. Your academic success is tied to how much time you spend studying and working on assignments. For every hour you spend in an in-person or online class, you need to put in two to three hours of studying per week. By these calculations, a student taking 12 credit hours would need to study 24 to 36 hours a week outside of class. If that seems like a lot, consider your former high school schedule: Most high school students are in school seven hours a day, five days a week, totaling 35 hours. Add a couple of hours of homework per night, including one weekend night, and you have 47 total hours—right in the ballpark of the 36 to 48 hours you need to spend in class and studying for a 12-credit college course load.

Schedule study time as you would class time or time on the job. Consider fitting it in throughout the day, between classes or during breaks, rather than all at once. Making it a top priority is a reasonable risk that will earn you enormous reward.

Self-Control

You live in a world of abundant choice: hundreds of courses, multiple majors, hundreds of television channels, millions of websites, multiple ways to order a coffee, thousands of food products. With increased choices comes more of an opportunity to get exactly what you want. However, there is also a price to pay.

Recent research indicates that making decision after decision takes a toll on your judgment and your ability to maintain your willpower in the face of temptation. When your brain begins to feel "decision fatigue," you are more likely to act impulsively or make no choice at all. Both of these situations can be highly problematic when you are trying to exercise self-control as a newly independent post-secondary student.[31]

Set yourself up to avoid the constant decision making that can sap your willpower and self-control. One researcher notes that successful people "establish habits that eliminate the mental effort of making choices. Instead of deciding every morning whether or not to force themselves to exercise, they set up regular appointments to work out with a friend."[32] They also are likely to schedule "tech breaks"—specific times when they allow themselves to surf the internet or check Facebook—during study or work time, rather than leaving the decision open about when to visit social networking sites.

Risk-Taking

You will find threaded through this text the concept of targeted, productive risk leading to a desired reward. In everything you approach at school a reward waits in exchange for your risk. Here are just a few examples of how to take action, earn rewards, and build your risk-taking habit for career and life success:

- Risk looking confused by asking a question in class or in an online class forum, for the reward of greater understanding.
- Risk the time it takes to match or exceed your abilities on a project, for the reward of increased knowledge and skill (and perhaps an excellent grade).
- Risk the awkwardness of reaching out to an instructor, for the reward of a relationship that can deepen your academic experience and perhaps provide career guidance.
- Risk the work required to prepare for a test rather than cheating, for the reward of learning you can use in higher-level courses or in the workplace, as well as the habit of integrity, which is essential for life success.
- Risk saying no to a substance or activity for the reward of greater health, even if it costs you a friend or an affiliation.

As psychologist Angela Duckworth says, "Learning is hard. True, learning is fun, exhilarating and gratifying—but it is also often daunting, exhausting and sometimes discouraging."[33] If you accept this from the start, you will have the best chance to approach your post-secondary journey as an optimistic learner with a growth mindset, willing to risk effort, exhaustion, and sometimes discouragement for the extraordinary rewards that education can provide.

revisit RISK AND REWARD

Courtesy of John Diaz

What happened to John? Finally, lightning struck—the tiny *Red Bluff Daily News* in Northern California needed a sports editor, and John took the job. After two years of a heavy workload and low pay, his risk paid off with a gig as a Washington, DC, correspondent for Red Bluff's parent company. He drove 5200 km across the country, arriving in DC on a winter night. "I remember looking at the Capitol and just being filled with amazement that I'm there," he says, "but also filled with determination and the resolve to make it work."

After four years covering Washington politics and a stint in the *Denver Post* newsroom, John returned to the Bay Area. He worked as assistant city editor at the *San Francisco Chronicle,* one of the nation's most esteemed daily newspapers. He was promoted to East Bay bureau chief and, in 1996, to a prominent role as editor of the editorial page. Although he and his staff have earned many awards, John is prouder of the legislative, social, and cultural progress inspired by the *Chronicle*'s editorials. The National Association of Hispanic Journalists honoured him in 2008 for opinion columns on topics including immigration and the terrorism "watch list."

What does this mean for you? John has endured changes, including the upheaval of the print industry in the new digital era. His ability to take risks and work hard has brought him enormous rewards. Honoured to be asked to address the graduates at his university's 2010 commencement ceremony, John said: "Some of you, perhaps most of you, before your careers are finished, will find yourselves in jobs that do not exist today. . . . Embrace change, be an agent of change, but recognize its limitations. Hold on to your values."

Think of how the world has changed since you began high school. Name a change you have embraced successfully, and one that has proven more challenging for you. Now consider what your world might be like 10 years from now. Identify three skills you have now that will help you weather the changes ahead.

What risk may bring reward beyond your world? The work that John and his staff do has helped revamp a flawed California foster-care system, overthrow an unethical district attorney, and trigger legislation to protect financial privacy for bank customers. "That is what we should be doing as journalists," John says, "giving voice to people who otherwise don't have the clout to lobby for themselves." Read one day's set of editorials on the *Chronicle*'s opinion page (find them at **www.sfgate.com**—click on "Index," and then under the "Sections" heading, click on "Opinion"). Then do the same on your local paper's online editorial page. Thinking about a local issue, consider what rewarding change you might work to make happen. Then write a compelling letter to the editor. Take the risk to send it in and see what far-reaching positive effects your words might have.

GLOBAL RISK AND REWARD

Irina Dmitrienko/Alamy Stock Photo

jannoon028/ Shutterstock

Looking for a low-cost, energy-saving transportation option in Montreal, and capitalizing on the widespread use of bicycles there, city transportation officials developed the BIXI bicycle sharing system. BIXI—a combination of BIcycle and taXI—provides bicycles for rent at stations all over the city. Users pay at a kiosk, unlock a bike, use it for up to 24 hours, and then return it at any BIXI station. BIXI bikers travel at low cost, release no toxins into the environment, and get great exercise to boot.[34]

RISK ACTION
FOR POST-SECONDARY, CAREER, AND LIFE REWARDS

KNOW IT
Blan-k/Shutterstock

WRITE IT
Blan-k/Shutterstock

WORK IT
Blan-k/Shutterstock

Left to Right: pio3/Shutterstock;
Viktor Gladkov/123RF;
MP_P/Shutterstock

Complete the following on paper or in digital format.

KNOW IT *Think Critically*

Activate Yourself

Robert Sternberg found that people who reach their goals successfully have 20 particular characteristics in common that motivate them to persist.[35] Each of the "I" statements in the list below identifies one of the characteristics.

Build basic skills. Use this self-assessment to see how well you think you can get motivated *right now*.

1	2	3	4	5
Not at All Like Me	Somewhat Unlike Me	Not Sure	Somewhat Like Me	Definitely Like Me

Please circle the number that best represents your answer:

1. I motivate myself well. 1 2 3 4 5
2. I can control my impulses. 1 2 3 4 5
3. I know when to persevere and when to change gears. 1 2 3 4 5
4. I make the most of what I do well. 1 2 3 4 5
5. I can successfully translate my ideas into action. 1 2 3 4 5
6. I can focus effectively on my goal. 1 2 3 4 5
7. I complete tasks and have good follow-through. 1 2 3 4 5
8. I initiate action—I move people and projects ahead. 1 2 3 4 5
9. I have the courage to risk failure. 1 2 3 4 5
10. I avoid procrastination. 1 2 3 4 5
11. I accept responsibility when I make a mistake. 1 2 3 4 5
12. I don't waste time feeling sorry for myself. 1 2 3 4 5
13. I independently take responsibility for tasks. 1 2 3 4 5
14. I work hard to overcome personal difficulties. 1 2 3 4 5
15. I create an environment that helps me concentrate on my goals. 1 2 3 4 5
16. I don't take on too much work or too little. 1 2 3 4 5

17. I can delay gratification to receive the benefits.   1 2 3 4 5
18. I can see both the big picture and the details in a situation.   1 2 3 4 5
19. I am able to maintain confidence in myself.   1 2 3 4 5
20. I can balance analytical, creative, and practical thinking skills.   1 2 3 4 5

Take it to the next level. Choose three characteristics you most want to develop throughout the term. Circle or highlight them on the self-assessment. Then, pretend to be an instructor recommending you for a job. On a separate sheet of paper or digital file, write a short email about the ways in which you display strength in those three characteristics. Set a goal to deserve those compliments in the future.

Move toward mastery. Select one of your three chosen characteristics. Then do the following:

1. Find material in your text that will help you develop this characteristic. If you wish to procrastinate less, for example, look for information on time management.
2. Skim the section you find and note a concept or strategy that catches your attention. Copy it onto paper or into an electronic file. Briefly describe how you plan to use it.
3. Take action in the next week based on your plan. You are on the road to growth.

In your course, you may have the opportunity to revisit this self-assessment and get more specific about actions you have taken, and plan to take, to promote personal growth.

WRITE IT *Communicate*

Emotional intelligence journal: Examine your readiness for success. Look at the characteristics of success starting on page 15—academic integrity, self-sufficiency, responsibility and planning, and self-control. Identify which is the most challenging for you. Describe the challenge—its causes, its effects on you, and how it makes you feel. Include ideas about what you can do to face the challenge, and how you feel when you think about taking those actions.

Real-life writing: Connect with your team. Compose an email to your advisor, your dean, and your instructors for the term. Your goal: to introduce yourself and inform them of your academic and personal goals for the term. Limit yourself to two paragraphs. Demonstrate your knowledge of email etiquette by using appropriate grammar, titles for your recipients, and acceptable greetings and signatures, as well as avoiding abbreviations. If and when you send it, your email may begin a relationship from which you can benefit as the term progresses.

WORK IT *Build Your Brand*

Assess Your Successful Intelligence. A "brand" is an image or concept that people connect with a product or service. A key factor in your ability to succeed in the modern workplace is your ability to "build your brand." Identify the qualities and skills that best define you, and emphasize them in how you market yourself. Seeing yourself as a product can help you work to package that product in the best possible way.

Compiling a portfolio of personal documents can help you build your brand as you work toward career exploration and planning goals. This is one of several that you may create throughout the term. Type your work and save the documents electronically in one file folder. Use loose paper for assignments that ask you to draw or make collages, and make copies of assignments that ask you to write in the text. For safekeeping, scan and save loose or text pages to include in your portfolio file.

As you begin this course, use this exercise to get a big-picture look at how you perceive yourself as an analytical, creative, and practical thinker. For the statements in each of the three-self-assessments, circle the number that best describes how often it applies to you.

Assess Your Analytical Thinking Skills

FOR EACH STATEMENT, CIRCLE THE NUMBER THAT FEELS RIGHT TO YOU, FROM 1 FOR "NOT AT ALL TRUE FOR ME" TO 5 FOR "VERY TRUE FOR ME."

1. I recognize and define problems effectively. 1 2 3 4 5
2. I see myself as a thinker and as analytical and studious. 1 2 3 4 5
3. When working on a problem in a group setting, I like to break down the problem into its components and evaluate them. 1 2 3 4 5
4. I need to see convincing evidence before accepting information as fact. 1 2 3 4 5
5. I weigh the pros and cons of plans and ideas before taking action. 1 2 3 4 5
6. I tend to make connections among bits of information by categorizing them. 1 2 3 4 5
7. Impulsive, spontaneous decision making worries me. 1 2 3 4 5
8. I like to analyze causes and effects when making a decision. 1 2 3 4 5
9. I monitor my progress toward goals. 1 2 3 4 5
10. Once I reach a goal, I evaluate the process to see how effective it was. 1 2 3 4 5

Total your answers here: _____

Assess Your Creative Thinking Skills

FOR EACH STATEMENT, CIRCLE THE NUMBER THAT FEELS RIGHT TO YOU, FROM 1 FOR "NOT AT ALL TRUE FOR ME" TO 5 FOR "VERY TRUE FOR ME."

1. I tend to question rules and regulations. 1 2 3 4 5
2. I see myself as unique, full of ideas, and innovative. 1 2 3 4 5
3. When working on a problem in a group setting, I generate a lot of ideas. 1 2 3 4 5
4. I am energized when I have a brand-new experience. 1 2 3 4 5
5. If you say something is too risky, I'm ready to give it a shot. 1 2 3 4 5
6. I often wonder if there is a different way to do or see something. 1 2 3 4 5
7. Too much routine in my work or schedule drains my energy. 1 2 3 4 5
8. I tend to see connections among ideas that others do not. 1 2 3 4 5
9. I feel comfortable allowing myself to make mistakes as I test out ideas. 1 2 3 4 5
10. I'm willing to champion an idea even when others disagree with me. 1 2 3 4 5

Total your answers here: _____

Assess Your Practical Thinking Skills

FOR EACH STATEMENT, CIRCLE THE NUMBER THAT FEELS RIGHT TO YOU, FROM 1 FOR "NOT AT ALL TRUE FOR ME" TO 5 FOR "VERY TRUE FOR ME."

1. I can find a way around any obstacle. 1 2 3 4 5
2. I see myself as a doer and the go-to person; I make things happen. 1 2 3 4 5
3. When working on a problem in a group setting, I like to figure out who will do what and when it should be done. 1 2 3 4 5
4. I apply what I learn from experience to improve my response to similar situations. 1 2 3 4 5
5. I finish what I start and don't leave loose ends hanging. 1 2 3 4 5
6. I note my emotions about academic and social situations and use what they tell me to move toward a goal. 1 2 3 4 5
7. I can sense how people feel and use that knowledge to interact with others effectively. 1 2 3 4 5
8. I manage my time effectively. 1 2 3 4 5
9. I adjust to the teaching styles of my instructors and the communication styles of my peers. 1 2 3 4 5
10. When involved in a problem-solving process, I can shift gears as needed. 1 2 3 4 5

Total your answers here: _____

With your scores in hand, use the Wheel of Successful Intelligence to look at all of the skills at once. In each of the three areas of the wheel, draw a curved line approximately at the level of the number of your score and fill in the wedge below that line. What does the wheel show about the balance you perceive in your three thinking skills? If it were a real wheel, would it roll?

Based on the appearance of the wheel, in which skill do you most need to build strength? Keep this goal in mind as you proceed through the term.

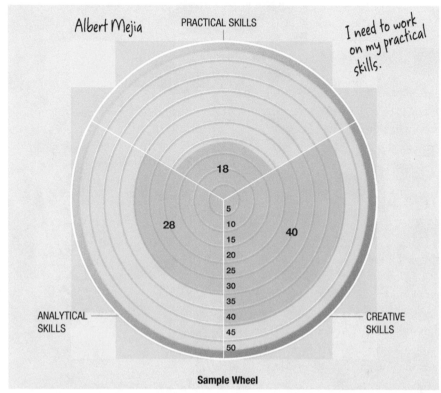

Sample Wheel

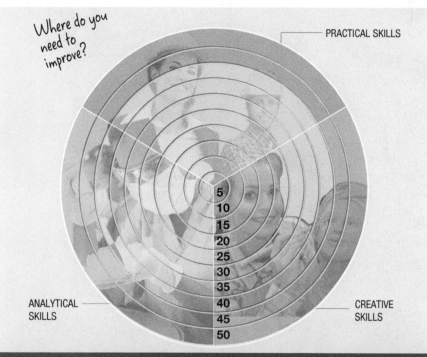

Wheel of Successful Intelligence
Source: Based on "The Wheel of Life" model developed by the Coaches Training Institute.
© Co-Active Space 2000.

2

Courtesy of Woody Roseland

Task management is stress management. Every goal-setting and time-management strategy you use contributes to your ability to cope with stress.

Goals, Time, and Stress Management

WHAT TRADE-OFFS ARE YOU WILLING TO MAKE?

What Would You Risk? *Woody Roseland*

THINK ABOUT THIS SITUATION AS YOU READ, AND CONSIDER WHAT ACTION YOU WOULD TAKE. THIS CHAPTER TAKES A CLOSER LOOK AT YOUR PERSONAL VALUES, THE GOALS YOU SET REFLECTING THOSE VALUES, AND HOW YOU MANAGE YOUR TIME AND STRESS TO ACHIEVE THOSE IMPORTANT GOALS.

A typical teenager, Woody Roseland grew up with two older brothers and a younger sister. Academics were not his focus and it showed at school, where he was not a great student. However, during grade 11, something happened that changed his perspective on everything and upended his value system.

Training for his high school football team, he felt a pain in his left leg, a pain that wouldn't go away. At first they thought that it was a knee ligament, but as the pain persisted, ultimately he learned that there was a malignant tumour in his left leg bone. He had osteosarcoma (bone cancer) at the age of 16.

Woody was thrown immediately into the world of a cancer patient, swirling with tests, doctors' appointments, and serious and detailed conversations about medical options and decisions. His first limb-salvaging procedure was a knee replacement, which doctors were hoping would remove the tumour and eliminate the cancer. Unfortunately this was not the end of the story. He needed chemotherapy, which he finished during grade 12.

Right after Woody started college the cancer recurred, and was found in Woody's lungs. He endured a gruelling series of chemotherapy treatments and lung surgery, only to have it come back again—four times—with four more courses of chemo and surgery. Then he began experiencing leg pain once again. A new and large cancerous tumour, 10 cm in length, was found in his leg. This presented an unwelcome challenge for Woody, his family, and his medical team. Every choice involved a high level of risk. Which would provide the greatest reward—the best chance at achieving the goal of keeping Woody alive and healthy?

To be continued . . .

CHANGE AND UNEXPECTED CHALLENGES CAN CALL YOUR VALUES INTO QUESTION. RESPONDING WITH FLEXIBILITY IN WHAT YOU VALUE CAN BRING YOU CLOSER TO A PRODUCTIVE, MEANINGFUL LIFE. YOU'LL LEARN MORE ABOUT WOODY, AND THE REWARD RESULTING FROM HIS ACTIONS, WITHIN THE CHAPTER.

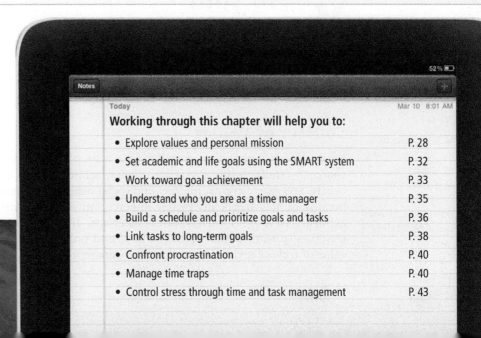

Notes

Today   Mar 10   8:01 AM

Working through this chapter will help you to:

status CHECK

Left to Right: Luis Santos/Shutterstock; Antonio Guillem/Shutterstock; antoniodiaz/Shutterstock; mimagephotography/Shutterstock; Djomas/Shutterstock; WAYHOME studio/Shutterstock

How Developed Are Your Self-Management Skills?

For each statement, fill in the number that feels right to you, from 1 for "not at all true for me" to 5 for "very true for me."

1. I am aware of my values and beliefs. ① ② ③ ④ ⑤

2. I have a system for reminding myself of what my goals are. ① ② ③ ④ ⑤

3. I find ways to motivate myself when I am working toward a goal. ① ② ③ ④ ⑤

4. When I set a long-term goal, I break it down into a series of short-term goals. ① ② ③ ④ ⑤

5. I am aware of my time-related needs and preferences. ① ② ③ ④ ⑤

6. I know how to use the SMART system to plan achievable goals. ① ② ③ ④ ⑤

7. I record tasks, events, and responsibilities in a planner and refer to it regularly. ① ② ③ ④ ⑤

8. Knowing how technology can act as a time trap, I manage my technology use. ① ② ③ ④ ⑤

9. When I procrastinate, I know how to get back on track. ① ② ③ ④ ⑤

10. I understand the hazards of multitasking and work to minimize it. ① ② ③ ④ ⑤

Each of the topics in these statements is covered in this chapter. Note those statements for which you filled in a 3 or lower. Skim the chapter to see where those topics appear, and pay special attention to them as you read, learn, and apply new strategies.

REMEMBER: NO MATTER HOW EFFECTIVELY YOU SET GOALS AND MANAGE TIME AND STRESS, YOU CAN IMPROVE WITH EFFORT AND PRACTICE.

WHAT IS IMPORTANT
to you?

VALUES ←
Principles or qualities that you consider important.

You make life choices—what to do, what to believe, what to buy, how and with whom to spend your time—based on your personal values. The choice to pursue a degree, for example, may reflect how you value the personal growth that comes from post-secondary education. If you pay credit card bills on time and work to keep your balance low, you may value financial stability.

Sources of Values

Your value system is complex, built piece by piece over time. It comes from many sources—family, friends, culture, media, school, work, neighbourhood, religious beliefs, and world events. Internet and social media are strong influences, in large part because of how frequently people interact with them. Positive effects of that include exposure to a great variety of perspectives, cultures, and ideas. Negative effects include exposure to destructive values, and potentially building an overdeveloped value of technology that can hamper in-person interaction.

MyLab Student Success
(www.mystudentsuccesslab.com) is an online solution designed to help you "Start Strong, Finish Stronger" by building skills for ongoing personal and professional development.

No matter how strong your influences, you have the power to choose what you value. Evaluate any value before you make it your own. Ask questions such as:

- What is the source of this value? Is it from the outside, or did I choose it on my own?
- What might happen if I adopt this value?
- Do my life goals and day-to-day actions reflect this value?
- What other, different value could I consider? What effects would it have on me?

Values often shift as you grow. A major life change can be a catalyst for reevaluation, making you step back and think about what's truly important to you. Woody's story is a perfect example of how a major upheaval can alter what you value and where you choose to focus your time and energy.

Expressing Values in Your Choices

Because what you value often determines the choices you make, your values also shape your life experiences. For example, colleges and universities have increasingly diverse student populations, a diversity that is often reflected in the workplace as well. If you value human differences, pursuing friendships with students from other cultures will prepare you to interact productively with diverse coworkers.

Interestingly, recent surveys indicate that many post-secondary students, especially men, value self-esteem more than money, friends, food, alcohol, and sex. For women, self-esteem rated equally high as money and friends.[1] Valuing self-esteem highly may stem from the idea that you need a strong sense of self-esteem to take action toward your goals. However, the reverse is true. Taking responsible action builds self-esteem because it gives you something to be proud of. Woody took action in response to his illness, and the self-esteem he earned empowered him toward achievements he couldn't have imagined.

SELF-ESTEEM Belief in your value as a person that builds as you achieve your goals.

HOW CAN YOU SET AND
achieve productive goals?

When you set a goal, you focus on what you want to achieve and then create a path to it. Goals exist in both long-term and short-term time frames. Long-term goals are broader objectives you want to achieve over a long period of time, perhaps a year or more. Short-term goals are smaller steps that move you toward a long-term goal, making it achievable piece by piece (see Key 2.1). Being able to "set goals and priorities balancing work and personal life" is one of the Personal Management Skills that make up the Conference Board of Canada's Employability Skills 2000+.[2]

GOAL An end toward which you direct your efforts.

Take Charge of Your Goals

Before college or university, most students have received a significant amount of guidance from parents, teachers, and other adults. Think about your life up until now: How much setting and pursuing of goals did you do on your own, and how much did you do because you "had to?" Chances are you spent most of your time fulfilling directives others laid out for you.

Transitioning to college or university involves increasing your command of the goal-setting and achievement processes, requiring you to take risks in ways that you may not be accustomed to. This includes making your own choices about what trade-offs, or sacrifices, you are willing to make to get where you want to go. Of course many students will still involve family members in determining big-picture goals, and instructors and advisors will define goals for coursework and majors. However, no one

get analytical

Darren Baker/
Shutterstock

EXPLORE YOUR VALUES

Dario Sabljak/Shutterstock

Rate each of the values in the list on a scale from 1 to 5, 1 being least important to you and 5 being most important. Write each rating next to the corresponding value.

Knowing myself	Being liked by others	Reading
Self-improvement	Taking risks	Time to myself
Improving physical/mental health	Time for fun/relaxation	Lifelong learning
Leadership and teamwork skills	Staying fit through exercise	Competing and winning
Pursuing an education	Spiritual/religious life	Making a lot of money
Good relationships with family	Community involvement	Creative/artistic pursuits
Helping others	Keeping up with the news	Getting a good job
Being organized	Financial stability	Other _____

Complete the following on a sheet of paper or digital file.

1. Write your top three values.

2. Choose one top value that is a factor in an educational choice you have made. Explain the choice and how the value was involved. Example: A student who values financial stability chooses to take a personal finance course.

3. Name an area of study that you think would help you live according to this value.

KEY **2.1** **Goals reinforce one another.**

Long-term		Earn a degree	
Yearlong	Declare major		Pass classes
Semester	Explore career areas	Work with study groups	Be in class and on time
One Month	Meet with academic advisor	Plan group meetings	Cut down on late-night socializing
This Week	Call advisor to set up appointment	Call friends from class about getting a group together	Study weeknights and go out on Friday nights

will set up the steps from start to finish and walk you through them. That's your responsibility now.

Defining your *personal mission*—a "longest-term goal" within which all post-secondary learning and life goals fit—will help you define a big-picture view of what you want. Personal development expert Steve Pavlina recommends that college students ask themselves: "Why am I going to college?" If your honest answer is something along the lines of "because it was expected," determining what you want may require some digging. "What are you there to learn? What do you want to experience?" asks Pavlina. If you can imagine your ideal post-secondary experience, he notes, you are "pre-programming yourself to succeed."[3]

Your personal mission can be spelled out in a *mission statement*, defined by Dr. Stephen Covey as a philosophy outlining what you want to be (character), the rewards you aim for (contributions and achievements), and the principles by which you live (your values).[4] For example, this mission statement was written by *Keys to Success* author Carol Carter:

> My mission is to use my talents and abilities to help people of all ages, stages, backgrounds, and economic levels achieve their human potential through fully developing their minds and their talents. I aim to create opportunities for others through work, service, and family. I also aim to balance work with people in my life, understanding that my family and friends are a priority above all else.

Think of your mission as a road map for your personal journey. It can give meaning to your daily activities, promote responsibility, and encourage you to take risks that lead you toward the long-term rewards you've laid out. In the Get Creative exercise and at the end of this chapter, you will explore your college or university experience and personal mission. Keep both flexible and open to revision so that they can change over time as you do.

Looking Short Term and Long Term

Long-term goals, such as earning a degree or having a particular career, outline the rewards you want in a way that reflects who you are and what you value. Defining such rewards in terms of the risks needed to achieve them—in other words, the steps that will take you toward them—makes them more achievable. For example, suppose your long-term goal is to become a family doctor and expose young people in your community to the medical field. Two years away from university graduation, you might prepare to move toward this reward with these one-year, long-term goals:

- Investigate medical practices in the area that could serve as a model for my practice.
- Research medical schools for application next year.

To determine long-term goals, consider the values that anchor your personal mission. For example, if you value health and fitness, possible long-term goals include working for an organic food company or training as a physical therapist. The stronger the link between your values and long-term goals, the more motivated and successful you are likely to be in achieving them.

Short-term goals narrow your focus and encourage progress toward long-term goals. They can last for as long

Kzenon/Shutterstock

Achieving academic goals requires focus. It helps to find a place to work that has the materials and technology you need and offers minimal distractions.

as several months or as little as an hour. For example, if you have a long-term goal of getting a nursing degree, you might set these short-term goals for the next six months:

- I will learn the names, locations, and functions of every human bone and muscle.
- I will work with a study group to understand the muscular-skeletal system.

You can break down these goals into even smaller parts, such as the following one-month goals:

- I will use on-screen tutorials of the muscular-skeletal system to memorize the material.
- I will spend three hours a week with my study partners.

To support your goal of regularly meeting with your study partners, you might set the following short-term goals:

- *By the end of today.* Text or email my study partners to ask them when they can meet.
- *One week from now.* Schedule each of our weekly meetings for this month.
- *Two weeks from now.* Hold our first meeting.
- *Three weeks from now.* Type and distribute notes; have second meeting.

These short-term goals might not seem risky to you. However, any action that requires energy and subjects your work to scrutiny is a risk. You can break down goals into parts of any size that work for you. The smallest ways in which you "put yourself out there" can lead, step by step, to the greatest rewards.

The SMART Goal-Achievement System

Use the SMART system to make rewarding long-term goals concrete and increase your chances of achieving them. SMART is an acronym for a five-part system that makes sure your goals are: **S**pecific, **M**easurable, **A**chievable, **R**ealistic, and attached to a **T**ime frame.

- *Specific.* Make your goal concrete by using as many details as possible. Focus on behaviours and events that are under your control and map out specific steps that will get you there.
- *Measurable.* Define your goal in measurable way, and set up a progress evaluation system such as keeping a journal, setting an alarm on your phone or computer, or reporting to a friend.
- *Achievable.* Determine whether the goal aligns with your interests and values. Then, reflect on whether you have the skills or resources needed. If you're missing something, plan how to get it.
- *Realistic.* Make sure your risks are reasonable and calculated. Create deadlines that will help you stay on track without making you feel rushed. Avoid the struggle of a timeline that is too short.
- *Time frame linked.* All goals need a time frame so you have something to work toward. If a goal is "a dream with a deadline," then without the deadline, your goal is only a dream (and may have only a dream's chance of coming to fruition).

MAJOR OR CONCENTRATION
An academic subject area chosen as a field of specialization, requiring a specific course of study.

Key 2.2 illustrates how to apply SMART goal setting to an important goal that nearly every post-secondary student needs to achieve: declaring a major or concentration (for the sake of simplicity, the term "major" will appear in this text).

Anyone can set a goal, of course. The real risk is in working toward it, and the real reward is in accomplishing it. Follow these steps, noting where your SMART system actions fit in.

- *Step 1: Define an achievable, realistic goal.* What do you want? Write out a clear description.
- *Step 2: Define an action plan.* How will you get there? Brainstorm different paths. Choose one; then map out its steps. Break a long-term goal into short-term subgoals.

GOAL: To decide on a major.

SMART GOAL CHARACTERISTICS	HOW TO ENGAGE EACH CHARACTERISTIC	EXAMPLE
Specific	Describe exactly how you will achieve your goal.	I will read the list of available majors, meet with my academic advisor, talk with instructors, and choose a major by the deadline.
Measurable	Find ways to measure your progress over time.	I will set alarms on my smartphone to remind me of when I should have accomplished each step. I will ask my mom to check in to make sure I'm getting somewhere.
Achievable	Set a goal that your abilities and drive can handle.	I'm driven to declare a major because I want to earn my degree, graduate, and gain work-ready skills.
Realistic	Define a goal that is workable given the resources (time and money) and other circumstances.	Because I'm starting early and already know how the process works, I should have time to think through this carefully.
Time frame	Set up a time frame for achieving your goal and identify the steps for working toward it.	I have a year until the deadline. I will read the catalog in the next month; I will meet with my advisor by the end of the term; I will talk with instructors at the beginning of next term; and I will declare a major by the end of next term.

- *Step 3: Link your goal to a time frame.* When do you want to accomplish your goal? Define a realistic time frame. Create specific deadlines for each step on the path.
- *Step 4: Identify resources and support.* What and who will keep you on track? Use helpful websites or apps. Find people who will push you in a supportive way.
- *Step 5: Be accountable.* How will you assess your progress? Create a system to measure how you move toward your goal, keeping your time frame in mind.
- *Step 6: Prepare to get unstuck.* What will you do if you hit a roadblock? Anticipate problems and define strategies for handling them. Reach out to people who can help you. Remind yourself of the benefits of your goal.
- *Step 7: Take action.* How will you persist? Follow the steps in your plan until you achieve your goal.
- *Step 8: Celebrate!* How will you recognize your accomplishments? Appreciate your hard work with something you enjoy— a movie night, an outing with friends, something you've been wanting to buy, maybe even a long nap.

At any given time, you may be working toward long-term and short-term goals of varying importance. You must first decide which goals offer you the most significant rewards and are most deserving of your focus. Then you can use the SMART system to make those goals concrete and increase your chances of achieving them.

Honzakrej/Fotolia

Goals, Time, and Stress Management

Academic Goals

Consider *learning* as your overarching "umbrella" academic goal, under which all other academic goals should fit. Your school provides resources that can help you set and achieve academic goals, if you can fulfill your end of the bargain, which is to use

get creative

Auremar/123RF

VISUALIZE YOUR POST-SECONDARY EXPERIENCE Astroid/123RF

Complete the following on paper or in digital format.

Take a cue from Steve Pavlina: Put your imagination to work and become, as he says, a "co-creator" of your life as a student "instead of a passive victim of it."[5]

1. First, come up with 10 words that come to mind when you imagine your ideal college or university experience. The words can be verbs, adjectives, nouns, whatever resonates with you.

2. The next step demands a little time. Mull over these words for a while and, write a paragraph or two describing more fully the rewards you envision gaining from post-secondary education. There is no obligation to fulfill every detail of your description, so don't restrict yourself. The picture you illustrate with your words will serve as a guide as you encounter decision-making points throughout your coursework.

those resources and take action. Key 2.3 illustrates basic academic goals and the resources that support you.

Look at each course separately at the beginning of the term. In addition to the objectives set by an instructor as outlined in a syllabus, students often want different outcomes from each course. For example, you are likely to have different goals for a course you are taking out of pure interest than for a prerequisite to a higher-level course in your chosen area of study. Your goals for any course will inform decisions about how much time and effort to devote to it.

Although declaring a major is an important academic goal for any student, you may or may not be ready to set that goal now. Some entering students know what they want, and transfer students who have accumulated a year or two's worth of credits

Courtesy of Woody Roseland

talk risk and reward

Risk asking tough questions to be rewarded with new insights. Use the following questions to inspire discussion with classmates, either in person or online.

- When you come up against a roadblock to an important goal, how do you react—with risk-taking or retreat? What is the result? If you want to change how you "get unstuck," what adjustments would you make?

- What time management issues do you see others face? How do they handle them? What happens when they take risks—or don't?

CONSIDER THE CASE: Woody's medical crisis demanded quick and decisive action because his life was at stake. Even if you never have a life-threatening illness, what can you take away from his experience that will help you face your own challenges?

get $mart

Racorn/123RF

FINANCIAL VALUES

Creativenv/Shutterstock

Complete the following on paper or in digital format.

Imagine yourself in five years . . .

1. What kind of work do you hope to be doing?
2. How much money do you hope to earn each year doing that work?
3. What type of major purchase might you make at that time? For ideas about this, consider your interests, needs, skills, and concerns.
4. How much might it cost (total cost or down payment)?
5. How much money would you have to save each month to have the money to make that major purchase at the end of five years? Monthly savings = total cost ÷ (5 years × 12 months per year)
6. Name two actions you can take to try to save that amount on a monthly basis.

KEY 2.3 Use resources to set and achieve academic goals.

ACADEMIC GOAL	RESOURCES THAT CAN HELP
Choose and register for classes each term	Advisor, course calendar, your school's website
Achieve objectives for each course	Instructor, syllabus, fellow students, course resources online, reading materials
Fulfill graduation requirements	Advisor, course calendar
Declare a major	Advisor, instructors from the department of your major, your school's website

may be further along in the process, but many students are just beginning to explore possibilities. When you are ready, refer to Key 2.2 to see how to apply SMART goal setting to declaring a major.

HOW CAN YOU MAKE
the most of your time?

Everyone has 24 hours in a day, and some of those hours should involve sleep if you want to remain healthy and alert enough to function. You can't manage how time passes, but you *can* manage how you use it. Start by looking at your personal relationship with time.

Analyze Yourself As a Time Manager

Some people are chronically late, while others work to get everything done ahead of time. Some people have lots of energy late at night, but others do their best work early in the day. The more you are aware of how you interact with time, the better you can create a schedule that moves you toward your goals.

Aleksandar Mijatovic/Shutterstock

Establish your personal time profile

The following steps will help you build a "profile" that illustrates how you relate to time:

- *Identify your energy patterns.* At what time of day does your energy tend to peak? When do you tend to have the least energy?

  - *Notice your on-time percentage.* Do you tend to be early, on time, or late? If you are early or late, by how many minutes are you normally off schedule?

    - *Look at your stamina.* Do you focus more effectively if you have a long block of time in which to work? Or do you need regular breaks in order to perform effectively?

With this information, you can establish an ideal schedule that reflects your preferences. If a student gets more done during the day and needs long blocks of time, for example, his schedule might read: "Classes bunched together on Mondays, Wednesdays, and Fridays. Tuesdays and Thursdays free for studying and research. Study primarily during day-time hours."

Of course, very few people are able to perfectly align their schedules to their profile and preferences. Use your ideal schedule as a tool to make choices that fit your preferences as much as possible. The student in the example, looking to schedule next term's classes on Monday, Wednesday, and Friday, may find that one class he has to take meets only on Tuesday and Thursday. He has a choice of 11 A.M. and 4 P.M., though, so he chooses 4 P.M. because that will give him a bigger block of time to study and do research during the day prior to the class.

Choose a planner

Find a planner that works for how you live. There are two major types:

- A book or notebook, showing either a day or a week at a glance, where you note your commitments. Some planners contain sections for monthly and yearly goals.
- An electronic planner, smartphone, or tablet, such as an iPhone or Android phone. Basic functions allow you to schedule days and weeks, note due dates, make to-do lists, perform mathematical calculations, and create and store an address book. Because most smartphone calendars have companion programs on computers, you can usually back up your schedule on a computer and view it there. You might also consider online calendars, such as Google calendar, which can communicate with your phone or other device.

Although electronic planners are handy, powerful, and capable of all kinds of functioning, they are not cheap, the software can fail, and their batteries can die. Analyze your preferences and finances and choose the best tool for you. A blank notebook, used consistently, may work as well as a top-of-the-line smartphone.

Build a Schedule

Scheduling is your central life control strategy and a necessity for goal achievement. The most clearly defined goal won't be achieved without being put into a time frame, and the most organized schedule won't move you toward long-term goals unless it is populated with tasks related to those goals. Be detailed and methodical about building your schedule, using the following strategies.

Prioritize tasks and goals

Prioritizing helps you focus the bulk of your energy and time on what is most important to you. Prioritizing is also where you consider the value of making trade-offs. Are you willing to trade an hour a day of social media time for an hour a day of study time that will help you improve your grades? Are you willing to trade a night out for an opportunity to get on top of a paper deadline? Think about what results your risks might bring, and what may result from taking *no* risks.

One way to assign priority is to use these three basic levels:

- *Priority 1.* These are crucial, high-reward items that you must do, usually at a specific time. They may include attending class, working at a job, picking up a child from day care, and paying bills.
- *Priority 2.* These are important items that have some flexibility in scheduling. Examples include study time and exercising.
- *Priority 3.* These are less important items that offer low-key rewards. Examples include calling a friend or downloading songs into iTunes.

Once you have set priority levels, schedule tasks using these steps. (Key 2.4 shows parts of both a daily schedule and a weekly schedule.)

KEY 2.4 Note daily and weekly tasks.

Monday, March 14

Time	Tasks	Priority
6:00 A.M.		
7:00		
8:00	Up at 8am — finish homework	
9:00		
10:00	Business Administration	
11:00	Renew driver's licence	
12:00 P.M.		
1:00	Lunch	
2:00	Writing Seminar (peer editing to	
3:00	↓	
4:00	check on Ms. Schwartz's office h	
5:00	5:30 work out	
6:00	↳6:30	
7:00	Dinner	
8:00	Read two chapters for	
9:00	Business Admin.	
10:00		
11:00		
12:00		

Monday, March 28

8		Call: Mike Blair		1
9	BIO 212	Financial Aid Office		2
10				3
11	CHEM 203	EMS 262	*Paramedic	4
12			role-play*	5
Evening	6pm yoga class			

Tuesday, March 29

8	Finish reading assignment!	Work @ library		1
9				2
10	ENG 112	(study for quiz)		3
11	↓			4
12				5
Evening		until 7pm		

Wednesday, March 30

8		Meet w/advisor	1
9	BIO 212		2
10		EMS 262	3
11	CHEM 203 *Quiz		4
12		Pick up photos	5
Evening	6pm Dinner w/study group		

1. *Enter Priority 1 items in your planner first.* This means class meetings for the term, including labs and other commitments; work hours; and key personal responsibilities. For someone like Woody, needing medical care, appointments and treatments fall into this category.

2. *Enter key dates from your course syllabi.* When you get your syllabi for the term, enter dates for tests and quizzes, assignments, presentations, holidays, and breaks in your planner right away. This will give you a big picture view and help you prepare for crunch times. For example, if you see that you have three tests and a presentation all in one week, you might rearrange your preceding week's schedule to create extra study time.

3. *Enter dates of events and commitments.* Put commitments in your schedule where you can see and plan for them. Include club and organizational meetings, events you need to attend for class or for other purposes, and personal commitments such as medical appointments, family events, fitness events such as a race, or important social events.

4. *Schedule Priority 2 items around existing items.* Once you have the essentials set, put in study time, workouts, study group meetings, and other important but flexible items. Schedule class prep time—reading and studying, writing, and working on assignments and projects—in the planner as you would any other activity. Keep this rule in mind when scheduling: You should allow two hours of preparation for every hour in class.

5. *Include Priority 3 items where possible.* Schedule these items, such as social time or doing errands, around the items already locked in.

When you are scheduling and evaluating the potential rewards of various tasks, be careful not to equate "reward" with "fun." They are not necessarily one and the same. For example, you might consider spending an hour on Snapchat a lot more fun than studying for a test for that same hour. However, the reward for working toward a good test grade may ultimately be more desirable to you than whatever you would gain from posting and liking photos.

Link tasks to long-term goals

Linking day-to-day events in your planner to your values and long-term goals gives meaning to your efforts and keeps you motivated. One important example is scheduling milestones toward major papers and assignments. If you know you have a huge project or research paper due at the end of the term, brainstorm a list of steps toward that goal—for example, research goals, different drafts, peer review—and set them up in your calendar.

Before each week begins, remind yourself of your most important long-term goals and what you can accomplish that week to move closer to achieving them. Every once in a while, take a hard look at your schedule to see if you are spending enough time on what you really value.

Make to-do lists

When you have a cluster of tasks to accomplish, you may find it useful to create a to-do list and check off the items as you complete them. A to-do list can be helpful during exam week, in anticipation of an especially busy day, for a long-term or complicated assignment, or when keyed to a special event. Some people keep a separate to-do list focused on low-priority tasks.

Use a code to prioritize the items on your list so that you address the most important items first. Some people just list items in priority order and number them. Some use letters (A, B, C) and some use different-coloured pens. Others use electronic planners, choosing different highlighting or font colours. Each time you complete a task, check it off your to-do list or delete it from your electronic scheduler. This physical action can enhance the feeling of confidence that comes from getting something done.

Manage Your Schedule

The most detailed schedule won't do you any good unless you actively manage it. Your most basic responsibility is to have your planner with you at all times (and, if it has a battery, keep it charged). Here are other strategies that can help:

- *Plan regularly.* Set aside a time each day to plan your schedule (right before bed, with your morning coffee, on your commute to or from school, or whatever time and situation works best for you). Check your schedule at regular intervals throughout the day or week.

- *Use monthly and yearly calendars at home.* A standard monthly or yearly wall calendar is a great place to keep track of your major commitments. A wall calendar gives you the "big picture" overview you need. Key 2.5 shows a monthly calendar.

- *Get ahead if you can.* If you can take the small risk of getting a task done ahead of time, get it done, and see how you appreciate the reward of avoiding pressure later. Focus on your growth mindset, reminding yourself that achievement requires persistent effort.

- *Schedule downtime.* It's easy to get so caught up in completing tasks that you forget to relax and breathe. Even a half-hour of downtime a day will refresh you and improve your productivity when you get back on task.

- *Schedule sleep.* Sleep-deprived bodies and minds have a hard time functioning, and research reports that one-quarter of all college students are chronically sleep-deprived.[6] Figure out how much sleep you need and do your best to get it. With adequate rest, your mind is better able to function, which has a direct positive impact on your schoolwork.

KEY 2.5 Keep track of your time with a monthly calendar.

MARCH

SUNDAY	MONDAY	TUESDAY	WEDNESDAY	THURSDAY	FRIDAY	SATURDAY
	1 WORK	2 Turn in English paper topic	3 Dentist 2 pm	4 WORK	5	6
7 Frank's birthday	8 Psych Test 9 am WORK	9	10 6:30 pm Meeting @ Acad Ctr	11 WORK	12	13 Dinner @ Ryan's
14	15 English paper due WORK	16 Western Civ paper	17	18 Library 6 pm WORK	19 Western Civ makeup class	20
21	22 WORK	23 2 pm meeting, psych group	24 Start running: 3 km.	25	26 WORK Run 3 km.	27
28 Run 4 km.	29 WORK	30 Western Civ paper due	31 Run 3 km.			

One last overarching strategy: *Be flexible.* Sudden changes can upset your plans. Although you cannot control all the events that occur, you can control how you respond to them. For changes that occur frequently, such as a job that tends to run into overtime, set up a backup plan (or two) ahead of time. For sudden changes, such as medical emergencies and car breakdowns, or serious changes, such as failing a course, use problem-solving skills to help you through (your course this term may include more detailed information about problem solving).

Your ability to evaluate situations, come up with creative options, and put practical plans to work will help you manage changes. So will your ability to reach out to people at your college—advisors, counsellors, deans, instructors—who can help you.

HOW CAN YOU
handle time traps?

Everyone experiences *time traps*—situations and activities that eat up time you could spend in a more productive way. Students just starting college and university, many of whom have never before been wholly responsible for their time, often fall deeply into time traps as they explore how much unproductive time they can spend and still get their work done. However, with the effort to think about what trade-offs might benefit them most, they can climb out and find a better balance.

Managing time traps doesn't mean *never* doing things like messaging friends on social media or watching videos on CraveTV or Netflix; it means making conscious decisions about when and how long you do certain activities so that they don't derail you. It also means thinking ahead about risks—both the risk of being unproductive, as well as the risk of prioritizing work over your social life—and what rewards may or may not come from them. It can be risky to put out the high level of attention and focus that your work may demand, but the reward is an education that can help you fulfill your life's most significant goals. Make your best choices by confronting procrastination, taking charge of technology, and minimizing multitasking.

Avoid Paying the Price of Procrastination

PROCRASTINATION
The act of putting off a task until another time.

It's human, and common for busy students, to leave difficult or undesirable tasks until later. However, if taken to the extreme, procrastination can develop into a habit that causes serious problems. For example, procrastinators who don't get things done in the workplace may prevent others from doing their work, sabotage a project, or even lose a promotion or a job because of it.

If procrastination can cause such major issues, why do it? One reason people procrastinate is to avoid the truth about what they can achieve. "As long as you procrastinate, you never have to confront the real limits of your ability, whatever those limits are,"[7] say procrastination experts Jane B. Burka and Lenora Yuen, authors of *Procrastination: Why You Do It and What to Do About It.* A fixed mindset also naturally leads to procrastination. A person with a fixed mindset thinks, "I can't do it, so what's the point of trying?"

Here are some strategies that can help you avoid procrastination and its negative effects:

- *Analyze the effects.* What reward will remain out of reach if you continue to put off a task? Chances are you will benefit more in the long term by facing the task head-on.

- *Set reasonable goals.* Because unreasonable goals can immobilize, take manageable risks. If you concentrate on one small step at a time, the task doesn't loom so large.

- *Get started whether you "feel like it" or not.* Break the paralysis of doing nothing by doing something—anything. Most people, once they start, find it easier to continue.

- *Ask for help.* Once you identify what's holding you up, find someone to help you face the task. Another person may come up with an innovative method to get you moving again.
- *Don't expect perfection.* People learn by approaching mistakes with a growth mindset. Richard Sheridan, President of Menlo Innovations, fosters a culture of exploration by telling his employees to "make mistakes faster."[8]
- *Acknowledge progress.* When you accomplish a task, celebrate with whatever feels like fun to you.

Take Charge of Technology

Many people find it challenging to resist the pull of relaxing and fun activities such as video games, YouTube surfing, and socializing virtually or in person. However, the fun stuff can run away with

Balance means getting your work done as well as finding time to have some fun with friends.

your time, preventing you from taking care of responsibilities and ultimately causing serious problems. Because technology is so much a part of modern life, it can seem risky to limit your exposure to it. However, controlling when and for how long you interface with technology will earn you the reward of its benefits minus the suffering from its drawbacks.

There is a saying that goes, "The river needs banks to flow." Within those banks—the reasonable limits you set on activities that tend to eat up time—you can be the thriving, healthy river, flowing toward the goals that are most important to you. Without the banks, and without the limits, you (the river) can spill out all over, losing the power to head in any single direction.

How can you make reasonable trade-offs that will empower you and provide balance? Consider the following:

- *Know what distracts you.* Be honest with yourself about what draws your attention and drains your time—chatting or texting on your cell phone, watching reality TV, visiting Facebook, reading tweets, and so on.
- *Set boundaries.* Determine when, and for how long, you can perform these activities without jeopardizing your studies. Then schedule them with built-in boundaries: "I will spend 10 minutes on Facebook for every 50 minutes of studying." "I will choose one TV show per day." Stick to your limits—use a cell phone alarm if you need it. You can even set up innovative browser plug-ins, such as LeechBlock (for Firefox) or StayFocused (for Google Chrome), to block certain time wasting sites for specific periods of time.
- *Think before you commit.* See "yes" and "no" as equally useful tools. Whatever you are asked to do— whether social, family-related, in connection with a school organization, or another activity—consider how the commitment will affect your schedule now and in the future. If you determine the reward isn't worth the risk, say "no" respectfully but firmly.
- *Be realistic about time commitments.* Many students who combine work and school find they have to trim

Kevin Eaves/Fotolia

get practical

binkski/123RF

CONQUER YOUR TIME TRAPS

Complete the following on paper or in digital format.

Think of two common time traps that you encounter. For each, come up with two ways to manage it effectively. Here's an example:

Time Trap: Texting

Response 1: Tell friend: "I'll get back to you in an hour. I need to finish this paper."

Response 2: Decide I will respond to my text messages after I've read two chapters.

1. Your turn: For each time trap of yours, name it and describe two possible responses.

2. Next, for each of the two time traps you identified, name which of the two responses will most help you to take control of the situation and why.

3. Finally, what did this exercise teach you about your personal time traps? Do you find yourself needing to be stricter with your time? Why, and how?

one or the other. Overloaded students often fall behind and experience high stress levels. Determine what is reasonable for you; you may find that taking longer to graduate is a viable option if you need to work while in school. You may also decide that you can handle easing up on work hours in order to spend more time on schoolwork.

Be Wary of Multitasking

Many modern post-secondary students think of themselves as master multitaskers and deliberately cram ever more activities, communication, and information into their days. However, multitasking is not without its price. Recent research has shown that the brain is biologically capable of doing only one thinking task at a time—at best, it can switch rapidly between tasks. When you think you are doing two tasks at once, you are actually "switch-tasking," not multitasking, meaning that you are interrupting the first activity with the second and then switching back.[9]

The time it takes to switch from one thinking activity to another is called *switching time*. Switching time increases errors and the amount of time it takes to finish tasks by an average of 50 percent. This means the more activities you juggle, the more your brain is interrupted, the more switching you do, the longer it takes to complete your activities, and the more mistakes you make.[10] The cost to the quality of your work may not be worth the juggling.

In the modern world, it is almost impossible *not* to do several things at once when managing constant input from texts, calls, emails, tweets, websites, blogs, visual media, and more. So how can you maintain the type of focus that will save you time, mistakes, and stress? Know what input leads you to multitask, and control it whenever you have a job that demands time and focus. Are you working on a big paper? Find a quiet corner of the library and put your phone on silent. Are you studying for a test by reading online materials? Use a browser plug-in to prevent yourself from surfing Facebook until after your study time. Minor risks in the moment will reward you with learning and accomplishment (and you will still find time to play).

WHAT WILL HELP YOU MANAGE
the stress of post-secondary life?

If you are feeling more stress in your everyday life as a student, you are not alone. Stress levels among post-secondary students have increased dramatically.[11] Stress factors for students include being in a new environment, increased workload, difficult decisions, and juggling school, work, and personal responsibilities. To help students manage time and stress, many Canadian universities and colleges now have a Fall Break, ranging from a couple of days to an entire week, to give students a chance to catch up on work or simply relax.

Dealing with stress can be an everyday challenge. The greater your stress, the greater the toll it may take on your health and on your ability to achieve your goals. However, this doesn't mean that you should try to get rid of *all* stress. Moderate stress—often brought on by reasonable risk-taking—can actually bring rewards, such as motivating you to do well on tests, finish assignments on time, and prepare for presentations. Key 2.6, based on research conducted by Drs. Robert M. Yerkes and John E. Dodson, shows that stress can be helpful or harmful, depending on how much you experience.

STRESS
Physical or mental strain or tension produced in reaction to pressure.

Goals, Time, and Stress Management

KEY 2.6 Stress levels can help or hinder performance.

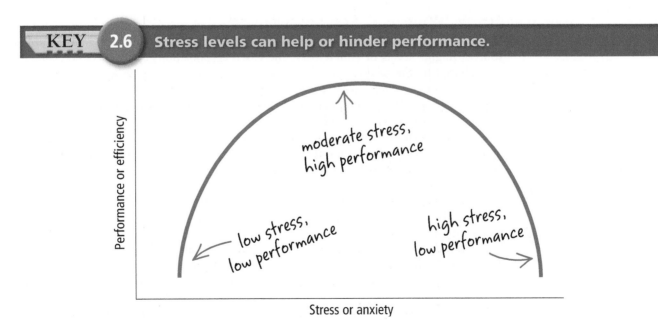

Source: From *Your Maximum Mind* by Herbert Benson M.D. Used by permission of Vicky Bijur Literary Agency.

Your course may go into more detail about emotional and physical wellness and how they connect to stress management. In the meantime, here are some stress management tools that are right at your fingertips.

Work to Delay Gratification

You may be aware that setting yourself up to make fewer decisions per day can help you to maintain your willpower. That willpower is necessary for delaying gratification. Recent studies reveal that the ability to make a sacrifice in the moment in exchange for a later reward is at least as important a factor in academic success as native intelligence.[12]

Following up on the well-known "marshmallow test" study that observed whether young children were able to resist eating a marshmallow in front of them in exchange for having more marshmallows 15 minutes later, research shows that people who respond strongly to cues in their environment—enticements around them, such as text messages popping up, for example, or games available on their computers—have a harder time delaying gratification.[13] In addition, the human brain is still developing its impulse control until around age 25. All of this can challenge many students to manage their responsibilities.

How does delaying gratification help you manage stress? When self-control slips and responsibilities pile up, so does stress, making it harder to get back on track. However, when you are able to take the risk of delaying gratification, keeping your focus on the rewards down the line, you are far more likely to perform your academic and life tasks on time. This reduces stress in two ways: One, it makes it less likely that you will fall behind in your responsibilities, and two, it builds your confidence, which helps to calm the stress reaction.

No one is able to sacrifice the immediacy of "fun" rewards all the time. Sometimes you will forgo the library and join your friends for some social time. However, you can commit to do your best to balance work and play. If you are able to maintain the right amount of each in your life, you will be likely to hit that "sweet spot" where you have just enough stress to perform well, but not so much that you shut down.

Go to Class and Use Your Syllabus

If the average student analyzed what percentage of stress came from unavoidable sources (higher levels of coursework, increased responsibility) and what percentage was created by the student (missing classes, not consulting a planner regularly, not using syllabi to schedule tasks), the latter percentage would likely be too high. Be honest with yourself: When you are overwhelmed with responsibilities, how much of that is a result of choices you've made?

Post-secondary school is challenging enough. Don't make it worse by blowing off classes and filing your syllabi out of sight. Your energy is much better spent moving ahead on the road toward your goals rather than crawling out of a ditch that you yourself dug and fell into.

The strategies are simple: One, go to class as consistently as you can. Two, refer to your syllabi regularly—whether the syllabi themselves or the syllabi due dates that you've put into your planner—to make sure you are on top of what's required of you. If you can do these two things you will save yourself an enormous amount of stress, and you will still find time for activities and relaxation outside of class.

Time and Goal Management = Stress Management

Here's the good news: Every goal-setting and time-management strategy you are reading in this chapter contributes to your ability to cope with stress. Remember that stress

student PROFILE

Peyton Campbell
FLEMING COLLEGE

About me:

I am a mature student pursuing my second diploma in law and justice studies. I am currently enrolled in the Customs and Border Services program at Fleming College.

What I focus on:

Having enough discipline to effectively implement time management and carry out your set schedule will highly impact your rate of success. Meeting deadlines is crucial as a student. Not allowing deadlines to creep up too quickly, getting up earlier in the morning, and following a visual grid of assignments coming due, all helped me feel like I was in control this semester. A poorly planned schedule or execution of priorities can throw off your entire week. Managing time goes much further than your class schedule or timetable. If you can manage your time and accomplish your goals within the time frame you allot yourself, you will still be able to enjoy down time, and have free time to go to the gym or out with friends. I would advise first-year students to find a method that works best for them and that they can stick to. This will ultimately aid your success in this semester and this course!

For me, the most successful strategy was to take all of my course outlines for the semester and to compile them into one visual grid that ran the fifteen weeks of my semester. I was able to track the marks of completed assignments and see my work successfully completed as the semester unfolded. This gave me a sense of accomplishment and allowed me to avoid the trap of receiving a zero on an assignment.

What will help me in the workplace:

It is important to have the ability and forward thinking to prioritize tasks in the workplace. Employers will look for strength in managing tasks and completing them within an appropriate amount of time. These employability skills are learned over time and build upon experience and past successes.

refers to how you *react* to pressure. When you make choices that reduce pressure, you have less to react to.

In this chapter you have explored stressbusters such as how to:

- Set productive, realistic goals based on what is important to you
- Break your goals into manageable tasks
- Make choices that take who you are as a time manager into account
- Create and follow a schedule that helps you gets tasks done and get to places on time
- Address your time traps by controlling distracting aspects of your environment

When you feel panic coming on, try to resist the urge to escape into a fun activity and forget what's causing you pressure. Instead, think: "How can I make a tradeoff that reduces the pressure? What task can I take care of?" Goal-setting and time-management skills are likely to bring you a more significant sense of calm and confidence than a night out partying. Save the night out for when the responsibilities are checked off and you can truly enjoy the rewards of effective self-management.

Goals, Time, and Stress Management

revisit RISK AND REWARD

What happened to Woody? Together, Woody, his family, and his medical team decided that the calculated risk most worth taking was to amputate his left leg above the knee. With a high-tech prosthetic, Woody regained his ability to walk. And with determination and humour, Woody took back his life, continuing to press on through his coursework toward a major in business marketing, which he plans to earn in the next year. Finding that his perspective on cancer and life resonated with others, he started a "side-hustle" in public speaking that has become his own business and a central focus in his life.

Woody travels around the country, speaking about his experience and raising money for cancer research and other pressing social problems. He has his own website, he blogs for the Huffington Post, he has started a video production business in addition to his work as a speaker, and he has spoken at TEDx Mile-High. He has appeared on CNN and ESPN. His willingness to continue to risk has brought enormous rewards and a career that he never could have imagined as a high school student on the football field. And his determination to take targeted medical risks continues to keep him living his life to the fullest. Woody is currently feeling great and working hard to make up for the time he lost because of cancer. In his free time he enjoys bike riding and playing golf, as well as sharing craft beers and baseball with his friends.

What does this mean for you? Woody discovered a whole new set of values through the course of his past few years. "I'm more concentrated on how I can achieve the goals I have set out for rather than the negatives, because there will always be reason to feel down about life." List three values that are important to you. Now look at your current academic and life goals. Do they support your values or not? Give specific examples. If you find that there isn't enough linkage between your values and current goals, think about risks you could take that could tie them closer.

Courtesy of Woody Roseland

What risk may bring reward beyond your world? "The most terrifying fact about the universe is not that it is hostile, but that it is indifferent," Woody says. "Your happiness is, and always has been, about you deciding to be happy . . . . At some point it comes down to a simple decision: happiness, or unhappiness. So if a one-legged, scar-riddled, chemotherapy-infused guy like me can figure it out, I like your chances." Check out www.woodyroseland.com to see how Woody risks choosing happiness by inspiring others. What risk and choice can you make that makes a difference for someone else? Putting your values into action can help you choose happiness in the face of the challenges of your own life.

GLOBAL RISK AND REWARD

Irina Dmitrienko/Alamy Stock Photo

imageflow/123RF

Sergio Castro initially came to Chiapas, Mexico, to build water infrastructure. The Mayan communities there came to see him as a healer, and he took the risk to accept the role and stay. With the art, clothing, and other items that patients gave him in exchange for his services, he created a museum that has helped to fund what is now a walk-in medical clinic. *El Andalón* (the one who never stops) continues to heal the bodies, minds, and hearts of poor and deprived people, experiencing the reward of making a difference for many who would otherwise have no access to care.[14]

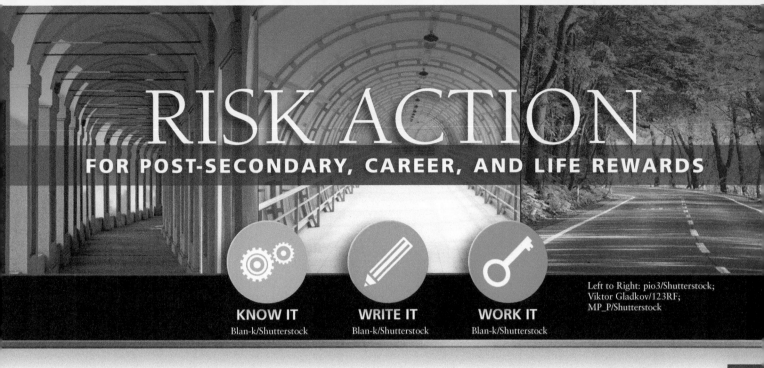

RISK ACTION
FOR POST-SECONDARY, CAREER, AND LIFE REWARDS

KNOW IT
Blan-k/Shutterstock

WRITE IT
Blan-k/Shutterstock

WORK IT
Blan-k/Shutterstock

Left to Right: pio3/Shutterstock; Viktor Gladkov/123RF; MP_P/Shutterstock

Complete the following on paper or in digital format; for the time management exercise, use the in-text grids.

KNOW IT *Think Critically*

Discover How You Spend Your Time

Build basic skills. Everyone has exactly 168 hours in a week. How do you spend your hours? Start by guessing or estimating the time you spend on three particular activities. How much time do you spend on each of these activities in a week?

Studying? _____ hours
Sleeping? _____ hours
Interacting with media and technology (computer, online services, cell phone, texting, video games, television) for nonacademic purposes? _____ hours

To find out the real story, record how you actually spend your time for seven days. The Weekly Time Log chart has blocks showing half-hour increments. As you go through the week, write down what you do each hour, indicating when you start and when you stop. Include sleep and leisure time. Record your *actual* activities instead of the activities you think you *should* be doing. There are no wrong answers.

Weekly Time Log

TIME	MONDAY	TUESDAY	WEDNESDAY	THURSDAY
	activity	activity	activity	activity
6:00 A.M.				
6:30 A.M.				
7:00 A.M.				
7:30 A.M.				
8:00 A.M.				
8:30 A.M.				
9:00 A.M.				
9:30 A.M.				
10:00 A.M.				
10:30 A.M.				
11:00 A.M.				
11:30 A.M.				
12:00 P.M.				
12:30 P.M.				
1:00 P.M.				
1:30 P.M.				
2:00 P.M.				
2:30 P.M.				
3:00 P.M.				
3:30 P.M.				
4:00 P.M.				
4:30 P.M.				
5:00 P.M.				
5:30 P.M.				
6:00 P.M.				
6:30 P.M.				
7:00 P.M.				
7:30 P.M.				
8:00 P.M.				
8:30 P.M.				
9:00 P.M.				
9:30 P.M.				
10:00 P.M.				
10:30 P.M.				
11:00 P.M.				
11:30 P.M.				
12:00 A.M.				
12:30 A.M.				
1:00 A.M.				
1:30 A.M.				
2:00 A.M.				

TIME	FRIDAY activity	SATURDAY activity	SUNDAY activity
6:00 A.M.			
6:30 A.M.			
7:00 A.M.			
7:30 A.M.			
8:00 A.M.			
8:30 A.M.			
9:00 A.M.			
9:30 A.M.			
10:00 A.M.			
10:30 A.M.			
11:00 A.M.			
11:30 A.M.			
12:00 P.M.			
12:30 P.M.			
1:00 P.M.			
1:30 P.M.			
2:00 P.M.			
2:30 P.M.			
3:00 P.M.			
3:30 P.M.			
4:00 P.M.			
4:30 P.M.			
5:00 P.M.			
5:30 P.M.			
6:00 P.M.			
6:30 P.M.			
7:00 P.M.			
7:30 P.M.			
8:00 P.M.			
8:30 P.M.			
9:00 P.M.			
9:30 P.M.			
10:00 P.M.			
10:30 P.M.			
11:00 P.M.			
11:30 P.M.			
12:00 A.M.			
12:30 A.M.			
1:00 A.M.			
1:30 A.M.			
2:00 A.M.			

Goals, Time, and Stress Management

After a week, note how many hours you spent on each activity using the Weekly Summary chart. Round off the times to half-hours—if you spent 31 to 44 minutes on an activity, mark it as a half-hour; if you spent 45 to 59 minutes, mark it as one hour. Log the hours in the boxes in the chart using tally marks, with a full mark representing one hour and a half-size mark representing a half-hour. In the third column, total the hours for each activity. Finally, add the totals in that column to make sure your grand total is approximately 168 hours (if it isn't, go back and check your grid and calculations and fix any errors you find). Leave the Ideal Time in Hours column blank for now.

Weekly Summary

Activity	Time Tallied Over One-Week Period	Total Time in Hours	Ideal Time in Hours
Example: Class	|||||||||||||||||	16.5	
Class			
Work			
Studying			
Sleeping			
Eating			
Family time/child care			
Commuting/travelling			
Chores and personal business			
Friends and important relationships			
Telephone time			
Leisure/entertainment			
Spiritual life			
Other			

Take it to the next level. Look over your results, paying special attention to how your *estimated* hours for sleep, study, and technology activities compare to your *actual* logged activity hours for the week. Use a separate sheet of paper or electronic file to answer the following questions:

- What surprises you about how you spend your time?
- Do you spend the most time on the activities that represent your most important values, or not?
- Where do you waste the most time? What do you think that is costing you?
- On which activities do you think you should spend *more* time? On which should you spend *less* time?

Move toward mastery. Go back to the Weekly Summary chart and fill in the Ideal Time in Hours column with the numbers of you think would make the most sense. Consider the difference between your actual hours and your ideal hours. What changes are you willing to make to get closer to how you want to ideally spend your time? Write a short paragraph describing, in detail, two time-management changes you plan to make this term so you focus your time more effectively on your most important goals and values.

WRITE IT *Communicate*

RECORD YOUR THOUGHTS ON A SEPARATE PIECE OF PAPER, IN A JOURNAL, OR ELECTRONICALLY.

Emotional intelligence journal: How you feel about your time management. Think and then write about how your most time-demanding activities make you feel. Paying attention to your feelings is a key step toward making time management choices that are more in line with your values. What makes you most fulfilled and satisfied? What makes you the most frustrated and drained? What do these feelings tell you about your choices? Describe how you could adjust your mindset or make different choices to feel better about how you spend your time.

Real-life writing: Examine two areas of academic specialty. Use your course catalog to identify two academic areas that look interesting to you. Write a short report comparing and contrasting the majors or concentrations in these areas. Consider GPA requirements, number of courses, relevance to career areas, campus locations of departments, "feel" of the departments, other requirements, and discussions with students and instructors. Conclude your report with observations about how this comparison and evaluation process has refined your thinking.

WORK IT *Build Your Brand*

Explore Career Goals Through Personal Mission

A successful career should be grounded in personal mission in some way. Draft yours, using Covey's three aspects of personal mission to think through it:

- *Character.* What aspects of character do you think are most valuable? When you consider the people you admire most, which of their qualities stand out?
- *Contributions and achievements.* What do you want to accomplish in your life? Where do you want to make a difference? What are you willing to risk to make it happen?
- *Values.* How do your values inform your life goals? How can you live according to what you value most highly? Consider what you would prioritize if you had one year to live.

With a personal mission statement to provide vision and motivation, think about your working life. Spend 15 minutes thinking about everything you wish you could be, do, or have in your career 10 years from now—skills, earnings, benefits, things or places you want to experience, anything you can think of. Depict your wishes by listing them, drawing them, cutting out images from magazines, or combining any of these ideas—whatever you like best.

Now, group your wishes in order of priority. Take three pieces of paper and label them: Priority 1, Priority 2, and Priority 3. Put each wish on the paper where it belongs, according to its priority (1 = high importance, 2 = medium importance, and 3 = low importance).

Look at the wishes on your priority lists. What do they tell you about what is most important to you? What fits into your personal mission and what doesn't? Identify those wishes that don't seem to have anything to do with your personal mission and cross them out. Circle or highlight three high-priority wishes that do mesh with your personal mission. For each wish, write down one action step you could take in the near future to make that wish come true.

You may want to look back at these materials at the end of the term to see what changes may have taken place in your priorities.

CHAPTER

3

Michael Paras Photography

Because stress and health are linked, every action you take to improve your physical and mental health can also increase your ability to cope with stress.

Emotional and Physical Wellness

HOW HEALTHY ARE YOU WILLING TO BE?

What Would You Risk? *Marlene Schwartz, Ph.D.*

THINK ABOUT THIS SITUATION AS YOU READ, AND CONSIDER WHAT ACTION YOU WOULD TAKE. THIS CHAPTER EXAMINES WAYS TO MANAGE STRESS THROUGH HEALTH MAINTENANCE, HOW TO HANDLE PHYSICAL AND MENTAL HEALTH ISSUES, AND HOW TO MAKE EFFECTIVE DECISIONS ABOUT SUBSTANCES AND SEX.

From her childhood days Marlene Schwartz was aware of nutrition. There was fruit and salad every night at the dinner table. There were no vending machines at her schools. After earning an undergraduate degree in psychology, a stint as a research assistant inspired her to earn her master's and doctoral degrees in clinical psychology. She was intent on changing the world, one person at a time.

"Psychology is the study of why people do what they do and how to get them to do better," Marlene says. Working with individuals at the Yale Center for Eating and Weight Disorders, she felt as though she really did help people improve—except in situations where she was addressing childhood obesity. With children, Marlene says, "I would do my best, then I felt like the world basically undid everything I was trying to accomplish. The environment was working against them as much as possible."

She had her own nutritional goals for her three young daughters. Marlene gathered the family for dinner as many nights as possible, serving whole grains and always including a fruit or vegetable. She avoided buying pop and candy, and fast food was rare. Still, Marlene found that society wasn't in unison with her mission. As she worked to instill good habits at home, her children's schools sold Pop Tarts, ice cream, and other sugary treats in the cafeteria. One day, Marlene's oldest daughter came home from first grade with a flyer announcing a cookie-eating contest. It was yet another example of how the school system was fuelling the childhood obesity epidemic, and it was the last straw for Marlene, who felt the school was undermining her efforts. She knew she had to take risks to turn the situation around.

To be continued . . .

YOU NEED DETERMINATION TO FOLLOW A LIFELONG WELLNESS PLAN. IF YOU ARE COMMITTED TO A GOAL, LIKE MARLENE, YOU WILL REAP PERSONAL REWARDS AND PERHAPS EVEN BENEFIT YOUR COMMUNITY. WITHIN THE CHAPTER, YOU'LL LEARN MORE ABOUT MARLENE, AND THE REWARD RESULTING FROM HER ACTIONS.

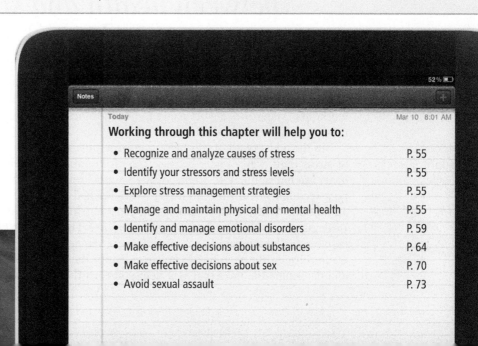

Today   Mar 10 8:01 AM

Working through this chapter will help you to:

statusCHECK

Left to Right: Luis Santos/Shutterstock; Antonio Guillem/Shutterstock; antoniodiaz/Shutterstock; mimagephotography/Shutterstock; Djomas/Shutterstock; WAYHOME studio/Shutterstock

How Effectively Do You Maintain Your Personal Wellness?

For each statement, fill in the number that best describes how often it applies to you.

1 = never   2 = seldom   3 = sometimes   4 = often   5 = always

1. I know that my health is a major factor in my success as a student.	① ② ③ ④ ⑤
2. I eat a healthy, balanced diet, and rarely overeat or undereat.	① ② ③ ④ ⑤
3. I make it a point to exercise regularly in some way.	① ② ③ ④ ⑤
4. I consistently get eight to nine hours of sleep per night.	① ② ③ ④ ⑤
5. I understand what constitutes sexual abuse, avoid abusive behaviours, and work to stay safe.	① ② ③ ④ ⑤
6. When I am feeling "out of it," I use healthy methods to elevate my mood.	① ② ③ ④ ⑤
7. I know the ways in which addiction can affect my life.	① ② ③ ④ ⑤
8. I understand the potential consequences of substance use and make choices based on that knowledge.	① ② ③ ④ ⑤
9. I am willing to ask for help with anxiety, depression, or other health problems.	① ② ③ ④ ⑤
10. I understand the potential consequences of sexual activity and feel comfortable with my choices.	① ② ③ ④ ⑤

Each of the topics in these statements is covered in this chapter. Note those statements for which you filled in a 3 or lower. Skim the chapter to see where those topics appear, and pay special attention to them as you read, learn, and apply new strategies.

REMEMBER: NO MATTER HOW WELL YOU TAKE CARE OF YOURSELF, YOU CAN IMPROVE WITH EFFORT AND PRACTICE.

WHAT IS THE LINK
between health and stress management?

In the modern media-saturated world, it's almost impossible to be unaware of the importance of health. TV shows feature medical professionals offering tips on healthy choices, chefs explaining how to eat well, and exercise gurus leading you through workouts. Magazines devote pages to health topics. Marketers of food and other products emphasize healthful effects.

In the midst of all of this helpful information, people are experiencing higher levels of stress than ever, in part because the proliferation of choice increases anxiety. Students are not immune to stress. A 2013 survey revealed that almost 9 in 10 Canadian post-secondary students often feel overwhelmed by all the responsibilities of young adulthood.[1] Which dinner item has the most nutritional value? What time of day should I exercise, and which activity should I choose? This chapter highlights the connection between wellness-related choices and stress management, with the goal of helping you wade through the myriad of choices, identify the rewards that are important to you, and determine the risks that will help you earn them. Managing your stress is also an

MyLab Student Success
(www.mystudentsuccesslab.com) is an online solution designed to help you "Start Strong, Finish Stronger" by building skills for ongoing personal and professional development.

important employability skill. The Conference Board of Canada lists the ability to "take care of your personal health" as an important personal management skill.[2]

More Stress, Less Health; More Health, Less Stress

Modern science definitively shows that chronic stress increases the incidence of heart disease and cardiac deaths, raises blood pressure and cholesterol, worsens asthma, dampens immune system function, and may increase the chance of cancer occurrence.[3] Excess stress can have a negative impact on your health in two general ways:[4]

1. *Stress can create an overactive endocrine system.* When your body is under stress, your endocrine system releases hormones such as cortisol and adrenaline that help you cope. These hormones activate the fight-or-flight response, which is a good thing. However, your body is designed to process a quick rise and fall of cortisol in response to a single event, not to manage a consistently high level over a long period of time. High levels of cortisol, often in reaction to chronic anxiety, can cause problems such as inflammation, immune system issues, and arthritis.

2. *Stress can lead to health-harming habits.* When stress rises above the helpful mid-level range, a natural response is to try to reduce it quickly. Often this means turning to habits such as drinking, smoking, addictive substances, and eating high-fat and high-sugar foods that may provide short-term relief but have long-term negative effects. In addition, high levels of stress can make helpful habits such as eating right, exercising, and getting adequate sleep seem too hard to maintain.

The strength of this connection is good news. Because you have significant control over many aspects of your health, you have several opportunities to positively affect your stress level.

Manage Stress by Managing Health

First of all, know that you are on your way to becoming more healthy simply by being in school. Scientists and researchers who study aging report that more education is linked to a longer life, perhaps because education teaches cause-and-effect thinking that helps people make better choices. Another link could be that educated people tend to be more able to delay gratification, which helps you to avoid harmful habits.[5]

Managing time helps you to manage stress. Similarly, managing your health can move your stress level into that mid-range zone where it will help you more than hurt you. Although you cannot always control what happens to you, you can respond to events in healthful ways.

Your ability to manage stress depends in part on your understanding of how it affects you. In the Get Practical exercise, you will complete a self-assessment that asks you how much stress you experience in different areas of your life. With the information it provides, you will have a clearer idea of what factors to focus on as you work to manage stress, and you will be more able to decide what strategies serve you best as you explore ways to improve your health.

HOW CAN YOU TAKE CHARGE OF
your physical health?

The key phrase here is *take charge*. Your health and fitness are your responsibility. You choose what you eat, how and when (and whether) you exercise, and how much sleep you get—and you live with the results of your choices, both good and bad. This section provides information about various options and their potential effects. Use it to consider your range of choices, thinking through what risks you are willing to take to earn the reward of a healthy body and mind.

Pay Attention to What You Eat

Eating well can lead to more energy, better general health, and an improved quality of life. However, this is easier said than done. One reason is that the cheapest choices are usually not the best. Post-secondary students often live on limited budgets, so such an environment does not support their efforts to choose well.[6]

Day-to-day student life is also an issue. Students spend hours sitting and tend to eat on the run, or sometimes not at all, build social events around food, and eat as a reaction to stress. Even though recent research has shown that students average less weight gain than the "freshman 15," they still tend to put on weight, and may experience low energy and health issues related to food choices.[7]

Healthy eating requires balance (varying your diet) and moderation (eating reasonable amounts). Key 3.1 presents some ways to incorporate both into your life. Following are some additional details.

Evaluate your eating habits. Before you can make a change, you need to know what and how you eat. Keep a food log for a week, writing down what you eat and when you eat it each day. Look over the log. What kinds of food are you eating? What time of day are you eating the most? Do you eat when you are hungry? Worried? Nervous? Are you eating more than you need? If you consistently have reactions to a

KEY 3.1   **Create positive food habits.**

- Vary what you eat, focusing on local, organic fruits and vegetables, when possible.
- Choose foods with limited fat, cholesterol, and trans fats.
- Replace sugary snacks with fresh or dried fruit.
- Keep healthy snacks within reach to avoid temptation.
- Limit calorie-heavy alcoholic drinks and sugar-heavy pop.
- Notice and reduce portion sizes.
- Plan meals and minimize late-night eating sprees.
- Substitute other activities for stress-related eating.
- Get help from weight-loss organizations and on-campus support.

Lilly Trott/Shutterstock

certain type of food, consult a doctor. You may have a condition such as celiac disease or a food allergy that requires you to change how you eat.

Eat a variety of foods. For guidance about the different types and amounts of food you should be eating, explore the information and helpful tools from Canada's Food Guide at http://www.hc-sc.gc.ca/fn-an/food-guide-aliment/basics-base/index-eng.php. For example, half of your daily food intake should be fruits and vegetables—ideally, five servings a day. However, data released by Statistics Canada in 2015 indicated that only four in ten Canadians ate five or more servings of fruit and vegetables every day.[8] Work to balance your diet so that you get the nutrients you need.

Understand the effects of obesity. The term *obese* refers to a person with a body mass index (BMI) of 30 or more (overweight refers to having a BMI of 25–29). According to the Canadian Medical Association, obesity rates in Canada have tripled since 1985. Their report, published in 2014, estimates that 18% of Canadians have a BMI of more than 30.[9] Obesity is a major factor in the development of adult-onset diabetes, coronary heart disease, high blood pressure, stroke, cancer, and other illnesses. In 2015, Statistics Canada reported that 1 in 5 Canadians is obese.[10] Additional studies show that overweight job applicants and workers experience discrimination in interviews and on the job.[11]

BODY MASS INDEX (BMI)
The ratio of your weight to your height.

Target your ideal weight. Visit the Diabetes Canada website at www.diabetes.ca and use its BMI calculator to find out if you fall within a healthy range or would be considered overweight or obese. If you want to lose weight, set a reasonable goal and work toward it at a pace of approximately no more than one kilo a week. You may also want to consult health professionals, enroll in a reputable and reasonable weight-loss program, and incorporate regular exercise into your life.

Prioritize Exercise

Evidence increasingly points to exercise as a key element of your health. The Mayo Clinic reports numerous positive effects of exercise, including reducing incidence of disease, easing depression, reducing fatigue, and maintaining a healthy weight.[12] During physical activity, the brain releases endorphins—chemical compounds that have a positive and calming effect on the body. In addition, regular exercise builds discipline, time-management skills, and motivation that can also contribute to academic success. Risking the time and effort to exercise brings enormous rewards.

Types of exercise

There are three general categories of exercise: cardiovascular (aerobic activity for your heart), strength, and flexibility (see Key 3.2). The type you choose depends on your exercise goals, personality, available equipment, your time and fitness level, and other factors. Some exercises fall primarily into one category. For example, weight lifting is a strength activity and biking is a cardiovascular activity. However, others, like power yoga or Pilates, combine elements of two or three categories. For maximum benefit, alternate and combine different types of exercise.

How much exercise do you need? Try to do both aerobic and muscle-strengthening activities and spread out your activity through the week. You may want to break it into smaller chunks of time throughout the day. Even 10 minutes at a time is just fine.[13] Dr. Mike Evans has a video on YouTube identifying 30 minutes of exercise a day as a more significant health intervention than any other. He asks a question: "Can you limit your sitting and sleeping to just 23½ hours a day?" When you think about it, that's a pretty minimal risk for a significant reward.[14]

KEY 3.2 Vary your exercise activities among three types of training.

Cardiovascular Training
• Strengthens your heart and lungs
• Examples: swimming, running, skating, aerobic dancing, and biking
Strength Training
• Strengthens different muscle groups
• Examples: weight machines, free weights, push-ups, and abdominal crunches
Flexibility Training
• Increases muscle flexibility
• Examples: yoga and stretching exercises such as dynamic, ballistic, static active, and static passive

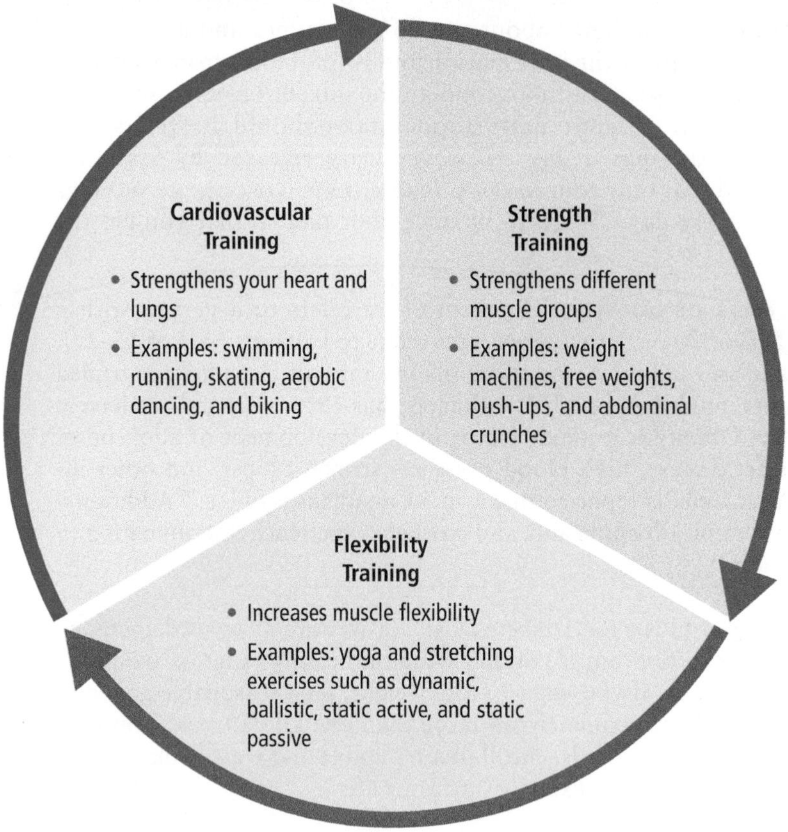

Find time for exercise

Busy students often have trouble getting to the gym, even when there is a fully equipped athletic centre on campus. Use the following ideas to make exercise a priority, even during the busiest weeks:

- Walk to classes and meetings. When you are inside buildings, use the stairs.
- Use your school's fitness facilities.
- Ride your bike instead of driving.
- Play team recreational sports at school or in your community.
- Take walks or bike rides for study breaks.
- Find activities you can do outside, such as running or pickup basketball.
- Work out with friends or family to combine socializing and exercise.
- Do a routine on your own with a DVD or on-demand TV exercise program.

Being fit is a lifelong pursuit that is never "done." Furthermore, since your body is constantly changing, reevaluate your exercise program on a regular basis to maximize its benefits.

Get Enough Sleep

Sleep is crucial for both stress reduction and normal development, but post-secondary students are often sleep deprived. While research indicates that they need eight to nine hours of sleep a night to function well, students average only six to seven hours—and often get much less.[15] Inadequate sleep hinders concentration, raises stress levels, and makes you more susceptible to illness. It can also increase the likelihood of auto accidents. According to Dr. Tracy Kuo at the Stanford Sleep Disorders Clinic, "A sleepy driver is just as dangerous as a drunk driver."[16]

Students, overwhelmed with responsibilities, often feel they have no choice but to prioritize schoolwork over sleep. Some regularly stay up until the wee hours of the morning to study. Others pull "all-nighters" from time to time to get through a tough project or paper. These habits affect your ability to learn and think, and can weaken your immune system. If you choose the risk of sleeping instead of putting in a few more hours of studying, you may experience a greater reward at test time than if you had studied all night.

For the sake of your health and your GPA, get some sleep. If you experience symptoms of sleep deprivation such as morning grogginess, dozing off in class, or needing caffeine to make it through the day, look to sleep expert Gregg D. Jacobs, Ph.D., for practical suggestions for improving sleep habits:[17]

- *Reduce consumption of alcohol and caffeine.* Caffeine may make you hungry (it drops your blood sugar level) or keep you awake, especially if you drink it late. Alcohol causes you to sleep lightly, making you feel less rested when you awaken.
- *Exercise regularly.* Regular exercise, especially in the afternoon or early evening, promotes sleep.
- *Take naps.* Taking short afternoon naps can reduce the effects of sleep deprivation.
- *Be consistent.* Try to establish somewhat regular times to wake up and go to bed.
- *Create a ritual.* Wind down and transition from work to sleep with a bedtime ritual. Read a book, listen to calming music, or drink a cup of herbal tea.
- *Manage your sleep environment.* Wear something comfortable, turn down the lights, and keep the room cool. Use earplugs or white noise to deal with outside distractions.

HOW CAN YOU TAKE CHARGE OF
mental and emotional health?

It is not enough to have a healthy body. Your well-being also depends on having a healthy mind, one that sees the world as it is and copes effectively. However, this is a challenge for many people, in part because of the exceptional power of the human brain.

Neurologist Robert Sapolsky explains that humans' ability to anticipate the future has a downside. "[For] a normal mammal, a stressor is a challenge to homeostatic balance—a real physical challenge in the world—and the stress-response is the adaptation your body mobilizes to re-establish homeostasis. For a cognitively complex species (like humans and other primates), a stressor is also the ANTICIPATION that a a real physical challenge is about to happen. If there really is not the threat of a physical stressor coming, then you are setting yourself up for increased risk of stress-related disease."[18] In other words, thinking about potential stressors makes your body react as though you are experiencing them. And if you can't stop thinking about them, being in a constant state of stress response will take a toll on your health over time.

Staying positive about who you are, making hopeful plans for the future, and building resilience to cope with setbacks will help you cultivate good mental health. However, some people experience emotional disorders that make it more difficult than usual to calm the stress response and cope. If you recognize yourself in any of the following descriptions, take practical steps to improve your health. Most student health and campus counselling centres provide medical and psychological help or referrals. Although asking for help may feel like a risk, most who do it find it is well worth the

Try to find productive ways to reduce stress. This student has chosen to spend time outdoors, eat a healthful lunch, and connect with a friend on the phone.

reward of feeling better and functioning more effectively. You won't be alone. Statistics Canada reports that in 2012, about 5 million Canadians felt they needed help with a mental health issue. Luckily, of those 5 million, two-thirds of them were able to find the help they needed.[19]

Be Aware of the Symptoms of Depression and Anxiety

It's common to experience negative emotions such as sadness after a breakup or anxiety over a low grade. However, depressive and anxiety disorders are illnesses, not temporary mental states that you can shake off, and sufferers need care and support. If you recognize these symptoms in someone you know, talk with the person about his or her feelings. Then try to convince the individual to see a doctor or mental health professional. Don't keep your concerns a secret; they may save someone. If you recognize these symptoms in yourself, reach out for help. There are people who care and can assist you. The right help can change or even save your life.

Depressive disorder

Depression is fairly common among post-secondary students. Research by the American Psychological Association (APA) found that 41 percent of students experience moderate to severe depression at some point in their academic careers.[20] Key 3.3 shows possible causes of depression, as well as some typical symptoms.

The Canadian Mental Health Association says depression isn't just someone feeling blue. It is a person "grappling with feelings of severe despair over an extended period of time. Almost every aspect of their life can be affected, including their emotions, physical health, relationships, and work. For people with depression, it does not feel like there is a light at the end of the tunnel—there is just a long, dark tunnel."[21]

Depression is treatable, but diagnosis requires a medical evaluation. Most student health and campus counselling centres provide both medical and psychological help, as well as referrals. For some people, adequate sleep, regular exercise, a healthy diet, and the passage of time can ease the disorder. For others, behavioural modification therapy and medication are important.

At its worst, depression can lead to suicide. SAVE (Suicide Awareness Voices of Education) lists the warning signs of an impending suicide:[22]

- Statements about hopelessness or worthlessness: "The world would be better without me."
- Loss of interest in people, things, or activities.
- Preoccupation with suicide or death.
- Visiting or calling family and friends and giving things away.
- Sudden sense of happiness or calm. A decision to commit suicide often brings a sense of relief that convinces others that the person "seemed to be on an upswing."

Risk sounding an alarm if someone you know exhibits any of these warning signs. And if you show signs yourself, don't let them go unnoticed. Consider visiting

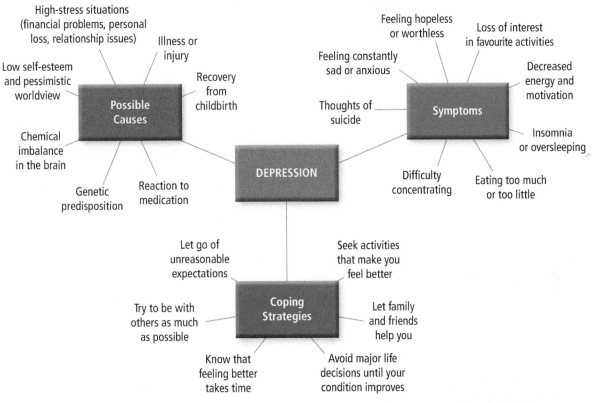

Source: Based on "Depression." National Institutes of Health publication 02-3561. National Institutes of Health, Bethesda, MD, 2002.

ULifeline, an organization dedicated to helping students manage mental health, at www.ulifeline.org. Complete its self evaluator to see what it tells you. Over 250 000 students have completed it to date—more evidence that troubled students are not alone.

Anxiety disorders

As with depression, anxiety disorders have been on the rise among students over the last decade. Potential causes include the struggling economy and job market, being constantly available via communication technology, and even the message of the modern world that you can be anything and do anything if only you work hard enough or get lucky, which can result in a disabling fear of failure.[23] Factors like these contribute to a consistently high stress response that can result in an anxiety disorder.

Types of anxiety disorders include:

- Generalized anxiety disorder (GAD), characterized by a nearly constant state of worry that is difficult to control and not always related to a cause
- Obsessive-compulsive disorder (OCD), characterized by obsessive thoughts that lead to compulsive behaviours
- Post-traumatic stress disorder (PTSD), which is especially common in war veterans or survivors of abuse, and involves flashbacks, avoidance, and heightened emotion and awareness
- Panic disorder, characterized by "panic attacks" that feature increased heart and breathing rates, dizziness, and a sense of impending doom

Recognizing an anxiety disorder can be challenging. In fact, many students who ultimately are diagnosed do not initially believe they have a medical problem, figuring that the anxiety they are experiencing is normal. This is especially true for students who have experienced high levels of anxiety all of their lives up until this point without any medical intervention. Any student who feels that anxiety is affecting his or her ability to function in or out of class should consult with a professional to see if an anxiety disorder is to blame.

Watch Out for Eating Disorders

Millions of people develop serious and sometimes life-threatening eating disorders every year, including anorexia nervosa, bulimia, and binge eating disorder. Negative effects of these disorders range from fertility and obesity issues to digestive tract and other organ damage, heart failure, and even death. There are three basic types of eating disorders:[24]

- *Anorexia nervosa.* People with anorexia nervosa restrict their eating and become dangerously underweight. They may also engage in over-exercising, vomiting, and abuse of diuretics and laxatives. Eventually, without proper nourishment, their internal organs begin to shut down, ending in death if no intervention occurs. Anorexia nervosa is often linked to excessive anxiety and perfectionism or the desire for control.
- *Bulimia nervosa.* People with bulimia engage in "binge episodes," which involve eating excessive amounts of foods and feeling out of control. Following the binge, the person feels remorseful and attempts to purge the calories through self-induced vomiting, laxative abuse, excessive exercise, or fasting. Bulimia is often linked to emotional distress that causes so much pain that an individual tries to "numb" the feeling by overeating.
- *Binge eating disorder.* Binge eating disorder is the most common eating disorder. People with this condition eat large amounts of food and feel out of control, similar to those with bulimia, but they do not purge after a binge episode. However, just like bulimics, they eat unusually fast, eat in secret, eat until they feel uncomfortably full, and feel ashamed of their eating behaviours.

Eating disorders are very difficult to cope with on your own, in part because you can't live without food, whereas avoiding tobacco or alcohol, for example, will not threaten your life. If you suffer from an eating disorder, risk asking for help from a counsellor who can offer the reward of care and understanding.

Increase Stability and Focus with Mindfulness Meditation

Many people's minds are overwhelmed with thoughts and worries on a daily basis. *Mindfulness* refers to paying focused attention, and meditation is a form of contemplation that helps you create that focus, reducing stress and anxiety and the damage they cause to your body. Meditation has measurable physical effects, such as reducing blood pressure, heart rate, and even inflammation.[25]

Pick a quiet time of day and a location where you can be alone and comfortable. Sit on a cushion or in a chair. Rest your hands in your lap, palms up, and close your eyes. Start by breathing deeply, in and out, preferably through your nose. Listen to your breathing.

Konstantin Sutyagin/Fotolia

How you meditate is up to you—it's your time. Some people like to set a timer and start with a one-minute meditation, then extend it to two, three, or more minutes.

binkski/123RF

Diego Cervo/
Shutterstock

EXPLORING YOUR STRESSORS

All sorts of situations and experiences can cause stress during college or university life. Furthermore, everyone has a unique response to any potential stressor. One way to assess your individual situation is to look at the different areas of your life and rate how much stress you are experiencing in each at the current time. Use a scale from 1 to 10, with 1 being the lowest possible level of stress and 10 being the highest possible level:

_____ 1. Increased independence and responsibility

_____ 2. Family relationships

_____ 3. Friend relationships

_____ 4. Academic relationships (instructors, student peers, administration, and so on)

_____ 5. Boyfriend/girlfriend/spouse relationships

_____ 6. Managing time and schedule

_____ 7. Managing money

_____ 8. Performance on assignments

_____ 9. Performance on tests

_____10. Physical health and fitness

_____11. Mental health and balance

_____12. Academic planning (major, and so on)

_____13. Career planning and vision for future

_____14. Work situation, if you have a job on or off campus

_____15. Current living situation (home, dorm, and so on)

Total your points here: 84

The lowest possible score is 15, and the highest possible 150. The higher your score, the more stress you perceive you are currently experiencing. Things to think about:

- Ponder what your total score says about your life at the moment. A score over 100 may indicate that reducing stress should be a top priority for you right now. A score under 50 may indicate that you are currently experiencing tolerable, and even productive, levels of stress.

- Take a look at how you rated each item, and consider putting particular energy into the areas that you rated the highest. There are two ways to determine where your energy would serve you best: One, focus on any area that you rated a 7 or higher. Two, focus on the five areas that you rated highest, no matter what number you gave them.

School and community resources can help you manage whatever level of stress you are experiencing. On a separate sheet of paper or digital file, write down names, locations, hours, phone numbers, URLs, and any other pertinent information for the following resources:

- Free counselling offered to students

- Exercise facility

- Sexual assault centre

- Other resource

Source: Adapted in part from Kohn, P.M., K. Lafreniere, and M. Gurevich, "The Inventory of College Students Recent Life Experiences: A Decontaminated Hassles Scale for a Special Population." *Journal of Behavioral Medicine*, vol. 13, no. 6, pp. 619–630, 1990.

Some people like to count as they inhale and exhale. When thoughts come up, let them pass by as if you were watching a movie. If you have a hard time sitting still, try an active meditation, breathing and counting while you walk, bike, or swim.

The stresses of school lead some students to experiment with alcohol, tobacco, and other potentially addictive substances. Although these substances may alleviate stress temporarily, they have potentially serious consequences.

Emotional and Physical Wellness

WHAT CHOICES WILL YOU MAKE
about substance use?

Abusing alcohol, tobacco, and drugs adds significantly to stress levels and can cause financial struggles, emotional traumas, family and financial upheaval, health problems, and even death. As you read the information in this section, think about the effects of your actions on yourself and others. Measure the risk of substance use against the social risk of going against what others are doing, and decide which reward is more valuable to you. Continually look for ways to make positive, life-affirming choices.

The frontal lobe of your brain is responsible for impulse control. It's the part that asks, "Is this really a good idea? What will happen if I take this action?" However, the frontal lobe does not reach full development until around the age of 25. This means that people under 25 are more likely to perform an action, such as taking drugs, without considering potential consequences.[26] Worse, those drugs are more likely to impair brain development and result in addiction in a younger person than in an older one.[27] Consider the information in this section.

Alcohol

Alcohol is a depressant and the most frequently abused drug on campus. Even a few drinks affect thinking and muscle coordination. Heavy drinking can damage the liver, digestive system, and brain cells, as well as impair the central nervous system. Prolonged use also leads to physical and emotional addiction, making it seem impossible to quit.

ADDICTION
The compulsive use of and need for a habit-forming substance.

According to the Centers for Disease Control (CDC), your tolerance and reaction to alcohol depends on a variety of factors including, but not limited to, age, gender, race or ethnicity, physical condition, the amount of food consumed before drinking, how quickly alcohol was consumed, use of drugs or prescription medications, and family history.[28] Key 3.4 shows the varying levels of drinking behaviours defined by the CDC.

Of all alcohol consumption, *binge drinking* (see Key 3.4) is associated with the greatest problems, and is consistently an issue on campuses, with over 42 percent of full-time students and over 35 percent of part-time students reporting a binge drinking episode in the month prior to the survey.[29] Students who binge drink are more likely to miss classes, perform poorly, experience physical problems (memory loss, headache, stomach issues), become depressed, and engage in unplanned or unsafe sex.[30]

If you drink, think carefully about the effects on your health, safety, and academic performance. The Get Analytical exercise on page 69 is a self-test that will help you analyze your habits.

Tobacco

Due to public education campaigns and a rise in smoking bans in Canada, smoking is becoming less common in Canada. While smoking is on the decline, 18 percent of Canadians over the age of 12, still smoke cigarettes. Men are more likely to smoke than women.[31]

Many students who use tobacco as a stress reliever become hooked on nicotine, a highly addictive drug found in all tobacco products. Nicotine's immediate effects may include an increase in blood pressure and heart rate, sweating, and throat irritation. Long-term effects may include high blood pressure, bronchitis and emphysema, stomach ulcers, heart disease, and cancer. Although advertisers spend millions of dollars a day trying to convince you smoking is sexy, an estimated 1 billion people will die from tobacco-related illnesses worldwide in the twenty-first century.[32]

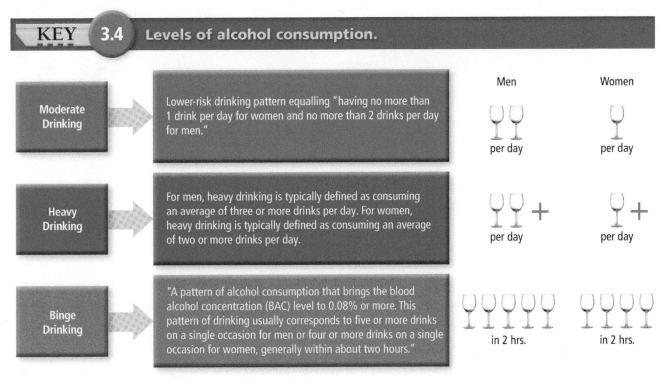

Source: Centers for Disease Control. "Alcohol and Public Health." Centers for Disease Control, October 14, 2011. Accessed on October 28, 2011, from http://www .cdc.gov/alcohol/index.htm.

In recent years, the health dangers of secondhand smoke have been recognized. According to Health Canada, living with smokers or being around them on a regular basis is linked to breathing problems (such as asthma, bronchitis and emphysema). It can also lead to heart problems.[33] This awareness has led many colleges and universities to ban smoking in dorm rooms, classrooms, and other public spaces. More and more companies, aware of the problem, ban smoking in the workplace or even refuse to hire people who smoke.[34]

SECONDHAND SMOKE
Smoke in the air exhaled by smokers or given off by cigarettes, cigars, or pipes.

If you smoke regularly, you know that quitting is challenging. However, if you seek help and persevere, you have a good chance of success. Practical suggestions for quitting include the following:[35]

- Try a nicotine patch or nicotine gum, and be sure to use it consistently.
- Get support and encouragement from a health care provider, a "quit smoking" program, a support group, and friends and family.
- Avoid situations that increase your desire to smoke, such as being around other smokers and drinking heavily.
- Find other ways to lower stress, such as exercise or other activities you enjoy.
- Set goals. Set a quit date and tell friends and family.

The positive effects of quitting include increased life expectancy and lung capacity, better skin, less body odour, and financial savings. If you're interested in quitting, investigate resources at the Canadian Cancer Society (BreakItOff.ca).

Drugs

Illicit drug use is a perennial problem on campuses. The NSDUH reports that 22% of students surveyed had used illicit drugs in the year prior to the survey.[36] Some students

get $mart

Racom/123RF

THE RELATIONSHIP BETWEEN WELLNESS AND FINANCIAL FITNESS

Creativenv/
Shutterstock

Complete the following on paper or in digital format.

Wellness has its costs—fitness club fees and healthy food often aren't cheap, although they can save you medical costs down the line. Track health-related expenses (both positive and negative) for one week and enter your daily and weekly totals in a grid you create with headers as shown here.

ITEM	MON	TUES	WED	THURS	FRI	SAT	SUN	TOTAL

In the "Item" column, include a row for each of the following items: Food + (healthful food), Food – (junk food), Alcohol, Tobacco, Fitness, Other. For monthly fees such as fitness memberships, divide by four and enter your result in the TOTAL box for fitness.

Looking at your grid when the week is over, answer the following questions.

1. Approximately how much did you spend on items that increase wellness?
2. Approximately how much did you spend on items that decrease wellness?
3. Are you spending more to increase or decrease wellness?
4. If you want to change how you spend money related to your wellness, describe your desired change here and be specific about how you plan to put it into action.

use drugs to relieve stress, others want to be accepted by peers, and other just want to try something new.

In most cases, however, the negative consequences of drug use outweigh any temporary high. You can jeopardize your reputation, your student status, and your ability to get a job if you are caught using drugs or if drug use impairs your performance. Finally, long-term drug use can damage your body and mind. Key 3.5 has comprehensive information about the most commonly used illicit drugs.

You are responsible for analyzing the potential consequences of what you introduce into your body. Ask yourself questions such as the following:

- What reward am I receiving from taking this risk, and it is worthwhile?
- Am I taking drugs to escape from other problems?
- What positive and negative effects might my behaviour have?
- Why do others want me to take drugs, and what do I really think of these people?
- How would my drug use affect the people in my life?

Use the self-test to assess your relationship with drugs. If you believe you have a problem, read the following section on steps that can help you get your life back on track.

DRUG	DRUG CATEGORY	USERS MAY FEEL . . .	POTENTIAL SHORT-TERM AND LONG-TERM PHYSICAL EFFECTS	DANGER OF DEPENDENCE
Alcohol	Depressant	Sedated, relaxed, loose	Impaired brain function, impaired reflexes and judgment, cirrhosis of the liver, impaired blood production, greater risk of cancer, heart attack, and stroke	Strong with regular, heavy use
Anabolic steroids (also called *roids, juice, hype*)	Steroid	Increased muscle strength and physical performance, energetic	Stunted growth, mood swings, male-pattern baldness, breast development (in men) or body hair development (in women), mood swings, liver damage, insomnia, aggression, irritability	Insubstantial
Cocaine (also called *coke, blow, snow*) and crack cocaine (also called *crack* or *rock*)	Stimulant	Alert, stimulated, excited, energetic, confident	Nervousness, mood swings, sexual problems, stroke or convulsions, psychoses, paranoia, coma at large doses	Strong
Ecstasy (also called *molly, X, XTC, vitamin E*)	Stimulant	Heightened sensual perception, relaxed, clear, fearless	Fatigue, anxiety, depression, heart arrhythmia, hyperthermia from lack of fluid intake during use	Insubstantial
Ephedrine (also called *chi powder, zest*)	Stimulant	Energetic	Anxiety, elevated blood pressure, heart palpitations, memory loss, stroke, psychosis, insomnia	Strong
Gamma hydroxyl butyrate (GHB) (also called *G, liquid ecstasy, goop*)	Depressant	Uninhibited, relaxed, euphoric	Anxiety, vertigo, increased heart rate, delirium, agitation	Strong
Glue, aerosols (also called *whippets, poppers, rush*)	Inhalants	Giddy, lightheaded, dizzy, excited	Damage to brain, liver, lungs, and kidneys, suffocation, heart failure	Insubstantial
Hallucinogenic mushrooms (psilocybin mushrooms or amanita muscaria) (also called shrooms, magic mushrooms)	Hallucinogen	Strong emotions, hallucinations, distortions of sight and sound, "out of body" experience	Paranoia, agitation, poisoning	Insubstantial
Heroin (also called *smack, dope, horse*) and **codeine**	Opiates	Warm, relaxed, without pain, without anxiety	Infection of organs, inflammation of the heart, convulsions, abscesses, risk of needle-transmitted diseases such as hepatitis and HIV	Strong, with heavy use
Ketamine (also called *K, Special K, vitamin K*)	Anesthetic	Dreamy, floating, having an "out of body" sensation, numb	Neuroses, disruptions in consciousness, reduced ability to move	Strong
Lysergic acid diethylamide (LSD) (also called *acid, blotter, trips*)	Hallucinogen	Heightened sensual perception, hallucinations, distortions of sight and sound, little sense of time	Impaired brain function, paranoia, agitation and confusion, flashbacks	Insubstantial
Marijuana and **hashish** (also called *pot, weed, herb*)	Cannabinol	Euphoric, mellow, little sensation of time, paranoid	Impaired judgment and coordination, bronchitis and asthma, lung and throat cancers, anxiety, lack of energy and motivation, hormone and fertility problems	Moderate

DRUG	DRUG CATEGORY	USERS MAY FEEL . . .	POTENTIAL SHORT-TERM AND LONG-TERM PHYSICAL EFFECTS	DANGER OF DEPENDENCE
Methamphetamine (also called *meth*, *speed*, *crank*)	Stimulant	Euphoric, confident, alert, energetic	Seizures, heart attack, strokes, vein damage (if injected), sleeplessness, hallucinations, high blood pressure, paranoia, psychoses, depression, anxiety, loss of appetite, severe dental decay	Strong, especially if taken by smoking
Nicotine (also called *smokes*, *cigs*)	Stimulant and depressant	Causes a release of adrenaline, speeding up breathing and heartrate; also causes the release of dopamine into the brain, resulting in feelings of pleasure and well-being. Heroin and "crack" have the same effects on the brain.	Lung cancer, emphysema, asthma, stroke, heart attack, miscarriage, ear infections and respiratory problems (in children exposed to secondhand smoke)	High
OxyContin (also called *Oxy*, *OC*, *legal heroin*)	Analgesic (containing opiate)	Relaxed, detached, without pain or anxiety	Overdose death can result when users ingest or inhale crushed time-release pills, or take them in conjunction with alcohol or narcotics	Moderate, with long-term use

Source: Based on "I Am a Parent." Drug Policy Alliance, 2011. Accessed on October 28, 2011, from http://www.safety1st.org/drugfacts.html; nicotine information from "NIDA InfoFacts: Cigarettes and Other Tobacco Products." National Institute of on Drug Abuse, September, 2010. Accessed on October 25, 2011, from http://drugabuse.gov/infofacts/tobacco.html.

Facing Addiction

Because substances often cause physical changes and psychological dependence, quitting may involve a painful withdrawal. Asking for help isn't a failure, but a risk calculated to earn you the reward of reclaiming your life. If you think you may be addicted, seek help. Even one "yes" answer on the self-test may indicate a need to evaluate alcohol or drug use and monitor it more carefully. If you answered "yes" to three or more questions, you may benefit from talking to a professional about your substance use and the problems it may be causing.

Working through substance-abuse problems can lead to restored health and self-respect. Helpful resources can help you generate options and develop practical plans for recovery.

- *Counselling and medical care.* You can find help from school-based, private, government-sponsored, or workplace-sponsored resources. Ask your school's counselling or health centre, your personal physician, or a local hospital for a referral.

- *Detoxification ("detox") centres.* If you have a severe addiction, you may need a controlled environment where you can separate yourself completely from drugs or alcohol, including the people and places associated with it.

- *Support groups.* Alcoholics Anonymous (AA) has led to other support groups for addicts such as Overeaters Anonymous (OA) and Narcotics Anonymous (NA). These groups are free, effective, anonymous, and meet in almost every city, almost every day of the week.

get analytical

Darren Baker/Shutterstock

EVALUATE YOUR SUBSTANCE USE

Dario Sabljak/Shutterstock

Even one "yes" answer to the following questions may indicate a need to examine your habits. Three or more "yes" answers indicate that you may benefit from discussing your substance use with a counsellor.

Within the last year:

- (Y) (N) 1. Have you tried to stop drinking or taking drugs but found that you couldn't do so for long?
- (Y) (N) 2. Do you get tired of people telling you they're concerned about your drinking or drug use?
- (Y) (N) 3. Have you felt guilty about your drinking or drug use?
- (Y) (N) 4. Have you felt that you needed a drink or drugs in the morning—as an "eye-opener"—to cope with a hangover?
- (Y) (N) 5. Do you drink or use drugs alone?
- (Y) (N) 6. Do you drink or use drugs every day?
- (Y) (N) 7. Have you found yourself regularly thinking or saying you "need" a drink or any type of drug?
- (Y) (N) 8. Have you lied about or concealed your drinking or drug use?
- (Y) (N) 9. Do you drink or use drugs to escape worries, problems, mistakes, or shyness?
- (Y) (N) 10. Do you find you need increasingly larger amounts of drugs or alcohol in order to achieve a desired effect?
- (Y) (N) 11. Have you forgotten what happened while drinking or using drugs because you had a blackout?
- (Y) (N) 12. Have you spent a lot of time, energy, or money getting alcohol or drugs?
- (Y) (N) 13. Has your drinking or drug use caused you to neglect friends, your partner, your children, or other family members, or caused other problems at home?
- (Y) (N) 14. Have you gotten into an argument or a fight that was alcohol- or drug-related?
- (Y) (N) 15. Has your drinking or drug use caused you to miss class, fail a test, or ignore schoolwork?
- (Y) (N) 16. Have you been choosing to drink or use drugs instead of attending social events or performing other activities you used to enjoy?
- (Y) (N) 17. Has your drinking or drug use affected your efficiency on the job or caused you to fail to show up at work?
- (Y) (N) 18. Have you continued to drink or use drugs despite any physical problems that your use has caused or made worse?
- (Y) (N) 19. Have you driven a car or performed any other potentially dangerous tasks while under the influence of alcohol or drugs?
- (Y) (N) 20. Have you had a drug- or alcohol-related legal problem or arrest (possession, use, disorderly conduct, driving while intoxicated, and so on)?

Source: Adapted from the Criteria for Substance Dependence and Criteria for Substance Abuse in the Diagnostic and *Statistical Manual of Mental Disorders*, Fourth Edition, published by the American Psychiatric Association, Washington, DC, and from materials entitled "Are You An Alcoholic?" developed by Johns Hopkins University.

HOW CAN YOU DEFINE AND
maintain sexual boundaries?

Your success in school depends as much on making choices that maintain health and safety—yours as well as those of others with whom you may be involved—as it does on managing time. Some of those important choices will be in the realm of sexual identity and activity.

Emotional and Physical Wellness

Sexual Choices and Consequences

Sexual identity in the modern world incorporates heterosexuality and homosexuality and goes beyond those designations into areas such as bisexuality and transgendered persons. Many people see sexual identity as a continuum, with places for individuals who don't feel that they fit squarely into one particular category. How you identify sexually is your personal business, as is what sexuality means to you and the role it plays in your life.

However, the decisions you make go beyond the personal realm. Because sexual conduct can result in an unexpected pregnancy or passing on sexually transmitted infections (STIs), consequences can extend for years and can affect both the people involved in the act and their families. Analyze sexual issues carefully. Look at potential effects of your choices, determine what rewards hold value for you, and consider what calculated risks can move you safely toward those rewards. Ask questions like the following:

- Is this what I really want? Does it fit with my values?
- Do I feel ready or do I feel pressured? Does this choice cause stress for me?
- Is this the right person/moment/situation? Does my partner truly care for me and not just for what we might be doing? Will this enhance or damage our emotional relationship?
- Do I have what I need to prevent pregnancy and exposure to STIs? If not, is having unprotected sex worth taking the chance?

Img Raj/Shutterstock

Using birth control is a choice that helps you decide when and if you want to be a parent. However, it is not for everyone. For some, using birth control goes against religious or personal beliefs. Others may not use birth control because they are ready to have children. Evaluate the pros and cons of each option. Consider cost, reliability, comfort, and protection against STIs. Communicate with your partner, then make a choice together. For more information, check your library, the internet, or a bookstore; talk to a doctor; or ask a counsellor at the student health centre. Key 3.6 describes established methods, with effectiveness percentages and STI prevention based on proper and regular use.

Protect Your Health

STIs spread through sexual contact, including intercourse or other sexual activity (oral or anal) that involves contact with the genitals, and cause a wide variety of health issues. All STIs are highly contagious. The only birth control methods that offer protection are the male and female condoms (latex or polyurethane only), which prevent skin-to-skin contact. Have a doctor examine any irregularity or discomfort as soon as you detect it. Key 3.7 describes common STIs.

The most serious STI is AIDS (acquired immune deficiency syndrome), caused by the human immunodeficiency virus (HIV). AIDS has no cure and can be fatal. People transmit HIV through sexual relations; by sharing hypodermic needles for drug use; by receiving infected blood transfusions; or through pregnancy, birth, or breastfeeding. Therefore, it is unlikely you can contract HIV from toilet seats, hugging, kissing, or sharing a glass. Other than not having sex, using condoms (latex only) is the best defence against AIDS. Avoid petroleum jelly, which can destroy latex. Although some people dislike condoms, using them is a small price to pay for preserving your life.

Make an educated decision about birth control.

METHOD	APPROXIMATE EFFECTIVENESS	PREVENTS STIs?	DESCRIPTION
Abstinence	100%	Only if no sexual activity occurs	Just saying no. No intercourse means no risk of pregnancy. However, alternative modes of sexual activity can still spread STIs.
Condom (Male)	85% (95% with spermicide)	Yes, if made of latex	A sheath that fits over the penis and prevents sperm from entering the vagina.
Condom (female)	95% if used correctly	Yes, if used correctly	A pouch with flexible rings at each end. It is inserted into the vagina, with the ring at the open end staying outside the vagina.
Diaphragm, cervical cap, or **shield**	85%	No	A bendable rubber cap that fits over the cervix and pelvic bone inside the vagina (the cervical cap and shield are smaller and fit over the cervix only). The diaphragm and cervical cap must be fitted initially by a gynecologist. All must be used with a spermicide.
Oral contraceptives (the pill)	99% with perfect use, 92% for typical users	No	A dosage of hormones taken daily by a woman, preventing the ovaries from releasing eggs. Side effects can include headaches, weight gain, and increased chances of blood clotting. Various brands and dosages; must be prescribed by a gynecologist.
Injectable contraceptives (Depo-Provera)	97%	No	An injection that a woman must receive from a doctor every few months. Possible side effects may resemble those of oral contraceptives.
Vaginal ring (NuvaRing)	92%	No	A ring inserted into the vagina that releases hormones. Must be replaced monthly. Possible side effects may resemble those of oral contraceptives.
Spermicidal foams, jellies, inserts	71% if used alone	No	Usually used with diaphragms or condoms to enhance effectiveness, they have an ingredient that kills sperm cells (but not STIs). They stay effective for a limited period of time after insertion.
Intrauterine device (IUD)	99%	No	A small coil of wire inserted into the uterus by a gynecologist (who must also remove it). Prevents fertilized eggs from implanting in the uterine wall. May or may not have a hormone component. Possible side effects include increased or abnormal bleeding.
Tubal ligation	Nearly 100%	No	Surgery for women that cuts and ties the fallopian tubes, preventing eggs from travelling to the uterus. Difficult and expensive to reverse. Recommended for those who do not want any, or any more, children.
Vasectomy	Nearly 100%	No	Surgery for men that blocks the tube that delivers sperm to the penis. Like tubal ligation, difficult to reverse and only recommended for those who don't want any, or any more, children.
Rhythm method	Variable	No	Abstaining from intercourse during the ovulation segment of the woman's menstrual cycle. Can be difficult to time and may not account for cycle irregularities.
Withdrawal	Variable	No	Pulling the penis out of the vagina before ejaculation. Unreliable, because some sperm can escape in the fluid released prior to ejaculation. Dependent on a controlled partner.

Source: Based on MayoClinic staff. "In-Depth birth control: Birth control basics." Mayo Clinic. Accessed on October 28, 2011, from http://www.mayoclinic.com/health/birthcontrol/MY01182/TAB=indepth.

Emotional and Physical Wellness

get creative

Auremar/123RF

EXPAND YOUR PERCEPTION OF FUN

Astroid/123RF

Complete the following on paper or in digital format.

Use your creativity to find things to do with friends that lie outside of the realm of potentially unsafe activities. Check your resources: What possibilities can you find at your student union, student activities centre, or local arts organizations, athletic organizations, various clubs, or nature groups? Could you go hiking or biking? Paint pottery? Check out a baseball game? Try a new kind of cuisine? Volunteer at a children's hospital? See a play? Have a book club? List 10 specific activities available to you.

Modern retroviral drugs can slow the progression of an HIV infection and extend life expectancy. However, one of the unfortunate consequences of the improvements in medications for HIV-positive patients is the mistaken notion that AIDS and HIV are no longer a danger. This has led to the phenomenon of "safe sex fatigue," in which young and healthy people grow tired of being vigilant about using condoms for every sexual encounter. Don't let your guard down.

KEY 3.7 To stay safe, know these facts about sexually transmitted infections.

DISEASE	SYMPTOMS	HEALTH PROBLEMS IF UNTREATED	TREATMENTS
Chlamydia	Discharge, painful urination, swollen or painful joints, change in menstrual periods for women	Can cause pelvic inflammatory disease (PID) in women, which can lead to sterility or ectopic pregnancies; infection; miscarriage; or premature birth.	Curable with full course of antibiotics; avoid sex until treatment is complete.
Gonorrhea	Discharge, burning while urinating	Can cause PID, swelling of testicles and penis, arthritis, skin problems, infections, sterility.	Usually curable with antibiotics; however, certain strains are becoming resistant to medication.
Genital herpes	Blister-like itchy sores in the genital area, headache, fever, chills	Symptoms may subside and then reoccur, often in response to high stress levels; carriers can transmit the virus even when it is dormant.	No cure; some antiviral medications can reduce and help heal the sores, as well as shorten outbreaks and reduce the chance of transmission.
Syphilis	A genital sore (often painless) lasting one to five weeks, followed by a rash, fatigue, fever, sore throat, headaches, swollen glands	If it lasts over four years, it can cause blindness, destruction of bone, dementia, or heart failure; can cause death or deformity of a child born to an infected woman.	Curable with full course of antibiotics. Important to receive treatment early; treatment will not reverse damage done by earlier stages of the disease.
Human Papilloma Virus (HPV, or genital warts)	Genital itching and irritation, small clusters of warts	Can increase risk of cancers including cervical cancer in women; virus may remain in body and cause recurrences even when warts are removed.	No treatment for virus, but warts are treatable with drugs or wart removal surgery. Vaccine available (three doses necessary); most effective when given before exposure to HPV.

student PROFILE

Mina Huang
WILFRED LAURER UNIVERSITY

Courtesy of Mina Huang

About me:

I am currently attending Wilfrid Laurier University as an Honours Business Administration candidate. During this time, I've had to deal with the stress of balancing school, family, a job, and the list goes on. Sometimes it's easy to forget your long-term goals when life gets too much to handle, but learning to deal with stress is a notoriously valuable skill that will help in my personal life and work life.

What I focus on:

Being a post-secondary student isn't always as easy and wonderful as movies seem to make it. Since entering university, I would say I've had to deal with the most stress and changes in my life so far. Where I am today is far from what I imagined life would be like after high school. At times it's taken a toll on my mental health. Post-secondary life means that you'll have assignments and exams being piled up all at once. I've broken down and cried many times. I had to learn how to cope with the stressors of going to school.

I've learned that if I'm stressed, I need to remove myself from academic life and revitalize. For example, I take 15 minutes out of my day to be away from technology. Disconnecting from social media helped me maintain a healthy mind. I also pull out my yoga mat and do a couple of exercises before I resume my work. There's really no point of working if you're just thinking about how stressed you are so you might as well find an outlet for that stress. I found this to be less daunting than spending an hour at the gym and it helps boost your mood.

What will help me in the workplace:

Right now I may be seeing assignments and exams as the greatest source of stress but imagine having to worry if you'll still be working the next day. I would describe myself as an anxious and sensitive person, so that isn't the best trait to have especially if your future employer isn't always going to be providing that extra support you would normally get from friends and family. Stress management is important because your job doesn't come with answers and you'll need to learn how to handle unexpected situations. Even if you can't solve the problem, when you're calm you can think of more creative ideas and maybe you can find the solution! Also, when your peers see how you respond in a stress situation, it can help them relax and improve your team's overall performance.

Used with permission of Mina Huang

To be safe, get an HIV test at your doctor's office or at a clinic. Consider requiring any of your sexual partners to be tested as well. If you are infected, inform all sexual partners and seek medical assistance. If you're interested in contacting support organizations in your area, call CATIE (Community AIDS Treatment Information Exchange) at 1-800-263-1638 or go to catie.ca for online support and information.

Stay Safe

One in four females is likely to be sexually assaulted in her lifetime, as is one in six males. Two-thirds of the people assaulted know their attacker—an acquaintance, a friend, or a family member.[38] Females between the ages of 18 and 24 are more likely to be stalked, harassed, or sexually assaulted than any other age group.

Rape—a person having nonconsensual sexual activity with another—is not about sex, it's about exerting power, and it's a crime. Rape is not caused by the victim's behaviour or clothing, any more than auto theft is caused by the owner of the car. It can happen on a date, at home, or at a party. If you find yourself in a situation where you feel powerless or threatened, leave immediately. If you feel afraid to leave by yourself, call a friend or call a cab. And if you see that someone is being inappropriate or offensive toward another, show your disapproval and publicly interrupt the behaviour as safely you can. If necessary, call for help.

If you are assaulted, tell someone you trust right away. If you want to report the assault to the police, you have the right to do that as well, preferably with a supportive person accompanying you. Get ongoing counselling to help you move from being a victim to being a survivor.

revisit RISK AND REWARD

Courtesy of Marlene Schwartz

What happened to Marlene? Risking opposition and anger from people ranging from the food industry to parents wanting to send cupcakes in for birthdays, Marlene set out to change the food culture in her daughters' schools. She rallied the principal and other parents to create the district's first health advisory committee. Now, as Director for the Rudd Center for Food Policy and Obesity at Yale University, Dr. Schwartz's research and community service address how home environments, school landscapes, neighbourhoods, and the media shape the eating attitudes and behaviours of children. She has collaborated with the Connecticut State Department of Education to evaluate school nutrition and physical activity policies. She co-chaired the Connecticut Obesity Task Force in 2010, and heads up vital research that has national implications for nutritional wellness.

One of the Rudd Center's studies found that cereal manufacturers were marketing the cereals with the most sugar and least fibre to kids. Most companies have since cut cereal sugar content by about a third, which is significant. Marlene's studies have even prodded corporate giant McDonald's to increase apple and milk offerings in Happy Meals.

What does this mean for you? The rewards of Marlene's work as a parent and a nutritional expert benefit people all over the country, and underscore the fact that you can make a difference. Think about her goal, as a psychologist, to figure out why people do what they do and help them do it better. How do you manage your physical wellness— eating, exercise, rest? Describe your approach and why you think you do what you do. Then, based on what you have read in the chapter, choose one thing you can do better. Describe what risk you can take and the specific reward that you seek, and create a 30-day plan to give it a try.

What risk may bring reward beyond your world? "Students need to realize they can influence what's sold in the dining hall or school stores," Marlene says, emphasizing that good nutrition is important to most people now. Consider the breakfast, lunch, dinner, and snack options at dining halls, stores, and other campus food services. What is the nutritional value of the food offered? What food brands and varieties would you like to see removed and added? What change would improve student health? Go to www.ruddcenter.org to see the latest research and initiatives that Marlene's organization is working on. Choose a topic relevant to your experience right now, and advocate for change in that area. Marlene encourages students to meet with the presidents of their institutions. As she says, "No one wants to be seen as the person who ignored the students."

GLOBAL RISK AND REWARD

Vinzenz Weidenhofer/123RF

ekler/Shutterstock

Former ballet dancer Xu Tingzhong is often referred to as the "inventor king" of China. He doggedly pursues multiple projects and holds over 100 patents. Although his work requires enormous risk—he has never sold anything he has created, and lives on approximately $30 (USD) per month—he takes action every day for the potential reward of making a difference in the world. One of his projects is an electric bicycle that converts to a small bed, which he envisions as a way for the poor to have both transportation and shelter.[37]

Emotional and Physical Wellness

RISK ACTION
FOR POST-SECONDARY, CAREER, AND LIFE REWARDS

KNOW IT
Blan-k/Shutterstock

WRITE IT
Blan-k/Shutterstock

WORK IT
Blan-k/Shutterstock

Left to Right: pio3/Shutterstock;
Viktor Gladkov/123RF;
MP_P/Shutterstock

Complete the following on paper or in digital format.

KNOW IT *Think Critically*

Move toward Better Health

Build basic skills. Pick a behaviour—eating, drinking, sleeping, sexual activity—that holds some kind of issue for you. Describe your behaviour and your attitude toward what you do.

Example: *Issue:* binge drinking
     Behaviour: I binge drink probably once a week.
     Attitude: I don't think it's any big deal. I like using it to escape.

Question to think about: Is it worth it?

Take it to the next level. Examine whether your behaviour is a problem by noting positive and negative effects. Be as objective as you can. To continue the example above:

Positive effects: I have fun with my friends. I feel confident, accepted, social.

Negative effects: I feel foggy the next day. I miss class. I'm irritable.

Move toward mastery. Based on the effects of your behaviour, think about where you want to make a difference, and why. Then describe changes you could make by answering the following questions. For example, the binge drinker might consider cutting back on one drinking outing a week and investigating one new social activity that does not involve drinking.

1. How might you change your behaviour?
2. How might you change your attitude?
3. What positive effects do you think these changes would have?
4. Commit to these actions to put positive change in motion. Describe your plan, including specific steps and a time frame.

WRITE IT *Communicate*

Emotional intelligence journal: Addiction. Discuss how you feel about addiction in any form—to alcohol, drugs, food, sex, the internet, gambling—whether or not it you have had direct or indirect experience with it. Imagine that a close friend or family member has a dangerous addiction of some kind. Use your emotional intelligence to describe how you would address the problem with that person to produce the best possible outcome.

Real-life writing: Health on campus. Think about what you consider to be the most significant health issue at your school—safety, substance abuse, anxiety and depression, weight management, and so on. Write a 500-word editorial for your school paper on the topic, describing the details of the problem and proposing one or more solutions. For example, if weight control is a problem, you might suggest changing the contents of the drink vending machines. When you are done, consider submitting your editorial to the paper (have an instructor or peer review it before you send it in).

WORK IT *Build Your Brand*

Wellness at Work

Taking responsibility for your health can make you a more valuable employee, in part because many companies are putting pressure on their employees to do more in less time. Increased work burdens, late nights, and work calls during weekends or off-hours create a great deal of stress for workers. In addition, health care costs are on the rise for companies.

Part of your responsibility involves getting routine screenings from a doctor or health clinic. Below is a list of health items commonly tested during screening. Using the internet or your library, research the listed items. For each, describe: (1) What the item is and why it is important to your overall health; (2) what the normal range is for the item and what numbers (high, low, or both) indicate a concern; and (3) what to do if you have abnormal results for this item.

- Hemoglobin
- Hematocrit
- Glucose
- Potassium
- Magnesium
- Calcium
- Iron
- Cholesterol

CHAPTER 4

Leadership vs. Management

- In groups of two (choose your partner) answer the following questions:

    What/who is a leader?
    What/who is a manager? Then make a list of at least five qualities that differentiate one from the other.
4. Share with the class

Courtesy of John Loblack

The more you know about yourself, the more effectively you can analyze courses; evaluate partners; and decide what, how, and where to study and work. With the information you discover, you can take the risks that will prove most productive for you.

Personality and Learning Preferences

WHO ARE YOU AND WHAT MAKES YOU UNIQUE?

What Would You Risk? *John Loblack, Ph.D.*

THINK ABOUT THIS SITUATION AS YOU READ, AND CONSIDER WHAT ACTION YOU WOULD TAKE. THIS CHAPTER HELPS YOU ASSESS YOUR PREFERENCES FOR LEARNING AND INTERACTION, AND SHOWS YOU HOW TO USE THIS INFORMATION TO MAKE PRACTICAL DECISIONS ABOUT WORK AND STUDYING.

John Loblack seemed destined for a life of poverty in his Caribbean homeland of Dominica. He skipped school, stole candy from a local market, and surrounded himself with friends who were dropouts or drug addicts—"dream killers," as he calls them, who didn't believe he had what it took to succeed. "The sad thing is, I believed them," says John of those people and that time. Despite his lack of faith in himself, his mother, Lucia, was determined to get him away from the dream killers and to help him discover and develop his abilities.

One day in elementary school, John cursed at one of his teachers after class. Later that day, while he played soccer at the park, the teacher went to John's home, sharing tea and stories with Lucia. Instead of discussing the meeting with John that night as he expected, Lucia showed up at school the next day and confronted John in front of the teacher and his friends, challenging him to take responsibility for his actions. "That singular incident changed my whole perspective on the value of teachers and education," John recalls. Suddenly, as a result of his mother's risky action, he felt how much she and his teacher cared, and realized that he had an opportunity to achieve something. Although she herself struggled to read and write, his mother had energized him with her support.

After getting through high school, John got his first job as an insurance salesman, but he lacked self-confidence. Still unsure of where his talents lay, he took a risk to try radio announcing, landing an interview after applying to five different jobs. Although the manager told him that his reading was not good enough, he liked John's voice and offered him a six-month probationary period. John wondered if this would be another dead-end path in his search for work that would inspire and motivate him.

To be continued . . .

DESPITE HIS DESIRE TO PERSIST IN SCHOOL, JOHN STRUGGLED WITH READING THROUGHOUT HIS EDUCATION, AND FOLLOWED A WINDING PATH TO SELF-KNOWLEDGE. YOU'LL LEARN MORE ABOUT JOHN, AND THE REWARD RESULTING FROM HIS ACTIONS, WITHIN THE CHAPTER.

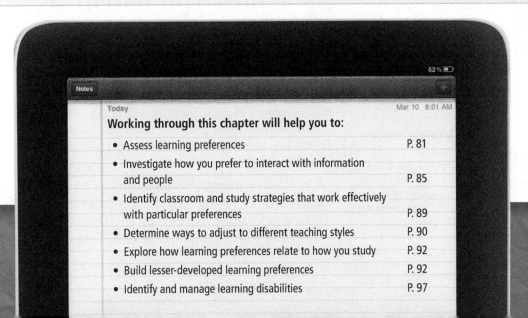

52%

Notes

Today   Mar 10 8:01 AM

Working through this chapter will help you to:

statusCHECK

Left to Right: Luis Santos/Shutterstock; Antonio Guillem/Shutterstock; antoniodiaz/Shutterstock; mimagephotography/Shutterstock; Djomas/Shutterstock; WAYHOME studio/Shutterstock

How Aware Are You of Your Learning Preferences?

For each statement, fill in the number that best describes how often it applies to you.

1 = never   2 = seldom   3 = sometimes   4 = often   5 = always

1. I believe I can develop my skills and abilities through self-knowledge and hard work.	① ② ③ ④ ⑤
2. I have a pretty clear idea of my strengths and abilities.	① ② ③ ④ ⑤
3. I understand which subjects and situations make it more difficult for me to learn.	① ② ③ ④ ⑤
4. I try to maximize what I do well in the classroom and outside of it.	① ② ③ ④ ⑤
5. I recognize that being comfortable with the subject matter isn't necessarily enough to succeed in a particular course.	① ② ③ ④ ⑤
6. I assess an instructor's teaching style and figure out how to maximize my learning.	① ② ③ ④ ⑤
7. I choose study techniques that tap into how I learn best.	① ② ③ ④ ⑤
8. I try to use forms of technology that work well with the way I learn.	① ② ③ ④ ⑤
9. I've taken a skills or interests inventory to help find a major or career area that suits me.	① ② ③ ④ ⑤
10. I understand what a learning disability is and am aware of several different types of disabilities.	① ② ③ ④ ⑤

Each of the topics in these statements is covered in this chapter. Note those statements for which you filled in a 3 or lower. Skim the chapter to see where those topics appear, and pay special attention to them as you read, learn, and apply new strategies.

REMEMBER: NO MATTER HOW WELL KNOW YOURSELF AS A LEARNER, YOU CAN IMPROVE WITH EFFORT AND PRACTICE.

WHY UNDERSTAND
how you learn?

You are one of a kind, born with a unique set of potentials, abilities, preferences, and challenges. As a student, you have one of the most significant opportunities of your life to explore how you learn, think, and function in the world. What you learn from this exploration can help you choose the risks that will most effectively lead you to rewards you value. Specifically, the more you know about yourself, the more effectively you can analyze courses; evaluate partners; and decide what, how, and where to study and work.

Of the countless aspects of your individuality, some affect your student and working life more than others. Take a moment to think through how you would answer the following questions:

- Which academic subjects make sense to you, and which seem more challenging?
- Which sports or other physical activities come naturally to you, and which feel more awkward or require extra effort?
- At what time of day do you generally have the most energy and focus? When do you have the least?

MyLab Student Success
(www.mystudentsuccesslab.com) is an online solution designed to help you "Start Strong, Finish Stronger" by building skills for ongoing personal and professional development.

- How do you manage your environment where you live? Do you prioritize order and neatness, comfort, entertainment, something else?
- With which instructors, friends, and family members do you connect easily? With whom is the relationship more of a struggle?

Even with just this basic array of details about who you are, you can see that you have more potential to succeed in certain settings and situations than in others. This chapter will increase and focus your self-knowledge, giving you more ability to realize your potential in favourable situations—and will improve your ability to make the most of less favourable circumstances. In its Employability Skills 2000+, the Conference Board of Canada recognizes the need for everyone to "learn and grow continuously." It also stresses the importance of assessing our own strengths and weaknesses to help us set goals for learning on our own terms. In other words, it is also important in the "real world" to know what your learning style is.[1]

Exploring Learning Preferences

You are born with particular learning preferences that combine with effort and environment to create a "recipe" for what you can achieve. In this case, the term *preference* refers to how your brain naturally tends to function. Part of this recipe comes from how you perceive yourself, which is affected by many factors and develops over time.

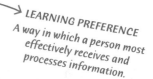

LEARNING PREFERENCE
A way in which a person most effectively receives and processes information.

Self-perception is strongly influenced by how others see you. Maybe your mother thinks you are "the funny one" or "the quiet one." An elementary-school teacher may have called you a "thinker" or "slacker," a "go-getter" or "shy." These labels influence your ability to set and achieve goals, and can prevent you from taking productive risks if you use them to define yourself too rigidly. Even as you accept that some truth lies within your labels, realize that you are not simply stuck with them. At any age, intelligence can grow when you work to keep learning.

Picture a bag of rubber bands of different sizes. Some are thick and some thin; some are long and some short—but all of them can stretch. A small rubber band, stretched out, can reach the length of a larger one that lies unstretched. In other words, with effort and focus, you can develop whatever raw material you start with, perhaps beyond the natural gifts of someone who makes no effort. As you'll see when you learn more about John at the end of the chapter, his story illustrates how far effort can stretch a person's natural abilities.

Givaga/Shutterstock

As you gather important information about yourself throughout this course, the understanding you build will improve your vision of where you are now, your projection of where you can go, and your toolkit of strategies for coping with all kinds of situations as you make progress. There may be much about yourself, your surroundings, and your experiences that you cannot control. However, with self-knowledge, you do have control over how you respond to circumstances. Get ready to define your rubber band and work to stretch it to its limit.

Use Assessments to Make Choices and to Grow

Ask yourself: Who am I right now? Where would I like to be in five years? Assessments focused on how you prefer to learn and interact with others can help you answer some of these big questions. Whereas a test attempts to identify a level of performance, an *assessment*, according to professor and psychologist Howard Gardner, is "the obtaining of information about a person's skills and potentials ... providing useful feedback to the person [emphasis added]."[2] Think of an assessment as an honest exploration that will produce interesting and helpful information.

POTENTIALS
Abilities that may be developed.

The assessments in this chapter provide questions to get you thinking about your strengths and challenges. *Note:* Learning disabilities are specific, diagnosed issues that differ from the learning challenges that all students face. They are discussed at the end of the chapter.

The two assessments in this chapter—Multiple Pathways to Learning and the Personality Spectrum—will give you greater insight into your strengths and weaknesses. The material following the assessments shows you how to maximize what you do well and compensate for challenging areas by making specific choices about what you do in class, during study time, and in the workplace. Understanding yourself and others as learners also helps you choose how to respond to people in a group situation. In a study group, classroom, or workplace, each person takes in material in a unique way. You can use what you know about others' learning preferences to improve communication and teamwork.

Remember, there are no "right" answers, no "best" scores. Completing a self-assessment is like wearing glasses to correct blurred vision. The glasses don't create new paths and possibilities, but they help you to see more clearly the ones in front of you at this moment. As you gain experience, build skills, and learn, your learning preferences are apt to change over time. If you take the assessments again in the future, your results may shift. Finally, to enjoy the reward of useful results, take the risk of answering questions honestly, reflecting who you *are* as opposed to who you *wish* you were.

WHAT TOOLS CAN HELP YOU
explore learning preferences?

A variety of tools exist to help you become more aware of different aspects of yourself. Some tools focus on learning preferences; some on areas of potential; and others on personality type. This chapter examines two assessments in depth. The first, Multiple Pathways to Learning, is a learning preferences assessment focusing on eight areas of potential, referred to as intelligences. It is based on Howard Gardner's Multiple Intelligences (MI) theory. The second, the Personality Spectrum, is a personality-type assessment based on the Myers-Briggs Type Indicator (MBTI). It helps you evaluate how you react to people and situations.

INTELLIGENCE
As defined by Gardner, an ability valued by a group of people for what it can produce.

Following each assessment is information about the typical traits of each type of intelligence and each personality spectrum dimension. As you will see from your scores, you have abilities in all areas, though some are more developed than others.

Assess Your Multiple Intelligences: Pathways to Learning

In 1983, Howard Gardner changed the way people perceived intelligence and learning with his theory of Multiple Intelligences. Like Robert Sternberg, Gardner believed that the traditional view of intelligence, based on mathematical, logical, and verbal measurements that made up an intelligence quotient (IQ), did not reflect the true spectrum of human ability. Sternberg focused on the spectrum of actions that help people achieve important goals, but Gardner chose to examine the idea that humans possess a number of different areas of natural ability and potential that he called *multiple intelligences*.

The theory of Multiple Intelligences

Gardner's research identified eight unique types of intelligence or areas of ability. These included two areas traditionally associated with the term *intelligence*—verbal and logic skills—but expanded beyond them, to encompass a wide range of potentials of the human brain.[3] These intelligences almost never function in isolation. You will almost always use several at the same time for any significant role or task.[4]

reflektastudios/Fotolia

Students drawn to the sciences may find that they have strengths in logical-mathematical or naturalistic thinking.

As you look at Key 4.1, study the description of each intelligence and then note the examples of people who have unusually high levels of ability in that area. Although few people have the verbal-linguistic intelligence of William Shakespeare or the interpersonal intelligence of Oprah Winfrey, everyone has some level of ability in every intelligence. Your goal is to identify what your levels are and to work your strongest intelligences to your advantage.

The way Gardner defines intelligence heightens the value of different abilities in different arenas, and debunks the notion that there are only one or two abilities that define intelligence and success more than others. In Tibet, for example, mountain

KEY 4.1   Each intelligence is linked to specific abilities.

INTELLIGENCE		DESCRIPTION AND SKILLS	HIGH-ACHIEVING EXAMPLE
Verbal-Linguistic		Ability to communicate through language; listening, reading, writing, speaking	• Author J.K. Rowling • CBC's Rick Mercer
Logical-Mathematical		Ability to understand logical reasoning and problem solving; math, science, patterns, sequences	• Physicist Stephen Hawking • Mathematician Svetlana Jitomirskaya
Bodily-Kinesthetic		Ability to use the physical body skillfully and to take in knowledge through bodily sensation; coordination, working with hands	• Olympic Gold Medal swimmer Penny Oleksiak • Edmonton Oiler Connor McDavid
Visual-Spatial		Ability to understand spatial relationships and to perceive and create images; visual art, graphic design, charts and maps	• Artist Walt Disney • Movie Director Deepa Mehta
Interpersonal		Ability to relate to others, noticing their moods, motivations, and feelings; social activity, cooperative learning, teamwork	• Media personality Marilyn Denis • "Me to We" founder Craig Kielburger
Intrapersonal		Ability to understand one's own behaviour and feelings; self-awareness, independence, time spent alone	• Animal researcher Jane Goodall • Philosopher Marshall McLuhan
Musical		Ability to comprehend and create meaningful sound; sensitivity to music and musical patterns	• Rapper, songwriter, and actor, Drake • Composer Andrew Lloyd Webber
Naturalist		Ability to identify, distinguish, categorize, and classify species or items, often incorporating high interest in elements of the natural environment	• Conservationist David Suzuki • Bird cataloger John James Audubon

Top to Bottom: TatsianaTur/Shutterstock; kak2s /Shutterstock; Alexander Raths/Shutterstock; Neelsky/ 123RF; Helder Almeida/ 123RF; focal point/ Shutterstock; Simeon Donov/123RF; Ambient Ideas/Shutterstock.

dwellers prize the bodily-kinesthetic ability of a top-notch Himalayan mountain guide. In Oshawa, automakers appreciate the visual-spatial talents of a master car designer. In a Vancouver hospital, a nurse's interpersonal intelligence is crucial for job success, as well as the health of the patients. Send the nurse up Mount Everest, or have the Sherpa design a car for General Motors, and suddenly a person who is exceptionally intelligent in one area will leave much to be desired in another.

Your own eight intelligences

Gardner believes that all people possess all eight intelligences, but each person has developed some intelligences more fully than others. When you find a task or subject easy, you are probably using a more fully developed intelligence. When you have trouble, you may be using a less developed intelligence.[5]

MULTIPLE PATHWAYS TO LEARNING

Each intelligence has a set of numbered statements. Consider each statement on its own. Then, on a scale from 1 (lowest) to 4 (highest), rate how closely it matches who you are right now and write that number on the line next to the statement. Finally, total each set of six questions. Enter your scores in the grid on page 85.

1. rarely   2. sometimes   3. usually   4. always

1. _____ I enjoy physical activities.
2. _____ I am uncomfortable sitting still.
3. _____ I prefer to learn through doing.
4. _____ When sitting I move my legs or hands.
5. _____ I enjoy working with my hands.
6. _____ I like to pace when I'm thinking or studying.
   13 TOTAL for BODILY-KINESTHETIC

1. _____ I enjoy telling stories.
2. _____ I like to write.
3. _____ I like to read.
4. _____ I express myself clearly.
5. _____ I am good at negotiating.
6. _____ I like to discuss topics that interest me.
   19 TOTAL for VERBAL-LINGUISTIC

1. _____ I use maps easily.
2. _____ I draw pictures/diagrams when explaining ideas.
3. _____ I can assemble items easily from diagrams.
4. _____ I enjoy drawing or photography.
5. _____ I do not like to read long paragraphs.
6. _____ I prefer a drawn map over written directions.
   12 TOTAL for VISUAL-SPATIAL

1. _____ I like math in school.
2. _____ I like science.
3. _____ I problem-solve well.
4. _____ I question how things work.
5. _____ I enjoy planning or designing something new.
6. _____ I am able to fix things.
   13 TOTAL for LOGICAL-MATHEMATICAL

1. 4 I listen to music.
2. 4 I move my fingers or feet when I hear music.
3. 2 I have good rhythm.
4. 4 I like to sing along with music.
5. 1 People have said I have musical talent.
6. 1 I like to express my ideas through music.
   16 TOTAL for MUSICAL

1. 4 I need quiet time to think.
2. 3 I think about issues before I want to talk.
3. 3 I am interested in self-improvement.
4. 3 I understand my thoughts and feelings.
5. 2 I know what I want out of life.
6. 2 I prefer to work on projects alone.
   17 TOTAL for INTRAPERSONAL

1. 3 I like doing a project with other people.
2. 4 People come to me to help settle conflicts.
3. 4 I like to spend time with friends.
4. 4 I am good at understanding people.
5. 3 I am good at making people feel comfortable.
6. 4 I enjoy helping others.
   23 TOTAL for INTERPERSONAL

1. 4 I like to think about how things, ideas, or people fit into categories.
2. 2 I enjoy studying plants, animals, or oceans.
3. 4 I tend to see how things relate to, or are distinct from, one another.
4. 1 I think about having a career in the natural sciences.
5. 3 As a child I often played with bugs and leaves.
6. 3 I like to investigate the natural world around me.
   17 TOTAL for NATURALISTIC

Multiple Pathways to Learning Assessment

Source: Developed by Joyce Bishop, PhD, Golden West College, Huntington Beach CA. Based on Howard Gardner. *Frames of Mind: The Theory of Multiple Intelligences.* New York: Harper Collins, 1993.

84

SCORING GRID FOR MULTIPLE PATHWAYS TO LEARNING

For each intelligence, shade the box in the row that corresponds with the range where your score falls. For example, if you scored 17 in bodily-kinesthetic intelligence, you would shade the middle box in that row; if you scored a 13 in visual-spatial, you would shade the last box in that row. When you have shaded one box for each row, you will see a "map" of your range of development at a glance.

A score of 20–24 indicates a high level of development in that particular type of intelligence, 14–19 a moderate level, and below 14 an underdeveloped intelligence.

	20–24 (HIGHLY DEVELOPED)	14–19 (MODERATELY DEVELOPED)	BELOW 14 (UNDERDEVELOPED)
Bodily-Kinesthetic			✓
Visual-Spatial		✓	
Verbal-Linguistic			✓
Logical-Mathematical			✓
Musical		✓	
Interpersonal	✓		
Intrapersonal		✓	
Naturalistic		✓	

Multiple Pathways to Learning Scoring Grid

Gardner also believes your levels of development in the eight intelligences can grow or recede throughout your life, depending on effort and experience. For example, although you will not become a world-class pianist if you have limited musical ability, you can develop what you have with focus and work. Conversely, even a highly talented musician will lose ability without practice. This reflects how the brain grows with learning and becomes sluggish without it.

VAK/VARK: A related self-assessment

A related self-assessment is the VAK or VARK questionnaire. VAK/VARK assesses learning preferences in three (or four) areas: visual, auditory, read/write (in VARK), and kinesthetic. This text focuses on the Multiple Intelligences (MI) assessment because it incorporates elements of VAK/VARK and expands upon them, giving you a comprehensive picture of your abilities. Keep in mind that auditory learning is part of two MI dimensions:

- Many auditory learners have strong verbal intelligence but prefer to hear words (in a lecture or discussion or on a recording) instead of reading them.
- Many auditory learners have strong musical intelligence and remember and retain information based on sounds and rhythms.

If you tend to absorb information better through listening, try study suggestions for these two intelligences. Some instructors convert their lectures into podcasts, which can be very helpful. For further information about VAK/VARK, go to www.vark-learn .com, or search online using the keywords "VAK assessment."

Complete the Multiple Pathways to Learning assessment and scoring grid to determine where you are right now in the eight intelligence areas. Then look at Key 4.2 to identify specific skills associated with each area. Elsewhere in your text, you may find information about how to apply your learning styles knowledge to key post-secondary success skills.

Assess How You Interact with Others: Personality Spectrum

Personality assessments help you understand how you respond to the world around you, including people, work, and school. They also can help guide you as you explore majors and careers.

TYPOLOGY
TYPOLOGY
A systematic classification or study of types.

The concept of dividing human beings into different "personality types" goes as far back as Aristotle and Hippocrates, two ancient Greek philosophers. In the early 20th century, psychologist and philosopher Carl Jung focused on personality typology based on these characteristics:[6]

■ *An individual's preferred "world."* Jung said that extroverts tend to prefer the outside world of people and activities, while introverts tend to prefer the inner world of thoughts, feelings, and fantasies.

■ *Different ways of dealing with the world, or "functions."* Jung defined four distinct interaction dimensions used to different degrees: sensing (learning through your senses), thinking (evaluating information rationally), intuiting (learning through an instinct that comes from many integrated sources of information), and feeling (evaluating information through emotional response).

KEY 4.2 Particular abilities and skills are associated with each intelligence.

Verbal-Linguistic		• Remembering terms easily • Mastering a foreign language • Using writing or speech to convince someone to do or believe something
Musical-Rhythmic		• Sensing tonal qualities • Being sensitive to sounds and rhythms in music and in spoken language • Using an understanding of musical patterns to hear music
Logical-Mathematical		• Recognizing abstract patterns • Using facts to support an idea, and generating ideas based on evidence • Reasoning scientifically (formulating and testing a hypothesis)
Visual-Spatial		• Recognizing relationships between objects • Representing something graphically • Manipulating images
Bodily-Kinesthetic		• Strong mind–body connection • Controlling and coordinating body movement • Using the body to create products or express emotion
Intrapersonal		• Accessing your internal emotions • Understanding your own feelings and using them to guide your behaviour • Understanding yourself in relation to others
Interpersonal		• Seeing things from others' perspectives • Noticing moods, intentions, and temperaments of others • Gauging the most effective way to work with individual group members
Naturalistic		• Ability to categorize something as a member of a group or species • Understanding of relationships among natural organisms • Deep comfort with, and respect for, the natural world

Later, in the 1960s and 1970s, Katharine Briggs and her daughter Isabel Briggs Myers developed an assessment based on Jung's typology, called the Myers-Briggs Type Inventory, or MBTI (information is available online at www.myersbriggs.org). One of the most widely used personality inventories in the world, it consists of 16 possible personality types from the four dimensions. David Keirsey and Marilyn Bates later condensed the MBTI types into four temperaments, creating the Keirsey Sorter (found at www.keirsey.com).

Psychologist Joyce Bishop adapted the Keirsey Sorter and MBTI material into four personality types—Thinker, Organizer, Giver, and Adventurer—to create the Personality Spectrum assessment. The Personality Spectrum helps you identify the kinds of interactions that are most and least comfortable for you, giving you a simplified overview of where you fall in the range of MBTI types.

Complete the Personality Spectrum assessment and then plot your results on the scoring diagram. As with multiple intelligences, these results may change over time as

---

PERSONALITY SPECTRUM

STEP 1   Rank-order all four responses to each question from most like you (4) to least like you (1) so that for each question you use the numbers 1, 2, 3, and 4 one time each. Place numbers on the lines next to the responses.

4. most like me	3. more like me	2. less like me	1. least like me

1. I like instructors who
   a. _____ tell me exactly what is expected of me.
   b. _____ make learning active and exciting.
   c. _____ maintain a safe and supportive classroom.
   d. _____ challenge me to think at higher levels.

2. I learn best when the material is
   a. _____ well organized.
   b. _____ something I can do hands-on.
   c. _____ about understanding and improving the human condition.
   d. _____ intellectually challenging.

3. A high priority in my life is to
   a. _____ keep my commitments.
   b. _____ experience as much of life as possible.
   c. _____ make a difference in the lives of others.
   d. _____ understand how things work.

4. Other people think of me as
   a. _____ dependable and loyal.
   b. _____ dynamic and creative.
   c. _____ caring and honest.
   d. _____ intelligent and inventive.

5. When I experience stress I would most likely
   a. _____ do something to help me feel more in control of my life.
   b. _____ do something physical and daring.
   c. _____ talk with a friend.
   d. _____ go off by myself and think about my situation.

6. I would probably not be close friends with someone who is
   a. _____ irresponsible.
   b. _____ unwilling to try new things.
   c. _____ selfish and unkind to others.
   d. _____ an illogical thinker.

7. My vacations could be described as
   a. _____ traditional.
   b. _____ adventuresome.
   c. _____ pleasing to others.
   d. _____ a new learning experience.

8. One word that best describes me is
   a. _____ sensible.
   b. _____ spontaneous.
   c. _____ giving.
   d. _____ analytical.

STEP 2   Add up the total points for each letter.

TOTAL FOR   a. _____ Organizer   b. _____ Adventurer   c. _____ Giver   d. _____ Thinker

STEP 3   Plot these numbers on the brain diagram on page 88.

Personality Spectrum Assessment

SCORING DIAGRAM FOR PERSONALITY SPECTRUM

Write your scores from page 87 in the four squares just outside the brain diagram—Thinker score at top left, Giver score at top right, Organizer score at bottom left, and Adventurer score at bottom right.

Each square has a line of numbers that go from the square to the centre of the diagram. For each of your four scores, place a dot on the appropriate number in the line near that square. For example, if you scored 15 in the Giver spectrum, you would place a dot between the 14 and 16 in the upper right-hand line of numbers. If you scored a 26 in the Organizer spectrum, you would place a dot on the 26 in the lower left-hand line of numbers. Connect the four dots to create a shape.

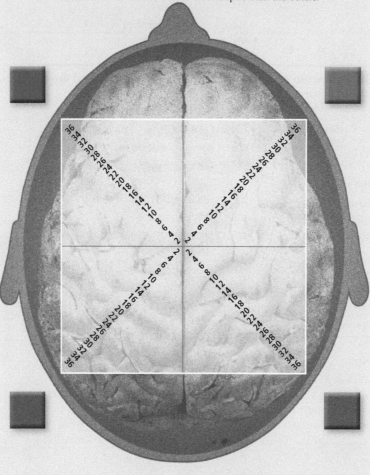

The more balanced the shape (closer to a square), the more equally developed the four spectrums of your personality. However, many people's shapes show one or two areas that are more developed than the others.

THINKER

Technical
Scientific
Mathematical
Dispassionate
Rational
Analytical
Logical
Problem Solving
Theoretical
Intellectual
Objective
Quantitative
Explicit
Realistic
Literal
Precise
Formal

GIVER

Interpersonal
Emotional
Caring
Sociable
Giving
Spiritual
Musical
Romantic
Feeling
Peacemaker
Trusting
Adaptable
Passionate
Harmonious
Idealistic
Talkative
Honest

ORGANIZER

Tactical
Planning
Detailed
Practical
Confident
Predictable
Controlled
Dependable
Systematic
Sequential
Structured
Administrative
Procedural
Organized
Conservative
Safekeeping
Disciplined

ADVENTURER

Active
Visual
Risking
Original
Artistic
Spatial
Skillful
Impulsive
Metaphoric
Experimental
Divergent
Fast-paced
Simultaneous
Competitive
Imaginative
Open-minded
Adventuresome

For the Personality Spectrum,
26–36 indicates a strong tendency in that dimension
14–25 indicates a moderate tendency
0–13 indicates a minimal tendency

Personality Spectrum Scoring Grid

KEY 4.3 Particular abilities and skills are associated with each Personality Spectrum dimension.

Thinker		• Solving problems • Developing models and systems • Analytical and abstract thinking
Organizer		• Responsibility, reliability • Neatness, organization, attention to detail • Comprehensive follow-through on tasks
Giver		• Successful, close relationships • Making a difference in the world • Negotiation, promoting peace
Adventurer		• Courageous and daring • Hands-on problem solving • Active and spontaneous style

Top to Bottom: onilmilk/Shutterstock; PHENPHAYOM/Shutterstock; Tatiana Popova/123RF; James Steidl/123 RF.

you experience new things, change, and continue to learn. Key 4.3 then shows the skills associated with each personality type.

Also based on Jung's work is the Golden Personality Assessment, which identifies sixteen personality types as does the MBTI. It is available to students using MyStudentSuccessLab, and can provide an interesting and detailed portrait of your traits.

HOW CAN YOU PUT
self-knowledge to work?

As you analyze learning preferences through completing the assessments, you develop a clearer picture of who you are and how you interact with others. Then, and most importantly, you figure out what to do with what this heightened self-knowledge. Use your creative and practical thinking skills to choose and use effective strategies for interacting in the classroom, managing study time, dealing with your workplace, and working with technology. These more targeted and personal efforts can help you earn the reward of deeper and more lasting learning.

Make Strategic Choices in the Classroom

Most students have to complete a set of "core curriculum" courses, as well as whatever courses their majors require. As you sign up for the sections that fit into your schedule, you may be asking, "How is it possible to make choices based on my learning preferences?" Well, it isn't always possible to choose courses with absolute freedom. However, your self-knowledge will always provide some way to improve your chances for success.

The primary opportunity for choice in the classroom lies in how you interact with your instructor and how you function during class. Instructors are unique individuals too, and they can't tailor classroom presentations to each of 15, 40, or 300 unique learners. As a result, you may find yourself in sync with one teacher and mismatched with another. Sometimes, the way the class is structured can affect your success more than the subject matter; for example, a strong interpersonal learner who has trouble writing may do well in a composition course emphasizing group work.

Just as you have learning preferences, instructors have ways they are most comfortable teaching. After several class meetings, you should be able to assess each instructor's preferred teaching styles (see Key 4.4) and determine how those fit with your learning preferences. As with learning preferences, most instructors will demonstrate a combination of teaching styles.

Although styles vary and instructors may combine styles, the word-focused lecture is still most common. For this reason, the traditional classroom generally works best for the verbal or logical learner or the Thinker and the Organizer. What can you do when your learning preferences don't match up with how your instructor teaches? Here are three suggestions:

- *Play to your strengths.* For example, if you're a kinesthetic learner, you might rewrite or type your lecture notes, make flash cards, or take walks while saying important terms and concepts out loud. Likewise, if you are a Giver with an instructor who delivers straight lectures, consider setting up a study group to go over details and fill in factual gaps.

KEY 4.4 Instructors often prefer one or more teaching styles.

TEACHING STYLE	WHAT TO EXPECT IN CLASS
Lecture, verbal focus	Instructor speaks to the class for the entire period, with little class interaction. Lesson is taught primarily through words, either spoken or written on the board, on PowerPoints in class or online, with handouts or text, or possibly through podcasts.
Lecture with group discussion	Instructor presents material but encourages class discussion.
Small groups	Instructor presents material and then breaks class into small groups for discussion or project work.
Visual focus	Instructor uses visual elements such as PowerPoint slides, diagrams, photographs, drawings, transparencies, in-class or "YouTube for Schools" videos, or movies.
Logical presentation	Instructor organizes material in a logical sequence, such as by steps, time, or importance.
Random presentation	Instructor tackles topics in no particular order, and may jump around a lot or digress.
Conceptual presentation	Instructor spends the majority of time on the big picture, focusing on abstract concepts and umbrella ideas.
Detailed presentation	Instructor spends the majority of time, after introducing ideas, on the details and facts that underlie them.
Hands-on presentation	Instructor uses demonstrations, experiments, props, and class activities to show key points.

get analytical

MAXIMIZE YOUR CLASSROOM EXPERIENCE

Complete the following on paper or in digital format.

Considering what you know about yourself as a learner and about your instructors' teaching styles this term, decide which classroom situation is the most challenging for you. Use this exercise to think analytically, creatively, and practically about the situation.

1. Name the course and describe the instructor's style.
2. Analyze the problem that is making this class challenging.
3. Generate and write down three ideas about actions you can take to improve the situation.
4. Finally, choose one action and put it to practical use. Briefly note what happened. Was there any improvement as a result?

- *Work to strengthen weaker areas.* As a visual learner reviews notes from a structured lecture, he could use logical-mathematical strategies such as outlining notes or thinking about cause-and-effect relationships within the material. An Organizer, studying for a test from notes delivered by an instructor with a random presentation, could organize her material using tables and timelines.

- *Ask your instructor for help.* Connect through email or during office hours. Communicating your struggle can feel like a risk, but building a relationship with an instructor or teaching assistant can be extremely rewarding. This is especially true in large lectures where you are anonymous unless you speak up. For example, a visual learner might ask the instructor to recommend figures or videos to study that illustrate the lecture.

The adjustments you make for your instructor's teaching style will build flexibility that you need for career and life success. Just as you can't hand pick your instructors, you will rarely, if ever, be able to choose your work colleagues. You will have to adjust to them, and help them adjust to you. Keep in mind, too, that research shows a benefit from learning in a variety of ways—kind of like cross-training for the brain. Knowing this, some instructors may challenge you to learn in ways that aren't comfortable for you.

A final point: Some students try to find out more about an instructor by asking students who have already taken the course or looking up comments online. Be cautious, as you may not be able to trust an anonymous poster. Even if you hear a review from a friend you trust, every student–instructor relationship is unique, and an instructor your friend loved may be a bad match for you. Prioritize the courses you need, and know that you can make the most of what your instructors offer, regardless of their teaching styles.

Broaden your experience in your courses, and your education, by interacting with instructors outside of class time.

Choose Your Best Study Strategies

Start now to use what you learned about yourself to choose the best study techniques. If you tend to learn successfully from a linear, logical presentation, look for order (for example, a timeline of information organized by event dates) as you review notes. If you are strong in interpersonal intelligence, you could work with study groups whenever possible.

When faced with a task that challenges your weaknesses, use strategies that boost your ability. For example, if you are an Adventurer who does *not* respond well to linear information, try applying your strengths to the material by using a hands-on approach. Or you could try developing your area of weakness by learning study skills that work well for Thinker-type learners.

KEY 4.5 Choose study techniques to maximize each intelligence.

Verbal-Linguistic		• Read text; highlight selectively • Use a computer to retype and summarize notes • Outline chapters • Recite information or write scripts/debates
Musical-Rhythmic		• Create rhythms out of words • Beat out rhythms with hand or stick while reciting concepts • Write songs/raps that help you learn concepts • Write out study material to fit into a wordless tune you have on a CD or MP3 player; chant or sing the material along with the tune as you listen
Logical-Mathematical		• Organize material logically; if it suits the topic, use a spreadsheet program • Sequentially explain material to someone • Develop systems and find patterns • Analyze and evaluate information
Visual-Spatial		• Develop graphic organizers for new material • Draw "think links" (mind maps) • Use a computer to develop charts and tables • Use color in your notes for organization
Bodily-Kinesthetic		• Move while you learn; pace and recite • Rewrite or retype notes to engage "muscle memory" • Design and play games to learn material • Act out scripts of material
Intrapersonal		• Reflect on personal meaning of information • Keep a journal • Study in quiet areas • Imagine essays or experiments before beginning
Interpersonal		• Study in a group • As you study, discuss information over the phone or send instant messages • Teach someone else the material • Make time to discuss assignments and tests with your instructor
Naturalistic		• Break down information into categories • Look for ways in which items fit or don't fit together • Look for relationships among ideas, events, facts • Study in a natural setting if it helps you focus

When you study with others, you and the entire group will be more successful if you understand one another's learning preferences, as in the following examples.

- An Interpersonal learner could take the lead in teaching material to others.
- An Organizer could coordinate the group schedule.
- A Naturalistic learner might organize facts into categories that solidify concepts.

Look at Key 4.5 for study strategies that suit each intelligence and Key 4.6 for study strategies that suit each Personality Spectrum dimension. Because you have some level of ability in each area and because you will sometimes need to boost your ability in a weaker area, you may find useful suggestions under any of the headings. Try different techniques. Pay attention to what works best for you. You may be surprised at what is useful.

Find Your Recipe for Technology Management

Technology is everywhere. People communicate using email, text messaging, and social networking sites; they read blogs, listen to podcasts, and use apps on their cell phones. Technology also plays a significant role in academic settings, where you may encounter:

- Instructors who communicate primarily via email
- Course websites and learning management systems where you can access syllabi and connect with resources and classmates
- Textbooks with associated websites through which you complete and email assignments
- Online research that takes you from website to website as you follow links
- Projects where students create media such as a YouTube video or social media campaign

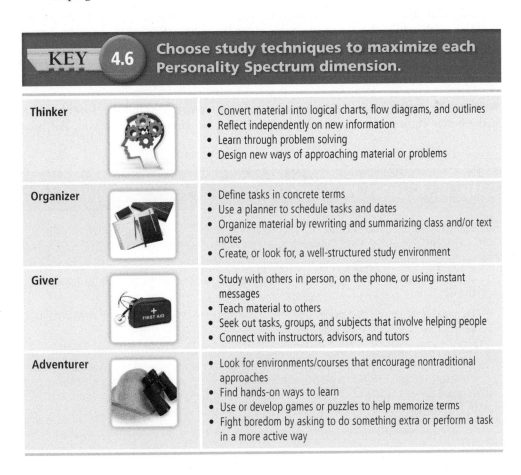

KEY 4.6 Choose study techniques to maximize each Personality Spectrum dimension.

Thinker	• Convert material into logical charts, flow diagrams, and outlines • Reflect independently on new information • Learn through problem solving • Design new ways of approaching material or problems
Organizer	• Define tasks in concrete terms • Use a planner to schedule tasks and dates • Organize material by rewriting and summarizing class and/or text notes • Create, or look for, a well-structured study environment
Giver	• Study with others in person, on the phone, or using instant messages • Teach material to others • Seek out tasks, groups, and subjects that involve helping people • Connect with instructors, advisors, and tutors
Adventurer	• Look for environments/courses that encourage nontraditional approaches • Find hands-on ways to learn • Use or develop games or puzzles to help memorize terms • Fight boredom by asking to do something extra or perform a task in a more active way

Technology has profoundly affected how we get information and share it with others. According to the Pew Research Center, it "is producing a fundamentally new kind of learner, one that is self-directed, better equipped to capture information, more reliant on feedback from peers, [and] more inclined to collaborate."[7] These "new learners" are more likely to research online, share content through social media sites, and create media content.

For some students, technology tools such as search engines and GoogleDocs come easily, but others may struggle. Knowing your learning preferences can help you fit technology tools to your assignment and use online resources effectively. Are you strong in the logical-mathematical intelligence or Thinker dimension? Working with an online tutorial may be a good choice. Are you an interpersonal learner? Find a tech-savvy modifies classmate to help you get the hang of it. An Adventurer may try out the features of a book or course website randomly, according to what looks interesting, whereas an Organizer may click through features in their listed order.

If you're having trouble with a particular type of technology, find a teaching assistant, instructor, or skilled classmate to help you understand how to use it. Finally, remember that technology cannot make you learn—it can simply make information accessible to you. Your job is to evaluate it carefully and use it in a way that works for you.

Improve Career Planning and Job Performance

Knowing how you learn and interact with others will help you work more effectively and take more targeted and productive career planning risks. How can an employee or job candidate benefit from self-awareness?

Better performance and teamwork. When you understand your strengths, you can find ways to use them on the job more readily, as well as determine how to compensate for tasks that take you out of your areas of strength. In addition, you will be better able to work with others. For example, a team leader might offer an intrapersonal team member the chance to take material home to think about before attending a meeting; an Adventurer might find ways to spearhead new projects, while delegating the detailed research to a Thinker on the team.

Better career planning. Exploring ways to use your strengths in school will help you make better choices about what internships, jobs, or careers will suit you. For most

talk risk and reward . . .

Risk asking tough questions to be rewarded with new insights. Use the following questions to inspire discussion with classmates, either in person or online.

- When you have trouble doing something, what is your first reaction—to risk trying again, or to give up? Do you say "I need a different approach" or "I'm no good at this"?

- Do people perceive their own strengths accurately, or do you often see strengths in others that they don't believe they have?

CONSIDER THE CASE: Imagine that you acted out in school as John Loblack did. If your mother had called you out at school in front of everyone, would that risk have had a good result for you? If that type of intervention doesn't motivate you, what does? When has a parent or friend found an effective way to get you going when you were down, and how did he or she do it?

Courtesy of John Loblack

get $mart

Racorn/123RF

YOUR FINANCIAL PREFERENCES

Creativenv/Shutterstock

As your unique preferences affect how you learn, they also influence how you approach your finances. Based on your learning preferences, take a look at how you think about and interact with money. Circle your answers to the following questions:

1. How often do you use a credit card?
   a. Never
   b. Less than twice a month
   c. Less than twice a week
   d. Daily

2. When you see something you like at the store, what do you do?
   a. Go to other stores to compare prices
   b. Think about it for a day or two
   c. Ask your friends what they think
   d. Purchase it immediately

3. How many credit cards do you have?
   a. 0
   b. 1
   c. 2
   d. 3 or more

4. How much credit card debt do you incur each month (in other words, how much money do you spend on credit monthly)?
   a. $0
   b. $1 to $100
   c. $101 to $500
   d. More than $500

5. How much of your credit card balance do you typically pay off each month?
   a. 100%
   b. 50% to 99%
   c. 25% to 49%
   d. Less than 24%

Now add up the number of a, b, c, and d answers:

a _____   b _____   c _____   d _____

- Thinkers and Organizers often have more a and b answers because they tend to be careful with money, thinking about the financial impact of their purchases and planning for the future.

- Givers may also be careful with their money, but often end up helping others or giving gifts, which might give them more c answers.

- Adventurers are usually risk-takers, which means they may be willing to take on more debt. They are likely to have more d answers.

95

KEY **4.7** Multiple Intelligences may open doors to majors and internships.

MULTIPLE INTELLIGENCE		CONSIDER MAJORING IN	THINK ABOUT AN INTERNSHIP AT A
Bodily-Kinesthetic		• Massage or physical therapy • Kinesiology • Construction engineering • Sports medicine • Dance or theatre	• Sports physician's office • Physical or massage therapy centre • Construction company • Dance studio or theatre company • Athletic club
Intrapersonal		• Psychology • Finance • Computer science • Biology • Philosophy	• Accounting firm • Biology lab • Pharmaceutical company • Publishing house • Computer or internet company
Interpersonal		• Education • Public relations • Nursing • Business • Hotel/restaurant management	• Hotel or restaurant • Social service agency • Public relations firm • Human resources department • Public or private elementary school
Naturalistic		• Geology • Zoology • Atmospheric sciences • Agriculture • Environmental law	• Museum • National park • Environmental law firm • Zoo • Geological research firm
Musical		• Music • Music theory • Voice • Composition • Performing arts	• Performance hall • Radio station • Record label or recording studio • Children's music camp • Orchestra or opera company
Logical-Mathematical		• Math • Physics • Economics • Banking/finance • Computer science	• Law firm • Consulting firm • Bank • Information technology company • Research lab
Verbal-Linguistic		• Communications • Marketing • English/literature • Journalism • Foreign languages	• Newspaper or magazine • PR/marketing firm • Ad agency • Publishing house • Network TV affiliate
Visual-Spatial		• Architecture • Visual arts • Multimedia designs • Photography • Art history	• Photo or art studio • Multimedia design firm • Architecture firm • Interior design firm • Art gallery

post-secondary students, majors and internships are more immediate steps on the road to a career. Internships can be extremely rewarding risks, giving you a chance to "try out" your major in a workplace setting. You might even discover you don't have an interest in a career in that area and need to switch majors.

INTERNSHIP
A temporary work program that allows you to gain supervised, practical experience in a job and career area.

Key 4.7 links majors and internships to the eight intelligences. This list is by no means complete; rather, it represents only a fraction of the available opportunities. Use what you see here to inspire thought and spur investigation. If something from this list or elsewhere interests you, consider looking for an opportunity to "shadow" someone (follow the individual for a day to see what he or she does) to see if you might want to commit to an internship or major.

Although all students have areas of strength and weakness, some challenges are more significant and are diagnosed as learning disabilities. Focused assistance can help students with learning disabilities to manage their conditions and succeed in school.

HOW CAN YOU IDENTIFY AND
manage learning disabilities?

Some learning disabilities cause reading problems, some produce difficulties in math, some cause issues that arise when working with others, and some make it difficult for students to process the language they hear. The following will help you understand learning disabilities as well as the tools people use to manage them.

Identifying a Learning Disability

The Learning Disabilities Association of Canada (LDAC) defines *learning disabilities* as "a number of disorders which may affect the acquisition, organization, retention, understanding, or use of verbal or non-verbal information. Learning disabilities result from impairments in one or more processes related to perceiving, thinking, remembering, or learning."[8]

How can you determine whether you should be evaluated for a learning disability? According to LDAC, persistent problems in any of the following areas may indicate a problem:[9]

- Oral language (listening, speaking, understanding)
- Reading (word recognition, comprehension)
- Written language (spelling, writing)
- Mathematics (computation, problem solving)

Details on specific learning disabilities appear in Key 4.8. For an evaluation, contact your school's learning centre or student health centre for a referral to a licensed professional. Note that a professional diagnosis is required in order for a person with a learning disability to receive government-funded aid.

Getting What You Need

If you are diagnosed with a learning disability, valuable information is available. Maximize your ability to learn by learning about and managing your disability.

- *Find information about your disability.* Search the library and the Internet—try the Learning Disabilities Association of Canada at www.ldac-acta.ca or LD

KEY 4.8 Learn how to recognize specific learning disabilities.

DISABILITY OR CONDITION	WHAT ARE THE SIGNS?
Dyslexia and related reading disorders	Problems with reading (spelling, word sequencing, comprehension, reading out loud) and with translating written language into thought or thought into written language
Dyscalculia (developmental arithmetic disorders)	Difficulty recognizing numbers and symbols, memorizing facts, understanding abstract math concepts, applying math to life skills (time management, handling money), and performing mental math calculations
Developmental writing disorders	Difficulty composing sentences, organizing a writing assignment, or translating thoughts coherently to the page
Handwriting disorders (dysgraphia)	Distorted or incorrect language, inappropriately sized and spaced letters, wrong or misspelled words, difficulty putting thoughts on paper or grasping grammar, large gap between spoken language skills and written skills
Speech and language disorders	Problems with producing speech sounds, using spoken language to communicate, or understanding what others say
LD-related social issues	Problems recognizing facial or vocal cues from others, understanding how others are feeling, controlling verbal and physical impulsivity, and respecting others' personal space
LD-related organizational issues	Difficulty scheduling and organizing personal, academic, and work-related materials

Source: Based on Information from the Language and Math section of the National Center for Learning Disabilities website. Accessed on December 24, 2011, from http://www.ncld.org/ld-basics/ld-explained.

Online at www.ldonline.org. If you have an individualized education program (IEP) (a document describing your disability and recommended strategies), read it and make sure you understand it.

- *Seek assistance from your school.* Speak with your advisor about getting a referral to the counsellor who can arrange specific assistance for your classes. Accommodations mandated by law for students who have learning disabilities include:
  - Extended time on tests
  - Note-taking assistance (for example, having another student take notes for you)
  - Assistive technology devices (screen readers, magnification software, adaptive keyboards)
  - Modified assignments
  - Alternative assessments and test formats

student PROFILE

Courtesy of Hongman Xu

Hongman Xu
SENECA COLLEGE, TORONTO, ONTARIO

About me:

I'm a mother of two and am originally from Jiujiang, a small and famous city in China. My mother and father are doctors. I have two sisters. Everyone in my family graduated from university in China. When my husband and I immigrated to Canada, I had 10 years of work experience in China but no idea of how to be a student in Canada. I'm enrolled in Seneca's International Transportation and Customs diploma program.

I plan to start my own customs brokerage company in the future.

What I focus on:

When I was younger, my dreams didn't include being a mature college student struggling with math in Canada. While it might be a common stereotype that Asians are good at math, it wasn't the case with me. I struggled. When I faced troubles in my studies, I was able to go to my professor for help. I also used both the textbook and online quizzes, which helped me practise over and over again. These were very useful for me and helped me study. Online studying was also helpful when my kids got sick and I couldn't get to class.

I also read the textbook step by step, a bit at a time, which helped me use what little time I had more effectively. Extra help from my professor, online quizzes, and the textbook were the keys for my success in accounting classes.

What will help me in the future:

Being able to overcome my struggles with math and accounting will help me reach my dream of starting my own customs brokerage firm. Succeeding in those classes has taught me that any problem can be solved with hard work. It's given me the confidence to succeed.

Used with permission of Hongman Xu

Other services that may be offered include tutoring, study skills assistance, and counselling.

- *Understand your legal rights.* In a unanimous 2012 decision, The Supreme Court of Canada declared that all Canadians have a right to an education. The decision stated that Canadian students with learning disabilities have the right "to receive an education that gives them an opportunity to develop their full potential." The ruling was based on the case of BC's Jeffrey Moore, a dyslexic student who did not receive the specialized educational help he required due to funding cutbacks.[10]
- *Be a dedicated student.* Be on time and attend class. Read assignments *before* class. Sit where you can focus. Review notes soon after class. Spend extra time on assignments. Ask for help.

Finally, build a positive attitude. Focus on what you have achieved and on how far you have come. Rely on support from others, knowing it will give you the best possible chance to succeed.

revisit RISK AND REWARD

What happened to John? John was still struggling with reading following his probationary period at the radio station, but his risk paid off when his high level of focus got him promoted to news editor. "I worked hard," says John. "I left Dominica as a government information service officer after nine years at the broadcasting corporation, and I have never stopped reading since." After emigrating in 1993 with $2000 in his pocket, John continued to earn rewards from his risk-taking. He cleaned toilets for minimum wage to help pay for his undergraduate degree. He earned a master's in human resource management, then a doctoral degree in organizational leadership. He now owns Goalmind Career Coaching and Consulting, a company that helps clients identify careers that suit their personalities. He's also a faculty member and dean at Strayer University, as well as a published author. Having had every excuse to fail, he chose the alternative and is experiencing the reward of a full expression of his abilities and talents.

What does this mean for you? John is currently working on a book entitled *Six Roads to Fulfilling Your Dreams*. The letters of the word "dreams" stand for each of the "roads:" **d**iscipline, (be) **r**esponsible, (no) **e**xcuses, **a**ccept (the hand you're dealt), (embrace) **m**istakes, **s**tick to it. As you work to discover and maximize your strengths, how can these roads help you? Choose two that you think will help you the most, noting what risks you will need to take in following them and what reward you hope will result. Then describe what you plan to do to begin moving down each road.

What risk may bring reward beyond your world? John Loblack overcame his challenges with reading to become a college dean, an author, and an inspiring force. Today, there are many more resources to help students overcome reading challenges. Check out the website www.literacyconnections.com, which offers a multitude of ways that people can get involved with improving literacy for adults and children. Find one that makes sense for your strongest learning preferences. Consider making a commitment, however small, to use how you learn best to help someone become a better reader.

GLOBAL RISK AND REWARD

Looking at the high cost of transporting water for many Africans, including time, effort, and injuries from carrying heavy water containers on the head or back, South Africans Pettie Petzer and Johan Jonker had an idea and took the risk to develop, build, and market it. Called the Hippo Water Roller, it enables people who do not live near a water source to transport water in a rolling container. As a result of this innovation, thousands of Africans experience the daily reward of saved time and energy as well as less physical wear and tear.[11]

MarcelClemens/ Shutterstock

RISK ACTION
FOR POST-SECONDARY, CAREER, AND LIFE REWARDS

KNOW IT
Blan-k/Shutterstock

WRITE IT
Blan-k/Shutterstock

WORK IT
Blan-k/Shutterstock

Left to Right: pio3/Shutterstock; Viktor Gladkov/123RF; MP_P/Shutterstock

Complete the following on paper or in digital format.

KNOW IT *Think Critically*

Link How You Learn to Coursework and Major

Apply what you know about yourself to some future academic planning.

Build basic skills. On paper or on the computer, summarize in a paragraph or two what you know about yourself as a learner. Focus on what you learned from the assessments.

Take it to the next level. Schedule a meeting with your academic advisor. Note the following:

- Name of advisor
- Office location/contact information
- Time/date of meeting

At the meeting, give the advisor an overview of your learning strengths and challenges based on the summary you wrote. Ask for advice about courses that might interest you and majors that might suit you. Take notes. As a result of your discussion, name two courses to consider in the next year.

Move toward mastery. Think about the courses you listed and other courses related to them. Toward what majors might each of them lead you? Based on those courses, name two majors to investigate. Then, create a separate to-do list of how you plan to explore one course offering and one major. Set a deadline for each task. If you are having trouble choosing a major because you are unsure of a career direction, see an advisor in the career centre for guidance.

WRITE IT *Communicate*

Emotional intelligence journal: Your interactions with others. With your Personality Spectrum profile in mind, think about how you generally relate to people. Describe the type(s) of people with whom you tend to get along. How do you feel when you are around these people? Then, describe the types that tend to irk you. How do those people make you feel? Use your emotional intelligence to discuss what those feelings tell you. Consider how you can adjust your mindset or take action to create the best possible outcome when interacting with people with whom you just don't get along.

101

Real-life writing: Ask an instructor for support. Reach out to an instructor of a course that clashes with your learning preference in terms of material, teaching style, or how the classroom is run. Draft a respectful email that introduces you, describes how you perceive yourself as a learner, and details your issue. Include any ideas you have about how the instructor might help you. Thank the instructor in advance. Finally, when you are done, make something happen: Send the email and follow through on any response you receive.

WORK IT *Build Your Brand*

Self-Portrait

Because self-knowledge helps you to shape your future, a self-portrait is an important exploration tool as you consider possible careers, as well as majors that may lead you to those careers. Use this exercise to synthesize what you've learned about yourself into one comprehensive portrait. Design it as a "think link" or mind map, using words and visual shapes to describe your (1) dominant Multiple Intelligences, (2) Personality Spectrum dimensions, (3) values, (4) abilities and interests, (5) personal characteristics, and (6) anything else that you have discovered through self-exploration. Key 4.9 shows an example. You can create it freehand or use a graphics program.

KEY 4.9

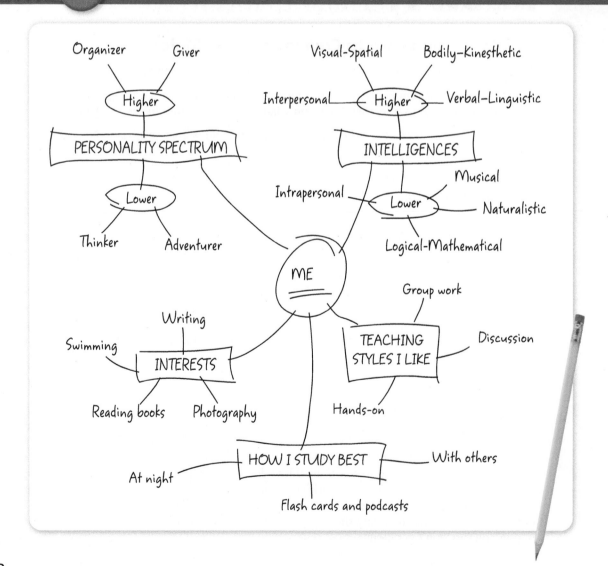

A *think link* is a visual presentation of related ideas, similar to a map or web, that represents your thought process. Put your ideas inside geometric shapes (boxes or circles) and attach related ideas and facts to those shapes using lines (you may find additional information on note taking elsewhere in your text).

To get started, try using the style shown in Key 4.9. Put your main idea ("Me") in a shape in the centre, and then create a wheel of related ideas coming off that central shape. Spreading out from each of those related ideas (interests, values, and so forth), draw lines connecting the thoughts that go along with each idea. For example, you might connect singing, stock market, and history with the "interests" idea.

Let your design reflect who you are, just as what you write does. You may want to look back at it at the end of the term to see how your self-image has changed and grown.

CHAPTER

5

Courtesy of Chanda Hinton

Brain cell function improves if you think actively – and can deteriorate if you don't. Risk the action of thinking to build a brain that can handle your most important problems and decisions.

Critical, Creative, and Practical Thinking

HOW CAN YOU MAXIMIZE BRAIN POWER?

What Would You Risk? *Chanda Hinton*

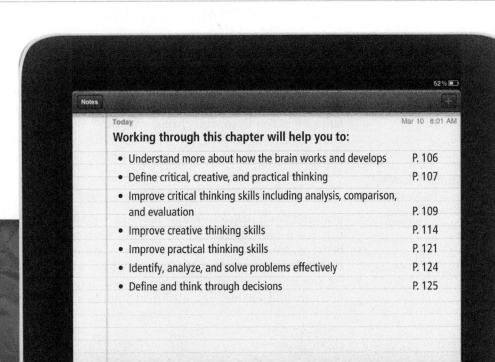

Courtesy of Chanda Hinton

THINK ABOUT THIS SITUATION AS YOU READ, AND CONSIDER WHAT ACTION YOU WOULD TAKE. THIS CHAPTER BUILDS METACOGNITION—"THINKING ABOUT THINKING"—AND PROBLEM-SOLVING SKILLS THAT WILL HELP YOU FACE CHALLENGES IN COLLEGE AND BEYOND.

Chanda Hinton was just 9 years old when her life path was forever altered. While visiting with family friends, Chanda and two 14-year-old boys were playfully arguing over popsicles. One of the boys picked up a gun, not knowing it was loaded. The gun discharged, the bullet striking Chanda in the back of her neck. The impact of the blow resulted in a spinal cord injury in the C5–C6 vertebrae, rendering Chanda a quadriplegic, unable to move or feel from the neck down.

Perhaps because she was so young, Chanda dealt with the transition and found meaning and fulfillment. "Elementary and high school were really great," Chanda recalls. "My outlook was super-positive." She had tons of friends. She was a role model.

Things changed when Chanda moved into adulthood. Her spinal cord injury had compromised her health, as her weight dropped to less than 30 kilos. The pain was chronic, the emergency 911 calls and doctor visits more frequent. Mentally, she struggled too, especially when her post-secondary education took her away from her comfort zone, the close-knit rural town where everyone cherished her.

Going to university was an enormous risk, and immensely difficult. "It was tough for me because they were looking upon me as a woman in a wheelchair as opposed to, 'Oh hey, there's Chanda.'" Worried about her health, her career prospects, and her future life, she dropped out and lost her will to take risks. At age 21 she was bedbound, dependent on medicine and painkillers, and inactive. She wondered if she had reached the end of her life expectancy.

To be continued . . .

NOT ALL LIFE PROBLEMS ARE AS EXTREME AS CHANDA'S; HOWEVER, EVERYONE FACES CHALLENGES THAT REQUIRE CRITICAL AND CREATIVE THINKING AND PRACTICAL ACTION. YOU'LL LEARN MORE ABOUT CHANDA, AND THE REWARD RESULTING FROM HER ACTIONS, WITHIN THE CHAPTER.

Notes

52% ▢

Today   Mar 10 8:01 AM

Working through this chapter will help you to:

statusCHECK

How Developed Are Your Thinking Skills?

For each statement, fill in the number that best describes how often it applies to you.

1 = never   2 = seldom   3 = sometimes   4 = often   5 = always

1. I discover and explore information by asking and answering questions.   ① ② ③ ④ ⑤

2. I try not to act impulsively.   ① ② ③ ④ ⑤

3. I don't take everything I read or hear as fact—I question how useful, truthful, and logical it is before I decide whether I can use it.   ① ② ③ ④ ⑤

4. Even if it seems like there is only one way to solve a problem, I try to generate other options.   ① ② ③ ④ ⑤

5. Knowing that effort is important to creativity, I persist when I'm stumped.   ① ② ③ ④ ⑤

6. I take time to "sit with" a problem or question in order to generate ideas.   ① ② ③ ④ ⑤

7. When working in a group, I try to manage my emotions and notice how I affect others.   ① ② ③ ④ ⑤

8. I think about different solutions before I choose one and take action.   ① ② ③ ④ ⑤

9. I spend time researching different possibilities before making a decision.   ① ② ③ ④ ⑤

10. When I make a decision, I consider how my choice will affect others.   ① ② ③ ④ ⑤

Each of the topics in these statements is covered in this chapter. Note those statements for which you filled in a 3 or lower. Skim the chapter to see where those topics appear, and pay special attention to them as you read, learn, and apply new strategies.

REMEMBER: NO MATTER HOW DEVELOPED YOUR THINKING SKILLS ARE, YOU CAN IMPROVE WITH EFFORT AND PRACTICE.

HOW IS YOUR BRAIN CHANGING
right now?

With the risk of effort comes the reward of positive change. When you spend four days a week in the gym doing weight training, for example, you grow and strengthen muscle fibres, ultimately increasing your ability to perform physically. Similarly, when you learn, you change your brain's cells and functioning, which develops your thinking skills. The actions of learning are your brain's workout. The result? A stronger, sharper brain that gets you where you want to go.

The Biology of Learning

Learning prods *neurons* (brain cells) to grow and strengthen *dendrites* (the branches that reach out to other neurons), and to increase and change *synapses* (the spaces between dendrites). Information moves through the brain in the form of electrical impulses that travel through dendrites and across synapses. Repeating and reinforcing something learned, such as an action, fact, or process, strengthens the cell connections and enables the electrical impulses to move more quickly and easily.

MyLab Student Success
(www.mystudentsuccesslab.com) is an online solution designed to help you "Start Strong, Finish Stronger" by building skills for ongoing personal and professional development.

An established "neural pathway" like this operates like a woodland path that has become well-worn and clear through frequent foot traffic.

Learning something new often feels risky and awkward, like cutting through bushes and brush to make a path that wasn't there before. That's because the neurons have to reach toward neurons that they may not have connected with much or at all. When you stop using something you've learned, your brain will reduce the clarity of that pathway by "pruning" unused cells.[1] Basically, it is a "use it or lose it" situation—your brain tissue literally changes shape and strength based on what you do or do not do.

Executive Function Under Construction

One of the most significant research findings of the last decade is that your brain's *prefrontal cortex*, which controls your most complex thinking actions, undergoes its last and most comprehensive phase of development from around 18 to 25 years of age. During this phase, dendrites grow thicker, frequently used synapses become stronger, and nerve fibres become more heavily insulated, making "the entire brain a much faster and more sophisticated organ."[2] The prefrontal cortex controls executive function, a crucial tool for school and life success.

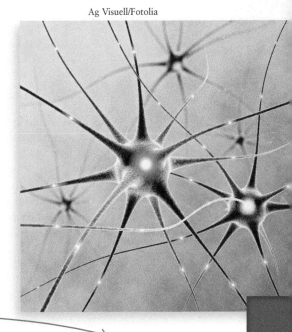

EXECUTIVE FUNCTION A set of higher-order behaviours and cognitive processes involving planning, prioritizing tasks, selecting the most important information, and evaluating potential future consequences of decisions.

Basically, executive function is what allows people to perceive possible future consequences of a choice, weigh the pros and cons of the consequences of different choices, and take the risk of putting one to work, based on what seems to offer the greatest reward. As the developing brain gets the "wiring upgrade" that improves executive function, that brain's owner becomes more skilled in each of these actions, more able to balance self-interest against other values and ultimately make more productive decisions.[3]

Because their executive function is still developing, many students tend toward impulsive choices and physically risky actions. However, this is not because they have shut off their brains, but because their thinking is highly focused on potential gain. Research shows that although younger people see and evaluate risk as do their older counterparts, they are more likely to take risks that adults would not because they value different types of rewards.[4]

Post-Secondary Education and Your Brain: An Ideal Team

Although it can be challenging, there is an advantage to being in this phase of brain development right now. Growing your thinking power often requires exposure to the unfamiliar, and university or college provides new turf that can stimulate an evolving brain. If you can apply the risk-taking tendencies your brain may exhibit now to the actions you take on behalf of your education, you may be more receptive to the relationships, information, and experiences college and university offer—the raw material you need to develop your mind.[5]

This chapter is focused on the development of your executive function, helping you to take advantage of how post-secondary learning and experiences can build richer networks among the neurons in your brain. You will increase your ability to solve problems and make decisions—your two most important and frequently used thinking processes. First, consider how to define thinking in terms of the thinker's intention and action.

WHAT IS A *thinking?*

According to experts, thinking is what happens when you ask questions and move toward the answers.[6] "To think through or rethink anything," says Dr. Richard Paul, director of research at the Center for Critical Thinking and Moral Critique, "one must ask questions that stimulate our thought. Questions define tasks, express problems and delineate issues. . . . only students who have questions are really thinking and learning."[7]

Thinking Means Questioning

As you answer questions, you turn information into material that you can use to achieve goals. A *Wall Street Journal* article entitled "The Best Innovations Are Those That Come from Smart Questions" relays the story of a cell biology student, William Hunter, whose professor told him that "the difference between good science and great science is the quality of the questions posed."[8] Now a physician, Dr. Hunter asks questions about new ways to use drugs. His risk-taking has helped his company reach the reward of developing a revolutionary product—a drug-coated mesh used to strengthen diseased blood vessels. How can you question effectively?

Know why you question. To ask useful questions, you need to know *why* you are questioning. Define your purpose by asking: "What am I trying to accomplish, and why?" For example, if Chanda's purpose for questioning her life expectancy were to extend it, that would generate an entirely different set of questions than if she intended to plan for end-of-life health needs.

Question in different ways. Use questions to:

- Analyze ("How bad is my money situation?")
- Come up with creative ideas ("How can I earn more money?")
- Apply practical solutions ("Whom do I talk to about getting a job on campus?")

Want to question. Knowing why you are questioning also helps you *want* to think. "Critical-thinking skills are different from critical thinking dispositions, or a willingness to deploy these skills," says cognitive psychologist D. Alan Bensley of Frostburg State University in Maryland. In other words, having the skills isn't enough—you also need the willingness to risk using them.[9] Having a clear understanding of your desired reward can motivate you to work to achieve it.

Metacognition: A Tool for Post-Secondary and Life Success

Metacognition is the foundation for the kind of self-knowledge and self-management that enables you to perform higher-level thinking skills. It is essential for successful lifelong learning.

One way to explain metacognition is to call it "thinking about thinking" or "knowing how you know," including taking action based on the information you have learned.[11] When you explore your learning preferences, you are being metacognitive. When you find a certain note-taking strategy more helpful for information retention than others and you use it in class, you are being metacognitive. Any time you examine what your brain is doing and consider how to do it better, you are putting metacognition to work toward accomplishing a meaningful goal.

This text uses the term *thinking skill*. Thinking is a skill that can be improved with focus and effort, much as shooting a basketball, drawing a face, chopping vegetables, organizing a schedule, or painting a room are improvable skills. Metacognition allows you to figure out how to deploy your skills to get where you want to go.

The Conference Board of Canada maintains that employers underline the importance of being able to "assess situations, identify problems, and then evaluate and implement solutions."[12]

When you need to solve a problem or make a decision, metacognitively combining all three thinking skills gives you the greatest chance of achieving your goal.[13]

METACOGNITION
An awareness and control of one's cognitive processes and the regulatory mechanisms used to solve problems.[10]

The rest of this chapter will explore analytical (or critical), creative, and practical thinking each individually, ultimately showing how they work together to help you to solve problems and make decisions effectively. Asking questions opens the door to each thinking skill, and in each section you will find examples of the kinds of questions that drive that skill. Begin by exploring analytical thinking skills.

HOW CAN YOU IMPROVE YOUR
analytical thinking skills?

Analytical thinking, also known as *critical thinking*, is the process of gathering information, breaking it into parts, examining and evaluating those parts, and making connections for the purposes of gaining understanding, solving a problem, or making a decision.

Through the analytical process, you look for how pieces of information relate to one another, setting aside any pieces that are unclear, unrelated, unimportant, or biased. You may also form new questions that change your direction. Be open to them and to where they may lead you.

Gather Information

Information is the raw material for thinking, so to start the thinking process you must first gather your raw materials. This requires analyzing how much information you need, how much time you should spend gathering it, and whether it is relevant. Say, for instance, that you have to write a paper on one aspect of the media (TV, radio, internet) and its influence on a particular group. Here's how analyzing can help you gather information for that paper:

- Reviewing the assignment terms, you note two important items: The paper should be approximately 10 pages and describe at least three significant points of influence.
- At the library and online, you find thousands of articles in this topic area. Analyzing your reactions to them and how many articles focus on certain aspects of the topic, you decide to focus your paper on how the internet influences young teens (ages 13 to 15).
- Examining the summaries of six comprehensive articles leads you to three in-depth sources.

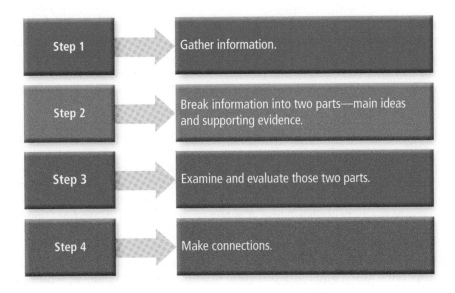

Step 1	Gather information.
Step 2	Break information into two parts—main ideas and supporting evidence.
Step 3	Examine and evaluate those two parts.
Step 4	Make connections.

Juniart/Fotolia

Many types of work, such as the construction project these architects are discussing, involve analytical thinking.

In this way you achieve a subgoal—a selection of useful materials—on the way to your larger goal of writing a well-crafted paper.

Break Information into Parts

The next step is to search for the two most relevant parts of the information: the main idea(s) (also called the argument or viewpoint) and the evidence that supports them (also called reasons or supporting details).

Separate the ideas. Identify each of the ideas conveyed in what you are reading. You can use lists or a mind map to visually separate ideas from one another. For instance, if you are reading about how teens aged 13 to 15 use the internet, you could identify the goal of each method of access they use (websites, blogs, messaging through social networking).

Identify the evidence. For each main idea, identify the evidence that supports it. For example, if an article claims that young teens rely on app-based messaging three times more than on emails, note the facts, studies, or other evidence cited to support the truth of the claim.

ARGUMENT
A set of connected ideas, supported by examples, made by a writer to prove or disprove a point.

Examine and Evaluate

The third step lies at the heart of analytical thinking. Now you examine the information to see if it is useful for your purposes. Keep your mind open to all useful information, setting aside personal prejudices. A student who thinks that the death penalty is wrong, for example, may have a hard time analyzing arguments that defend it, or may focus his research on materials that support his perspective. Set aside personal prejudices when you analyze information. The extra time you risk with careful evaluation will reward you with the most accurate and useful information available.

Here are four different questions that will help you examine and evaluate effectively.

1. Do examples support ideas? When you encounter an idea or claim, examine how it is supported with examples or *evidence*—facts, expert opinion, research, personal experience, and so on (see Key 5.1). How useful an idea is may depend on whether, or how well, it is supported with evidence or made concrete with examples. For example, a blog written by a 13-year-old might make statements about what kids do on the internet. The word of one person, who may or may not be telling the truth, is not adequate support; however, a study of youth technology use released by Statistics Canada or the CRTC may be more reliable.

2. Is the information factual and accurate, or is it opinion? A *statement of fact* is information presented as objectively real and verifiable (e.g., "The internet is a research tool"). In contrast, a *statement of opinion* is a belief, conclusion, or judgment that is inherently difficult, and sometimes impossible, to verify (e.g., "The internet is always the best and most reliable research tool"). When you critically evaluate materials, one test of the evidence is whether it is fact or opinion. Key 5.2 defines important characteristics of fact and opinion.

3. Do causes and effects link logically? Look at the reasons given for why something happened (causes) and the explanation of its consequences (effects, both positive

KEY 5.1   Support an idea with evidence.

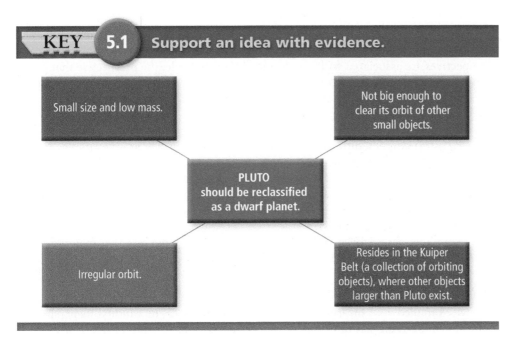

Small size and low mass.		Not big enough to clear its orbit of other small objects.
	PLUTO should be reclassified as a dwarf planet.	
Irregular orbit.		Resides in the Kuiper Belt (a collection of orbiting objects), where other objects larger than Pluto exist.

and negative). For example, an article might detail what causes young teens to use the internet after school, and the effects that this has on their family life. The cause-and-effect chain in the article should make sense to you.

Analyze carefully to seek out *key* or *"root" causes*—the true and significant causes of a problem or situation. For example, many factors may be involved in why young teens spend time on the internet, including availability of service, previous experience, and education level of parents, but on careful examination one or two factors may be more significant than others.

BIAS
A preference or inclination, especially one that prevents even-handed judgment.

4. Is the evidence biased? Evidence with a bias is evidence that is slanted in a particular direction. Searching for a bias involves looking for hidden perspectives or assumptions that lie within the material.

KEY 5.2   Examine how fact and opinion differ.

FACTS INCLUDE STATEMENTS THAT . . .	OPINIONS INCLUDE STATEMENTS THAT . . .
. . . deal with actual people, places, objects, or events. Example: "In 2002, the European Union introduced the physical coins and banknotes of a new currency—the euro—that was designed to be used by its member nations."	**. . . show evaluation.** Any statement of value indicates an opinion. Words such as *bad, good, pointless,* and *beneficial* indicate value judgments. Example: "The use of the euro has been beneficial to all the states of the European Union."
. . . use concrete words or measurable statistics. Example: "The charity event raised $50 862."	**. . . use abstract words.** Complicated words like *misery* or *success* usually indicate a personal opinion. Example: "The charity event was a smashing success."
. . . describe current events in exact terms. Example: "Mr. Barrett's course has 378 students enrolled this semester."	**. . . predict future events.** Statements about future occurrences are often opinions. Example: "Mr. Barrett's course is going to set a new enrollment record this year."
. . . avoid emotional words and focus on the verifiable. Example: "Citing dissatisfaction with the instruction, seven out of the twenty-five students in that class withdrew in September."	**. . . use emotional words.** Emotions are unverifiable. Words such as *delightful* or *miserable* express an opinion. Example: "That class is a miserable experience."
. . . avoid absolutes. Example: "Some students need to have a job while in school."	**. . . use absolutes.** Absolute qualifiers, such as *all, none, never,* and *always,* often express an opinion. Example: "All students need to have a job while in school."

Source: Adapted from Ben E. Johnson. Stirring Up Thinking. New York: Houghton Mifflin, 1998, pp. 263–270.

PERSPECTIVE
A characteristic way of thinking about people, situations, events, and ideas.

ASSUMPTION
A judgment, generalization, or bias influenced by experience and values.

A perspective can be broad (such as a generally optimistic or pessimistic view of life) or more focused (such as an attitude about whether students should own cars). Perspectives are associated with assumptions. For example, the perspective that people can control technology leads to assumptions such as "Parents can control children's exposure to the internet." Having a particular experience with children and the internet can build or reinforce a perspective.

Assumptions often hide within questions and statements, blocking you from considering information in different ways. Take this classic puzzler as an example: "Which came first, the chicken or the egg?" Thinking about this question, most people assume that the egg is a chicken egg. If you think past that assumption and come up with a new idea—such as, the egg is a dinosaur egg—then the obvious answer is that the egg came first. Key 5.3 offers examples of how perspectives and assumptions can affect what you read or hear through the media.

Examining perspectives and assumptions helps you judge whether material is *reliable*. The less bias you can identify, the more reliable the information.

After the questions: What information is most useful to you?

You've examined your information, looking at its evidence, its validity, its perspective, and any underlying assumptions. Now, based on that examination, you evaluate whether an idea or piece of information is important or unimportant, relevant or not, strong or weak, and why. You then set aside what is not useful and use the rest to form an opinion, possible solution, or decision.

In preparing your paper on young teens and the internet, for example, you've analyzed a selection of information and materials to see how they applied to the goal of your paper. You then selected what you believe will be most useful, in preparation for drafting.

Make Connections

The last part of analytical thinking is when, after you have broken information apart, you find new and productive ways to connect pieces together. This step is crucial for research papers and essays because it is where your original ideas are born and your creative skills get involved (more on that in the next section). When you begin to write, you focus on your new ideas, supporting them effectively with information you've learned from your analysis. Here are some ways to make connections.

Compare and contrast. Look at how ideas are similar to, or different from, each other. You might explore how different young teen subgroups (boys vs. girls, for example) have

---

KEY 5.3 Different articles may present different perspectives on the same topic.

Topic: *How teens' grades are affected by internet use*

STATEMENT BY A TEACHING ORGANIZATION	STATEMENT BY A PR AGENT FOR AN INTERNET SEARCH ENGINE	STATEMENT BY A PROFESSOR SPECIALIZING IN NEW MEDIA AND EDUCATION
"Too much internet use equals failing grades and stolen papers."	"The internet use allows students access to a plethora of information, which results in better grades."	"The effects of the internet on young students are undeniable and impossible to overlook."

different purposes for setting up pages on sites such as Facebook or creating Twitter handles.

Look for themes, patterns, and categories. Note connections that form as you look at how bits of information relate to one another. For example, you might see patterns of internet use that link young teens from particular cultures or areas of the country together into categories.

Come to new information ready to hear and read new ideas, think about them, and make informed decisions about what you believe. The process will educate you, sharpen your thinking skills, and give you more information to work with as you encounter life's problems. See Key 5.4 for some questions you can ask to build and use analytical thinking skills.

Pursuing your goals, in school and in the workplace, requires not just analyzing information but also thinking creatively about how to use what you've learned from your analysis.

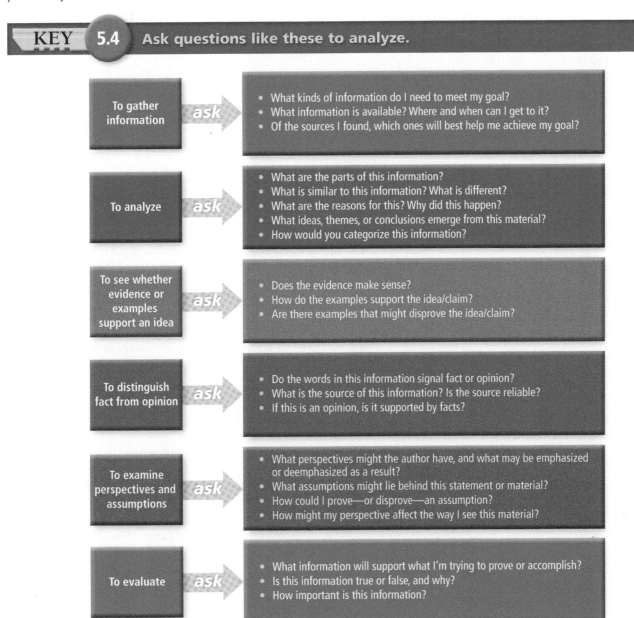

KEY 5.4 Ask questions like these to analyze.

To gather information *ask*
- What kinds of information do I need to meet my goal?
- What information is available? Where and when can I get to it?
- Of the sources I found, which ones will best help me achieve my goal?

To analyze *ask*
- What are the parts of this information?
- What is similar to this information? What is different?
- What are the reasons for this? Why did this happen?
- What ideas, themes, or conclusions emerge from this material?
- How would you categorize this information?

To see whether evidence or examples support an idea *ask*
- Does the evidence make sense?
- How do the examples support the idea/claim?
- Are there examples that might disprove the idea/claim?

To distinguish fact from opinion *ask*
- Do the words in this information signal fact or opinion?
- What is the source of this information? Is the source reliable?
- If this is an opinion, is it supported by facts?

To examine perspectives and assumptions *ask*
- What perspectives might the author have, and what may be emphasized or deemphasized as a result?
- What assumptions might lie behind this statement or material?
- How could I prove—or disprove—an assumption?
- How might my perspective affect the way I see this material?

To evaluate *ask*
- What information will support what I'm trying to prove or accomplish?
- Is this information true or false, and why?
- How important is this information?

Source: Adapted from www-ed.fnal.gov/trc/tutorial/taxonomy.html (Richard Paul, *Critical Thinking: How to Prepare Students for a Rapidly Changing World,* 1993) and from www.kcmetro.edu/longview/ctac/blooms.htm (Barbara Fowler, Longview Community College "Bloom's Taxonomy and Critical Thinking").

Critical, Creative, and Practical Thinking

get analytical

ANALYZE A STATEMENT

Dario Sabljak/Shutterstock

Complete the following on paper or in digital format.

Consider the statement below; then analyze it by answering the questions that follow.

> *"There's no point in pursuing a career area that you love*
> *if it isn't going to earn you a living."*

1. Is this statement fact or opinion? Why?
2. What examples can you think of that support or negate this statement?
3. What perspective(s) are guiding this statement?
4. What assumption(s) underlie the statement? What negative effects might result from accepting these assumptions and therefore agreeing with the statement?
5. As a result of your critical thinking, what is your evaluation of this statement?

HOW CAN YOU IMPROVE YOUR
creative thinking skills?

When you think of the word *creativity,* do painters, musicians, and actors come to mind? Although creativity is often equated with visual and performing arts, it is actually a universal human capability, reflected in every aspect of human experience. "The human mind . . . has the creative impulse built into its operating system, hardwired into its most essential programming code," says Jonah Lehrer, author of *Imagine: How Creativity Works.*[14] To begin to grasp the range of accomplishment that depends on creative thinking, look at the examples in Key 5.5.

How can you define creativity? Basically, to think creatively is to generate new ideas that promote useful change, whether the change consists of world-altering communication technology or a tooth-brushing technique that prevents cavities. Such functional ideas can come from:

- Combining existing elements in an innovative way (using a weak adhesive to mark pages in a book, a 3M scientist created Post-it Notes).
- Generating *analogies*—comparisons based on a resemblance of things otherwise unlike—from looking at how things are related (after examining how burrs stuck to his dog's fur after a walk in the woods, the inventor of Velcro imagined how a similar system of hooks and loops could make two pieces of fabric stick to each other).
- Pondering a longstanding problem (after viewing hundreds of hours of video of labour-intensive mopping, members of a design firm came up with the idea of having a disposable floor cleaning material, and the Swiffer was born).

Understand the Process

More than just a flash of insight, creativity is a *process.* Scientists track this "insight experience" through stages including the *impasse* (a period of frustration and blockage in the face of a problem or goal), the *revelation* (the moment when the idea bursts

Solar streetlights powered by solar panels attached to the poles

Packaging for Sun Chips that is biodegradable in a backyard compost pile

B Cycles, a bicycle-sharing modifies system operating in cities all over the world, saving energy and providing mobility and exercise

The ownership of the Green Bay Packers, consisting of 112 158 devoted fans who provide financial stability and ensure the team will stay in Wisconsin

Think-Pair-Share, a teaching innovation that gets students involved in the classroom

Office design featuring central meeting places such as Google's café, providing a place for people from different teams to connect and share ideas

Creativity is everywhere

Bead for Life, a group of African women who make jewellery out of recycled materials and use income to help combat poverty

National No-Screen Week, which gets kids playing games and running around outside

Hybrid cars that save money and reduce the carbon footprint

Clockwise from Top: anemad/Shutterstock; Andriy Popov/123RF; Fotofermer/Shutterstock; gbh007/123rf; Michael Shake/Shutterstock; Swapan Photography/Shutterstock; Helder Almeida/123RF; Ruslan Grigolava/123RF. Center: valengilda/123RF.

Critical, Creative, and Practical Thinking

into being), and then the *refining* of the idea. The process often involves stretches of time and multiple stumbles along the way.[15]

The challenging aspect of the creative experience often gets cast aside when the spotlight is focused on the brilliant final product. However, there is no product without the challenge. "Creativity is . . . about taking an idea in your head, and transforming that idea into something real," says graphic designer Milton Glaser, who developed the "I ♥ NY" slogan. "And that's always going to be a long and difficult process. If you're doing it right, it's going to feel like work."[16]

Examining the creative process reveals that it requires both divergent and convergent thinking. *Divergent thinking* is the stage leading up to the revelation of the idea, where you let your mind diverge—wander in different directions—in search of solutions. *Convergent thinking* is the more focused, systematic refining stage where you sift through and adjust ideas until you narrow it down to what works. These thinking actions are separate dimensions of creativity.[17] Look at Key 5.6 for ways to diverge and converge on your path to creative insight.

Gather Five Ingredients of Creativity

Growing your creativity starts with a receptive mindset. Combine the five attitudes in this creativity "recipe" to produce a mindset that promotes creative thinking:

1. *Belief that you can develop creativity.* Some people have more innate ability to think creatively than others. However, as with any skill, you can build and expand creative thinking ability. In an essay about creativity in medicine, Jennifer Gibson, PharmD, notes, "While not everyone will paint a masterpiece or write a great novel, everyone can be curious, seek change and take risks."[18]

2. *Receptiveness to new ideas.* Seeking out new information, experiences, and people will give you more raw materials with which to build creative ideas.[19] Research shows that people who interact with many people in large human networks are significantly more innovative than people who tend to stick with smaller, more familiar groups of friends.[20]

3. *Comfort with time alone.* Disconnecting is another crucial part of the creative process. Research indicates that creativity demands time and independent thinking

KEY 5.6 **Prepare your brain to diverge and converge.**

Peter Waters/Fotolia

Alle/Fotolia

Peter Waters/Fotolia

Peter Waters/Fotolia

Aleks/Fotolia

Converge

Creative ideas can fly out of your mind as quickly as they enter. Get in the habit of recording ideas as you think of them. Keep a pen and paper by your bed, your smartphone in your pocket, a notepad in your car, or a recorder in your backpack.

Diverge

Often, your mind will be most able to form unexpected connections when you have shifted into a more relaxed mode. People find that their best ideas come while on a long run, after a nap, in the shower, or in any environment that gives their brains permission to chill out.

Smileus/Fotolia

Peter Waters/Fotolia

(think of the stereotype of the writer alone in a cabin).[21] Business offers examples such as Apple founder Steve Jobs's collaborator, Steve Wozniak, who worked solo over many months to develop the personal computer that Mr. Jobs marketed so ingeniously. Wozniak strongly recommends that would-be inventors spend time working alone.[22]

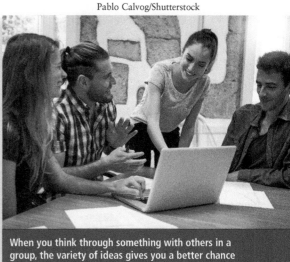

4. *Risk-taking and hard work.* Creativity demands that you risk time, ideas, and enormous effort in the quest for reward. "All creative geniuses work passionately hard and produce incredible numbers of ideas, most of which are bad," reports creativity expert Michael Michalko, recounting the fact that Picasso created more than 20 000 pieces of art. He also advocates regular practice, noting that "the more times you try to get ideas, the more active your brain becomes."[23] Like any other consistent action, working on ideas builds new neural pathways in your brain.

When you think through something with others in a group, the variety of ideas gives you a better chance of finding a workable solution to a problem.

5. *Acceptance of mistakes as part of the process.* When you can risk messing up, you open yourself to ideas and promote productivity. Thomas Edison tried over 2000 filaments before he found the best one for the tungsten electric bulb. Michalko repackages failure as a learning experience. "Whenever you try to do something and do not succeed," he says, "you do not fail. You have learned something that does not work."[24]

With your brain primed for creativity, explore actions that will build creative thinking skill: braingaming, shifting perspective, and being an outsider.

Go Beyond Brainstorming

You've likely heard of *brainstorming*—letting your mind freely associate to come up with different ideas or answers to a question. This longstanding creative technique demands that you generate ideas without regard to usefulness, and evaluate their quality later. New research calls the value of brainstorming into question, showing that avoiding evaluating idea quality can result in fewer and less effective ideas. Researchers report that constructive criticism and dissent generate *more* ideas and promote the rethinking and refining that lead to an idea's most productive form.[25] "All these errant discussions add up," says Lehrer. "In fact, they may even be the most essential part of the creative process. . . . It is the human friction that makes the sparks."[26]

Teamwork is crucial in today's workplace, and most modern problems are so complex that to tackle them with any measure of success requires the cooperation of many individuals. However, the most productive teamwork will incorporate constructive dissent and questioning. Instead of brainstorming, think of it as *braingaming*—a term that incorporates the challenges and back-and-forth that can take groups to new heights of creativity.[27] Remember that you don't have to sacrifice civility to have a successful braingaming session. At Pixar, groups use a technique called "plussing," which refers to crafting criticism that includes a productive way of improving on the idea in question—as in, "That might work, and consider adjusting it in this way. . . ."[28] Keep the "plus" in mind as you contribute and evaluate.

Shift Your Perspective

If no one ever questioned established opinion, people would still think the sun revolved around the Earth. Here are some ways to change how you look at the world:

Challenge assumptions. Taking the risk of going against what people assume to be true can lead you down innovative paths. In the late 1960s, for example, most people assumed that school provided education and television provided entertainment. Jim Henson, a pioneer in children's television, asked, "Why can't we use TV to educate young children?" From that question, the characters of Sesame Street, and many other

KEY 5.7 Use perception puzzles to experience a shift in perspective.

There are two possibilities for each image. What do you see? (See page 133 for answers.)

imagewriter/Shutterstock

Christos Georghiou/Shutterstock

educational programs, were born. Another example is the company 2Kool and the clothing and workshops it produces, founded by artists Bimmer Torres and Ratha Sok, who challenged the assumption that graffiti is simply defacement of property.

Seek out and connect with new and different people. Highly productive companies and places owe much of their creative bounty to frequent and diverse human interactions. For example, behind the astounding rate of invention at Bell Labs beginning in the 1940s was deliberate building design, in which researchers were across the hall from engineers and employees had to travel long hallways—encountering people and ideas—on the way to lunch.[29]

Try on another point of view. Ask others for their perspectives, read about new ways to approach situations, or risk going with the opposite of your first instinct. Then use what you learn to inspire creativity. For a political science course, for example, you might craft a position paper for a parliamentary candidate that goes against your position on that particular issue. For a fun example of how looking at something in a new way can unearth a totally different idea, look at the perception puzzles in Key 5.7.

Ask "what if" questions. Set up imaginary environments in which new ideas can grow, such as "What if I had unlimited money or time?" For example, the founders of Seeds of Peace, faced with long-term conflict in the Middle East, took the risk to ask: What if Israeli and Palestinian teens met at a summer camp in Maine to build mutual understanding and respect? Based on the ideas that came up, they created an organization that provides enormous reward to teenagers from the Middle East, helping them to develop leadership and communication skills.

Take a break. When you are stumped by a challenging academic or personal problem, you can benefit from the shift in perspective that some downtime can provide. In fact, a "brain break" is often an essential part of the creative process. Go for a walk or run, take a shower, watch a YouTube video, play a game—whatever sends the "off duty" message to your brain. You may be surprised at what ideas come to the surface when you are not actively trying to generate them.[30]

Risk Being an Outsider

Although humans naturally seek belonging and expertise, mastery and being part of the "in crowd" can stifle creative thinking. The more you know, the less your brain

get creative

ACTIVATE YOUR CREATIVE POWERS

Complete the following on paper or in digital format.

Think about your creativity over the past month.

1. First, describe three creative acts you performed – one in the process of studying course material, one in your personal life, and one at work or in the classroom.
2. Now think of a problem or situation that is on your mind. Generate one new idea for how to deal with it.
3. Then think of another perspective: How would someone else you know react to the situation? Write down an idea that reflects a choice someone else might make.
4. Next, do something unfamiliar—listen to a new type of music, eat a style of food you've never tried, go somewhere on campus you've never been. Then train your mind back on the problem and write an idea that comes to mind.
5. Finally, get some distance. Write down one more idea ONLY after you have been away from this page for 24 to 48 hours.

Keep these ideas in mind. You may want to use one soon!

feels the need to innovate. For this reason, "outsiders" with little knowledge often come up with game-changing ideas. Here are some ideas on how to be an outsider, even in areas where you are firmly established.

Risk leaving your comfort zone. Your creative mind benefits when you leave areas of competence and come into contact with the unknown.[31] Go somewhere you've never been. Play music you've never heard. Check out an international or independent film or documentary that is completely outside of your experience. Think about what sparks your curiosity and take a course in it, read a book about it, check out a website. Explore things you *don't* think you'd like.

Go against established ideas. For example, the founders of Etsy.com went against the idea that the North American consumer prefers cheap, mass-produced items. In 2005, they took the risk of creating an online company that allows artisans to offer one-of-a-kind, handmade products to the consumer, and were rewarded with a thriving site that has also created a community of artists and personally connects each artist to his or her customers.

Think young. Young people can be considered "natural outsiders" because they haven't yet learned enough to decide that they know it all. In a recent study, college students who imagined they were young children and then performed creativity tests generated twice as many ideas as other students who were not asked to think of themselves as younger.[32]

Take time and get distance. Too much closeness and familiarity can hamper your ability to think about things in a fresh way. If you take time to "sit with" a problem or put away a draft of a writing assignment for a day or two, you can relax and come up with new ideas, essentially becoming an outsider to your own work.

Throughout your course you will explore real-life, day-to-day ways that creative thinking makes a difference: solving financial issues, deciding how to handle

To brainstorm → ask	• What do I want to accomplish? • What are the craziest ideas I can think of? • What are ten ways that I can reach my goal? • What ideas have worked before and how can I apply them?
To shift your perspective → ask	• How has this always been done—and what would be a different way? • How can I approach this task or situation from a new angle? • How would someone else do this or view this? • What if . . . ?
To set the stage for creativity → ask	• Where, and with whom, do I feel relaxed and inspired? • What music helps me think out of the box? • When in the day or night am I most likely to experience a flow of creative ideas? • What do I think would be new and interesting to try, to see, to read?
To take risks → ask	• What is the conventional way of doing this? What would be a totally different way? • What would be a risky approach to this problem or question? • What is the worst that can happen if I take this risk? What is the best? • What have I learned from this mistake?

communication problems, creative ways to manage your time, and much more. Later in this chapter you will see the starring role that creativity plays in problem solving and decision making.

As with analytical thinking, asking questions powers creative thinking. See Key 5.8 for examples of the kinds of questions you can ask to get your creative juices flowing.

Creativity connects analytical and practical thinking. When you generate ideas, solutions, or choices, you need to think analytically to evaluate their quality. Then, you need to think practically about how to make the best solution or choice happen.

Courtesy of Chanda Hinton

talk risk and reward . . .

Risk asking tough questions to be rewarded with new insights. Use the following questions to inspire discussion with classmates, either in person or online.

■ What problem(s) do you see others avoid? What problem(s) do you avoid? What do you risk when avoiding these problems? What might result from the different risk you take to address them?

■ What is your opinion of yourself as a creative person? What effect does that opinion have on your creative thinking skills?

CONSIDER THE CASE: What problems do you think Chanda may have experienced in her first term as a university student? If you had known her at school, what risks would you have advised her to take that may have helped her adjust to post-secondary life?

CHAPTER 5

HOW CAN YOU IMPROVE YOUR
practical thinking skills?

You've analyzed a situation. You've come up with ideas. Now, with your practical skill, you make things happen. Practical thinking—also called *common sense* or *street smarts*—refers to how you adapt to your environment (both people and circumstances), or shape or change your environment to adapt to you, to pursue important goals.

Let's say your goal is to pass first-year composition. You learn most successfully through visual presentations. To achieve your goal, you can use the instructor's PowerPoints or other visual media to enhance your learning (adapt to your environment) or enroll in a heavily visual internet course (change your environment to adapt to you)—or both.

Real-world problems and decisions require you to add understanding of experiences and social interactions to your analytical abilities. Your success in a sociology class, for example, may depend almost as much on getting along with your instructor as on your academic work. The workplace also demands practical skills. For example, while students majoring in elementary education might successfully quote child development facts on an exam, their career success depends on their ability to evaluate and address real children's needs in the classroom.

Through Experience, You Build Emotional Intelligence

You gain much of your ability to think practically from personal experience, rather than from formal training.[33] What you learn from experience answers "how" questions—how to talk, how to behave, how to proceed.[34] For example, after completing several papers for a course, you may learn what your instructor expects, or, after a few arguments with a roommate, you may learn how to manage "hot button" topics more effectively. See Key 5.9 for ways in which this kind of knowledge can be shown in "if–then" statements.

Emotional intelligence promotes success. For example, when first recovering from her accident, Chanda experienced a wide range of emotions. Over time, her response involved practical and emotionally intelligent actions that made her more likely to thrive in high school:

- *Perceiving emotions:* After getting over the initial shock of what happened, recognizing her feelings of confusion and loss
- *Thinking about emotions:* Noting what perception arose from those feelings (at first, "I'm not going to be able to live like other kids") and how it affected her mindset (at first, made her feel shy and unmotivated)
- *Understanding emotions:* Determining that the emotions diminished her motivation, and considering how to adjust that mindset to increase self-worth and determination
- *Managing emotions:* Using what she learned, deciding she could have a fulfilling experience despite her disability, and getting involved with friends and school activities

If you know that social interactions are difficult for you, enlist someone to give you some informal coaching. As Dr. Norman Rosenthal reports in "10 Ways to Enhance Your Emotional Intelligence," you may not realize how much others can tell what you are feeling. "Ask someone who knows you (and whom you trust) how you are coming across," he recommends.[35] For example, ask a friend to role-play the meeting with your instructor (with the friend playing the instructor) and give you feedback on words, tone, and body language.

Practical Thinking Means Action

Action is the logical result of practical thinking. Basic student success strategies that promote action—staying motivated, making the most of your strengths, managing time,

get practical

binkski/123RF

Diego Cervo/Shutterstock

TAKE A PRACTICAL APPROACH TO BUILDING SUCCESSFUL INTELLIGENCE

Complete the following on paper or in digital format.

Considering the three thinking skills, write the one in which you most need to build strength (look back at your Wheel of Successful Intelligence if you completed one in your text). Then, name and describe two practical actions you can take that will improve your skills in that area. For example, someone who wants to be more creative could take a course focused on creativity; someone who wants to be more practical could work on paying attention to social cues; someone who wants to be more analytical could decide to analyze one newspaper article every week. Be as specific as you can about your plans, noting what you will do, when, and how.

KEY 5.9   One way to map out what you learn from experience.

Goal: You want to talk to the soccer coach about your status on the team.

IF the team has had a good practice and IF you've played well during the scrimmage and IF the coach isn't rushing off somewhere, THEN grab a moment with him right after practice ends.

IF the team is having a tough time and IF you've been sidelined and IF the coach is in a rush and stressed, THEN drop in during his office hours tomorrow.

CHAPTER 5

get $mart

THINKING ANALYTICALLY ABOUT MONEY

Analyzing potential purchases helps you decide whether the pros outweigh the cons. To practise, write down your thoughts on three potential purchases and their consequences. Use this format: "If I buy [fill in the blank] for [$ amount], I will be able to [whatever this purchase will allow you to do] but I won't [whatever sacrifice you will have to make because of the expenditure].

Here is an example to get you started:

If I buy <u>the latest iPhone</u> for **$899**, I will be able to <u>access the internet, take videos, and store music and photos</u>, but I won't <u>have money for my sociology books, and I won't be able to buy coffee every morning</u>.

seeking help from instructors and advisors, and believing in yourself—will keep you moving toward your goals.[36] Learning from mistakes and failure is an especially important part of practical thinking. As psychologist Barry Schwartz points out, "Wisdom comes from experience, and not just any experience. You need permission to be allowed to improvise, to try new things, occasionally to fail, and to learn from your failures."[37]

The key to making practical knowledge work is to use what you discover, assuring that you will not have to learn the same lessons over and over again. As Sternberg says, "What matters most is not how much experience you have had but rather how much you have profited from it—in other words, how well you apply what you have learned."[38]

See Key 5.10 for some questions you can ask in order to apply practical thinking to your problems and decisions.

KEY 5.10	Ask questions like these to activate practical thinking.

To learn from experience	**ask**	• What worked well, or not so well, about my approach? My timing? My tone? My wording? • What did others like or not like about what I did? • What did I learn from that experience, conversation, event? • How would I change things if I had to do it over again? • What do I know I would do again?
To apply what you learn	**ask**	• What have I learned that would work here? • What have I seen others do, or heard about from them, that would be helpful here? • What does this situation have in common with past situations I've been involved in? • What has worked in similar situations in the past?
To boost your ability to take action	**ask**	• How can I get motivated and remove limitations? • How can I, in this situation, make the most of what I do well? • If I fail, what can I learn from it? • What steps will get me to my goal, and what trade-offs are involved? • How can I manage my time more effectively?

WHAT PROCESS CAN HELP YOU SOLVE
problems and make decisions?

Successful problem solvers and decision makers put their analytical, creative, and practical thinking skills together to solve problems and make decisions. Problem solving and decision making follow similar paths, both requiring you to identify and analyze a situation, generate possibilities, choose one, follow through on it, and evaluate its success. Key 5.11 gives an overview of the paths, indicating how you think at each step. Later in the chapter, Keys 5.13 and 5.14 show how to use this path, and a visual organizer, to map out problems and decisions effectively.

Understanding the differences between problem solving and decision making will help you know how to proceed. See Key 5.12 for more information. Whereas all problem solving involves decision making, only some decision making requires you to solve a problem.

Solve a Problem

Use these strategies as you move through the problem-solving process outlined in Key 5.11.

Use probing questions to define problems. Ask: What is the problem? And what is *causing* the problem? Engage your emotional intelligence. If you determine that you are not motivated to do your work for a class, for example, you could ask questions like these:

- Do my feelings stem from how I interact with my instructor or classmates?
- Is the subject matter difficult? Uninteresting? Is the volume of work too much?

Chances are that how you answer one or more of these questions may help you define the problem—and ultimately solve it.

Analyze carefully. Gather information that will help you examine the problem. Consider how the problem is similar to, or different from, other problems. Clarify facts. Note your own perspective, and look for others. Make sure your assumptions are not getting in the way.

KEY 5.11   Solve problems and make decisions using successful intelligence.

PROBLEM SOLVING	THINKING SKILL	DECISION MAKING
Define the problem—recognize that something needs to change, identify what's happening, look for true causes.	STEP 1 DEFINE	**Define the decision**—identify your goal (your need) and then construct a decision that will help you get it.
Analyze the problem—gather information, break it down into pieces, verify facts, look at perspectives and assumptions, evaluate information.	STEP 2 ANALYZE	**Examine needs and motives**—consider the layers of needs carefully, and be honest about what you really want.
Generate possible solutions—use creative strategies to think of ways you could address the causes of this problem.	STEP 3 CREATE	**Name and/or generate different options**—use creative questions to come up with choices that would fulfill your needs.
Evaluate solutions—look carefully at potential pros and cons of each, and choose what seems best.	STEP 4 ANALYZE (EVALUATE)	**Evaluate options**—look carefully at potential pros and cons of each, and choose what seems best.
Put the solution to work—persevere, focus on results, and believe in yourself as you go for your goal.	STEP 5 TAKE PRACTICAL ACTION	**Act on your decision**—go down the path and use practical strategies to stay on target.
Evaluate how well the solution worked—look at the effects of what you did.	STEP 6 ANALYZE (RE-EVALUATE)	**Evaluate the success of your decision**—look at whether it accomplished what you had hoped.
In the future, apply what you've learned—use this solution, or a better one, when a similar situation comes up again.	STEP 7 TAKE PRACTICAL ACTION	**In the future, apply what you've learned**—make this choice, or a better one, when a similar decision comes up again.

SITUATION	YOU HAVE A PROBLEM IF . . .	YOU NEED TO MAKE A DECISION IF . . .
PLANNING SUMMER ACTIVITIES	Your low GPA means you need to attend summer school—and you've already accepted a summer job.	You've been accepted into two summer abroad internship programs.
DECLARING A MAJOR	It's time to declare, but you don't have all the prerequisites for the major you want.	There are three majors that appeal to you and you qualify for them all.
HANDLING COMMUNICATIONS WITH INSTRUCTORS	You are having trouble following the lecture style of a particular instructor.	Your psychology survey course has seven sections taught by different instructors; you have to choose one.

Generate possible solutions based on causes, not effects. Addressing a cause provides a lasting solution, whereas "putting a Band-Aid on" an effect cannot. Say, for example, that your shoulder hurts when you type. Getting a massage is a helpful but temporary solution, because the pain returns whenever you go back to work. Changing your keyboard height is a better idea and a lasting solution to the problem, because it eliminates the cause of your pain.

Consider how possible solutions affect you and others. Which risk rewards you most? Which takes other people's needs into consideration? Is it possible to maximize reward for all involved?

Evaluate your solution and act on it. Once you choose a solution and put it into action, ask yourself: What worked? What would you avoid or change in the future?

What happens if you don't work through a problem comprehensively? Take, for example, a student having an issue with an instructor. He may get into an argument with the instructor, stop showing up to class, or do half-hearted work on assignments. All of these choices have negative consequences. Now look at how the student might work through this problem using analytical, creative, and practical thinking skills. Key 5.13 shows how his effort can pay off.

Make a Decision

As you use the steps in Key 5.11 to make a decision, remember these strategies.

Look at the given options—then try to think of more. Some decisions have a given set of options. For example, your school may allow you to major, double major, or major and minor. However, you may be able to work with an advisor to come up with more options, such as an interdisciplinary major. Consider similar situations you've been in or heard about, what decisions were made, and what resulted from those decisions.

Think about how your decision affects others. What you choose might have an impact on friends, family, and others around you.

Gather perspectives. Talk with others who made similar decisions. If you listen carefully, you may hear ideas you never thought about. Consider choices with different levels of risk.

Look at the long-term effects. As with problem solving, the quality of future choices depends on your examining what happened after you put the decision into action. For important decisions, do a short-term evaluation and another evaluation after a period of time.

What happens when you make important decisions too quickly? Consider a student deciding whether to transfer schools. If she decides

IQoncept/Fotolia

DEFINE PROBLEM HERE:	ANALYZE THE PROBLEM
I don't like my Sociology instructor	We have different styles and personality types—I am not comfortable working in groups and being vocal. I'm not interested in being there, and my grades are suffering from my lack of motivation.

Use boxes below to list possible solutions:

POTENTIAL POSITIVE EFFECTS	SOLUTION #1	POTENTIAL NEGATIVE EFFECTS
List for each solution: Don't have to deal with that instructor Less stress	Drop the course	List for each solution: Grade gets entered on my transcript I'll have to take the course eventually; it's required for my major
Getting credit for the course Feeling like I've honoured a commitment	SOLUTION #2 Put up with it until the end of the semester	Stress every time I'm there Lowered motivation Probably not such a good final grade
A chance to express myself Could get good advice An opportunity to ask direct questions of the instructor	SOLUTION #3 Schedule meetings with advisor and instructor	Have to face instructor one-on-one Might just make things worse

Now choose the solution you think is best—circle it and make it happen.

ACTUAL POSITIVE EFFECTS	PRACTICAL ACTION	ACTUAL NEGATIVE EFFECTS
List for chosen solution: Got some helpful advice from advisor Talking in person with the instructor actually promoted a fairly honest discussion I won't have to take the course again	I scheduled and attended meetings with both advisor and instructor and opted to stick with the course.	List for chosen solution: Still have to put up with some group work I still don't know how much learning I'll retain from this course

FINAL EVALUATION: Was it a good or bad solution?
The solution has improved things. I'll finish the course, and I got the chance to fulfill some class responsibilities on my own or with one partner. I feel more understood and more willing to put my time into the course.

student PROFILE

Kayla Brogan

NOVA SCOTIA COMMUNITY COLLEGE

SPRINGHILL, NOVA SCOTIA

About me:

I am a single mother of two daughters and a Women Unlimited Graduate of the 14-week Career Exploration Program, which promotes diversity, confidence building, and eventually mentoring young women. I am an honours student, in my second year of Metal Fabrication. I am a NSCC Board of Governors Award recipient, as well as Women Innovating in Nova Scotia Award recipient.

What I focus on:

My practical thinking skills are essential while I am continuing my education. I have learned to successfully conquer school work with my two small daughters, aged three and seven. I have struggled and overcome barriers I never thought I could have. I truly believe that my post-secondary education has given me the ability to succeed in any way I want now as a woman in Metal Fabrication. It was a risk that I took and it paid off.

The most valuable thing I learned is to use my time wisely at school and at home, as I have small children who have needs and wants when I leave school for the day. I use the library frequently as I have access to every resource I need. I make sure to pay attention when there is an instruction being given. I ask questions, lots of them! I also make great use of my agenda and my work record book. I write in it every class, every day. I use point form style just to jot my thoughts, stuff we did in class, and reflections as I'm not going to remember everything once I get home to my busy children. I've learned to think ahead in order to solve problems before they happen.

What will help me in the workplace:

Being positive each day has played and will continue to play a role in my success. Some days there are not enough hours in the day, I can't do it all, but tomorrow is a new day. I wake up each day to celebrate who I am and what I do.

Critical, Creative, and Practical Thinking

based on a reason that ultimately is not the most important one for her (for example, a boyfriend or close friends go to the other school), she may regret her choice later. Now look at how this student might make an effective decision. Key 5.14 shows how she worked through the analytical, creative, and practical parts of the process.

Successfully intelligent thinkers are able to analyze their abilities, come up with creative ideas about how to maximize their strengths and build their weaknesses, and put them to practical use in solving problems and making decisions. These executive function skills have never been more important. Says neurologist Judy Willis:

> The qualifications for success in today's ever-changing world will demand the ability to think critically, communicate clearly, use continually changing technology, be culturally aware and adaptive, and possess the judgment and open-mindedness to make complex decisions based on accurate analysis of information. . . . The best jobs will go to applicants who analyze information as it becomes available, adapt when new information makes facts obsolete, and collaborate with other experts on a global playing field.[39]

Use it, don't lose it. Continue to build and strengthen your thinking power by using your analytical, creative, and practical thinking skills, and you'll be one of the applicants getting that best job, and continuing to win great jobs for as long as you are in the workplace.

DEFINE PROBLEM HERE:	EXAMINE NEEDS AND MOTIVES
Whether or not to transfer schools	My father has changed jobs and can no longer afford my tuition. My goal is to become a physical therapist, so I need a school with a full physical therapy program. My family needs to cut costs. I need to transfer credits.

Use boxes below to list possible solutions:

POTENTIAL POSITIVE EFFECTS	SOLUTION #1	POTENTIAL NEGATIVE EFFECTS
List for each solution: No need to adjust to a new place or new people / Ability to continue course work as planned	Continue at the current college	List for each solution: Need to finance most of my tuition and costs on my own / Difficult to find time for a job / Might not qualify for aid
Some coursework available that would apply toward physical therapy degree / Reasonable tuition / Parents have a friend who works in advising there	SOLUTION #2 Transfer to less expensive school	No personal contacts there that I know of / Will have to investigate whether credits will transfer / No full physical therapy program
Opportunity to earn tuition money / Could live at home / Status should be intact	SOLUTION #3 Take a break for a year	Could forget so much that it's hard to go back / Could lose motivation / A year might turn into more

Now choose the solution you think is best—circle it and make it happen.

ACTUAL POSITIVE EFFECTS	PRACTICAL ACTION	ACTUAL NEGATIVE EFFECTS
List for chosen solution: Money saved / Opportunity to spend time on studies rather than on working to earn tuition money / Availability of classes I need	Go to less expensive school for two years; then transfer to a school that offers complete physical therapy coursework in connection with a B.A.	List for chosen solution: Less contact with friends / Will need to transfer again at some point / Additional time and effort required to map out new academic plan

FINAL EVALUATION: Was it a good or bad solution?

I'm satisfied with the decision. It can be hard adjusting to a new place and making new friends, but with fewer social distractions I'm getting more work done. And the reduced cost suits my needs perfectly right now.

What happened to Chanda? "One of my healing mantras," says Chanda, "is that everything happens for a purpose." First, her sister suggested she try integrative therapies, specifically physical therapy, massage therapy, adaptive yoga, and acupuncture. Chanda took that risk and began thriving on those treatments. She also got a service dog, Flint, who performs tasks for her and knows her so well that he can sense if something is wrong. As her health improved, she returned to college, joined activities, and rediscovered her outgoing nature.

Chanda's renewed energy inspired an idea for her life's mission. Vowing "Here's my passion, here's my dream, let's get it done," she took the risk to create and run her own foundation. Today The Chanda Plan Foundation provides extensive rewards for persons with physical disabilities, working to improve quality of life through education and programs to access integrative therapies. Since 2006, The Chanda Plan Foundation has provided the opportunity for increased health and hope by covering 11 600 integrative therapies for participants in the Quality of Life program. She's also actively pushing legislation for federal funding of integrative therapies. In short, Chanda's a risk-taker, and it is paying off for her and for many.

What does this mean for you? Although your problems are most likely different than Chanda's, you too can benefit from support when you are at a low point. Chanda puts trust in her family, and her beloved service dog, for a helping hand. First, think of a problem of yours that is sapping your energy. Now, consider whom you can turn to for help in untangling this problem. Identify the reward this person's perspective and motivation may help you attain. Get in contact with this person and see what can result from the risk of asking for help.

What risk may bring reward beyond your world? One of the goals of The Chanda Plan is to raise funds to provide access to integrative therapies. However, you don't have to contribute money to support a cause. Explore the lists of reputable charities at www.canadahelps.org. Research three charities that have a special appeal to you. Do they offer volunteer opportunities or other nonmonetary ways to contribute? Consider one way you could contribute, and how it would reward you as well as those you serve.

Critical, Creative, and Practical Thinking

GLOBAL RISK AND REWARD

A graphic designer from the Netherlands named Christian Boer risked a great deal of time and energy on a project that has brought a very personal reward. As a dyslexic college student, his struggle led him to the idea of creating a font that he could read more easily. Boer completed work on his font as a project in graduate school, and research has proven that the changes he made to the shapes and sizes of letters significantly improve reading skills for dyslexics. The font, Dyslexie, is now available in both Dutch and English.[40]

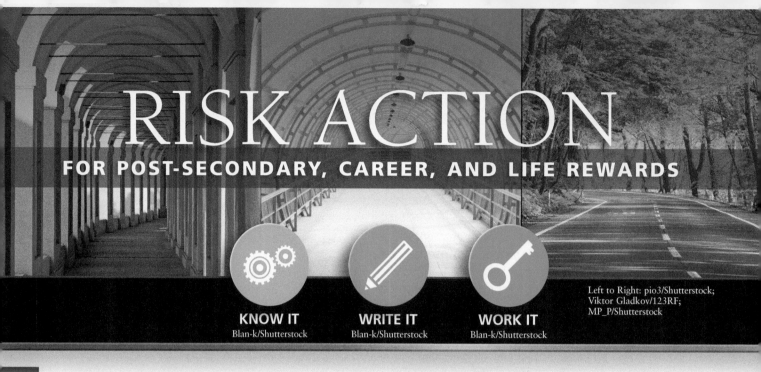

RISK ACTION
FOR POST-SECONDARY, CAREER, AND LIFE REWARDS

KNOW IT
Blan-k/Shutterstock

WRITE IT
Blan-k/Shutterstock

WORK IT
Blan-k/Shutterstock

Left to Right: pio3/Shutterstock;
Viktor Gladkov/123RF;
MP_P/Shutterstock

Complete the following on paper or in digital format.

KNOW IT *Think Critically*

Make an Important Decision

Build basic skills. List the steps of the decision-making process.

Take it to the next level. Think about how you would put the decision-making process to work on something that matters to you. Write an important long-term goal that you have, and define the decision that will help you fulfill it. Example: "My goal is to become a nurse. My decision: What to specialize in."

Move toward mastery. Use the empty flowchart (Key 5.15) to apply the decision-making process to your goal. Follow the steps below.

- *Examine needs and concerns.* What are your needs, and how do your values come into play? What is most needed in the health market, and how can you fulfill that need? What road-blocks might be involved? List what you come up with in the "Analyze problem/decision" section. For example, the prospective nurse might list needs like: "I need to feel that I'm help-ing people. I intend to help with the shortage of perinatal or geriatric nurses. I need to make a good living."

- *Generate options.* Ask questions to imagine what's possible. Where might you work? What might be the schedule and pace? Who might work with you? What would you see, smell, and hear on your job? What would you do every day? Make a separate list of all of the options you know of. The prospective nurse, for example, might list perinatal surgery, neonatal intensive care unit, geriatric nursing in a hospital or in a retirement community, and so forth.

- *Evaluate options.* Think about how well your options will fulfill your needs. Select three options to analyze. Write potential positive and negative effects (pros and cons) of each.

- *Imagine acting on your decision.* Choose one practical course of action, based on your thinking so far, that you might follow. List the specific steps you would take. For example, the prospective nurse might list actions that help him determine what type of nursing suits him best, such as interning, summer jobs, academic goals, and talking to working nurses. If you eventually act on this choice, you can fill in actual positive and negative effects in the flow-chart, as well as a final evaluation.

KEY 5.15 Work through a decision or problem using this flowchart.

DEFINE PROBLEM/DECISION

ANALYZE PROBLEM/DECISION

Use centre boxes to list possible options:

POTENTIAL POSITIVE EFFECTS

List for each:

OPTION #1

OPTION #2

OPTION #3

POTENTIAL NEGATIVE EFFECTS

List for each:

Now choose the one you think is best—circle it and make it happen.

ACTUAL POSITIVE EFFECTS

List for chosen option:

PRACTICAL ACTION

ACTUAL NEGATIVE EFFECTS

List for chosen option:

FINAL EVALUATION: Did your action, overall, have a positive or negative result?

Source: Based on heuristic created by Frank T. Lyman Jr. and George Eley, 1985.

An additional practical action is to go where the job is and talk to people. The prospective nurse might go to a hospital, a clinic, and a health centre at a retirement community. Get a feel for what the job is like day to day so that can be part of your decision.

WRITE IT *Communicate*

Emotional intelligence journal: Make a wiser choice. Think about a decision you made that you wish you had handled differently. Describe the decision and what feelings resulted from it. Then, describe what you would do if you could approach the decision again, thinking about what mindset and actions might produce more positive feelings and a better outcome.

Real-life writing: Address a problem. Think about a problem you have right now—difficulty with a course, a scheduling nightmare, conflict with a classmate. Write a letter—to an advisor, instructor, friend, or someone else—asking for support. Be specific about what you need and how the person can help. Assess the effect that the letter may have, and if you decide that it may help, have someone you trust review it for you and then send it via mail or email.

WORK IT *Build Your Brand*

Generate Ideas for Internships

Pursuing internships is a practical way to get experience, learn what you like and don't like, and make valuable connections. Even if you intern in a career area that you don't ultimately pursue, you build skills that are useful in any career. The creative thinking skills you've built will help you generate ideas for where you might intern at some point during your post-secondary career.

First, use personal contacts to gather information about career fields. Generate the names of two people whom you want to interview about their fields or professions. Note the following for each:

- Name and contact information
- Field
- Why you want to interview him or her

Then talk to the people you have listed, and take notes.

Next, look for more information on Youth Jobs and Internships (online at www
.canada.ca/en/services/culture/cultural-youth-programs/jobs-internships.html). You'll
find information about internships at home and abroad.

Then consult someone in the career office about local companies that offer
internships. Note specific information about internship descriptions, time frames,
and compensation.

Finally, analyze what you have learned from your reading, interviews, and the
career office information. Based on your analysis, name what field or fields in which
you would like to intern and why. Then, describe what practical action you plan to
take to secure an internship within the next two years.

Answers to perception puzzles on page 118

First puzzle: A goblet or two faces
Second puzzle: A tree or a man and woman's face

Your future success in a knowledge economy demands that you be able to read, understand, evaluate, and write about information. How can you build reading and writing skills? The short answer: Read more and write more.

Reading, Research, and Writing

HOW CAN YOU DEVELOP DEEP UNDERSTANDING?

What Would You Risk? *Mary Haynes*

THINK ABOUT THIS SITUATION AS YOU READ, AND CONSIDER WHAT ACTION YOU WOULD TAKE. THIS CHAPTER FOCUSES ON HOW TO UNDERSTAND AND ANALYZE WHAT YOU READ, BE AN INFORMATION-LITERATE RESEARCHER, AND KNOW WHAT POST-SECONDARY WRITING DEMANDS.

A communication major from a politically active family, Mary Haynes thrived in the post-secondary environment, heading up campus organizations, serving as a resident assistant, and routinely challenging professors on racial and socioeconomic issues.

Mary was a bookworm and a high-achieving student. She loved learning and research, spending countless hours in the "stacks." However, she was less successful when it came to writing papers. She preferred to talk about information rather than organize her thoughts on paper. As she recalls, "I loved the learning and figured the professor already knew the information, so why couldn't we just discuss?"

Early in her post-secondary career, Mary encountered a greater challenge: coping with tragedy. Her boyfriend's brother had lost his spleen in a childhood accident, and when he contracted chicken pox as a freshman, his body could not fight off the illness and he died. Months later, her boyfriend's father died of a massive heart attack. These deaths shattered both him and Mary.

"I wanted to understand more about what was going on for him," Mary says, "when this opportunity came up in sociology class." Assigned to research the sociological aspects of grief and write a paper on it, her desire to know more bumped up against her lack of experience as a writer. She gathered more research than needed and found it tough to risk letting her thoughts out onto paper. Now she had both emotional *and* academic hurdles to overcome.

To be continued . . .

EXPRESSING LITERACY IN THE WRITTEN FORM DEMANDS WELL-HONED SKILLS IN READING, RESEARCHING, AND ORGANIZING THOUGHTS AND EMOTIONS. WRITING ABOUT A SUBJECT MATTER THAT IS INTENSELY PERSONAL CAN HELP THOSE SKILLS EVOLVE. YOU'LL LEARN MORE ABOUT MARY, AND THE REWARD RESULTING FROM HER ACTIONS, WITHIN THE CHAPTER.

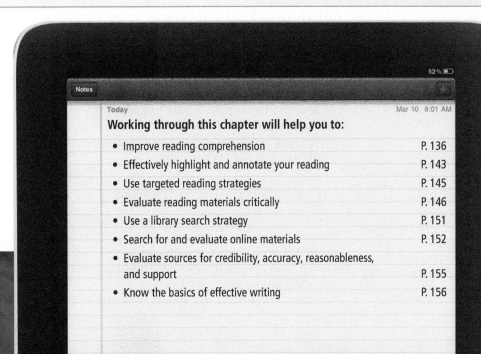

Notes

Today   Mar 10   8:01 AM

Working through this chapter will help you to:

status CHECK

Left to Right: Luis Santos/Shutterstock; Antonio Guillem/Shutterstock; antoniodiaz/Shutterstock; mimagephotography/Shutterstock; Djomas/Shutterstock; WAYHOME studio/Shutterstock

How Developed Are Your Reading, Research, and Writing Skills?

For each statement, fill in the number that best describes how often it applies to you.

1 = never   2 = seldom   3 = sometimes   4 = often   5 = always

1. To improve my comprehension, I make choices about when and how I read.	① ② ③ ④ ⑤
2. Before reading a textbook chapter, I develop questions to guide me.	① ② ③ ④ ⑤
3. I turn materials into study tools by taking notes and highlighting key information.	① ② ③ ④ ⑤
4. I have an effective process for reading on-screen assignments and articles.	① ② ③ ④ ⑤
5. When I have a high volume of reading assignments, I prioritize and schedule them.	① ② ③ ④ ⑤
6. When I get a research or writing assignment, I go first to general references for an overview.	① ② ③ ④ ⑤
7. I don't just rely on the internet for research; I also consult library materials.	① ② ③ ④ ⑤
8. I carefully evaluate any online resource to determine if it is useful.	① ② ③ ④ ⑤
9. I use a specific process when I write a paper.	① ② ③ ④ ⑤
10. I do not copy anything from a written or online resource without a proper citation.	① ② ③ ④ ⑤

Each of the topics in these statements is covered in this chapter. Note those statements for which you filled in a 3 or lower. Skim the chapter to see where those topics appear, and pay special attention to them as you read, learn, and apply new strategies.

REMEMBER: NO MATTER HOW DEVELOPED YOUR READING, RESEARCH, AND WRITING SKILLS ARE, YOU CAN IMPROVE THEM WITH EFFORT AND PRACTICE.

WHAT SETS YOU UP FOR *reading comprehension?*

You already know how to read, of course. However, most reading assignments in college or university are a few notches up in complexity from what you may be used to. The reward of a deep *understanding* of what you read in these materials—the kind of understanding that both helps you remember information and allows you to use it— requires you to risk a significant level of focus and commitment. How can you prepare to make the most of your reading?

Know Why You Are Reading

When you get ready to read an assignment, first ask yourself: Why am I reading this? What do I need to get out of it? A clear purpose will allow you to decide how much time and effort to spend on your assignment, and will increase your engagement in the material. Key 6.1 illustrates three reading purposes commonly in use for materials. Depending on materials and expectations, you may have one or more for a single assignment. As you read for your classes, you're also developing an important job skill.

James Woodson/DigitalVision/Getty Images

According to the Conference Board of Canada, being able to "read and understand information presented in a variety of forms (words, graphs, charts, diagrams)"[1] is a fundamental employability skill. Why? Because if you can read and understand something, you'll be able to learn it and use it.

Choose When and Where You Read

When and where you study has a significant effect on your success. Drawing on your self-knowledge, choose the following.

Your best locations. Find settings that distract you least: in your room, at a library, outdoors, in an empty classroom, whatever works. Your schedule may inform your choices. For example, if you need to study primarily at night, you may be restricted to safe spaces such as your room or a well-used library; if you commute, mass transit may be your best study spot.

You may be more able to concentrate in some locations than in others. Try many, at different times of day, and see what works best for you. This student enjoys reading in her room in the daytime.

Your best times. Pay attention to your body's natural rhythms, and try to read when you tend to be most alert and focused. For example, night owls tend to be productive when everyone else is sleeping, but morning people may have a hard time reading late at night. The times you choose depend on what your schedule allows.

Manage Heavy Workloads

Assigned reading piles up fast. When you have a pile of diverse assignments including a world history textbook chapter, an original study on sleep deprivation, and three chapters of a novel, how do you get to it all (and actually retain information)? Here are some strategies that will help:

- *Set priorities.* Consult your syllabi. When are your reading assignments due? Which are the most challenging? Prioritize first by time, reading assignments in the order that they are due. Then, if more than one assignment is due on the same day, prioritize the longer or more complex assignments over other lighter ones.

KEY 6.1 Establish why you are reading a given piece of material.

PURPOSE	GOAL	OFTEN USED WHEN READING . . .
1. To understand	Read to comprehend concepts and details, and to explain them in your own words. Concepts provide a framework for details and details help explain or support general concepts.	Any textbook
2. To evaluate analytically	Read to develop a level of understanding that goes beyond recall. Examine causes and effects, evaluate ideas, and test arguments and assumptions (see pages 146–147 for more on this topic).	Primary sources such as journal articles, opinion essays, and studies
3. For practical application	Read to find information to help reach a specific goal or perform a particular action.	Lab manuals or explanations of math operations

Reading, Research, and Writing

- *Schedule carefully.* Be realistic about how much time it will take you to do any reading assignment. Try not to cram a chapter that requires an hour and a half into a 30-minute between-classes break.
- *Set reasonable expectations.* Don't expect to master challenging material on the first pass. Use the first reading as an overview, and build understanding on subsequent readings.
- *Build course-specific vocabulary.* Your vocabulary influences how well you understand complex materials. The more you read, the more words you are exposed to, and the greater your comprehension becomes. When reading a textbook, search the end-of-book glossary explaining technical words and concepts (if applicable). Definitions there are usually limited to the meanings used in the text. Standard dictionaries provide broader information. Buy one or use websites such as www.dictionary.com or dictionary.canadaspace.com.

Manage Distractions

Even well-written textbooks and other high-level materials require a lot of focus, and distractions are a major issue. Don't underestimate the power of hunger or fatigue to derail you at study time. Some distractions you can actively avoid; others require management.

- *Internal distractions.* When you are cold or hungry, get a sweatshirt or a snack. When worries come up, write them down to deal with later. If you are feeling jumpy, take an exercise break to release energy.
- *External distractions.* You can't always control the noise around you, but you can control where you study. Politely ask people to keep the noise down if you are within your rights (for example, on a weeknight in a dorm or study area), ignoring any unhelpful response you may receive (your academic success is worth the risk of seemingly overly studious). If that doesn't work, use headphones, or move elsewhere if you can.
- *Technology.* Web surfing, emailing, texting, and instant messaging are enormously distracting. Plus, forcing your brain to switch between tasks can increase work time and errors. Set boundaries that save technology for breaks or after you finish your work.

Remember, too, that some of the strongest motivation comes from within. When you see how what you study will help you reach important personal goals, you will be better able to focus and resist distraction.

HOW CAN YOU MAKE
the most of reading?

Reading is an interactive form of communication. The author communicates ideas to you and invites your response, and that response is where true learning happens—remembering information, critical thinking, and application. How can you respond?

Use the SQ3R Reading System

One answer is provided by the SQ3R reading strategy, which stands for Survey, Question, Read, Recite, and Review.[2] This technique requires that you interact with reading material by asking questions, marking ideas, discovering connections, and more. In return, it rewards you with greater ability to take in, understand, and remember what you read.

SQ3R works best with textbook-based courses such as science, math, social sciences, and humanities, and is not recommended for literature courses.

As is true with so many strategies, SQ3R works best if you adapt it to your own needs. Explore the techniques, evaluate what works, and then make the system your own.

Step 1: Survey

Surveying, the first stage in SQ3R, is the process of previewing a book before you study it. Compare surveying to looking at a map before a road trip; determining the route and stops along the way will save time and trouble while you travel. Surveying tools include the following.

Front matter. Skim the table of contents for chapter titles, topic order, main topics in each chapter, and features. Consider reading the preface (even if you have never before looked at a textbook preface in your life), which usually provides a comprehensive description of both coverage and point of view. For example, the preface for the American history text *Out of Many* states that it highlights "the experiences of diverse communities of Americans in the unfolding story of our country."[3] This tells you that cultural diversity is a central theme.

Chapter elements. Text chapters use devices to structure and highlight content. Titles establish focus; chapter introductions may list objectives or key topics; headings break material down into bite-size chunks. Tables and charts illustrate concepts visually; margin materials may include quotes and questions; boxed features present supplemental discussions or stories. Finally, exercises help you understand and apply the content.

Back matter. Some texts include a glossary that defines text terms, an index to help you locate topics, and a bibliography that lists additional readings.

Key 6.2 on the next page shows a typical page from the textbook *Psychology: An Introduction,* by Charles G. Morris and Albert A. Maisto. As you examine it, how many chapter elements do you recognize? How do these elements help you grasp the subject even before reading it?

> **SKIMMING**
> Rapid, superficial reading of material to determine central ideas and main elements.

Step 2: Question

The next step in SQ3R is to ask questions about your assignment. Questioning leads you to discover knowledge on your own and gets you more invested in the material. Here's the process.

Ask yourself what you know. Before you begin reading, think about, and summarize in writing if you can, what you already know about the topic. Bringing your previous knowledge into the forefront of your consciousness makes your brain more receptive to learning new material, and prepares you to apply what you already know to what you are about to learn.

Write questions linked to chapter headings. The goal of questioning is to guide your reading so you learn more from it. Examine the chapter headings and, on a separate page or in the text margins, write questions about them. When an assignment has no headings, divide the material into sections and develop questions based on what you think is the main idea of each section.

Key 6.3 on page. 141 shows how questioning works. The column on the left contains primary and secondary headings from a section of *Out of Many*. The column on the right rephrases these headings in question form.

Classical (or Pavlovian) conditioning The type of learning in which a response naturally elicited by one stimulus comes to be elicited by a different, formerly neutral stimulus.

Unconditioned stimulus (US) A stimulus that invariably causes an organism to respond in a specific way.

Unconditioned response (UR) A response that takes place in an organism whenever an unconditioned stimulus occurs.

Conditioned stimulus (CS) An originally neutral stimulus that is paired with an unconditioned stimulus and eventually produces the desired response in an organism when presented alone.

Conditioned response (CR) After conditioning, the response an organism produces when only a conditioned stimulus is presented.

you are experiencing insight. When you imitate the steps of professional dancers you saw last night on television, you are demonstrating observational learning. Like conditioning, cognitive learning is one of our survival strategies. Through cognitive processes, we learn which events are safe and which are dangerous without having to experience those events directly. Cognitive learning also gives us access to the wisdom of people who lived hundreds of years ago, and it will give people living hundreds of years from now some insight into our experiences and way of life.

Our discussion begins with *classical conditioning*. This simple kind of learning serves as a convenient starting point for examining what learning is and how it can be observed.

Classical Conditioning

How did Pavlov's discovery of classical conditioning help to shed light on learning?

Ivan Pavlov (1849–1936), a Russian physiologist who was studying digestive processes, discovered classical conditioning almost by accident. Because animals salivate when food is placed in their mouths, Pavlov inserted tubes into the salivary glands of dogs to measure how much saliva they produced when they were given food. He noticed, however, that the dogs salivated before the food was in their mouths: The mere sight of food made them drool. In fact, they even drooled at the sound of the experimenter's footsteps. This aroused Pavlov's curiosity. What was making the dogs salivate even before they had the food in their mouths? How had they learned to salivate in response to the sound of the experimenter's approach?

To answer these questions, Pavlov set out to teach the dogs to salivate when food was not present. He devised an experiment in which he sounded a bell just before the food was brought into the room. A ringing bell does not usually make a dog's mouth water but, after hearing the bell many times just before getting fed, Pavlov's dogs began to salivate as soon as the bell rang. It was as if they had learned that the bell signaled the appearance of food, and their mouths watered on cue even if no food followed. The dogs had been conditioned to salivate in response to a new stimulus—the bell—that would not normally have prompted that response (Pavlov, 1927). Figure 5–1, shows one of Pavlov's procedures in which the bell has been replaced by a touch to the dog's leg just before food is given.

Elements of Classical Conditioning

Generally speaking, **classical (or Pavlovian) conditioning** involves pairing an *involuntary* response (for example, salivation) that is usually evoked by one stimulus with a different, formerly neutral stimulus (such as a bell or a touch on the leg). Pavlov's experiment illustrates the four basic elements of classical conditioning. The first is an **unconditioned stimulus (US)**, such as food, which invariably prompts a certain reaction—salivation, in this case. That reaction—the **unconditioned response (UR)**—is the second element and always results from the unconditioned stimulus: Whenever the dog is given food (US), its mouth waters (UR). The third element is the neutral stimulus—the ringing bell—which is called the **conditioned stimulus (CS)**. At first, the conditioned stimulus is said to be "neutral" with respect to the desired response (salivation), because dogs do not salivate at the sound of a bell unless they have been conditioned to react in this way by repeatedly presenting the CS and US together. Frequent pairing of the CS and US produces the fourth element in the classical conditioning process: the **conditioned response (CR)**. The conditioned response is the behavior that the animal has learned in response to the conditioned stimulus. Usually, the unconditioned response and the conditioned

Darren Baker/
Shutterstock

SURVEY A TEXT

Dario Sabljak/Shutterstock

Complete the following on paper or in digital format.

Improve surveying skills by practising on a textbook currently assigned for one of your courses.

1. Skim the front matter, including the table of contents and preface. What does this material tell you about the book's focus and point of view?

2. Are there unexpected topics listed in the table of contents, or expected topics that are missing?

3. Now look at a typical chapter. List the devices that provide structure for the content.

4. Name an idea that pops out at you after skimming the chapter. What device communicated that idea to you?

5. Finally, skim the back matter. What elements can you identify?

6. How do you plan to use each of the elements you identified in your text survey when you begin studying?

Using Bloom's Taxonomy can help you understand and ask a variety of questions that engage different levels of thinking. This system was developed by educational psychologist Benjamin Bloom, whose research focused on the varying levels of effort and thinking required by different types of questions.[4] Key 6.4 on the next page shows the six levels identified by Bloom. The three-column table explains what each level is and provides associated verbs and examples linked to headings from *Out of Many*. When you read, use these verbs to create specific questions.

KEY 6.3 Create questions from headings.

HEADINGS	QUESTIONS
The Meaning of Freedom	What did freedom mean for both slaves and citizens in the United States?
Moving About	Where did African Americans go after they were freed from slavery?
The African American Family	How did freedom change the structure of the African American family?
African American Churches and Schools	What effect did freedom have on the formation of African American churches and schools?
Land and Labor After Slavery	How was land farmed and maintained after slaves were freed?
The Origins of African American Politics	How did the end of slavery bring about the beginning of African American political life?

Reading, Research, and Writing

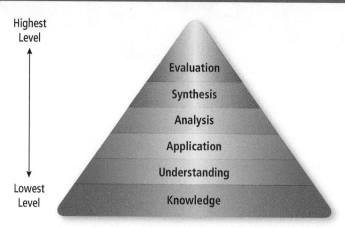

Highest Level

Lowest Level

The table below explains each level in the taxonomy illustration, provides common verbs to help you recognize each level, and provides a sample question you might ask at that level. The questions are based on the headings from *Out of Many*.

LEVEL OF LEARNING	COMMON VERBS THAT INDICATE THE LEVEL	SAMPLE QUESTIONS DEMONSTRATING THE LEVEL OF LEARNING
Knowledge. Memorize words and ideas.	average, define, duplicate, label, list, memorize, name, order, recognize, relate, recall, repeat, reproduce, state	*List* three main characters of the early African American political scene.
Understanding. Explain ideas in your own words.	classify, describe, discuss, explain, express, identify, indicate, locate, recognize, report, restate, review, select, translate	*Explain* the struggles faced by African American politicians.
Application. Apply what you learn.	apply, choose, demonstrate, dramatize, employ, illustrate, interpret, operate, practise, schedule, sketch, solve, use, write	*Interpret* the impact of slavery on the early African American politicians.
Analysis. Analyze information and look at similarities and differences.	analyze, appraise, calculate, categorize, compare, contrast, criticize, differentiate, discriminate, distinguish, examine, experiment, question, test	*Compare and contrast* the White political environment of the time with that of the emerging African American politicians.
Synthesis. Put together information "from scratch."	arrange, assemble, collect, compose, construct, create, design, develop, formulate, manage, organize, plan, prepare, propose, set up, write	*Arrange* the major events of the era as they corresponded with the emerging political movement.
Evaluation. Examine different ideas and make decisions about their merit.	appraise, argue, assess, attach, choose, compare, defend, estimate, evaluate, judge, predict, rate, score, select, support, value	*Rate* the effectiveness of the first African American political campaign and note any changes since.

Step 3: Read

Your text survey and questions give you tools for active reading, the first R in SQ3R. With these tools you can dig into the text, ask more questions, and identify important information.

Focus on the key points of your survey. Pay special attention to information in the headings, in boldface type, in chapter objectives, in the summary, and in other emphasized text.

Focus on your Q-stage questions. Read the material with the purpose of answering each question. Write down or highlight ideas and examples that relate to your questions.

Annotate your text. If the book is yours, write directly on it. If using an ebook, use the "insert comments" feature. Annotations boost memory and help you study. Consider these tips:

- Use pencil so you can erase questions answered later.
- Write your Q-questions in the margins next to text headings.
- Circle main ideas and underline supporting details.
- Mark critical sections with marginal notations such as "e.g." for a helpful example.
- Write notes at the bottom of the page connecting the text to what you learned in class or in research. You can also attach adhesive notes with your comments.
- Circle the topic sentence in a paragraph to focus on the most important information.

> TOPIC SENTENCE
> A statement describing the main idea of a paragraph.

Key 6.5 shows an annotated page from an introduction to business textbook.

Consider learning preferences. Explore the Multiple Intelligence Strategies for Reading on page 145.

Highlight your text. Although highlighting does not equal learning, it helps you identify concepts and information that are important to learn. Use these tips to make it work:

- *Develop a system and stick to it.* Decide how you will highlight different elements such as important ideas or long passages (overmarking vs. bracketing, using different colours, and so on). With ebooks, use the highlighting function.
- *Consider using a pencil or pen instead of, or in addition to, a highlighter pen.* The copy may be cleaner and easier to follow.
- *Mark text carefully if you are using a rented book or a book to be re-sold.* Use pencil and erase your marks at the end of the course. Write on sticky notes. Make copies of important chapters or sections and mark up the pages.
- *Avoid overmarking.* Underlining or highlighting everything makes it impossible to tell what's important. Read an entire paragraph before deciding which ideas and details are important to highlight. If you decide that a whole passage is important to call out, try marking it with brackets.

Yes, annotating your textbook carries the risk that you will not be able to sell it back. However, students who interact with material stand to gain greater depth of learning than those who don't. If you aim to learn, the reward of annotating your text is worth the financial risk.

Step 4: Recite

Once you finish reading a section of text, recite answers to the questions you raised in the Q stage—say them aloud, silently speak them to yourself, "teach" them to someone, or write them in note form. The action of speaking or writing anchors material in your brain. This is the second R in SQ3R. Repeat the question-read-recite cycle until you complete the chapter you are reading.

Writing is often the most effective way to learn new material. Write responses to your Q-stage questions and use your own words to explain new concepts. Save your writing as a study tool for review. Writing also gives you immediate feedback. When your writing agrees with the material you are studying, you know the information. When it doesn't, you still need work.

Keep your learning preferences in mind when exploring strategies. For example, an intrapersonal learner may prefer writing, while an interpersonal learner may recite answers aloud to a classmate. A logical-mathematical learner may benefit from organizing material into charts, while a musical learner might want to chant information to a rhythm.

Reading, Research, and Writing

How does target marketing and market segmentation help companies sell product?

■ TARGET MARKETING AND MARKET SEGMENTATION

Marketers have long known that products cannot be all things to all people. Buyers have different tastes, goals, lifestyles, and so on. The emergence of the marketing concept and the recognition of consumer needs and wants led marketers to think in terms of **target markets**—groups of people with similar wants and needs. Selecting target markets is usually the first step in the marketing strategy.

Target marketing requires **market segmentation**—dividing a market into categories of customer types or "segments." Once they have identified segments, companies may adopt a variety of strategies. Some firms market products to more than one segment. General Motors *(www.gm.com)*, for example, offers compact cars, vans, trucks, luxury cars, and sports cars with various features and at various price levels. GM's strategy is to provide an automobile for nearly every segment of the market.

In contrast, some businesses offer a narrower range of products, each aimed toward a specific segment. Note that segmentation is a strategy for analyzing consumers, not products. The process of fixing, adapting, and communicating the nature of the product itself is called *product positioning*.

How do companies identify market segments?

Identifying Market Segments

By definition, members of a market segment must share some common traits that affect their purchasing decisions. In identifying segments, researchers look at several different influences on consumer behavior. Three of the most important are *geographic, demographic,* and *psychographic variables.*

What effect does geography have on segmentation strategies?

Geographic Variables Many buying decisions are affected by the places people call home. The heavy rainfall in Washington State, for instance, means that people there buy more umbrellas than people in the Sun Belt. Urban residents don't need agricultural equipment, and sailboats sell better along the coasts than on the Great Plains. **Geographic variables** are the geographical units, from countries to neighborhoods, that may be considered in a segmentation strategy.

These patterns affect decisions about marketing mixes for a huge range of products. For example, consider a plan to market down-filled parkas in rural Minnesota. Demand will be high and price competition intense. Local newspaper ads may be

Definitions

target market
Group of people that has similar wants and needs and that can be expected to show interest in the same products

← *GM eg*

market segmentation
Process of dividing a market into categories of customer types

GM makes cars for diff. market segments

Buying decisions influenced by where people live

geographic variables
Geographical units that may be considered in developing a segmentation strategy

— good eg —
selling parkas in Minnesota

Thought
Geographical variables change with the seasons

multiple intelligence strategies

Name an upcoming reading assignment (material, course, date due): _____.
In the right-hand column, record specific ideas for how MI strategies can help you complete it.

INTELLIGENCE	USE MI STRATEGIES TO BECOME A BETTER READER	IDENTIFY MI READING STRATEGIES THAT CAN HELP YOU IMPROVE COMPREHENSION
Verbal-Linguistic	• Use the steps in SQ3R, focusing especially on writing Q-stage questions, summaries, and so on. • Make marginal text notes as you read.	
Logical-Mathematical	• Logically connect what you are reading with what you already know. Consider similarities, differences, and cause-and-effect relationships. • Draw charts showing relationships and analyze trends.	
Bodily-Kinesthetic	• Use text highlighting to take a hands-on approach to reading. • Take a hands-on approach to learning experiments by trying to re-create them yourself.	
Visual-Spatial	• Make charts, diagrams, or think links illustrating difficult ideas you encounter as you read. • Take note of photos, tables, and other visual aids in the text.	
Interpersonal	• Discuss reading material and clarify concepts in a study group. • Talk to people who know about the topic you are studying.	
Intrapersonal	• Apply concepts to your own life; think about how you would manage. • Try to understand your personal strengths and weaknesses to lead a study group on the reading material.	
Musical	• Recite text concepts to rhythms or write a song to depict them. • Explore relevant musical links to the material.	
Naturalistic	• Tap into your ability to notice similarities and differences in objects and concepts by organizing reading materials into relevant groupings.	

Top to Bottom: TatsianaTur/Shutterstock; kak2s /Shutterstock; Alexander Raths/Shutterstock; Neelsky/123RF; Helder Almeida/ 123RF; focal point/ Shutterstock; Simeon Donov/123RF; Ambient Ideas/Shutterstock.

Reading, Research, and Writing

CHAPTER 6

Step 5: Review

Reviewing is the final R in SQ3R. When you review early and often in the days and weeks after you read, you will better memorize, understand, and learn material. *Reviewing is your key to learning.* Reviewing the same material over several short sessions will also help you identify knowledge gaps. It's natural to forget material between study sessions, especially if it's complex. When you come back after a break, you can focus on where you need the most help.

Try the following reviewing techniques, and use the ones that work best for you. Consider using more than one strategy when you study. Switching among several different strategies tends to strengthen learning and memory.

- Reread your notes, then summarize them from memory.
- Review and summarize in writing the text sections you highlighted or bracketed.
- Scan for key points and main concepts and rewrite them in your own words.
- Answer the end-of-chapter review, discussion, and application questions.
- Reread the preface, headings, tables, and summary.
- Recite important concepts to yourself (although you may risk looking silly, this technique's high effectiveness may be a worthwhile reward).
- Record information and play it back.
- Listen to MP3 audio recordings of your text and other reading materials on your iPod.
- Make hard-copy or electronic flash cards and test yourself daily.
- Quiz yourself, using the questions you raised in the Q-stage.
- With a classmate or in a study group, answer one another's Q-stage questions.

SCANNING
Reading material in an investigative way to search for specific information.

Refreshing your knowledge is easier and faster than learning it the first time. Make a weekly review schedule and stick to it. A combination of short daily reviews in the morning, between classes, or in the evening is more effective than an all-night cramming session before a test.

Respond with Critical Thinking

Question everything you read—books, articles, online documents, and even textbooks (which are supposed to be as accurate as possible). Think of the critical reading process as an archaeological dig. First, you excavate a site and uncover the artifacts. Then you sort what you've found, make connections among items, and judge their importance. This process of questioning, analysis, and evaluation rewards you with the ability to focus on the most important materials.

Reading for different purposes engages different parts of critical reading. When you read to learn and retain information or to master a skill, you focus on important information (analyzing and evaluating how the ideas are structured, how they connect, and what is most crucial to remember). When you read to evaluate, you question arguments (analyzing and evaluating the author's point of view as well as the credibility, accuracy, reliability, and relevancy of the material).

Focus on important information

Before, during, and after reading content, ask yourself what is important to remember. According to Adam Robinson, co-founder of *The Princeton Review*, "The only way you can effectively absorb the relevant information is to ignore the irrelevant information."[5] Use the following questions to evaluate any segment of content (a "yes" answer means it's probably relevant):

- Does it contain key terms and definitions or an introduction or summary? (For a textbook, check mid-chapter or end-of-chapter exercises.)
- Does it offer crucial concepts, examples, an explanation of a variety or type, critical relationships, or comparisons?
- Does it mirror or reinforce what your instructor emphasizes?
- Does it spark questions and reactions as you read?
- Does it surprise or confuse you?

It can be challenging to decide what is important. If you are unsure about what to pull out of a piece of content, email your instructor and ask for clarification.

Ask questions to evaluate arguments

An *argument* refers to a persuasive case—a set of connected ideas supported by examples—made to prove or disprove a point. Many scholarly books and articles, in print form or on the internet, are organized around particular arguments. However, other online articles, websites, and blogs offer *claims* instead—arguments without adequate support. Just because you read it does not mean it's true. Evaluate arguments and claims to determine whether they are accurate and logical. When quality evidence combines with sound logic, the argument is solid.

> EVIDENCE
> Facts, statistics, and other materials that are presented in support of an argument.

Evaluating an argument involves investigating the following:

- The quality of the evidence
- Whether the evidence fits the idea concept
- The logical connections

To understand an argument and determine its validity, first read it with healthy skepticism and an open mind. Avoid the common trap of accepting or rejecting it according to whether it fits with your point of view. Then, risk asking questions such as those listed in Key 6.6 to gain the reward of greater depth of understanding, regardless of your opinion.

KEY 6.6 — Ask questions like these to evaluate arguments.

EVALUATE THE VALIDITY OF THE EVIDENCE	DETERMINE WHETHER THE EVIDENCE SUPPORTS THE CONCEPT
Is the source reliable and free of bias?	Is there enough evidence?
Who wrote this and with that intent?	Do examples and ideas logically connect?
What assumptions underlie this material?	Is the evidence convincing?
Is this argument based on opinion?	Do the examples build a strong case?
How does this evidence compare with evidence from other sources?	What different and perhaps opposing arguments seem equally valid?

Reading, Research, and Writing

get $mart

Racorn/123RF

READ THE FINE PRINT

Creativenv/Shutterstock

Complete the following on paper or in digital format.

Use your reading skills to make sure you understand your bank's policies about the account you use most (chequing or savings). Look up your type of account on your bank's website, and read the rules. Then answer the following questions.

1. Can you make withdrawals and deposits online without a fee?
2. Can you make withdrawals and deposits in the bank without a fee?
3. Can your transfer money electronically between accounts?
4. Is there a monthly fee? If so, how much is it?
5. Is there a limit for cheques, debits, or ATM transactions? If so, describe it.
6. Describe any other fees or rules involved (such as minimum balance).
7. What happens if a cheque you write bounces? What if someone else's cheque bounces?
8. What happens if you overdraw your account? If overdraft protection is available, how much does it cost?

Match Strategies to Different Subjects

If your school has general education (Gen Ed) requirements, you may have to take a wide variety of courses. Know how to approach reading materials in different academic areas.

Math and science

Math and science textbooks move sequentially, so your understanding of later material depends on how well you learned material in earlier chapters. Try the following strategies to get the most from your textbooks, and get extra help right away when you are confused.

Interact with math material by writing. As you read through problems and solutions, highlight important information and examples. Work out missing problem steps on paper. Draw sketches to help visualize the material. Write questions for your instructor or fellow students.

Pay attention to formulas. Math and science texts contain formulas that express general rules and principles. Try to learn the ideas behind each formula. Always do the practice problems, using the formulas to make sure your understanding sticks.

Use memory strategies to learn science. Science textbooks are packed with field-specific vocabulary (for example, an environmental science text may refer to the greenhouse effect). Use mnemonic devices, test yourself with flash cards, and rehearse aloud or silently.

Consider solving all sample problems. Risk a little extra work for the reward of greater comprehension. The more problems you do, the more solid your understanding will be.

Social sciences and humanities

Courses in the social sciences and humanities prepare you to be a well-rounded person, able and ready to fulfill your responsibilities to yourself, your family, and a free democracy. They also prepare you for the workplace by focusing on critical-thinking skills, civic and historic knowledge, and ethical reasoning. As you study these disciplines, use critical thinking to identify themes and connect what you know to learn new material.

Note themes. The U.S. National Council for the Social Studies organized the study of the social sciences and humanities into ten themes:[6]

- Culture
- Time, continuity, and change
- People, places, and environment
- Individual development and identity
- Individuals, groups, and institutions
- Power, authority, and governance
- Production, distribution, and consumption
- Science, technology, and society
- Global connections
- Ideals and practices of citizenship

One or more of these themes underscores everything you read in these disciplines, even if they are not spelled out. For example, a political science chapter on the history of Canadian political parties may make you think of the history of elections or how the internet is changing electoral politics.

Think critically. Courses in the social sciences ask hard questions about ethics, human rights and freedoms, and personal and community responsibility, looking at these topics over time across cultures. Critical thinking helps you ask questions about what you read, think of material in terms of problems and solutions, look for evidence for arguments, consider possible bias of the writers, and examine big-picture statements for cause-and-effect logic.

Literature

Even if you're not an English major, you will probably take one or more literature courses. Books you read for these courses let you experience other times and cultures, build your understanding of how others react to the problems of daily life, and provide insight into your own thinking. Literature courses ask you to look at different literary elements to find meaning on various levels. As you read, use critical-reading skills to consider:

- *Character.* How do characters reveal who they are? How are the main characters similar or different? How do a character's actions change the course of the story?
- *Plot.* How would you evaluate the power of the story? Did it hold your interest?
- *Setting.* How does the setting relate to the actions of the major and minor characters?
- *Point of view.* How are the author's views expressed through the characters' actions?
- *Style.* How would you describe the writing style?
- *Imagery.* How does the author use imagery as part of the theme?
- *Theme.* What is the goal of the work? What is it trying to communicate?

Online materials

Many (but not all) reading materials are available in digital formats and applications that can be used on computers, smartphones, and tablets such as the iPad. Although college and university students are more likely to use digital devices for research and studying than for reading, a recent survey of students who own digital devices indicated that over 60% had used them to read an electronic textbook at least once, and almost half did so regularly.[7]

Frequent screen readers tend to notice heads and subheads, bullet points, and visuals, scanning material for the important points instead of staying focused through long paragraphs or articles.[8] They may also develop what Web researcher Jakob Nielsen calls *F-pattern reading*—reading across the line at the beginning of a document, then

Jasminko Ibrakovic/123RF

reading less and less of the full width of the line as they move down the page, and only seeing the left-hand text by the time they reach the bottom of the document.[9]

Nielsen suggests making the most of screen reading using a step-by-step process, which includes aspects of SQ3R:

1. *Skim through the article.* See whether it contains important ideas.
2. *Before reading in depth, save the article on your computer or device.* This gives you the ability to print the article if you prefer to highlight and add notes on hard copy.
3. *Survey the article.* Read the title, subtitle, headings, figures, charts, and tables.
4. *Come up with questions to guide your reading.* Ask yourself what general and specific information you want to learn from the article.
5. *Read the article in depth.* Take it slower than you normally would.
6. *Highlight and take notes.* Use the program's highlighter and comment functions.
7. *Print out articles you would rather study on hard copy.* Make sure printouts include any electronic highlighting and comments you've created.
8. *Review your notes.* Combine them with your class and text notes.

Finally, remember that "it is not so much about the tool and what it can do, but more about the purpose for using the tool," says educator Mary Beth Hertz.[10] Every choice, from the latest iPad to a book and a pencil, has pros and cons. Evaluate on a case-by-case basis and see what works best for you, especially if you are a "digital native" who gravitates toward technology.

Take a Specific Approach to Primary Sources

SECONDARY SOURCES *Other writers' interpretations of primary source documents.*

PRIMARY SOURCES *Original, uninterpreted documents or works.*

Reading requires a lot of focus whether you are working with secondary sources such as textbooks or primary sources. However, primary sources require some particular strategies.

Primary sources were created at or near the time of the circumstances or events they document. They include letters, financial documents, photographs, journals, articles, video or audio recordings, scientific studies, email records, and more. You will read primary sources for a wide range of coursework, including history (descriptions of historical events), literature (original poetry, novels, essays), and sociology (studies and interviews).

Careful evaluation of primary sources will allow you to derive useful information from them. One evaluation strategy is to use journalists' questions—the who, what, when, where, why, and how that are useful for all kinds of investigations.[11]

Define the context. Ask questions such as:

- When and where was it created? Time and location shape a source. A letter from a Jewish citizen of France in 1935 will differ from one from a Jewish citizen of Israel in 1957.
- How was it created (what format)? For example, a photograph of an event in 1923 is more likely to be accurate than a written description.
- Who produced it, and for whom is it created—in other words, what is the intended audience? A letter from a British loyalist will describe pre–Revolutionary War conditions differently than one from a colonist determined to declare independence.

Define the purpose. Ask questions such as:

- Why did the creator produce this source? In other words, what is the goal of the source?
- What does the creator want to convey to the intended audience? The loyalist may have wanted to move to Canada whereas the colonist may have wanted letter recipients to rally to his cause of independence.

Compare and contrast the sources. Ask questions such as:

- How does the information from this source compare to what you already know or to other information about the event or time? A primary source may or may not reinforce accepted fact, and it can be interesting to consider why.
- What surprises you? History professor Zachary Schrag recommends asking this question, seeing what information and observations emerge as you compare a source to other primary or secondary sources.[12]

Secondary sources provide comprehensive overviews, but necessarily leave out pieces of information and often add a layer of interpretation. Primary sources allow a more direct experience of an event, providing a chance to discover and consider information that a secondary source author may have set aside. With a primary source in hand, you are the interpreter.

HOW CAN YOU BE AN INFORMATION
literate reader and researcher?

When it comes to research, most students' first instinct is to power up the computer and start jumping around on Google. However, there are a myriad of research resources at your fingertips. Library materials have been evaluated by librarians and researchers and are likely to be solid and credible—a definite time-saver compared to the myriad of internet sources that may turn out to be nothing more than conjecture, opinion, and rants. Risking time and effort to search carefully will reward you with the most useful, accurate, and reliable information.

Know the Basics of Library Research

To select the most useful information for your research, get an overview of what is available. Attend an in-person library orientation session to familiarize yourself

Courtesy of Mary Haynes

talk risk and reward . . .

Risk asking tough questions to be rewarded with new insights. Use the following questions to inspire discussion with classmates, either in person or online.

- How can reading be a risk, and what reward would it bring? What risk do you take if you do *not* read?
- What steps do you take to ensure that you understand what you read? Have those strategies worked for you so far? Why or why not?

CONSIDER THE CASE: What step (or steps) from SQ3R could help Mary improve her ability to choose the most important information to use and set the rest aside? What step or steps do you think will be most helpful to *you* as you read materials in preparation for a writing assignment?

with the library layout and resources. Get to know a librarian who can assist you in locating unfamiliar or hard-to-find sources, navigating catalogs and databases, uncovering research shortcuts, and dealing with unpredictable equipment. At most schools, you can query a librarian by email or text. Know what you want to accomplish before asking a question.

To avoid being overwhelmed, use a practical, step-by-step search method. Key 6.7 shows how to start wide and then narrow your search for a closer look at specific sources.

When using virtual or online catalogs, you will need to adjust your research methods. Searching library databases requires a *keyword search*—an exploration that uses a topic-related, natural-language word or phrase as a starting point to locate other information. To narrow your search and reduce the number of *hits* (results returned by your search), add more keywords to your search criteria. For example, instead of searching through the broad category "art," focus on "French art" or, more specifically, "nineteenth-century French art." Key 6.8 shows how to use the keyword system to narrow your search with what is called *Boolean logic*.

Know the Basics of Online Research

Unlike your library collection or databases, internet resources are not always evaluated by anyone who vouches for their quality. As a result, you need critical thinking to sort out the valid, credible materials from the invalid, not-so-credible ones.

Start with search engines

Among the most popular and effective search engines are Google (www.google.ca) and Yahoo! (ca.yahoo.com). Search engines aimed at Canadian academic audiences include

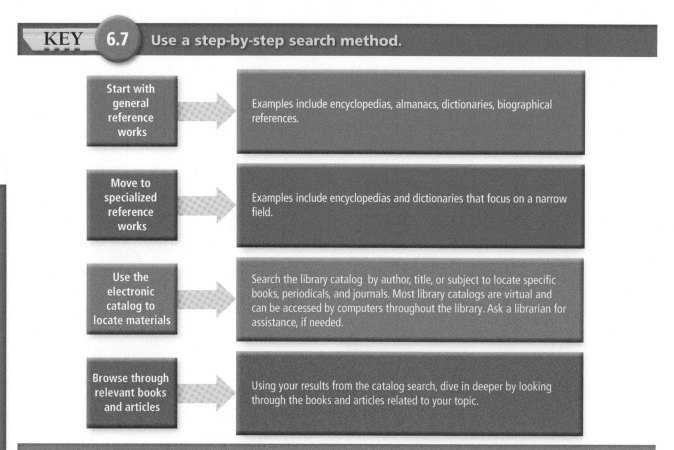

KEY 6.7 **Use a step-by-step search method.**

Start with general reference works
Examples include encyclopedias, almanacs, dictionaries, biographical references.

Move to specialized reference works
Examples include encyclopedias and dictionaries that focus on a narrow field.

Use the electronic catalog to locate materials
Search the library catalog by author, title, or subject to locate specific books, periodicals, and journals. Most library catalogs are virtual and can be accessed by computers throughout the library. Ask a librarian for assistance, if needed.

Browse through relevant books and articles
Using your results from the catalog search, dive in deeper by looking through the books and articles related to your topic.

IF YOU ARE SEARCHING FOR . . .	DO THIS . . .	EXAMPLE
A word	Type the word normally.	aid
A phrase	Type the phrase in its normal word order (use regular word spacing) or surround the phrase with quotation marks ("x"). Quotation marks ensure the search engine finds the words together in the same phrase, rather than the individual words on the same page.	financial aid, "financial aid"
Two or more keywords without regard to order	Type the words in any order, surrounding the words with quotation marks. Use *and* to separate the words.	"financial aid" and "scholarships"
Topic A *and* topic B	Type the words in any order, surrounding the words with quotation marks. Use *and* to separate the words. The search engine will list a result only if it contains BOTH topics A and B.	"financial aid" and "scholarships"
Topic A *or* topic B	Type the words in any order, surrounding the words with quotation marks. Use *or* to separate the words. The search engine will list a result if it contains EITHER A or B.	"financial aid" or "scholarships"
Topic A *but not* topic B	Type topic A first within quotation marks, and then topic B within quotation marks. Use *not* to separate the words. The search engine will list a result if it contains only Topic A and does not contain Topic B.	"financial aid" not "scholarships"

EBSCO's Canadian Reference Centre (www.ebscohost.com/canadian-schools/ canadian-reference-centre) and ProQuest's Canadian Business and Current Affairs Database (www.proquest.com/libraries/academic/databases/cbca.html). At these well-vetted academic directories, only reputable and regularly updated sources are listed.

In addition, your school may provide access to nonpublic academic search engines. LexusNexus, InfoTrac, GaleGroup, OneFile, and other such reputable sites catalog vast amounts of information. Check with your school's library to see how to access these sites.

Use a search strategy

The World Wide Web has been called "the world's greatest library, with all its books on the floor." With no librarian in sight, you need to master a practical internet search strategy.

1. *Use natural language phrases or keywords to identify what you are looking for.* University of Michigan professor Eliot Soloway recommends phrasing your search in the form of a question, identifying the important words in the question as well as related words. You then have a collection of terms to use in different combinations as you search (see example below).[13]

   Initial question: What vaccines are given to children before age 5?

   Important words: vaccines, children, before age 5

   Related words: polio, shot, pediatrics

   Final search criteria (important + related words): vaccines children "before age 5" "polio shot" pediatrics

   Note: By putting terms in quotes, you tell the search engine that the words *must* appear next to one another, rather than at different locations on the same web page.

2. *Use a search engine to isolate valuable sites.* Enter your questions, phrases, and keywords in various combinations to generate lists of hits. Vary word order

Much, although not all, research can be done using online databases. Get to know the databases and other resources your school makes available to students.

Cathy Yeulet/123RF

to see what you can generate. If you get too many hits, try using more specific keywords.

3. *Evaluate the results.* The first links on your search results may or may not be the most relevant. Often, top hits belong to individuals or companies that have paid to have their sites show up first. Scan through the results, reading the short synopsis of each. You may need to look further, perhaps to the second or third page of results, to find what you need.

4. *Skim sites to evaluate what seems most useful.* Once you identify a potentially useful link, go to the site and evaluate it. Does the site seem relevant and reputable? What is its purpose? For example, a blog is apt to focus on opinion; a company's site is likely to promote its products; an article in a scholarly journal may focus on research findings.

5. *Save, or bookmark, the sites you want to focus on.* Make sure you can access them again. You may want to copy URLs and paste them into a separate document. Consider printing internet materials that you know you will need to reference over and over again.

6. *When you think you are done, start over.* Choose another search engine and search again. Different systems access different sites.

Your need to be an effective researcher doesn't stop at graduation. The skills you develop as you research school projects will serve you well in any job that requires use of the internet and other resources to find and evaluate information.

Evaluate Every Source

Because the reliability of internet content varies widely, your internet research is only as strong as your critical thinking. Robert Harris, professor and Web expert, has developed a system for evaluating internet information called the CARS test for information quality (**C**redibility, **A**ccuracy, **R**easonableness, **S**upport). Use the information in Key 6.9 to question sources as you conduct research. You can also use it to test the reliability of non-internet sources.

Vary Strategies and Sources

The limitations of internet-only research make it smart to combine internet and library research. Search engines cannot find everything for several reasons:

- Not all sources are in digital format.
- The internet prioritizes current information and may not find older information.
- Some digital sources may not be part of your library's subscription offerings.
- Internet searches require electricity or battery power and an online connection.

Use the internet as a starting point to get an idea of the various documents you may want to locate in the library and read in print. When you find a blog or website that provides only a short extract of important information and then references the rest, find that original article or book and read the information in its entirety. Often, risking the time and effort that extra searching takes will reward you with more accurate, in-depth, and useful information.

KEY 6.9 Use the CARS test to determine information quality on the internet.

CREDIBILITY	ACCURACY	REASONABLENESS	SUPPORT
Examine whether a source is believable and trustworthy.	*Examine whether information is correct—i.e., factual, comprehensive, detailed, and up to date (if necessary).*	*Examine whether material is fair, objective, moderate, and consistent.*	*Examine whether a source is adequately supported with citations.*
What are the author's credentials?	*Is it up to date, and is that important?*	*Does the source seem fair?*	*Where does the information come from?*
Look for education and experience, title or position of employment, membership in any known and respected organization, reliable contact information, biographical information, and reputation.	If you are searching for a work of literature, such as Shakespeare's play *Macbeth*, there is no "updated" version. However, you may want reviews of its latest productions. For most scientific research, you will need to rely on the most updated information you can find.	Look for a balanced argument, accurate claims, and a reasoned tone that does not appeal primarily to your emotions.	Look at the site, the sources used by the person or group who compiled the information, and the contact information. Make sure that the cited sources seem reliable and that statistics are documented.
Is there quality control?	*Is it comprehensive?*	*Does the source seem objective?*	*Is the information corroborated?*
Look for ways in which the source may have been screened. For example, materials on an organization's website have most likely been approved by several members; information coming from an academic journal has to be screened by several people before it is published.	Does the material leave out any important facts or information? Does it neglect to consider alternative views or crucial consequences? Although no one source can contain all of the available information on a topic, it should still be as comprehensive as is possible within its scope.	While there is a range of objectivity in writing, you want to favour authors and organizations who can control their bias. An author with a strong political or religious agenda or an intent to sell a product may not be a source of the most truthful material.	Test information by looking for other sources that confirm the facts in this information—or, if the information is opinion, sources that share that opinion and back it up with their own citations. One good strategy is to find at least three sources that corroborate one another.
Is there any posted summary or evaluation of the source?	*For whom is the source written, and for what purpose?*	*Does the source seem moderate?*	*Is the source externally consistent?*
You may find abstracts of sources (summary) or a recommendation, rating, or review from a person or organization (evaluation). Either of these—or, ideally, both—can give you an idea of credibility before you decide to examine a source in depth.	Looking at what the author wants to accomplish will help you assess whether it has a bias. Sometimes biased information will not be useful for your purpose; sometimes your research will require that you note and evaluate bias (such as if you were to compare Civil War diaries from Union soldiers with those from Confederate soldiers).	Do claims seem possible, or does the information seem hard to believe? Does what you read make sense when compared to what you already know? While wild claims may turn out to be truthful, you are safest to check everything out.	Most material is a mix of both current and old information. External consistency refers to whether the old information agrees with what you already know. If a source contradicts something you know to be true, chances are higher that the information new to you may be inconsistent as well.
Signals of a potential lack of credibility:	*Signals of a potential lack of accuracy:*	*Signals of a potential lack of reasonableness:*	*Signals of a potential lack of support:*
Anonymous materials, negative evaluations, little or no evidence of quality control, bad grammar or misspelled words	Lack of date or old date, generalizations, one-sided views that do not acknowledge opposing arguments	Extreme or emotional language, sweeping statements, conflict of interest, inconsistencies or contradictions	Statistics without sources, lack of documentation, lack of corroboration using other reliable sources

Source: Based on Harris, Robert. "Evaluating Internet Research Sources." VirtualSalt, November 22, 2010. From http://www.virtualsalt.com/evalu8it.htm.

Reading, Research, and Writing

get practical

binkski/123RF

GENERATE AND EVALUATE A LIST OF HITS

Complete the following on paper or in digital format.

Use a topic being covered in one of your courses to practise generating hits for online research.

1. Name the topic and the course.

2. Identify two or three keywords related to this topic.

3. Identify two search engines that you plan to use.

4. Using the keywords, generate a list of hits with each of the two search engines.

5. Identify two particular hits: one hit that comes up with both engines, and one that is unique to a single engine.

6. Analyze each of these two hits according to the CARS criteria.

7. Finally, note whether you believe each hit would be useful for your coursework, and support your decision with information from your CARS analysis.

WHAT DOES POST-SECONDARY
writing demand of you?

There is much more to say about writing in college or university than can fit here, and nearly every student will take a composition course that covers writing in detail. To lay the foundation for your studies, here is an overview of the writing process (planning, drafting, revising, and editing) followed by some important points about citations and plagiarism.

Planning

The planning process involves five steps that help you think about the assignment:

1. *Note logistics.* Confirm how long the paper should be, how much time you have, what kind of research is needed, and what level of depth is expected.

2. *Brainstorm topic ideas.* Begin by writing down anything on the assigned subject that comes to mind, in no particular order. To jump-start your thoughts, scan your text and notes, check library or internet references, or meet with your instructor to discuss ideas.

3. *Use prewriting strategies to narrow your topic.* Prewriting strategies[14] help you develop a topic that is broad enough for investigation but narrow enough to handle.
   - *Freewrite.* Jot down whatever comes to mind without censoring ideas or worrying about grammar, spelling, punctuation, or organization.
   - *Ask journalists' questions.* Ask who, what, where, when, why, and how to explore potential topics.

4. *Conduct research and take notes.* Create source notes and content notes to organize your work, keep track of your sources, and avoid plagiarism.
   - Source notes should include all identifying details of the work (author, title, year, URL, and so on) as well as a short summary and critical evaluation.

get creative

Auremar/123RF

Astroid/123RF

FREEWRITE ON A TOPIC

Complete the following on paper or in digital format.

Ramp up your freewriting skills by practising on a topic from one of your courses.

1. Review your syllabi and find one that lists a writing assignment that is already linked to a general or specific topic. Write the assignment topic at the top of your paper or digital document.
2. Then, on paper or an electronic device of your choosing, freewrite three paragraphs, writing whatever thoughts you have related to your topic, in whatever order they occur. Don't do any research beforehand, and free yourself from self-censorship so that ideas can flow. Keep this document in your materials for that course and use it as a starting point for your assignment when the time comes.

■ Content notes are taken during a thorough reading and are where you put the information you want to use. To supplement your content notes, annotate photocopies of sources.

5. *Write a working thesis statement and outline.* Next, write a thesis statement that declares your subject and point of view and reflects your purpose. This working thesis may change as you research and develop your draft. Finally, create a working outline to guide your writing.

Drafting

No first draft comes out of the gate ready to hand in. You may write many drafts, each version moving you closer to what you want to say and how you want to say it.

Freewrite a draft. Don't think yet about your introduction, conclusion, or organizational structure. Using your planning stage information as your raw material, get your thoughts down on paper. Only then should you begin to shape your work.

Write an introduction. The introduction tells readers what the paper contains and includes a thesis statement, which is often found at the end of the introduction.

Create the body. The body of the paper presents your central ideas and supporting evidence (facts, statistics, and examples). Try to find a structure that helps you organize your ideas and evidence into a clear pattern. Options include arranging ideas by time, according to importance, by problem and solution, or according to cause and effect.

Write the conclusion. A conclusion brings your paper to a natural ending by summarizing your main points, perhaps showing the significance of your thesis and how it relates to larger issues.

Revising and Editing

First, critically evaluate the content, organization, word choice, paragraph structure, and style of your first draft. Consider whether your evidence proves your thesis, and look for logical holes. Consider feedback from a peer reviewer or your instructor. Ask yourself these questions:

■ Does the paper fulfill the requirements of the assignment?
■ Do I prove my thesis?

revisit RISK AND REWARD

Courtesy of Mary Haynes

What happened to Mary? Mary focused her reading skills on materials on grief including *On Death and Dying* by Dr. Elizabeth Kübler-Ross. Understanding grief from a scientific perspective helped her grasp the emotional component. Then she took the risk of showing her drafts to others and staying open to the feedback she received. Her deep connection to the subject matter, combined with her hard work, resulted in the reward of an outstanding paper.

After graduation, Mary worked at Stanford for eight years as an associate director of admissions and later as assistant dean of students. As "a gatekeeper," Mary recalls, "my job was to get the gate open."

What does this mean for you? Years after graduation, Mary shared her paper with two co-workers who were grieving, and it helped them. "It felt great to have that kind of impact," she says. Your writing, too, can have a lasting impact on others. For an upcoming writing assignment, strive for a reward beyond a good grade. Consider writers who make you think, inspire you, or help you. Imagine saying something that has a lasting impact on others or, at the very least, on the quality of your own thinking. Write down three things: The assignment as stated, how you plan to craft an important message, and finally, three authors and/or books that represent the kind of writing that you strive to create.

What risk may bring reward beyond your world? As assistant dean of students Mary also supervised new student orientation, hiring a staff of up to 14 students each summer to help plan the orientation activities. "Many of those students who worked for me still keep in touch," she says. "They tell me they still remember the life lessons I helped instill in them." Consider volunteering for your campus's orientation program. What reward can your small risk of personal time have for newcomers? Think back to your first days on campus and what information you benefited from—or would have, had it been made available to you. Find a way to bring that information to those who need it.

GLOBAL RISK AND REWARD

Fotogroove/Shutterstock

Startup companies exist because people took a risk to spend money and time on a product they believe in, in the hopes that great reward lies ahead. A Japanese startup called Whill has created an electric add-on that converts a conventional wheelchair into a motorized vehicle. The prizewinning product has a bright future, especially with a growing elderly population.[15]

Vinzenz Weidenhofer/123RF

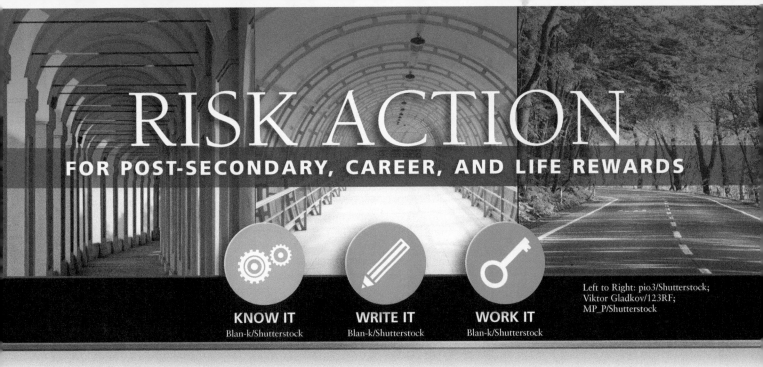

RISK ACTION
FOR POST-SECONDARY, CAREER, AND LIFE REWARDS

KNOW IT
Blan-k/Shutterstock

WRITE IT
Blan-k/Shutterstock

WORK IT
Blan-k/Shutterstock

Complete the following on paper or in digital format.

KNOW IT *Think Critically*

Study a Text Page

Build basic skills. The excerpt on page 162 is from the chapter "Groups and Organizations" in the sixth edition of John J. Macionis's *Sociology*.[16] Skim the excerpt. Identify the headings on the page and the relationships among them. Mark primary-level headings with a numeral 1, secondary headings with a 2, and tertiary (third-level) headings with a 3.

Take it to the next level. Analyze the headings and text by answering the following questions.

1. Which heading serves as an umbrella for the rest?
2. What do the headings tell you about the content of the page?
3. Name three concepts that seem important to remember.
4. Based on the three concepts you pulled out, write three study questions that you can review with an instructor, a teaching assistant, or a fellow student.

Move toward mastery. Read the excerpt, putting SQ3R to work. Use a marker pen to highlight key phrases and sentences. Write short marginal notes to help you review the material later. After reading this page thoroughly, write a short summary paragraph.

WRITE IT *Communicate*

Emotional intelligence journal: Reading challenges. Which current course presents your most difficult reading challenge? Describe what makes the reading tough: the type of material, the length of the assignments, the level of difficulty, or something else. What feelings come up for you when you read, and what effect do they have on your reading? Describe techniques you learned in this chapter that can help you get into a growth mindset and read productively.

Reading, Research, and Writing

Getty Images

SOCIAL GROUPS

Virtually everyone moves through life with a sense of belonging; this is the experience of group life. A social group refers to *two or more people who identify and interact with one another.* Human beings continually come together to form couples, families, circles of friends, neighborhoods, churches, businesses, clubs, and numerous large organizations. Whatever the form, groups encompass people with shared experiences, loyalties, and interests. In short, while maintaining their individuality, the members of social groups also think of themselves as a special "we."

Groups, Categories, and Crowds

People often use the term "group" imprecisely. We now distinguish the group from the similar concepts of category and crowd.

■ *Category.* A *category* refers to people who have some status in common. Women, single fathers, military recruits, homeowners, and Roman Catholics are all examples of categories.

Why are categories not considered groups? Simply because, while the individuals involved are aware that they are not the only ones to hold that particular status, the vast majority are strangers to one another.

■ *Crowd.* A *crowd* refers to a temporary cluster of individuals who may or may not interact at all. Students

sitting in a lecture hall do engage one another and share some common identity as college classmates; thus, such a crowd might be called a loosely formed group. By contrast, riders hurtling along on a subway train or bathers enjoying a summer day at the beach pay little attention to one another and amount to an anonymous aggregate of people. In general, then, crowds are too transitory and impersonal to qualify as social groups.

The right circumstances, however, could turn a crowd into a group. People riding in a subway train that crashes under the city streets generally become keenly aware of their common plight and begin to help one another. Sometimes such extraordinary experiences become the basis for lasting relationships.

Primary and Secondary Groups

Acquaintances commonly greet one another with a smile and the simple phrase, "Hi! How are you?" The response is usually a well scripted, "Just fine, thanks, how about you?" This answer, of course, is often more formal than truthful. In most cases, providing a detailed account of how you are *really* doing would prompt the other person to beat a hasty and awkward exit.

Sociologists classify social groups by measuring them against two ideal types based on members' genuine level of personal concern. This variation is the key to distinguishing primary from secondary groups.

According to Charles Horton Cooley (1864–1929), a **primary group** is a *small social group whose members share personal and enduring relationships.* Bound together by primary relationships, individuals in primary groups typically spend a great deal of time together, engage in a wide range of common activities, and feel that they know one another well. Although not without periodic conflict, members of primary groups display sincere concern for each other's welfare. The family is every society's most important primary group.

Cooley characterized these personal and tightly integrated groups as *primary* because they are among the first groups we experience in life. In addition, the family and early play groups also hold primary importance in the socialization process, shaping attitudes, behavior, and social identity.

Source: Macionis, Clarke, and Gerber, *Sociology* 2Ce, pp. 171-173, 1997, Prentice-Hall Canada Inc. Reprinted by permission of Pearson Canada Inc.

Real-life writing: Ask for help. Self-help plans often involve reaching out to others. Draft an email to your instructor that describes the difficulties you are facing in your challenging course, as well as specific help you need to move to the next step. Make sure your message is clear and accurate; your grammar, spelling, and punctuation are correct; and your tone is appropriate. Whether you send the email or not is up to you. In either case, writing it will help you move forward in your reading-improvement plan.

WORK IT *Build Your Brand*

Reading Skills on the Job As the Conference Board of Canada's Employability Skills 2000+ tells us,[17] excellent reading skills are a requirement for almost every 21st century job. Employers expect you to read independently and master new skills to keep up with change. For example, working in the field of sociology requires you to keep on top of case reports, government regulations, court documents, and research materials. Plus, nearly every job requires you to read memos, emails, and reports from your co-workers and managers.

Prepare yourself by honestly assessing your practical skills *right now*. Copy the following list on your paper or in your document. For each item, rate your ability on a scale of 1 to 10, with 10 being the highest:

- Concentrate, no matter the distractions.
- Define your reading purpose and use it to guide your focus and pace.
- Use specific vocabulary-building techniques to improve comprehension.
- Use every aspect of SQ3R to master content.
- Skim and scan.
- Use analytical thinking skills when reading.
- Use highlighting and notes to help you master content.

Identify the two skill areas where you rated yourself lowest and think about how you can improve. Make a problem-solving plan for each (you may want to use a flowchart like the one in Key 6.7). Check your progress in one month and again at the end of the term. Finally, write one short paragraph describing how you anticipate using reading skills in your chosen career.

Courtesy of Chandra McQueen

Whatever you study, your goal is to anchor important information in long-term memory so that you can use it – for both short-term goals like tests and long-term goals like performing effectively on the job.

Note Taking, Memory, and Studying

HOW CAN YOU RETAIN WHAT YOU LEARN?

What Would You Risk? *Chandra McQueen*

THINK ABOUT THIS SITUATION AS YOU READ, AND CONSIDER WHAT ACTION YOU WOULD TAKE. THIS CHAPTER PRESENTS NOTE-TAKING, MEMORY, AND STUDYING STRATEGIES THAT WILL HELP YOU SUCCESSFULLY RECORD AND REMEMBER KNOWLEDGE THAT YOU CAN USE.

Understanding the risks her single mother took to provide for her and her three brothers, Chandra McQueen was determined to become the first in her family to graduate from post-secondary school. That ambition blossomed in high school, where she played first chair clarinet in the concert band, was a cheerleader, played tennis, and ran track. "I was really driven to change my situation," she says. "One of my favourite activities was going to the library and reading about different places and people. This nurtured a desire for me to make a difference in the world."

As an undergraduate she risked aiming for a double major in American politics and sociology. She dove into post-secondary life, working in student government and as a resident assistant. However, she was initially a bit overwhelmed academically and was heartbroken when

she got her first D. "I was my worst critic," she said. "I wanted to make honours, like I did in high school."

Used to more intimate class settings than the large lectures, Chandra struggled to record lecture highlights. Because she found it tough to discern what information was valuable enough to write down, her notes were frequently missing key points—an issue in coursework that applied to her double major. With her note-taking skills lacking, she had trouble converting her knowledge into success on papers and exams, and rewards seemed out of reach. As Chandra says, "It was sink or swim."

To be continued . . .

MANY STUDENTS STRUGGLE TO TAKE IN THE MASSIVE AMOUNTS OF MATERIAL FROM LECTURES AND LESSONS. WHAT WORKED IN HIGH SCHOOL OFTEN DOES NOT WORK AT THE POST-SECONDARY LEVEL. YOU'LL LEARN MORE ABOUT CHANDRA, AND THE REWARD RESULTING FROM HER ACTIONS, WITHIN THE CHAPTER.

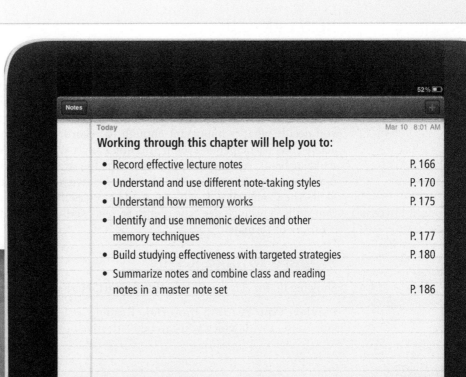

Notes

Today   Mar 10 8:01 AM

Working through this chapter will help you to:

status CHECK

Left to Right: Luis Santos/Shutterstock; Antonio Guillem/Shutterstock; antoniodiaz/Shutterstock; mimagephotography/Shutterstock; Djomas/Shutterstock; WAYHOME studio/Shutterstock

How Developed Are Your Note-Taking, Memory, and Studying Skills?

For each statement, fill in the number that best describes how often it applies to you.

1 = never   2 = seldom   3 = sometimes   4 = often   5 = always

1. I believe that good preparation is essential for taking comprehensive notes.	① ② ③ ④ ⑤
2. I generally review notes within 24 hours of taking them.	① ② ③ ④ ⑤
3. I use different note-taking systems depending on my instructor's teaching styles and the material being taught.	① ② ③ ④ ⑤
4. I write, rewrite, and summarize information to remember it.	① ② ③ ④ ⑤
5. When I am studying, I focus on what I consider most important to remember.	① ② ③ ④ ⑤
6. I use flash cards and other active memory strategies to remember what I study.	① ② ③ ④ ⑤
7. I create mnemonic devices with images and associations as memory hooks.	① ② ③ ④ ⑤
8. I try to review material in several sessions over time rather than cram the night before a test.	① ② ③ ④ ⑤
9. I know how to combine class and text notes effectively to prepare for tests.	① ② ③ ④ ⑤
10. My study strategies work for me; after a test is over, I retain much of what I had to know.	① ② ③ ④ ⑤

Each of the topics in these statements is covered in this chapter. Note those statements for which you filled in a 3 or lower. Skim the chapter to see where those topics appear, and pay special attention to them as you read, learn, and apply new strategies.

REMEMBER: NO MATTER HOW DEVELOPED YOUR NOTE-TAKING, MEMORY, AND STUDYING SKILLS ARE, YOU CAN IMPROVE WITH EFFORT AND PRACTICE.

HOW CAN YOU *take useful notes?*

Taking notes provides you with a record of what happened in class and generates study materials. Note taking also builds critical thinking. Because it is virtually impossible to write down every word of a lecture, you constantly evaluate what you hear as you decide what is important enough to record. Finally, note taking makes you an active class participant—even if you don't say a word. This essential tool, frankly, can make or break your academic success. Use the strategies outlined here to prepare, take notes in class, and review notes. Taking effective notes is a Fundamental Employability Skill. The Conference Board of Canada stresses the importance of strong communication skills. This includes "the ability to read and understand information presented in a variety of formats."[1]

Prepare to Take Notes

Showing up for class on time is just the start. Here's more about preparing to take notes:

Preview your reading material. Reading assigned materials before class will provide context with which you can take effective notes, and is one of the most rewarding

MyLab Student Success (www.mystudentsuccesslab.com) is an online solution designed to help you "Start Strong, Finish Stronger" by building skills for ongoing personal and professional development.

possible study strategies. Check your class syllabi daily for when assignments are due, and plan your reading time with these deadlines in mind.

Review what you know. Taking 15 minutes before class to review previous notes and reading will help you to follow the lecture from the start.

Set up your environment. Find a comfortable seat, away from friends if sitting with them distracts you. Set up your notebook or, if you use a laptop, open the file containing your class notes. Be ready to write (or type) as soon as the instructor begins speaking.

Gather support. In each class, set up a support system with one or two students so you can look at their notes after an absence. Find students whose work you respect.

Choose the best note-taking system. Take instructor style, the course material, and your learning preferences into account. Discussion of various systems appears later in this chapter.

Record Information During Class

The following practical suggestions will help you record information to review later:

- Record what your instructor emphasizes by paying attention to verbal and nonverbal cues.
- Write down all key terms and definitions.
- For difficult concepts, note relevant examples, applications, and links to other material.
- If questions are welcome during class, ask them. If you prefer to ask questions after class, jot down questions as you think of them through the class period.
- Write down every question your instructor raises, since these questions may be on a test.
- Be organized, but not fussy. Remember that you can always improve your notes later.
- Draw pictures and diagrams to illustrate ideas.
- Be consistent. Use the same system to show importance—such as indenting, spacing, or underlining—on each page.
- If you have trouble with a concept, leave space for an explanation and flag it with a question mark. After class, consult your text or ask a classmate or instructor for help.
- Go beyond the PowerPoint. When instructors use electronic resources, expand on the main points listed there with details from the lecture.
- Consider learning preferences. The Multiple Intelligences table in this chapter (see page 168) suggests MI-related note-taking strategies.

Using a personal shorthand helps you write faster when taking notes in class. Consider these shorthand suggestions. You may already use some of them to speed up texting or tweeting.

1. Use standard abbreviations in place of complete words (see Key 7.1 for ideas)
2. Shorten words by removing vowels from the middle of words (prps = purpose)
3. Substitute word beginnings for entire words (info = information)
4. Make up your own symbols and use them consistently (b4 = before)

Good listening powers note taking. When taking notes in class, listen carefully to the information before deciding what to write down.

Wavebreakmedia/Shutterstock

multiple intelligence strategies

FOR NOTE-TAKING

Name an upcoming class meeting (date, time, course): _____.

In the right-hand column, record specific ideas for how MI strategies can help you take notes in this class.

INTELLIGENCE	USE MI STRATEGIES TO IMPROVE TOUR NOTES	IDENTIFY MI TEST-PREP STRATEGIES THAT CAN HELP YOU TAKE NOTES
Verbal-Linguistic	• Rewrite your class notes in an alternate note-taking style to see connections more clearly. • Combine class and text notes to get a complete picture.	
Logical-Mathematical	• When reviewing or rewriting notes, put information into a logical sequence. • Create tables that show relationships.	
Bodily-Kinesthetic	• Think of your notes as a crafts project that enables you to see "knowledge layers." Use coloured pens to texture your notes. • Study with your notes spread in sequence around you so that you can see knowledge building from left to right.	
Visual-Spatial	• Take notes using coloured markers or pens. • Rewrite lecture notes in think link format (see page 171), focusing on the most important points.	
Interpersonal	• Try to schedule a study group right after a lecture to discuss class notes. • Review class notes with a study buddy. Compare notes to see what the other missed.	
Intrapersonal	• Schedule some quiet time soon after a lecture to review and think about your notes. • As you review your notes, decide whether you grasp the material or need help.	
Musical	• To improve recall, recite concepts in your notes to rhythms. • Write a song that includes material from your class and text notes. Use the refrain to emphasize what is important.	
Naturalistic	• Notice similarities and differences in concepts by organizing material into natural groupings.	

KEY 7.1 Save time with standard abbreviations.

w/, w/o	with, without	Cf	compare, in comparison to
Ur	you are	Ff	following
→	means; resulting in	Q	question
←	as a result of	gr8	great
↑	increasing	Pov	point of view
↓	decreasing	<	less than
∴	therefore	>	more than
b/c	because	=	equals
≈	approximately	b&f	back and forth
+ or &	and	Δ	change
Y	why	2	to; two; too
No. or #	number	Afap	as far as possible
i.e.	that is	e.g.	for example
cos	change of subject	c/o	care of
Ng	no good	k	kilogram
POTUS	President of the United States	hx	history

5. Use abbreviations for proper nouns such as places, people, companies, scientific substances, events, and so on (CAN = Canada).

6. If you know that a word or phrase will be repeated, write it once, and then establish an abbreviation for the rest of your notes.

Sometimes, using shorthand results in forgetting what your writing means. To avoid this problem, review your notes shortly after class and spell out words that are confusing. Also, don't forget to eliminate shorthand from any work that you turn in.

Finally, don't stop taking notes when your class engages in a discussion. Even though it isn't part of the instructor's planned presentation, important information often surfaces. If you can focus on important concepts better when involved in a discussion, like Chandra, you may benefit significantly from staying focused at these times.

Review and Revise Your Notes

Class notes are works in progress, incomplete in some places, confusing in others, and illegible in still others. Getting what you need out of notes requires that you review and revise them as soon as possible after class. Read your notes over and revise by filling in gaps, clarifying sloppy handwriting, and raising questions.

If you can review your notes within 24 hours of taking them down in class, you are likely to reactivate and strengthen the new neural pathways you created when you learned the material. Waiting longer increases the possibility that you will forget what you worked so hard to record.

WHAT NOTE-TAKING *systems can you use?*

Now that you have gathered some useful note-taking strategies, take a look at different systems for how to approach note taking. Keep these questions in mind as you read, so that you begin to think about how you would use specific systems:

- What class or type of instruction would this system be best suited for? Why?
- Which system seems most comfortable to me?
- What system might be most compatible with my learning preferences? Why?

Outlines

Outlines use a standard structure to show how ideas and supporting details relate and to indicate levels of importance. *Formal outlines* indicate idea dominance and subordination with Roman numerals, uppercase and lowercase letters, and numbers. In contrast, *informal outlines* show the same associations but replace the formality with a system of consistent indenting and dashes. Key 7.2 shows how the structure of an informal outline helps a student take notes on the topic of tropical rain forests.

From time to time, an instructor may provide *guided notes*—an outline on the board, a projected PowerPoint, or a handout—at the beginning of class. Guided notes are general and minimal, and they require that you fill in the details during the lecture.

Cornell T-Note System

The Cornell note-taking system, also known as the *T-note system,* consists of three sections you create before class on paper and fill in during class time. Picture an upside-down letter T as you follow these directions:[2]

- Set up your paper by picturing an upside-down letter T. Create the cue column by drawing a vertical line about 6 cm from the left side of the paper. End the line about 4 cm from the bottom of the sheet. Create the summary area by drawing a horizontal line that spans the entire paper about 4 cm from the bottom of the page. Notes, the largest section, is to the right of the cue column.

Courtesy of Chandra McQueen

talk risk and reward . . .

Risk asking tough questions to be rewarded with new insights. Use the following questions to inspire discussion with classmates, either in person or online.

- Every student experiences the frustration of needing to work hard to remember something that you think is completely unimportant and irrelevant to your life. How do you handle this, and what is the result? How *should* you handle it?

- When you are in class, what percent of your brain is focused on class, and what percent is distracted and focused elsewhere? If you want the reward of increased focus, what are you willing to risk to be more focused in the classroom?

CONSIDER THE CASE: How do you respond when, like Chandra, you discover that a goal presents much more of a challenge than you had expected? Do you forge ahead, do the minimum, give up? How do the people in your life advise you to proceed—and what do you think of the advice?

| KEY | 7.2 | An informal outline is useful for taking notes in class. |

Tropical Rain Forests

- What are tropical rain forests?
    - Areas in South America and Africa, along the equator
    - Average temperatures between 25° and 30° C
    - Average annual rainfalls range between 250 and 400 centimetres
    - Conditions combine to create the Earth's richest, most biodiverse ecosystem.
        - A biodiverse ecosystem has a great number of organisms coexisting within a defined area.
        - Examples of rain forest biodiversity
            - one hectare in the Amazon rain forest has 283 species of trees
            - a 7.77 square km section of a Peruvian rain forest has more than 1300 butterfly species and 600 bird species.
            - Compare this biodiversity to what is found in Canada
                - only 275 butterfly species and 426 bird species
- How are humans changing the rain forest?
    - Humans have already destroyed about 40% of all rain forests.
        - They are cutting down trees for lumber or clearing the land for ranching or agriculture.
    - Biologist Edwin O. Wilson estimates that this destruction may lead to the extinction of 27 000 species.
    - Rainforest removal is also linked to the increase in atmospheric carbon dioxide, which worsens the greenhouse effect.
        - The greenhouse effect refers to process in which gases such as carbon dioxide trap the Sun's energy in the Earth's atmosphere as heat resulting in global warming.
    - Recognition of the crisis is growing, as are conservation efforts.

Source: Audesirk, Teresa, Gerald Audesirk, and Bruce E. Byers. *Life on Earth,* 9th ed. Upper Saddle River, NJ: Prentice Hall, 2011, pp. 559–561.

- Record your notes in the notes section during class, in whatever form you choose.
- When reviewing the notes, fill in the cue column with key words or comments, questions, examples, links to ideas, or diagrams—whatever expands or clarifies your notes.
- In the summary area, rewrite the most critical points from the notes section.

    Key 7.3 shows how the Cornell system is used in a business course.

Think Links

A think link, also known as a *mind map* or *word web,* is a visual and flexible form of note taking that links ideas with supporting details and examples using lines and shapes. To create a think link, start by circling or boxing your topic in the middle of the paper. Next, draw a line from the topic and write the name of one major idea at the end of the line. Circle that idea. Then, jot down specific facts related to the idea, linking them to the idea with lines. Continue the process, connecting thoughts to one another with circles, lines, and words. Key 7.4, a think link on the sociological concept called *stratification,* follows this structure.

Think links can take a wide variety of forms. Designs include stair steps showing connected ideas that build toward a conclusion, and a tree with trunk and roots as central concepts and branches as examples. Another type, called a "jellyfish," shows a central idea at the top with connecting ideas and examples hanging down from it like tentacles.

Create the cue column by drawing a vertical line about 6 cm from the left side of the paper. End the line about 4 cm from the bottom of the sheet.

Label a sheet of paper with the date and title of the lecture. October 3, 2019, p. 1

UNDERSTANDING EMPLOYEE MOTIVATION

Cue	Notes
Why do some workers have a better attitude toward their work than others?	Purpose of motivational theories —To explain role of human relations in motivating employee performance —Theories translate into how managers actually treat workers
	2 specific theories
Some managers view workers as lazy; others view them as motivated and productive.	—Human resources model, developed by Douglas McGregor, shows that managers have radically different beliefs about motivation. —Theory X holds that people are naturally irresponsible and uncooperative —Theory X holds that people are naturally irresponsible and uncooperative
Maslow's Hierarchy	—Maslow's Hierarchy of Needs says that people have needs in 5 different areas, which they attempt to satisfy in their work.
self-actualization needs (challenging job) esteem needs (job title) social needs (friends at work) security needs (health plan) physiological needs (pay)	—Physiological need: need for survival, including food and shelter —Security need: need for stability and protection —Social need: need for friendship and companionship —Esteem need: need for status and recognition —Self-actualization need: need for self-fulfillment Needs at lower levels must be met before a person tries to satisfy needs at higher levels. —Developed by psychologist Abraham Maslow

Two motivational theories try to explain worker motivation. The human resources model includes Theory X and Theory Y. Maslow's Hierarchy of Needs suggests that people have needs in 5 different areas: physiological, security, social, esteem, and self-actualization.

Create the summary area by starting where the vertical line ends (about 4 cm from the bottom of the page) and drawing a horizontal line across the paper.

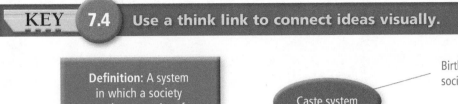

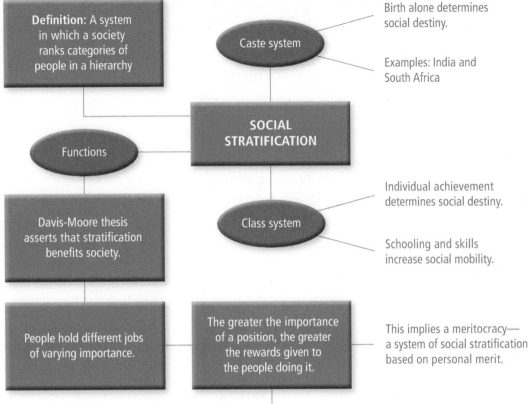

Definition: A system in which a society ranks categories of people in a hierarchy

Caste system

Birth alone determines social destiny.

Examples: India and South Africa

SOCIAL STRATIFICATION

Functions

Davis-Moore thesis asserts that stratification benefits society.

Class system

Individual achievement determines social destiny.

Schooling and skills increase social mobility.

People hold different jobs of varying importance.

The greater the importance of a position, the greater the rewards given to the people doing it.

This implies a meritocracy— a system of social stratification based on personal merit.

Example: A surgeon earns more than an auto mechanic.

A think link may be difficult to construct in class, especially if your instructor talks quickly. If this is the case, transform your notes into think link format later when you review.

Other Visual Strategies

Other strategies that help organize information are especially useful to visual learners, although they may be too involved to complete during class. Use them when taking text notes or combining class and text notes for review.

Charting notes. Determine the topic of the lecture, then create a chart or table, separating your paper into distinct columns according to the information you expect to gather. Then fill in your chart in class. Shown is a section of a set of charting notes for a history class:

Time Period	Important People	Events	Importance
1968–1984	Pierre Trudeau	FLQ Crisis, Quebec Separatist Movement	Replaced Canadian Bill of Rights with The Canadian Charter of Rights and Freedoms.

Pictures and diagrams. Copy diagrams from the board and create your own. Make complex concepts into images or cartoons.

get analytical

FACE A NOTE-TAKING CHALLENGE

Dario Sabljak/Shutterstock

Darren Baker/Shutterstock

Complete the following on paper or in digital format.

Analyze the note-taking task ahead of you in your most difficult class.

1. What is the name of the course that is most challenging for you right now?
2. What factors make this class challenging?
3. Consult your syllabus, and then list what you have to read (text sections and/or other materials) before your next class meeting.
4. Which note-taking strategy will best help you make meaning from your reading assignments for this class?
5. Which note-taking system is best suited to the material and instructor for use in class, and why?
6. Name three note-taking strategies that will best help you address the challenge of this class.

Timelines. Use a timeline to organize information into chronological order. Draw a vertical or horizontal line on the page and connect each item to it in order, noting dates and descriptions.

Hierarchy charts. Charts showing an information hierarchy can help you visualize how pieces fit together. For example, use a hierarchy chart to show classification levels of plants.

Electronic Strategies

If you take notes using an electronic device, saving them safely is essential. You can save notes on your device or on a remote server (known as "the cloud") connected to the internet. Evernote is a software package that lets you take notes using any computer or Android phone. These notes include text, webpage URLs and content, photographs, or voice memos—all of which can have attachments. You can save your notes on your own computer or on a special Evernote server.

Google Drive is another example of a documentation and note-taking tool that lets you save text to the cloud. With Google Drive, you need only connect to the internet, open Google Drive, and start typing. When you're done, you save your work to a collection (folder) of your choice, hosted on a Google server. You can also download the file to your own computer. You can allow other people in a study group to access your file in Google Drive and edit it, adding new information where necessary. Dropbox and Microsoft's One Drive are two other options for cloud storage.

Finally, recent note-taking technology has added recording capabilities to your arsenal. The Livescribe "smartpen" records exactly what you hear and write with the pen on a specialized notebook that saves everything electronically, enabling you to store and review the lecture and your notes on a computer. SoundNote is a similar application that works with tablet computers. When you type notes on a tablet, SoundNote will record everything you type, as well as what you are hearing if you are attending the class in person. Students who have challenges similar to Chandra's may find that recording devices help them go back through the lecture to find the key points they missed.

WHAT WILL STRENGTHEN
your memory?

All learning and performance depends on memory, because the information you remember—concepts, facts, processes, formulas, and more—is the raw material with which you think, write, create, build, and perform your day-to-day actions in school and out. Memorization also forms a foundation for higher-level thinking, because you need to recall and understand information before you can apply, analyze, synthesize, or evaluate it.

Understand the Brain Science of Memory

Memory refers to the way the brain stores and recalls information or experiences that are acquired through the five senses. While you take in thousands of pieces of information every second—everything from the shape and colour of your chair to how your history text describes Canada's Fathers of Confederation—you remember few. Unconsciously, your brain sorts through stimuli and stores only what it considers important.

Look at Key 7.5 as you read how the brain forms lasting memories:

1. Raw information, gathered through the five senses, reaches the brain (for example, the tune of a song you're learning in your jazz ensemble class).

KEY 7.5 Information processing model of memory.

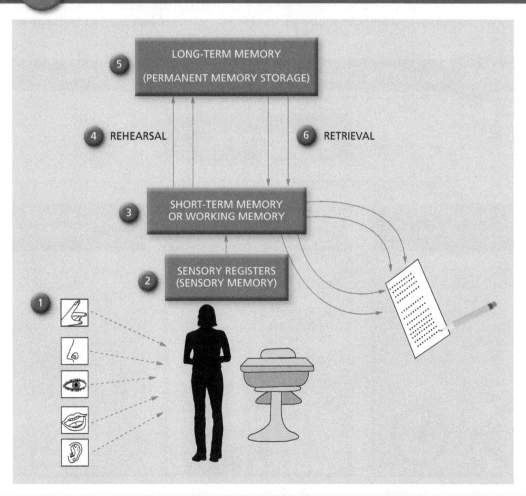

2. This information enters sensory registers, where it stays for only seconds (as you play the notes for the first time, the sounds stop in short-term memory).

3. You then pay attention to the information that seems most important to you. This moves it into short-term memory or working memory, which contains what you are thinking at any moment and makes information available for further processing (the part of the song that you're responsible for, for example the clarinet solo, will likely take up residence in your working memory). To do this, your brain improves the functioning of synapses (the gaps between cells across which electrical pulses carry messages) through chemical changes, but doesn't yet make more permanent changes to neurons.[3] You can temporarily keep information in short-term memory through *rote rehearsal*—the process of repeating information to yourself or even out loud.

4. Information moves to long-term memory through focused, active rehearsal repeated over time (as you practise the song, your brain stores the tone, rhythm, and pace in your long-term memory where you will be able to draw on it again). To create these memories, brain cells grow new dendrites and build new synapses, which grow stronger the more times the same electrical signal passes through them (created by your repetition).[4] Long-term memory is the storage house for everything you know from War of 1812 battle dates to the location of your elementary school. Most people retain memories of personal experiences and procedures longer than concepts, facts, formulas, and dates.

Long-term memory has three separate storage houses, as shown in Key 7.6. When you need a piece of information from long-term memory, the brain retrieves it and places it in short-term memory. On test day, this enables you to choose the right answer on a multiple-choice question or lay out a fact-based argument for an essay question.

SENSORY REGISTER
Brain filters through which sensory information enters the brain and is sent to short-term memory.

SHORT-TERM MEMORY
The brain's temporary information storehouse in which information remains for a limited time (from a few seconds to half a minute).

LONG-TERM MEMORY
The brain's permanent information storehouse from which information can be retrieved.

KEY 7.6 Long-term memory has three separate storage houses.

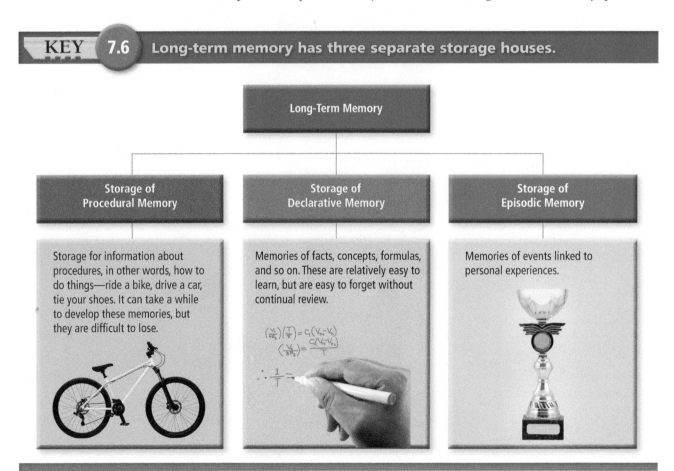

Long-Term Memory

Storage of Procedural Memory

Storage for information about procedures, in other words, how to do things—ride a bike, drive a car, tie your shoes. It can take a while to develop these memories, but they are difficult to lose.

Storage of Declarative Memory

Memories of facts, concepts, formulas, and so on. These are relatively easy to learn, but are easy to forget without continual review.

Storage of Episodic Memory

Memories of events linked to personal experiences.

Left to Right: Arina Zaiachin/123RF; Noppasin Kortungsap/123RF; Diablophotos/Shutterstock.

176

The movement of information from short-term to long-term memory and back again strengthens the connections. Learning happens and memories are built when neurons grow new dendrites and form new synapses. When you learn an algebra formula, for example, your brain forms new connections. Every time you review it, the connections get stronger.

Why You Forget

Issues with health, nutrition, and stress can cause memory problems. Research shows that even short-term stress can interfere with cell communication in the learning and memory regions of the brain.[5] However, the most common reason that information fails to stay in long-term memory is ineffective studying—not risking the effort necessary to earn the reward of retention.

Retaining information requires continual review. If you review the material over time—after 24 hours, a week, a month, six months, and more—your reward is knowledge retention. If you do not review, the neural connections will weaken, and eventually you will forget. In a classic study conducted in 1885, researcher Herman Ebbinghaus memorized a list of meaningless three-letter words such as CEF and LAZ. He then examined how quickly he forgot them. Within one hour he had forgotten more than 50% of what he had learned; after two days, he knew less than 30% of the memorized words. His experiment shows how fragile memory can be without regular review.[6]

Neuroscientist Karim Nader's research shows that once a memory is solidified in the brain, it is to some extent rebuilt each time it is remembered and can be altered by environment or circumstances.[7] For example, people often recall an event from the past inaccurately because they've heard someone else tell the story or want to forget some aspect of it. For your purposes as a student, this emphasizes the importance of both regular repetition and studying in as consistent an environment as you can manage.

Now that you know more about how memory works, get down to the business of how to retain the information you think is important and access that information when you need it.

Use Mnemonic Devices

Mnemonic devices (pronounced neh-MAHN-ick) work by linking new information to what you already know. They depend on vivid associations that engage your emotions and give you a "hook" on which to hang facts and retrieve them later. Because mnemonics take effort to create and motivation to remember, use them only when necessary—for instance, to distinguish confusing concepts that consistently trip you up. Also know that no matter how clever they are and how easy they are to remember, mnemonics have nothing to do with understanding. Their sole objective is to help you memorize.

Mnemonics all involve some combination of *imagination* (coming up with vivid images that are meaningful to you), *association* (connecting information you need to know with information you already know), and *location* ("locating" pieces of information in familiar places). They offer the reward of lasting memory in exchange for the risk of getting a little wacky. Here are some common types to try.

Visual images and associations

Imagining a compelling visual image and connecting it to information helps improve memory, especially for visual learners. To remember that the Spanish artist Picasso painted *The Three Women,* for example, you might imagine the women in a circle dancing to a Spanish song with a pig and a donkey (pig-asso). The most effective images involve bright colours, three dimensions, action scenes, inanimate objects with human traits, and humour.

get creative

CRAFT YOUR OWN MNEMONIC

Complete the following on paper or in digital format.

Create a mnemonic to help you remember some facts.

1. Identify a group of facts that you have to memorize—for example, the names of all the world's major religions, or a series of elements in the periodic table.
2. Now create your own mnemonic to remember the grouping, using any of the devices in this chapter. Write the mnemonic out in detail.
3. Describe your mnemonic. What type is it? How does it rely on imagination, association, and/or location?
4. Considering your learning preferences, describe why you think this particular mnemonic will help you retain the information.

The method of loci

This technique involves imagining storing new ideas in familiar locations. Say, for example, that on your next biology test you have to remember the body's major endocrine glands. Think of the route you travel through campus to the library. You pass the campus theatre, the physics building, the bookstore, the cafeteria, the gym, and the social science building before reaching the library. At each spot along the way, you "place" a concept you want to learn. You then link the concept with a similar-sounding word that brings an image to mind (see Key 7.7):

- At the campus theatre, you imagine bumping into the actor Brad Pitt (pituitary gland).
- At the science centre, you visualize a body builder with bulging thighs (thyroid gland).
- At the campus bookstore, you envision a second body builder with his thighs covered in mustard (thymus gland).
- In the cafeteria, you bump into Dean Al (adrenal gland).
- At the gym, you think of the school team, the Panthers—nicknamed the Pans— and remember the sound of the cheer "Pans-R-Us" (pancreas).
- At the social science building, you imagine receiving a standing ovation (ovaries).
- And at the library, you visualize sitting at a table taking a test that is easy (testes).

You can use all kinds of locations with the method of loci. Try locating information at buildings in a city you know well, places in your bedroom, or locations on a familiar game board.

ACRONYM
A word formed from the first letters of a series of words created to help you remember the series.

Acronyms

Another helpful association method involves acronyms. In history class, you can remember the allies during World War II—Britain, America, and Russia—with the acronym BAR. This is an example of a *word acronym*, because the first letters of the items you want to remember spell a word. The word (or words) spelled don't necessarily have

KEY **7.7** **The method of loci helps you remember items in a list.**

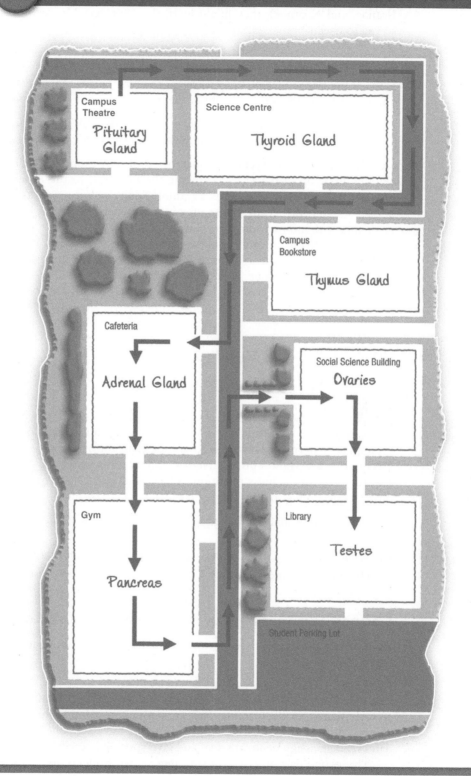

Campus Theatre — **Pituitary Gland**

Science Centre — **Thyroid Gland**

Campus Bookstore — **Thymus Gland**

Cafeteria — **Adrenal Gland**

Social Science Building — **Ovaries**

Gym — **Pancreas**

Library — **Testes**

Student Parking Lot

to be real words. For example, the acronym Roy G. Biv is a made-up name that will help you remember the colours of the rainbow.

Other acronyms take the form of an entire sentence, in which the first letter of each word in each sentence stands for the first letter of the memorized term. This is called a *list order acronym*. When astronomy students want to remember the list of planets in order of their distance from the sun (Mercury, Venus, Earth, Mars, Jupiter, Saturn, Uranus, and Neptune), they might learn this sentence: My very elegant mother just served us nectarines.

Songs and rhymes

Some of the classic mnemonic devices are rhyming poems that stick in your mind. One you may have heard is the rule about the order of "i" and "e" in spelling:

> I before E, except after C, or when sounded like "A" as in "neighbour" and "weigh." Four exceptions if you please: either, neither, seizure, seize.

Music can be an exceptional memory tool. For example, a whole generation of children grew up in the 1970s knowing the Preamble to the American Constitution because of the Schoolhouse Rock Preamble Song (look it up on YouTube and see if it doesn't stick in your head). Make up your own poems or songs, linking familiar tunes or rhymes with information you want to remember.

Improving your memory requires energy, time, and work. It also helps to master the SQ3R textbook study technique. By going through the steps in SQ3R and using the specific memory techniques described in this chapter, you will be able to learn more in less time—and remember what you learn long after exams are over.

HOW CAN YOU REMEMBER
what you study?

Whatever you study—textbooks, course materials, notes, primary sources—your goal is to anchor important information in long-term memory so that you can *use it*, for both short-term goals like tests and long-term goals like being an information technology specialist. Take a productive risk and try out a variety of strategies to see which reward you with the most retention. Journalists' questions provide a way to organize strategies according to how they help.

1. **When, where,** and **who:** Determine the times, places, and company (or none) that suit you.
2. **What** and **why:** Choose what is important to study, and set the rest aside.
3. **How:** Find the specific tips and techniques that work best for you.

Choose When, Where, and (with) Whom to Study

Figuring out the when, where, and who of studying is all about self-management.

When

The first part of *when* is *how much*. Having the right amount of time for the job is crucial. Remember the formula: For every hour you spend in the classroom each week, spend at least two to three hours preparing for the class. Check your syllabus for the dates reading assignments are due, and give yourself enough time to complete them.

The second part of *when* is *what time*. If two students go over their biology notes from 8 to 9 a.m., but one is a morning person who went to bed at 11 p.m. and one is a night owl who hit the sack around 2 a.m., you can guess who has more of a chance of remembering the information. First, determine what time is available to you in between classes, work, and other commitments. Then, thinking about when you function best, choose your study times carefully. You may not always have the luxury of being free during your peak energy times, but do the best you can.

get $mart

STAY AWARE OF YOUR MONEY

Complete the following on paper or in digital format.

How good is your memory is when it comes to bills and due dates? Find out by answering the following questions. First, create a hard-copy or digital table with headers as shown.

BILL	EST. AMOUNT	ACTUAL AMOUNT	EST. DUE DATE	ACTUAL DUE DATE

1. Off the top of your head, list your typical monthly bills, their estimated amount and estimated due date. Do this quickly and do NOT worry if you are wrong.
2. Now go through your actual bills to fill in the actual amount and actual due date. Then complete the following:
   a. Name any bills you forgot to include in your first list.
   b. For any bill where your estimate did not match the actual values, identify how far off you were in dollars and whether your estimate was high or low.

The third part of *when* is *how close to original learning*. Because most forgetting happens right after learning, the review that helps you retain information most effectively happens close to when you first learn the material. If you can, review notes the same day you took them in class, make an organizer of important information from a text chapter shortly after you read it, or write a summary of a group study session within 24 hours of the meeting.

The final part of *when* is *when to stop*. Take a break, or go to sleep, when your body is no longer responding. Forcing yourself to study when you're not focused won't reward you with increased retention, and may in fact have detrimental effects.

Where

Where you study matters. As with time, consider your restrictions first—there may be only so many places that are available to you, close by, and open when you have study time free. Also, analyze previous study sessions to determine what places work best for you.

Many students like to study in a library. Your main library may have a variety of possibilities such as quiet rooms that don't allow talking, social areas where study groups can discuss materials, rooms where computer terminals are available for research, and so on. Also, keep in mind that many discipline-specific buildings have their own smaller libraries where you might consider spending some study time.

Dorms or other living spaces (rooms or common areas) and outdoor areas can be useful study spots. At home, find times to study when distractions are at a minimum. Explore your campus to find outdoor locations that are secluded enough to allow you to focus. An empty classroom is another great option. If you know a classroom will be unused for a period of time, it can provide a quiet space with room to spread out materials.

Every campus has a variety of study locations available. Explore outdoors and inside buildings to find your favourite spots.

Who

Some students prefer to study alone, and some in pairs or groups. Many mix it up, doing some kinds of studying (such as first reading) alone, and others (such as problem sets) with one or more people. Some find that they prefer to study certain subjects alone and others with a group. Even students who prefer to study alone might risk working with others from time to time to see what reward can result.

One final part of *who* is dealing with *who might be distracting*. Do you want to hang out with a group of friends you can see anytime, even if it compromises your ability to do well in an important course? Tell your friends why studying is important to you. Friends who truly care about you are likely to support your goals.

What and Why: Evaluating Study Materials

There is no need to study every word and bit of information. Engage your analytical thinking skills: Decide *what* is important to study by examining *why* you need to know it. Here's how:

Choose materials to study. Put away materials or notes you know you do not need to review. Looking at the notes, textbooks, and other materials left, determine what chapters or sections are important to know and why. Thinking about the "why" can increase your focus. If like Chandra you have a sense that your notes are missing key points, review them with a classmate who can help you fill in the gaps.

Prioritize materials. Determine what you need the most work on and put it first, then save easier materials for later. Almost every student has more steam at the beginning of a study session than at the end; plus, fatigue or an interruption may prevent you from covering everything.

Set specific goals. Look at what you need to cover and the time you have available, and decide what you will accomplish—for example, you will read a certain textbook chapter, review three sets of class notes, and create a study sheet. Make a list so you can check things off as you go.

How: Using Study Strategies

Now that you have figured out the *when*, *where*, *who*, *what*, and *why* of studying, focus on the *how*—the strategies that will anchor the information you need in your brain. You may already use several of them. Try as many as you can, and keep what works. Key 7.8 shows all of the strategies that follow.

Take notes on readings

Taking notes on a reading assignment helps you learn the material, because you are repeating information in writing and thinking critically about it as you decide what is important to include in your notes. Before you start, identify what goal you want your notes to achieve. Are you looking for the basic topics from a chapter? An in-depth understanding of a particular concept? Then choose a note-taking system, and keep your goal in mind as you work.

Put your notes to work

It is common to let notes sit in a notebook unread until just before midterms or finals. Even the most comprehensive, brilliant notes offer no reward if you don't refer back to them. Regularly reread your notes in batches (for example, every one or two weeks) to build your recall of information. As you reread, do the following:

- Fill in any gaps or get help with trouble spots.
- Mark up your notes by highlighting main ideas and key supporting points.
- Add recall or practice test questions in the margins.

KEY 7.8 The "how" of study success.

Use strategies for math and science

Take notes on readings

Put your notes to work

Use the information

Understand what you memorize

Use learning styles strategies

How to Study Effectively

Study during short, frequent sessions

Use audio strategies

Use flash cards

Recite, rehearse, and write

Organize the items you are processing

Use analytical thinking skills

Understand what you memorize

It sounds kind of obvious, but something that has meaning is easier to recall than something that makes little sense. This basic principle applies to everything you study. Figure out logical connections, and use these connections to help you learn. For example, in a plant biology course, memorize plants in family groups; in a history course, link events in a cause-and-effect chain.

When you have trouble remembering something new, think about how the new idea fits into what you already know. A simple example: If you can't remember what a word means, look at the word's root, prefix, or suffix. Knowing that the root *bellum* means "war" and the prefix *ante* means "before" will help you recognize that *antebellum* means "before the war."

Syda Productions/Shutterstock

Study during short, frequent sessions

You can improve your chances of remembering material if you learn it more than once. A pattern of short sessions, say three 20-minute study sessions followed by brief periods of rest, is more effective than continual studying with little or no rest. Try studying on your own or with a classmate during breaks in your schedule. Although studying between classes isn't for everyone, you may find that it can help you remember more.

In addition, scheduling regular, frequent review sessions over time will help you retain information more effectively. If you have two weeks before a test, set up study sessions three times per week instead of putting the final two days aside for hours-long study marathons.[8]

Use analytical thinking skills

Analytical, or critical, thinking encourages you to associate new information with what you already know. Imagine you have to remember information about the signing of the Treaty of Versailles, the peace settlement signed after World War I ended. How can critical thinking help?

- Recall everything that you know about the topic.
- Think about how this event is similar to other events in history.
- Consider what is different and unique about this treaty in comparison to other treaties.
- Explore the causes that led up to this event, and look at the event's effects.
- Evaluate how successful you think the treaty was.

This critical exploration makes it easier to remember the material you are studying.

Organize the items you are processing

There are a few ways to do this:

- *Divide material into manageable sections.* Master each section, put all the sections together, and then test your memory of all the material.
- *Use the chunking strategy.* Chunking increases the capacity of short-term and long-term memory. For example, while it is hard to remember these 10 digits—4808371557—it is easier to remember them in three chunks—480 837 1557. In general, try to limit groups to 10 items or fewer.
- *Use organizational tools.* Put your note-taking knowledge to work using an outline, a think link, or another tool to record material and make connections among the elements.
- *Be careful when studying more than one subject.* When studying for several tests at once, avoid studying two similar subjects back-to-back. Your memory may be more accurate when you study history after biology rather than chemistry after biology.
- *Notice what ends up in the middle, and practise it.* When you are studying, you tend to remember what you study first and last. The weak link is likely to be what you study in the middle. Knowing this, try to give this material special attention.

CHUNKING Placing disconnected information into smaller units that are easier to remember.

Recite, rehearse, and write

The more you can repeat, and the more ways you can repeat, the more likely you are to remember. Reciting, rehearsing, and writing help you diversify your repetition and maximize memory. When you *recite* material, you repeat key concepts aloud, in your own words, to aid memorization. *Rehearsing* is similar to reciting but is done silently. *Writing* is reciting on paper. Use these steps to get the greatest benefit:

- As you read, focus on central ideas. Then recite, rehearse, or write the ideas down.
- Convert each main idea into a key word, phrase, or visual image—something that is easy to recall and that will set off a chain of memories that will bring you back to the original material. Write each key word or phrase on an index card.
- One by one, look at the key words on your cards and recite, rehearse, or write all the associated information you can recall. Check your recall against the original material.

These steps are part of the process of consolidating and summarizing lecture and text notes as you study—a key study strategy you will read more about later in this chapter.

Use flash cards

Flash cards give you short, repeated review sessions that provide immediate feedback. Use the front of a 3-by-5-inch index card to write a word, idea, or phrase you want to remember, or find an online site on which you can create electronic flash cards.

KEY 7.9 Flash cards help you memorize important facts.

Theory

- Definition: Explanation for a phenomenon based on careful and precise observations
- Part of the scientific method
- Leads to hypotheses

Hypothesis

- Prediction about future behaviour that is derived from observations and theories
- Methods for testing hypotheses: case studies, naturalistic observations, and experiments

Use the back for a definition, explanation, example, and other key facts. Key 7.9 shows two flash cards used to study for a psychology exam.

Here are some suggestions for making the most of your flash cards:

- *Use the cards as a self-test.* As you go through them, divide them into two piles—the material you know and the material you are learning.
- *Carry the cards with you and review them frequently.* You'll learn the most if you start using cards early in the course, well ahead of exam time.
- *Shuffle the cards and learn the information in various orders.* This will help you avoid putting too much focus on some items and not enough on others.
- *Test yourself in both directions.* First, look at the terms and provide the definitions or explanations. Then turn the cards over and reverse the process.
- *Reduce the stack as you learn.* Eliminate cards when you know them well. As the pile shrinks, your motivation may grow. Do a final review of all the cards before the test.

Use audio strategies

Although all students can benefit from these strategies, they are especially useful if you learn best through hearing.

- *Create audio flash cards.* Record short-answer study questions by leaving 10 to 15 seconds between questions blank, so you can answer out loud. Record the correct answer after the pause to give yourself immediate feedback. For example, part of a recording for a writing class might say: "Three elements that require analysis before writing are . . . [pause] topic, audience, and purpose."
- *Use podcasts.* An increasing amount of information is presented in podcasts—knowledge segments that are downloadable to your computer or MP3 player. Ask your instructors if they intend to make any of their lectures available in podcast format.

Use learning preference strategies

Thinking about any learning preference self-assessments you have completed in this course, identify your strongest areas and locate study techniques applicable for each. For example, if you scored highly in bodily-kinesthetic learning, try reciting material aloud while standing or listening to it on an MP3 player while walking. Be open to trying something new—even if it sounds a little odd to begin with. Effective studying is about finding what works, often by any means necessary.

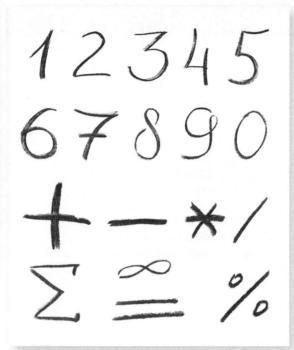

Nomad Soul/Fotolia

Use the information

In the days after you learn something new, try to use the information in every way you can. Apply it to new situations and link it to problems. Explain the material to a classmate. Test your knowledge to make sure the material is in long-term memory. "Don't confuse recognizing information with being able to recall it," says learning expert Adam Robinson. "Be sure you can recall the information without looking at your notes for clues. And don't move on until you have created some sort of sense-memory hook for calling it back up when you need it."[9]

Use strategies for math and science

Recalling what you learn in math and science courses can demand particular attention and some specific techniques.

- *Review processes and procedures.* Much of math and science involves knowing how to work through each step of a proof, a problem-solving process, or a lab experiment.
- *Do problems, problems, and more problems.* Working through problems provides examples that will help you understand concepts and formulas.
- *Work with others.* Working with one or more classmates can be particularly helpful. When the work is really tough, try to meet daily.
- *Focus on learning preferences.* Use strategies that activate your strengths. A visual learner might draw pictures to illustrate problems, and musical learners might create songs describing math concepts.

Summarize and Create Master Note Sets

Especially in the later stages of review, strategies that help you combine and condense materials provide significant reward for the extra time they require. They help you connect information in new ways and boost analytical and creative thinking, things that are especially important for essay exams.

Create a summary of reading material

When you summarize main ideas in your own words, you engage analytical thinking, considering what is important to include as well as how to organize it. Don't include your own ideas or evaluations at this point. Your summary should simply condense the material.

First, choose material to summarize—a textbook chapter, for example, or an article. Identify the main ideas and key supporting details by highlighting or annotating the material. Then, in your own words whenever possible, write down those ideas and details in a concise, cohesive way—in a paragraph or two, or perhaps in an outline or think link.

Combine class and reading notes into a master set

MASTER NOTE SET
The complete, integrated note set that contains both class and text notes.

The process of combining class and text notes enables you to see patterns and relationships among ideas, find examples for difficult concepts, and much more. It strengthens memory and offers a cohesive and comprehensive study tool, especially useful at midterm or finals time. Follow these steps to use a master note set:

Step 1: Condense down to what's important. Combine and reduce your notes so they contain only main ideas and key supporting details, such as terms, dates, formulas, and examples. Tightening and summarizing forces you to critically evaluate which

ANSWER YOUR JOURNALISTS' QUESTIONS

Complete the following on paper or in digital format.

Think about a study session you've had in the past that you believe did not prepare you well for a test, and recall what strategies you used—if any. Now, plan a study session that will take place within the next seven days—one that will help you learn something important to know for one of your current courses. Answer the questions below to create your session:

1. *When* will you study, and for how long?

2. *Where* will you study?

3. *Who* will you study with, if anyone?

4. *What* will you study?

5. *Why* is this material important to know?

6. *How* will you study it—what strategy (or strategies) do you plan to use?

7. How do you think the journalists' questions, and this structure, would have helped you get more out of your previous study session?

8. Final step—put this plan to work. Name the date you will use it.

ideas are most important. Key 7.10 shows a comprehensive outline and a reduced key term outline of the same material.

Step 2: Recite what you know. Use the terms in your combined notes as cues for reciting what you know about a topic. Make the process more active by reciting out loud during study sessions, writing your responses on paper, making flash cards, or working with a partner.

Step 3: Use critical thinking. Reflect on ideas as you review your master note set:

- Brainstorm examples from other sources that illustrate central ideas.
- Think of ideas from your readings or from class that support or clarify your notes.
- Consider what in your class notes differed from your reading notes and why.
- Apply concepts to problems at the end of text chapters or real-world situations.

Step 4: Create study sheets. This step puts your master notes in their shortest, most manageable (and portable) form. A study sheet is a one-page synthesis of all key points on one theme, topic, or process. Use critical thinking skills to organize information into themes or topics that you will need to know on an exam.

Step 5: Review and review again. To ensure learning and prepare for exams, review your condensed notes, study sheets, and critical thinking questions until you know every topic cold. Try to vary your review methods, focusing on active involvement. Recite the material to yourself, have a Q and A session with a study partner, create and take a practice test. Another helpful technique is to summarize your notes in writing from memory after you review them. This will give you a fairly good indication of your ability to recall the information on a test.

revisit RISK AND REWARD

What happened to Chandra? As Chandra says, "Sinking was not an option, so of course I had to swim." Not about to let the reward of education slip away, she found a productive risk: learning, and using, different note-taking approaches for different courses. Courses like math required focus on equations and formulas. To absorb facts and concepts for American politics, she used topic headers and bullet points underneath. Sometimes, a highlighter helped her isolate important points. Other times, she wrote down large chunks of information to help her remember it. "I had to experiment along the way," she said.

Chandra proudly graduated with her double major, and later embarked on a career in corporate communications and public relations, working as an associate producer at Black Entertainment Television (BET) and a publicist at HBO. During the 9/11 terrorist attacks, she worked as press secretary for the New Jersey Secretary of State. Today, Chandra runs her own public relations firm, Moona Inc., using listening and note-taking skills to help clients construct effective media kits. Her entrepreneurial risks have rewarded her with several high-profile clients including Simone (daughter of music icon Nina Simone), actress Samaria Graham, celebrity makeup artist Kim Baker, producer Pamm Malveaux, President Obama's Fatherhood and Mentoring Initiatives Fatherhood Buzz Tour, and Kenneth Braswell, executive director of Fathers Incorporated and director of the National Responsible Fatherhood Clearing House.

What does this mean for you? Thriving in the classroom requires patience, focus, and the ability to adapt. You might feel insignificant in a large lecture class. You might rely too heavily on technology when you would benefit more from taking down key points with pen and paper. You might find that what works in one class might not work in another. Experiment until you find the right strategies for any given course. Risk spending a week using a new strategy or technique in all of your classes to see if it suits one or more of them. Evaluate what reward you experienced in each case. If it made a positive difference for one or more classes, continue using it.

What risk may bring reward beyond your world? A career in public relations can give you the opportunity to make a difference for others, as can many career areas. Check out the websites of two companies or organizations that interest you. Read their online media kits to learn more about them. Consider the risk of pursuing work with one of them at some point, or at least see if what you read inspires you to make a difference with your career path. Finally, if you are interested in public relations, earn the reward of ground-level experience by volunteering to develop a media kit for a local business.

Courtesy of Chandra McQueen

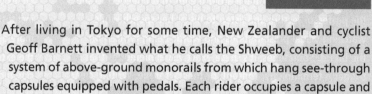

GLOBAL RISK AND REWARD

foxroar/123RF

After living in Tokyo for some time, New Zealander and cyclist Geoff Barnett invented what he calls the Shweeb, consisting of a system of above-ground monorails from which hang see-through capsules equipped with pedals. Each rider occupies a capsule and propels him- or herself by pedaling as though on a recumbent bike. The prototype was built in Rotorua, New Zealand. Barnett's risk has already earned him the reward of a $1 million prize from Google in recognition of the Shweeb's potential to address transportation issues in crowded urban areas.[10]

Vinzenz Weidenhofer/123RF

RISK ACTION
FOR POST-SECONDARY, CAREER, AND LIFE REWARDS

KNOW IT
Blan-k/Shutterstock

WRITE IT
Blan-k/Shutterstock

WORK IT
Blan-k/Shutterstock

Left to Right: pio3/Shutterstock;
Viktor Gladkov/123RF;
MP_P/Shutterstock

Complete the following on paper or in digital format.

KNOW IT *Think Critically*

Evaluate Your Memory

Build basic skills. For each of these classifications of information in long-term memory, write down an example from your personal experience:

- *Episodic memory (events).* Example: I remember the first time I conducted an experiment in chemistry class.
- *Declarative memory (facts).* Example: I know that the electoral college must vote before a new U.S. president is officially elected.
- *Procedural memory (motion).* Example: I know how to type without looking at the keyboard.

Take it to the next level. Answer the following:

1. Which type of information (events, facts, motion) is easiest for you to remember? Why?
2. Which type of information is hardest for you to remember? Why?

Move toward mastery. Address the type of information that you said you find most difficult to remember.

1. Name an example, from your life, of some information in this category that you need to be able to recall and use.
2. Name two actions from the chapter that you believe will help you strengthen it.
3. Now use both during your next study session. Afterward, identify the one that worked best.

WRITE IT *Communicate*

Emotional intelligence journal: How feelings connect study success. Think about how you were feeling at times when you were most able to recall and use information in a high-stress situation—a test, a workplace challenge, a group presentation. What thought, action, or situation put you in this productive mindset that helped you succeed? Did you go for a run, talk to your best friend, take 30 minutes for yourself? Create a list of thoughts or actions you can call on when you will want the best possible outcome from your studying efforts.

Real-life writing: Combining class and text notes. Choose a course for which you have a test coming up in the next four weeks. Create a master set of notes for that course that combines one week's classes and reading assignments (make sure it is material you need to know for your test). Your goal is to summarize and connect all the important information covered during the period.

WORK IT *Build Your Brand*

Memory and Networking

Your ability to remember people you meet or interact with in the workplace—their names, what they do, other relevant information about them—is an enormous factor in your career success.

Consider this scenario: You are introduced to your supervisor's new boss, someone who could help you advance in the company, and you both exchange small talk for a few minutes. A week later you run into him outside the building. What if you greet him by name and ask if his son is over the case of the flu he had? You have made a good impression that is likely to help you in the future. What if you call him by the wrong name, realize your mistake, and slink off to work? You've set up a bit of a hurdle for yourself as you try to get ahead.

With what you know about memory strategies and what works for you, set up a system to record and retain information about people you meet whom you want to remember. For your system, decide on a tool (address book, set of notecards, electronic organizer, computer file), what to record (name, phone, email, title, how you met, important details), and how you will update. Choose a tool that you are most likely to use and that will be easy for you to refer to and update.

1. Name your tool of choice.
2. List the information you will record for each entry.
3. Describe when you will record information and how often you will check/update it.

Finally, get started by putting in information for all of the people you consider to be important networking contacts at this point. These could be family, friends, instructors and advisors, or work colleagues and supervisors. Make this the start of a database that will serve you throughout your career.

The best test preparation is learning, because the goal of a test is to see what you have learned. As you attend class, work on assignments, and participate in discussions, you become ever more ready to succeed in testing situations.

Test Taking

HOW CAN YOU SHOW WHAT YOU KNOW?

What Would You Risk? *Suzanne Malveaux*

Courtesy of Suzanne Malveaux

THINK ABOUT THIS SITUATION AS YOU READ, AND CONSIDER WHAT ACTION YOU WOULD TAKE. THIS CHAPTER HELPS YOU USE PREPARATION, PERSISTENCE, AND STRATEGY TO CONQUER TEST ANXIETY, SHOW WHAT YOU KNOW, AND LEARN FROM TEST MISTAKES.

Suzanne Malveaux (pronounced mal-VOH) grew up as a social, ambitious child in a family of achievers. Although she loved school, Suzanne struggled with stuttering—an issue that would seem to rule out a future in front of a television camera. "I wasn't aware of it until kindergarten or first grade," she says. "They took me out of class and put me in a speech class for stutterers."

To add to this test of her will, Suzanne needed support in reading and math in her early elementary years and scored low on standardized testing. In Grade 5, something finally clicked for Suzanne. She began to soak up learning like a sponge and joined her twin sister in the gifted and talented program. She excelled in high school and kept up the momentum in her post-secondary career, graduating cum laude in sociology from Harvard before earning a master's in journalism from Columbia.

Her first real job was with the Boston-based New England Cable News Channel. She remembers well her first "test" in the workforce—her on-camera debut covering a crime as a general assignment reporter. Overcome with nerves at the risk of doing her first live shot, Suzanne trembled as the cameras rolled. "You could see the microphone going back and forth from my shaking," she says. "After I was done I thought for sure I was going to get fired. They had hired me for my potential. I had travelled overseas, I had done documentaries, I was highly motivated, but they had taken a big chance on me."

To be continued . . .

FACING LIFE TESTS TAUGHT SUZANNE THAT THE VALUE OF TEST-TAKING SKILLS EXTENDS FAR BEYOND THE CLASSROOM. WHATEVER YOUR TESTS, IN SCHOOL AND ELSEWHERE, YOU WILL NEED SKILL AND FORTITUDE TO PASS THEM. YOU'LL LEARN MORE ABOUT SUZANNE, AND THE REWARD RESULTING FROM HER ACTIONS, WITHIN THE CHAPTER.

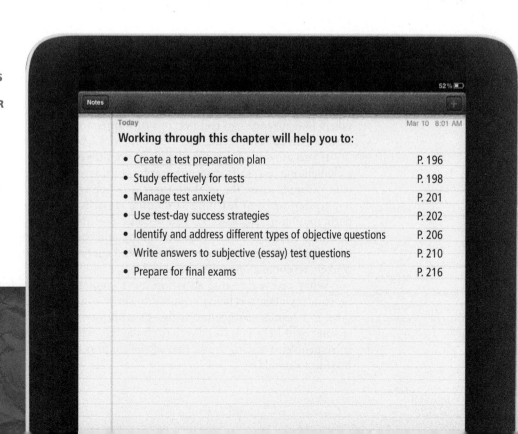

Notes

Today   Mar 10 8:01 AM

Working through this chapter will help you to:

status CHECK

How Prepared Are You for Taking Tests?

For each statement, fill in the number that best describes how often it applies to you.

1 = never   2 = seldom   3 = sometimes   4 = often   5 = always

1. I use strategies to help me predict what will be on tests.	① ② ③ ④ ⑤
2. I actively prepare and review before taking exams.	① ② ③ ④ ⑤
3. I do anything to avoid cramming.	① ② ③ ④ ⑤
4. When I recognize signs of test anxiety, I use relaxation methods to calm down.	① ② ③ ④ ⑤
5. I read test directions before beginning.	① ② ③ ④ ⑤
6. I use certain strategies to answer questions for which I'm unsure of the answers.	① ② ③ ④ ⑤
7. I don't think cheating is worth the price.	① ② ③ ④ ⑤
8. I know the difference between objective and subjective questions and how to answer each.	① ② ③ ④ ⑤
9. I look for action verbs when answering essay questions.	① ② ③ ④ ⑤
10. I learn from my testing mistakes and actively grow from them.	① ② ③ ④ ⑤

Each of the topics in these statements is covered in this chapter. Note those statements for which you fill in a 3 or lower. Skim the chapter to see where those topics appear, and pay special attention to them as you read, learn, and apply new strategies.

REMEMBER: NO MATTER HOW PREPARED YOU ARE FOR TAKING TESTS, YOU CAN IMPROVE WITH EFFORT AND PRACTICE.

WHAT WILL GET YOU READY TO
perform well on tests?

Testing is one of the unavoidable realities of education, and even seasoned test-takers like Suzanne can feel nervous or unprepared when faced with a new test. Many students dread tests, seeing them as roadblocks, contests, or insurmountable obstacles.

If you are one of these students, or even if you are just occasionally thrown off by a challenging test, shift your mindset by considering this idea: The best test preparation is *learning*, because the goal of a test is to see what you have learned. As you do the day-to-day work of learning (attending class, working on assignments and projects, participating in discussions), you become ever more ready to succeed in testing situations. Re-envision the risk you are taking and the reward you seek. If learning is your reward and you are willing to risk time and energy to earn it, effective test performance is likely to come along with the package.

What makes a testing situation more challenging than demonstrating knowledge on your own terms is being required to show what you know during a preset period of time, in a certain setting, and with—or without—particular tools. The strategies in this chapter will help you handle that challenge. Remember, test taking prepares you to solve problems and to think, two of the Employability Skills listed by The Conference Board of Canada.[1]

MyLab Student Success
(www.mystudentsuccesslab.com) is an online solution designed to help you "Start Strong, Finish Stronger" by building skills for ongoing personal and professional development.

Identify Test Type, Topics, and Study Materials

As the saying goes, forewarned is forearmed. Before you begin studying, find out about the test. Investigate the following:

- *Types of questions.* Will the questions be objective (multiple choice with only one correct answer, multiple choice with more than one correct answer, true–false, sentence completion), subjective (essay), or a combination?
- *Test logistics.* What is the date, time, and location of the test? Is it an in-class or a take-home exam? Will you complete it in person or online?
- *Supplemental information and tools.* Is the test open book (meaning you can use your class text), open note (meaning you can use any notes you've taken), both, or neither? Can you use a graphing calculator or any other tool?
- *Value of the test.* All tests are not created equal in terms of how they affect your final course grade. For example, a quiz is generally not as important as a midterm or final. Plan and prioritize your study time and energy according to the value of the quiz or test.

Part of successful test preparation is knowing when to stop. To avoid overload, study in shorter segments over a period of time, and get the sleep you need before test day.

Pressmaster/Fotolia

Don't be fooled into thinking that online tests and open-book tests are easier than traditional tests in the classroom. In reality, the fact that you have access to resources usually leads instructors to create challenging tests that require more critical thinking. Prepare as you would for any other test if you want a successful result.

How can you predict what will be on a test? First, read your syllabus and talk to your instructor to get a clear idea of the topics that will be covered and the material (text chapters, readings, lectures, and so on) that you will be tested on. Furthermore:

- *Use your textbook.* Check features such as summaries, vocabulary terms, and study questions for clues about what's important to remember.
- *Listen at review sessions.* Many instructors offer review sessions before midterms and finals. Bring your questions to these sessions and listen to the questions others ask.
- *Talk to your instructor in person.* Spending a few minutes talking about the test one on one may clarify misunderstandings and help you focus on what to study.
- *Get information from people who already took the course.* Try to get a sense of test difficulty, whether tests focus primarily on assigned readings or class notes, what materials are usually covered, and the types of questions that are asked.
- *Examine old tests, if the instructor makes them available.* You may find old tests in class, online, or on reserve in the library.

Also, your practical thinking skills will help you learn from experience. After taking the first exam in a course, you will have a better idea of what to expect over the rest of the term.

Finally, knowing what will be covered on the test; decide what to study.

- *Sort through materials.* Go through your notes, texts, related primary sources, and handouts. Choose what you need to study, and set aside materials you don't need.
- *Prioritize materials.* Arrange your chosen materials in order of priority so that you focus the bulk of your time on the information you most need to understand.

When you have figured out your topics and materials, time management and goal-setting skills will allow you to use them to the best of your ability.

Manage Your Study Time and Goals

Want to be as ready as possible for a test? Don't wait until the night before to study for it, and don't assume that paying attention during class time is enough. The most effective studying takes place in consistent segments over time. Use time management skills to lay out a study schedule.

- *Consider relevant factors.* Note the number of days until the test, when in your days you have time available, and how much material you have to cover.
- *Schedule a series of study sessions.* If you need to, define what materials you will focus on for each session.
- *Enter study sessions in your planner.* Do this ahead of time, just as you would for class, work, or any other important appointment. Then stick to your commitment.

Your goal-setting skills are likewise essential to test success. Make getting ready for a test a SMART goal by making it:

- *Specific.* Get clear on what you need to study.
- *Measurable.* Acknowledge when you accomplish each study session.
- *Achievable.* Stay up-to-date with coursework so that you have knowledge you can use.
- *Realistic.* Give yourself enough time and resources to get the job done.
- *Time frame.* Anchor each step toward the test in your schedule.

To work SMART, try using a comprehensive study plan like the one in Key 8.1. Consider making several copies and filling one out for each major test you have this term. Alternately, you can create your own version by modifying Key 8.1 according to your specific needs. Format your version on a computer so that you can print out copies.

Review Using Study Strategies

Put your plan and schedule to work. Use what you have learned about learning, thinking, reading, memory, and studying during this course to understand and remember material.

- *Think analytically.* Exams often ask you to analyze and apply material in more depth than you experienced in high school. For example, your history instructor may ask you to place a primary source in its historical context. Prepare by continually asking analytical thinking questions and using the higher levels of Bloom's taxonomy.
- *Use SQ3R.* This reading method provides an excellent structure for reviewing your reading materials.
- *Consider your learning preferences.* Use study strategies that engage your strengths. When necessary, incorporate strategies that boost your areas of challenge.
- *Remember your best settings.* Use the locations, times, and company that suit you best.
- *Employ specific study strategies.* Consider your favourites. Use flash cards, audio strategies, chunking, or anything else that suits you and the material (see pages 182–186).
- *Create mnemonic devices.* These work exceptionally well for remembering lists or groups of items. Use mnemonics that make what you review stick.
- *Actively review your combined class and text notes.* Summaries and master sets of combined text and class notes provide comprehensive study tools.
- *Make and take a pretest.* Use end-of-chapter text questions to create a pretest. If your course doesn't have a text, develop questions from notes, assigned readings, and old homework problems. Some texts provide a website with online activities and pretests to help you review. Answer questions under test-like conditions—in a quiet place, with no books or notes (unless the exam is open book), and with a clock to tell you when to quit.

KEY 8.1 Prepare for a test.

Complete the following checklist for each exam to define your study goals, get organized, and stay on track:

Course: _____ Instructor: _____

Date, time, and place of test: _____

Type of test (Is it a midterm or a minor quiz?): _____

What instructor said about the test, including types of test questions, test length, and how much the test counts toward your final grade:

_____

_____

Topics to be covered on the test, in order of importance (information should also come from your instructor):

1. _____

2. _____

3. _____

4. _____

5. _____

Study schedule, including materials you plan to study (texts, class notes, homework problems, and so forth) and dates you plan to complete each:

Material	Completion Date
1. _____	_____
2. _____	_____
3. _____	_____
4. _____	_____
5. _____	_____

Materials you are expected to bring to the test (textbook, sourcebook, calculator, and so on):

_____

_____

_____

Special study arrangements (such as planning study group meeting, asking the instructor for special help, getting outside tutoring):

_____

_____

_____

Life-management issues (such as rearranging work hours):

_____

_____

_____

Source: Adapted from Fry, Ron. "Ace" Any Test, 3rd ed., Franklin Lakes, NJ: Career Press, 1996, pp. 123–124.

Test Taking

get creative

WRITE YOUR OWN TEST

Astroid/123RF

Complete the following on paper or in digital format.

Create a pretest that helps you prepare for a specific upcoming test in one of your courses. Use the tips in this chapter to predict the material that will be covered, the types of questions that will be asked (multiple choice, essay, and so on), and the nature of the questions (a broad overview of the material or specific details). Then be creative. Write interesting questions that tap into what you have learned and make you think about the material in different ways. Go through the following steps:

1. Create your questions on paper or in a digital file.

2. Use what you created as a pretest. Set up test-like conditions—a quiet, timed environment—and see how you do.

3. Evaluate your pretest answers against your notes and the text. How did you do?

4. Finally, after you take the actual exam, evaluate whether you think this exercise improved your performance. Would you use this technique again? Why or why not?.

Prepare Physically

Your brain is an organ in your body, and like other organs, it works best when you are taking care of yourself. First of all, get some sleep—at the very least the night before the exam, and ideally for a few nights beforehand. Sleep improves your ability to remember what you studied before you went to bed. By contrast, research has shown that sleep deprivation, which is rampant among college and university students, results in lower levels of recall, impaired contextual memory (you remember a fact but can't recall how it connects to other information), and a decrease in cognitive performance.[2] Taking a test while sleep deprived can be compared to driving drunk; although it may not endanger your life, it involves a similar level of impairment and is likely to bring unwanted consequences.

Eating a light, well-balanced meal that is high in protein (eggs, milk, yogurt, meat and fish, or nuts) will keep you full longer than carbohydrates (breads, candy, and pastries). Keep some high-energy foods such as peanut butter, energy bars, or bananas in your room so that you can grab something when you can't get to your habitual meal spot before a test.

Cram if You Must

Cramming—studying intensively and around the clock right before an exam—often results in information popping out of your head as soon as the exam is over. If learning is your goal, cramming will not help you reach it. The reality, however, is that almost every student crams for tests from time to time. Sometimes you just end up in a time crunch; sometimes you don't use your planner effectively and get caught by surprise; sometimes anxiety may lead you to avoid studying. Use these hints to make the most of last-minute study time:

- *Focus on crucial concepts.* Summarize the most important points and try to resist reviewing notes or texts page by page.
- *Create a last-minute study sheet to review right before the test.* Write down key facts, definitions, and formulas on a single sheet of paper or on flash cards.
- *Arrive early.* Review your study aids until you are asked to clear your desk.

After your exam, step back and evaluate your performance. Did cramming help, or did it load your mind with disconnected details? Did it increase or decrease anxiety at test time? If you find that in a few days you remember very little, know that this will work against you in advanced courses and careers that build on this knowledge. Plan to start studying earlier next time.

HOW CAN YOU

A *manage test anxiety?*

A moderate amount of stress can make you alert, ready to act, and geared up to do your best. Some students, however, experience incapacitating stress before and during exams, especially midterms and finals. *Test anxiety* can cause sweating, nausea, dizziness, headaches, and fatigue. It can reduce concentration and cause you to go blank when trying to recall information. Sufferers may get lower grades because their performance does not reflect what they know or because their fear has affected their ability to prepare effectively.

Two Sources of Test Anxiety

Test anxiety has two different sources, and students may experience one or both:[3]

- *Lack of preparation:* Not having put in the work to build knowledge of the material
- *Dislike of testing situations:* Being nervous about a test because of its very nature

For anxiety that stems from being unprepared, the answer is straightforward: Get prepared. All of the information in this chapter about creating and implementing a study plan and schedule is designed to give you the best possible chance of doing well on the test. If you are able to stay calm when you feel ready for a test, effective preparation is your key test anxiety strategy.

Unfortunately, being prepared doesn't necessarily ensure confidence. For students who dread the event no matter how prepared they are, having a test—any test—causes anxiety. Because testing is unavoidable, this anxiety is more challenging to manage. Such students need to shift their mindset and build a positive attitude that says: "I know this material and I'm ready to show it," although this is often easier said than done. Personal or situational factors may also increase the challenge, as Suzanne found out when she worked through stuttering (a personal factor) and experienced her first time on camera (a situational factor).

Anxiety is defined as an emotional disturbance, meaning that it tends to be based on an imagined risk rather than an actual one, and often leads you away from your goals rather than toward them.[4] If you experience test anxiety, analyze your situation to build a more realistic view of your risk and get back on track toward your goal of test success:

- Reconceive the negative risk and costly result you think you are facing, looking at the risk in a positive sense with a focus on the potential reward. Downplay the negative by considering the possibility that you may be more prepared than you realize, or that the test is not as important as it seems, or not as difficult as you believe it to be.
- Define your goal for this test. Identify the physical and mental issues affecting your ability to reach that goal, and see which of them you can attribute to your anxiety.

Courtesy of Sarah Lyman Kravits

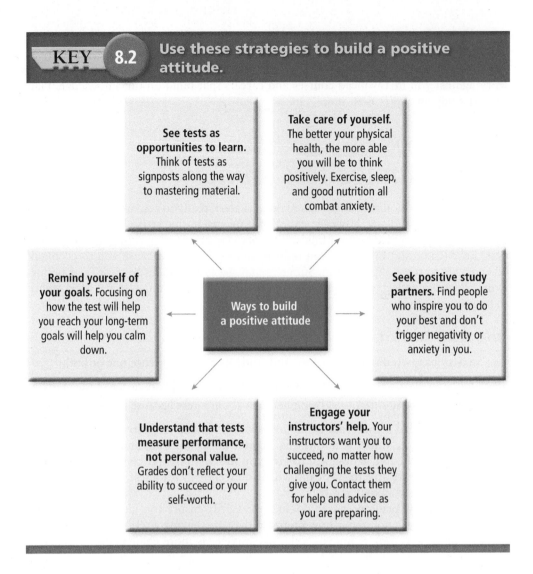

KEY 8.2 Use these strategies to build a positive attitude.

See tests as opportunities to learn. Think of tests as signposts along the way to mastering material.

Take care of yourself. The better your physical health, the more able you will be to think positively. Exercise, sleep, and good nutrition all combat anxiety.

Remind yourself of your goals. Focusing on how the test will help you reach your long-term goals will help you calm down.

Ways to build a positive attitude

Seek positive study partners. Find people who inspire you to do your best and don't trigger negativity or anxiety in you.

Understand that tests measure performance, not personal value. Grades don't reflect your ability to succeed or your self-worth.

Engage your instructors' help. Your instructors want you to succeed, no matter how challenging the tests they give you. Contact them for help and advice as you are preparing.

- Build a realistic, positive, and productive attitude that says "I know this material and I'm ready to show it." Key 8.2 provides several ways to do this.
- Assess your level of anxiety around test-taking situations. Use the test anxiety assessment on page 203 to determine if you have anxiety that preparation alone cannot eliminate.

Calm and Focus Your Mind at Test Time

It's test time, and you have arrived at the testing location (ideally a few minutes early) and you are waiting for the cue to begin. How can you be calm and focused? These strategies may help.

Manage your environment. Make a conscious effort to sit away from students who might distract you. If it helps, listen to relaxing music on an MP3 player while waiting for class to begin.

Reassure yourself with positive self-talk. Tell yourself that you can do well and that it is normal to feel anxious, particularly before an important exam.

Write down your feelings. Researchers have found that if students take a few minutes before an exam to put their feelings in writing, they post higher grades and have less anxiety. Without worrying about the quality of your writing, express your fears and

get practical

Diego Cervo/
Shutterstock

binkski/123RF

ASSESS TEST ANXIETY WITH THE WESTSIDE TEST ANXIETY SCALE

The first step toward becoming a fearless test-taker is understanding your personal level of test anxiety. Answer the questions below as honestly as possible.

Rate how true each of the following is of you, from extremely or always true, to not at all or never true. Use the following 5 point scale. Circle your answers.

1 = never true   2 = seldom true   3 = sometimes true   4 = usually true   5 = always true

1. The closer I am to a major exam, the harder it is for me to concentrate on the material.	1 2 3 4 5
2. When I study for my exams, I worry that I will not remember the material on the exam.	1 2 3 4 5
3. During important exams, I think that I am doing awful or that I may fail.	1 2 3 4 5
4. I lose focus on important exams, and I cannot remember material that I knew before the exam.	1 2 3 4 5
5. I finally remember the answer to exam questions after the exam is already over.	1 2 3 4 5
6. I worry so much before a major exam that I am too worn out to do my best on the exam.	1 2 3 4 5
7. I feel out of sorts or not really myself when I take important exams.	1 2 3 4 5
8. I find that my mind sometimes wanders when I am taking important exams.	1 2 3 4 5
9. After an exam, I worry about whether I did well enough.	1 2 3 4 5
10. I struggle with written assignments, or avoid doing them, because I want them to be perfect.	1 2 3 4 5

Sum of the 10 questions _____.

Now divide the sum by 10. Write it here _____. This is your test anxiety score.

Compare your score against the scale below. How does your level of test anxiety rate? In general, students who score a 3.0 or higher on the scale tend to have more test anxiety than normal and may benefit from seeking additional assistance.

1.0–1.9   Comfortably low test anxiety

2.0–2.5   Normal or average test anxiety

2.5–2.9   High normal test anxiety

3.0–3.4   Moderately high (some items rated 4)

3.5–3.9   High test anxiety (half or more of the items rated 4)

4.0–5.0   Extremely high anxiety (items rated 4 and 5)

Reflect on your results. Are you considered to have high levels of test anxiety? Normal levels? On paper or in a digital file, write a paragraph describing your anxiety-management plan for your next test using what you've learned about yourself and test anxiety-reducing strategies.

Source: "Westside Test Anxiety Scale" from Test Anxiety Instrument by Richard Driscoll. Copyright © 2004 by Richard Driscoll, Ph.D. Used by permission of Richard Driscoll.

Test Taking

anxieties about the test on a piece of paper or your computer. "It's almost as if you empty the fears out of your mind," says researcher and psychology professor Sian Beilock.[5]

Practice relaxation. Close your eyes, breathe deeply and slowly, and visualize positive mental images like finishing the test confidently. Or, try a more physical tensing-and-relaxing method:[6]

1. Put your feet flat on the floor.
2. With your hands, grab underneath the chair.
3. Push down with your feet and pull up on your chair at the same time for about five seconds.
4. Relax for five to ten seconds.
5. Repeat the procedure two or three times.
6. Relax all your muscles except the ones that are actually used to take the test.

Bring a special object. If an object has special meaning for you—a photograph, a stone or crystal, a wristband, a piece of jewelry, a hat—it may provide comfort at test time. Bring it along and hold it, look at it, or wear it during the test. Let its presence settle and inspire you.

Some of these strategies may seem odd or embarrassing. However, they might also make a difference for you. Consider whether you are willing to risk a little embarassment for the reward of doing well on a test. It just might be worth it.

HOW CAN YOU DO YOUR
best on test day?

When it's time to show what you know, these general strategies can help you handle almost any type of test, including short-answer and essay exams.

Test Day Strategies

Choose the right seat. Find a seat that will help you maximize focus and minimize distractions. Know yourself—for many students, it's better to avoid sitting near friends.

Courtesy of Suzanne Malveaux

talk risk and reward . . .

Risk asking tough questions to be rewarded with new insights. Use the following questions to inspire discussion with classmates, either in person or online.

- What did you learn about yourself from the test anxiety questionnaire? If you experience test anxiety, what effect do you think it will have on your future?

- Which suggestions for reducing test anxiety are you likely to use? How do you think they will help you feel more comfortable at test time? What other risks, however small, might reward you with better test performance?

CONSIDER THE CASE: Do you have any personal factors that cause anxiety, as Suzanne did when she struggled with stuttering? Do you have any situational factors, such as Suzanne's first time reporting on camera? What risks can you take to manage these factors in a way that brings rewards?

Write down key facts. Before you even look at the test, write down key information, including formulas, rules, and definitions, that you don't want to forget. (Use the back of the question sheet so your instructor knows that you made these notes after the test began.)

Start with the big picture. Scan the questions—how many in each section, types, difficulty, point values—and use what you learn to schedule your time. For example, if for a two-hour test you think the writing section will take you more time than the short-answer section, you can budget an hour and a quarter for the essays and 45 minutes for the short-answer questions.

Directions count, so read them. Reading test directions carefully can save you trouble. For example, you may be required to answer only one of three essay questions; you may also be told that you will be penalized for incorrect responses to short-answer questions.

Mark up the questions. Mark up instructions and key words to avoid careless errors. Circle qualifiers such as *always, never, all, none, sometimes,* and *every;* verbs that communicate specific instructions; and concepts that are tricky or need special attention.

Be precise when taking a machine-scored test. Use the right pencil (usually a #2) on machine-scored tests, and mark your answer in the correct space, filling it completely. Periodically, check the answer number against the question number to make sure they match.

Work from easy to hard. Begin with the easiest questions and answer them quickly but accurately. This will boost your confidence and leave more time for harder questions. Mark tough questions as you reach them, and return to them after answering the questions you know.

Stay aware of time. Wear a watch so you don't have to wonder if the room has a working clock (although mobile phones have the time, you may not be permitted to have your phone in view during the test). Try not to rush. If you finish early, take time to check over your work. If, on the other hand, you are falling behind, make focused choices about how to use the remaining time.

Take a strategic approach to questions you cannot answer. Even if you are well prepared, you may face questions you do not understand or cannot answer. Key 8.3 has ideas to consider.

Use particular techniques for math tests. In addition to these general test-taking strategies, the techniques in Key 8.4 can help you achieve better results on math exams.

Maintain Academic Integrity

While cheating has the immediate gain of possibly passing a test or at the least getting a few answers right, its long-term consequences aren't so beneficial. If you cheat, you may be caught and disciplined (with consequences that can go as far as expulsion). Furthermore, cheating that goes on your record can damage your ability to get a job.

In recent years, cheating has become high-tech, with students putting all kinds of devices to dishonest uses. Examples include:[7]

- Texting answers from cell phones or smartphones
- Using in-phone cameras to take pictures of tests to send to friends or sell online
- Using graphing calculators to save formulas that were supposed to have been memorized
- With an internet connection, finding answers on crowd-sourcing sites such as Quora
- Sharing answers on private all-student groups connected to social media platforms

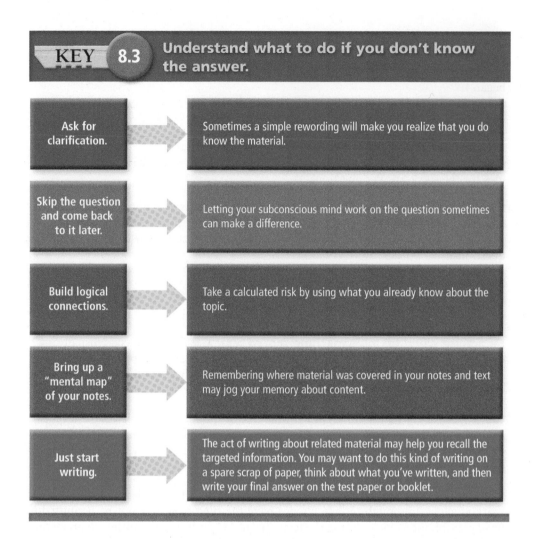

KEY 8.3 Understand what to do if you don't know the answer.

Ask for clarification.	Sometimes a simple rewording will make you realize that you do know the material.
Skip the question and come back to it later.	Letting your subconscious mind work on the question sometimes can make a difference.
Build logical connections.	Take a calculated risk by using what you already know about the topic.
Bring up a "mental map" of your notes.	Remembering where material was covered in your notes and text may jog your memory about content.
Just start writing.	The act of writing about related material may help you recall the targeted information. You may want to do this kind of writing on a spare scrap of paper, think about what you've written, and then write your final answer on the test paper or booklet.

Because this type of cheating can be difficult to discover when exams are administered in large lecture halls, some instructors ban all electronic devices from the room.

Valid concerns can put students under pressure: "I have to do well on the final. I am in a constant time crunch. I need a good grade to qualify for the next course in my major. I can't fail because I'm already in debt and I have to graduate and get a job." Compounded, these worries can often drive students to thoughts of academic dishonesty. However, feeling the drive to cheat generally means you haven't learned the material. Ask yourself: Am I in post-secondary school to learn information that I can use? Or to cheat my way to a decent GPA and breathe a sigh of relief when the term is done? If you aim to complete future coursework and to thrive in a job that requires you to use what you've learned, cheating will not move you toward that goal.

Remember that there is often more than one solution to the problem, and that every possible solution has potential positive and negative effects. Your decisions will have lasting impacts on your future and your life. The risk of cheating may bring a starkly different reward than the risk of staying honest even in the face of a lack of preparation. The next time you are tempted to break the rules of academic integrity, remember: The choice is yours, and so are the consequences.

Handling Objective Questions

Every type of test question has a different way of finding out how much you know. First, look at *objective questions*. Objective questions generally have you choose or write a short answer, often selecting from a limited number of choices. They can include multiple-choice, fill-in-the-blank, matching, and true-or-false questions.

Read through the exam first. When you receive an exam, read through every problem quickly and make notes on how you might attempt to solve the problems.

Analyze problems carefully. Categorize problems according to type. Take the "givens" into account, and write down any formulas, theorems, or definitions that apply. Focus on what you want to find or prove.

Estimate to come up with a "ballpark" solution. Then work the problem and check the solution against your estimate. The two answers should be close. If they're not, recheck your calculations.

Break the calculation into the smallest possible pieces. Go step by step and don't move on to the next step until you are clear about what you've done so far.

Recall how you solved similar problems. Past experience can provide valuable clues.

Draw a picture to help you see the problem. Visual images such as a diagram, chart, probability tree, or geometric figure may help clarify your thinking.

Be neat. Sloppy numbers can mean the difference between a right and a wrong answer. A 4 that looks like a 9 will be marked wrong.

Use the opposite operation to check your work. Work backward from your answer to see if you are right.

Look back at the question to be sure you did everything. Did you answer every part of the question? Did you show all required work?

Probably the most important objective question strategy is an obvious one: Know your material! If you haven't studied, all of the tricks in the world won't help you ace the test. However, if you arrive at the test with a fairly solid baseline of knowledge, the following strategies will help you handle the different ways that a test can ask you to show it.

As you review the sample questions in the following section, look also at the Multiple Intelligence Strategies for Test Preparation on page 208. Harness the strategies that fit your learning strengths to prepare for exams. Note that some suggestions are repeated in the following sections, in order to reinforce the importance of these suggestions and their application to different types of test questions.

Multiple-choice questions

Multiple-choice questions, in which you read a question "stem" (a complete or partial question) and choose the most likely response or completion, are the most popular type of question on standardized tests. The following strategies will help you choose as effectively as possible:

- *Read the directions carefully and try to think of the answer before looking at the choices.* Then read the choices and make your selection.
- *Underline key words and phrases.* If the question is complicated, try to break it down into small sections that are easy to understand.
- *Make sure you read every word of every answer.* Focus especially on qualifying words such as *always, never, tend to, most, often,* and *frequently.* Look also for negatives in a question ("Which of the following is *not* . . . ").
- *When questions are linked to a reading passage, read the questions first.* This will help you focus on the information you need to answer the questions.

multiple intelligence strategies

FOR TEST PREPARATION

Describe an upcoming exam (date, course, exam type): _____.
In the right-hand column, record specific ideas for how MI strategies can help you prepare for it.

INTELLIGENCE		USE MI STRATEGIES TO IMPROVE TEST PREPARATION	IDENTIFY MI TEST-PREP STRATEGIES THAT CAN HELP YOU PREPARE
Verbal-Linguistic		• Write test questions your instructor might ask. Answer the questions and then try rewriting them in a different format (essay, true/false, and so on). • Underline important words in review or practice questions.	
Logical-Mathematical		• Logically connect what you are studying with what you know. Consider similarities, differences, and cause-and-effect relationships. • Draw charts that show relationships and analyze trends.	
Bodily-Kinesthetic		• Use text highlighting to take a hands-on approach to studying. • Create a sculpture, model, or skit to depict a tough concept that will be on the test.	
Visual-Spatial		• Make charts, diagrams, or think links illustrating concepts. • Make drawings related to possible test topics.	
Interpersonal		• Form a study group to prepare for your test. • In your group, come up with possible test questions. Then use the questions to test each other's knowledge.	
Intrapersonal		• Apply concepts to your own life; think about how you would manage. • Brainstorm test questions and then take the sample "test" you developed.	
Musical		• Recite text concepts to rhythms or write a song to depict them. • Explore relevant musical links to reading material.	
Naturalistic		• Try to notice similarities and differences in objects and concepts by organizing your study materials into relevant groupings.	

The following examples show the kinds of multiple-choice questions you might encounter in an introductory psychology course (the correct answer follows each question):

1. Although you know that alcohol is a central nervous system depressant, your friend says it is actually a stimulant because he does things that he wouldn't otherwise do after having a couple of drinks. He also feels less inhibited, more spontaneous, and more entertaining. The reason your friend experiences alcohol as a stimulant is that:

   a. alcohol has the same effect on the nervous system as amphetamines.
   b. alcohol has a strong placebo effect.
   c. the effects of alcohol depend almost entirely on the expectations of the user.
   d. alcohol depresses areas in the brain responsible for critical judgment and impulsiveness.

   (answer: d)

2. John drinks five or six cups of strong coffee each day. Which of the following symptoms is he most likely to report?

   a. nausea, loss of appetite, cold hands, and chills
   b. feelings of euphoria and well-being
   c. anxiety, headaches, insomnia, and diarrhea
   d. time distortion and reduced emotional sensitivity

   (answer: c)

Source: Morris, Charles G.; Maisto, Albert A., *Understanding Psychology,* 10th Ed., p. 145. ©2013. Reprinted and Electronically reproduced by permission of Pearson Education, Inc., New York, NY.

True-or-false questions

Read true-or-false questions carefully to evaluate what they are asking. Look for absolute qualifiers (such as *all, only,* and *always* that often make an otherwise true statement false) and conservative qualifiers (*generally, often, usually,* and *sometimes* that often make an otherwise false statement true). For example, "The grammar rule 'I before E except after C' is *always* true" is false, whereas "The grammar rule 'I before E except after C' is *usually* true" is true.

Be sure to read *every* word of a true-or-false-question to avoid jumping to an incorrect conclusion. Common problems in reading too quickly include missing negatives (*not, no*) that would change your response, and deciding on an answer before reading the complete statement.

Marekuliasz/Shutterstock

The following examples show the kinds of true–false questions you might encounter in an introductory psychology course (the correct answer follows each question):

Indicate whether the following statements are true (T) or false (F):

1. Alcohol is implicated in more than two-thirds of all automobile accidents.   *(true)*

2. Caffeine is not addictive.   *(false)*

3. Recurring hallucinations are common among users of hallucinogens.   *(true)*

4. Marijuana interferes with short-term memory.   *(true)*

Source: Morris, Charles G.; Maisto, Albert A., *Understanding Psychology,* 10th Ed., p. 145. ©2013. Reprinted and Electronically reproduced by permission of Pearson Education, Inc., New York, NY.

Matching questions

Matching questions ask you to match the terms in one list with the terms in another list. For example, the directions may tell you to match a communicable disease with the microorganism that usually causes it. The following strategies will help you handle these questions.

- *Make sure you understand the directions.* The directions tell you whether each answer can be used only once (common practice) or more than once.
- *Work from the column with the longest entries.* The column on the left usually contains terms to be defined or questions to be answered, while the column on the right has definitions or answers. As a result, entries on the right are usually longer than those on the left. Reading those items only once will save time.
- *Start with the matches you know.* On your first run through, pencil in these matches.
- *Finally, tackle the matches of which you're not sure.* Think back to your class lectures, text notes, and study sessions as you try to visualize the correct response. If one or more phrases seem to have no correct answer and you can use answers only once, consider the possibility that one of your sure-thing answers is wrong.

Fill-in-the-blank questions

Fill-in-the-blank questions, also known as sentence completion questions, ask you to supply one or more words or phrases. These strategies will help you make successful choices.

- *Be logical.* Insert your answer, then reread the sentence from beginning to end to be sure it makes sense and is factually and grammatically correct.
- *Note the length and number of the blanks.* If two blanks appear right after one another, the instructor is probably looking for a two-word answer. If a blank is longer than usual, the correct response may require additional space.
- *If there is more than one blank and the blanks are widely separated, treat each one separately.* Answering each as if it is a separate sentence-completion question increases the likelihood that you will get at least one answer correct.
- *If you are uncertain, guess.* Have faith that after hours of studying, the correct answer is somewhere in your subconscious mind and that your guess is not completely random.

The following examples show fill-in-the-blank questions you might encounter in an introductory psychology course (correct answers follow questions):

1. Our awareness of the mental processes of our everyday life is called _____. *(consciousness)*

2. The major characteristic of waking consciousness is _____. *(selective attention)*

3. In humans, sleeping and waking follow a _____ cycle. *(circadian)*

4. Most vivid dreaming takes place during the _____ stage of sleep. *(REM)*

Source: Morris, Charles G.; Maisto, Albert A., *Understanding Psychology*, 10th Ed., p. 130. ©2013. Reprinted and Electronically reproduced by permission of Pearson Education, Inc., New York, NY.

Creating Effective Answers to Subjective Questions

Subjective questions demand the same information recall as objective questions, but they require you to plan, organize, draft, and refine a more lengthy response that expresses your knowledge and views. All essay questions are subjective. With freedom of thought and expression comes the challenge to organize your ideas and write well under time pressure. These steps—a shortened version of the writing process—will help you plan, draft, revise, and edit your responses.

> **The following examples show essay questions you might encounter in an introductory psychology course:**
>
> 1. Experts disagree about how many different kinds of memory there are. Recently, some psychologists have suggested that the classification of memories into different types is artificial and merely confuses matters. They suggest that we should consider memory a unitary thing. What arguments can you come up with to support the practice of making distinctions among different kinds of memory?
> 2. Primary drives are, by definition, unlearned. But learning clearly affects how these drives are expressed: We learn how and what to eat and drink. Given that information, how might you design a research study to determine what aspects of a given drive, say hunger, are learned and which are not?
> 3. Obviously, war is not the only cause of extreme stress and trauma. Do you think an individual's response to a personal attack, such as a rape, is similar to or different from that caused by serving in combat?

Source: Morris, Charles G.; Maisto, Albert A., *Understanding Psychology*, 10th Ed., pp. 196, 260, 385. ©2013. Reprinted and Electronically reproduced by permission of Pearson Education, Inc., New York, NY.

1. *Read every question.* Decide which to tackle (if there's a choice). Read carefully, and use critical thinking to identify exactly what the question is asking.

2. *Map out your time.* Schedule how long to allot for each answer, and then break your time down into smaller segments for each part of the process; for example, if you have 20 minutes to answer a question, use 5 to plan, 10 to draft, and 5 to review and finalize. Be flexible and ready to adjust how you use your time if things don't go as planned.

3. *Focus on action verbs.* Action verbs like those in Key 8.5 tell you what to do to answer the question. Underline these words and use them to guide your writing.

4. *Plan.* Thinking about what the question is asking and what you know, define your goal—what you intend to say in your answer. On scrap paper, outline or map your ideas and supporting evidence. Then develop a thesis statement that outlines the goal you've set, illustrating both the content and, if applicable, your point of view. Don't skimp on planning: Not only does planning result in a better essay, it also reduces stress because it helps you get the process under control.

5. *Draft.* Note the test directions before drafting your answer. Your essay may need to be of a certain length, for example, or may need to take a certain format. Then, use the following guidelines as you work:

   - State your thesis, and then get right to the evidence that backs it up.
   - Structure your essay so that each paragraph presents an idea that supports the thesis.
   - Use clear language and tight logic to link ideas to your thesis and to create transitions between paragraphs.
   - Look back at your planning notes periodically to make sure you cover everything.
   - Wrap it up with a short, to-the-point conclusion.

6. *Revise.* Although you may not have the time to rewrite your entire answer, you can improve it with minor changes. Check word choice, paragraph structure, and style. If you notice anything missing, use editing marks to insert it (neatly so it remains legible) into the text. When you're done, make sure it's the best possible representation of your ideas.

   As you check over your essay, ask yourself these questions:

   - Have I answered the question?
   - Does my essay begin with a clear thesis statement, and does each paragraph start with a strong topic sentence that supports the thesis?
   - Have I provided adequate support—in the form of examples, statistics, and relevant facts—to prove my argument? Have I used tight logic?
   - Have I covered all the points in my original outline or map?
   - Is my conclusion an effective wrap up?

Test Taking

KEY 8.5 Focus on action verbs in essay tests.

ANALYZE	Break into parts and discuss each part separately.
COMPARE	Explain similarities and differences.
CONTRAST	Distinguish between items being compared by focusing on differences.
CRITICIZE	Evaluate the issue, focusing on its problems or deficiencies.
DEFINE	State the essential quality or meaning.
DESCRIBE	Paint a complete picture; provide the details of a story or the main characteristics of a situation.
DIAGRAM	Present a drawing, chart, or other visual.
DISCUSS	Examine completely, using evidence and often presenting both sides of an issue.
ELABORATE ON	Start with information presented in the question, and then add new material.
ENUMERATE/LIST/IDENTIFY	Specify items in the form of a list.
EVALUATE	Give your opinion about the value or worth of a topic and justify your conclusion.
EXPLAIN	Make meaning clear, often by discussing causes and consequences.
ILLUSTRATE	Supply examples.
INTERPRET	Explain your personal views and judgments.
JUSTIFY	Discuss the reasons for your conclusions or for the question's premise.
OUTLINE	Organize and present main and subordinate points.
PROVE	Use evidence and logic to show that a statement is true.
REFUTE	Use evidence and logic to show that a statement is not true or tell how you disagree with it.
RELATE	Connect items mentioned in the question, showing, for example, how one item influenced another.
REVIEW	Provide an overview of ideas and establish their merits and features.
STATE	Explain clearly, simply, and concisely.
SUMMARIZE	Give the important ideas in brief, without comments.
TRACE	Present a history of a situation's development, often by showing cause and effect.

7. *Edit.* Check for mistakes in grammar, spelling, punctuation, and usage. Correct language—and neat, legible handwriting—leaves a positive impression and helps your grade.

Even the most prepared and accomplished student can hit a wall during an essay test and have trouble continuing, or even starting, an essay. If it happens to you, your best bet is just to start writing, even if you are unsure of what you want to say. You don't want to be sitting in front of an empty page when time is called. One way to get moving is to begin writing on the second page of your test booklet, leaving the first page blank so that you can go back and create an introduction once you have a clearer idea of where your essay is going.[8]

Key 8.6 shows a student's completed response to an essay question on body language including word changes and inserts she made while revising her draft.

Before she began writing the answer to this essay question, this student created the planning outline shown in Key 8.7. Notice how abbreviations and shorthand help her write quickly.

As you plan and write, remember that neatness is crucial. No matter how good your ideas are, if your instructor can't read them, your grade will suffer. Most essay

---

KEY 8.6 Response to an essay question with revision marks.

QUESTION: Describe three ways that body language affects interpersonal communication.

Body language plays an important role in interpersonal communication and helps shape the impression you make. Two of the most important functions of body language are to contradict and reinforce verbal statements. When body language contradicts verbal language, the message ~~conveyed~~ *delivered* by the body is dominant. For example, if a friend tells you that she is feeling "fine," but her posture is slumped, *her eye contact minimal,* and her facial expression troubled, you have every reason to wonder whether she is telling the truth. If the same friend tells you that she is feeling fine and is smiling, walking with a bounce in her step, and has direct eye contact, her body language is ~~telling the truth.~~ *accurately reflecting and reinforcing her words.*

The nonverbal cues that make up body language also have the power to add shades of meaning. Consider this statement: "This is the best idea I've heard all day." If you were to say this three different ways—in a loud voice while standing up; quietly while sitting with arms and legs crossed and looking away; and while ~~maintening~~ *maintaining* eye contact and taking the receiver's hand—you might send three different messages.

Finally, the impact of nonverbal cues can be greatest when you meet someone for the first time. When you meet someone, you tend to make assumptions based on nonverbal behaviour such as posture, eye contact, gestures, and speed and style of movement.

In summary, nonverbal communication plays a ~~crucial~~ *crucial* role in interpersonal relationships. It has the power to send an accurate message that may ~~destroy~~ *belie* the speaker's words, offer shades of meaning, and set the tone of a first meeting.

, especially when you meet someone for the first time

Although first impressions emerge ~~from a combination of nonverbal cues, tone of voice, and choice of words,~~ nonverbal elements (cues and tone) ~~usually come~~ across first and strongest.

Test Taking

213

get analytical

WRITE TO THE VERB

Dario Sabljak/Shutterstock

Complete the following on paper or in digital format.

Focusing on the action verbs in essay test instructions can mean the difference between giving instructors what they want and wandering off track. Get to know action verbs a little more closely. Choose three verbs from Key 8.5 that you've seen used in essay questions. List each verb. Then, for each, write out what the verb inspires you to do *without reusing the verb*. In other words, avoid saying that "Describe" asks you to describe.

Now put your choices to work.

1. Name a topic you learned about in this text—for example, the concept of successful intelligence or different barriers to listening.

2. Put yourself in the role of instructor. Write an essay question on this topic, using one of the action verbs you listed above to frame the question. For example, "List the three aspects of successful intelligence" or "Analyze the classroom-based challenges associated with internal barriers to listening."

3. Now rewrite your original question twice more, using the other two action verbs you chose, and adjusting the question to the verb each time.

4. Finally, analyze how each new verb changes the focus of the essay. Describe the goal of each essay question and note how they differ.

KEY 8.7 Create an informal outline during essay tests.

> Essay question: Describe three ways in which body language affects interpersonal communication.
>
> Roles of BL in IC
>
>   1.To contradict or reinforce words
>   —e.g., friend says "I'm fine"
>   2.To add shades of meaning
>   —saying the same sentence in 3 diff. ways
>   3.To make lasting 1st impression
>   —impact of nv cues and voice tone greater than words
>   —we assume things abt person based on posture, eye contact, etc.

tests are taken in *blue books*—small blank paper booklets available at the bookstore or provided by your instructor on test day. If your handwriting is a problem, try printing or skipping every other line, and write on only one side of the page in your blue book. Use an extra blue book if you need it. Students with documented learning disabilities may be able to get permission to take the test on a computer.

The purpose of a test is to see how much you know, not merely to get a grade. Embrace this attitude to learn from your mistakes.

WHAT IS THE UPSIDE OF
poor performance?

You've finished the exam, handed it in, gone home to a well-deserved night of sleep. At the next class meeting you've returned refreshed, rejuvenated, and ready to accept a great score. As you receive the test back from your instructor, you look wide-eyed at your grade. *How could that be?*

No one aces every test or understands every piece of material perfectly. Making mistakes on tests and learning from them is an essential part of the academic experience. Instead of beating yourself up about a bad grade, take the risk of looking realistically at what you could have done better. Identify what you can correct, and you may be rewarded with better study choices and an improved performance on your next exam.

Examining test results will help these students evaluate their performance, as well as learn from their mistakes.

Montgomery Martin/
Alamy Stock Photo

Ask yourself global questions that may help you identify correctable patterns. Honest answers can help you change the way you study for the next exam.

- What were your biggest problems? Did you get nervous, misread the question, fail to study enough, study incorrectly, neglect to go beyond recall to analysis?
- Did your instructor's comments clarify where you slipped up? Did your answer lack specificity? Did you fail to support your thesis well? Was your analysis weak?
- Were you surprised by the questions? For example, did you expect them all to be from the lecture notes and text instead of from your notes and text and supplemental readings?
- Did you make careless errors? Did you misread the question or directions, blacken the wrong box on the answer sheet, skip a question, write illegibly?
- Did you make conceptual or factual errors? Did you misunderstand a concept? Did you fail to master facts or concepts?

Rework the questions you got wrong. Based on instructor feedback, try to rewrite an essay, recalculate a math problem from the original question, or redo questions following a reading selection. If you discover a pattern of careless errors, redouble your efforts to be more careful, and save time to double-check your work.

After reviewing your mistakes, fill in your knowledge gaps. If you made mistakes because you didn't understand important concepts, develop a plan to learn the material.

Talk to your instructor. Focus on specific mistakes on objective questions, or if you were marked down on an essay, ask what you could have done better. If you feel that

get $mart

TEST YOUR FINANCIAL LITERACY

Creativenv/Shutterstock

Racorn/123RF

As with any academic area of study, knowledge of basic terms is a necessary foundation on which to build understanding. Test your knowledge of some financial literacy terminology with this matching exercise. In the blank next to each term, write the letter that corresponds with the correct definition. An answer key is provided at the end of this chapter.

1. ___ finance charge
2. ___ net worth
3. ___ TFSA
4. ___ debit card
5. ___ overdraft

6. ___ credit score
7. ___ interest
8. ___ APR
9. ___ down payment
10. ___ identity theft

A. A number assigned to you based on your credit activity—higher numbers are better.
B. Using more money than you have available in a bank account.
C. Your total financial assets—cash, savings, property—minus your debt.
D. A percentage charged annually on the amount of a loan or credit card debt.
E. A first payment on a large purchase that you cannot cover all at once.
F. When someone acquires and uses your personal information without your consent.
G. When you use it, the purchase amount is subtracted from your bank account.
H. A percentage that you earn on savings or pay on borrowed money or credit.
I. What it costs you to use credit; can be a percentage of what you owe, or a flat fee.
j. An account designed to help you save money for retirement.

Fotopak/Fotolia

an essay was unfairly graded, ask for a rereading. Approach your instructor in a non-defensive way and you will be more likely to receive help. Frankly, the fact that you care enough to review your errors will make a good impression on its own.

Rethink the way you studied. Make changes to avoid repeating your errors. Use varied techniques to study more effectively so that you can show yourself and your instructors what you are capable of doing. The earlier in the term you make positive adjustments the better, so make a special effort to analyze and learn from early test mistakes.

If you fail a test, don't throw it away. Use it to review troublesome material, especially if you will be tested on it again.

The importance of learning from experience applies to life tests as well as academic ones. Suzanne, for example, could not have ascended to the position of anchorperson at CNN without assessing her performances over time, deciding what could be improved, and implementing plans to do things differently next time she appeared on camera.

HOW CAN YOU PREPARE FOR
final exams?

Studying for final exams, which usually take place the last week of the term, is a major commitment. Avoid thinking that you can approach them as you would any other test. Because a final exam typically requires you to recall information from the entire scope of the course, it requires efforts above and beyond your regular exam preparation.

Manage Your Schedule

Studying for finals requires careful time management. Your school may schedule study days (also called a "reading period") between the end of classes and the beginning of finals. Lasting from a day or two to a couple of weeks, these days give you time to prepare for exams and finish papers. As tempting as it may be to blow off work for a portion of your reading period, try to take advantage of this precious study time. With no class meetings in your calendar, you have that much more time to work and prepare, and you will benefit from the extra effort.

Plan out your reading period at least a week before it starts, beginning with a look at your final exam schedule. Generally, all finals will take place within one week, and each final happens on a specific day and at a specific time (often a different day and time from when the course usually meets). Note exactly when each final takes place, and plan several study sessions in the days before each final exam time, setting aside blocks of time assigned to specific subject areas. If you have a day when you are taking more than one final, make sure you factor that into your study plan for the days leading up to it. Finally, as you would with challenging material, devote more time to courses that are tougher for you.

Scheduling your study time may require location flexibility. Libraries are often packed, and students may need to find alternative locations. Consider outdoor settings (if weather permits), smaller libraries (many departments have their own libraries), and empty classrooms. Set up times and places that will provide the atmosphere you need to focus well.[9]

Use Targeted Strategies

Use these finals-specific versions of test preparation strategies to get ready for final exam success.

Know what to study. Some finals cover the entire term's material, some cover from midterm on, and some address a particular topic that was part of the course coverage. Get a clear answer from your instructor on what the final will cover so that you can target your study time.

Take advantage of review sessions and study groups. If your instructor offers them, review sessions are certain to focus you on what you need to know. If studying in a group works for you and with the course material, get together with classmates to go over material.

Start early and start small. As Professor Robert Talbert recommends, begin when you have at least several days until a final and do short reviews at first, basically skimming your notes and study materials. This approach eases your brain back into the information it learned earlier in the term. Then once you have a decent overview, you should go into more depth as the date of the final nears.[10]

Get some sleep. Save your all-nighters for writing papers; you need sleep in order for your brain to function on test day. Professor Talbert recommends that you stop studying the night before, in fact, to give your brain time off and allow it to process everything you've been studying in the days up until the final.[11]

Your Priorities

Finals are a temporary but top-priority item in your schedule. Giving them the time and attention they need usually means that something else will have to give, and busy students will need to temporarily reduce their commitments. Look ahead to study days

student PROFILE

Kelcy McNally

UNIVERSITY OF PRINCE EDWARD ISLAND, CHARLOTTETOWN, PEI

About me:

I just successfully completed my first year at university and am looking forward to the next. While attending university I played on the varsity basketball team, which kept me on a tight schedule. I really wanted to focus on being a strong student as well as an athlete, and I believe I accomplished that by keeping my average in the 90s. Although my time was limited, I tried to do other things aside from school and basketball to have a good balance in my life. I am attending university in the hopes of getting a degree in Business Administration. After that, I plan to continue my education to become a chartered accountant.

What I focus on:

In university, I focused mainly on studying and making sure that I had a good balance of everything else in my life. Studying was difficult because of the limited amount of time I had; I was on the road almost every weekend for basketball. Also, some of the information was not interesting to me so I had to really focus in order to remember and understand it. Distractions are difficult to overcome when you are studying. To handle distractions, I usually isolate myself from anything that may cause me not to focus 100 percent. For example, I turn off my cellphone, shut off my laptop, and just focus on the subject at hand. Also, once I begin studying, I make sure to take short breaks so that I can refocus when I find it difficult to concentrate on the subject.

Knowing the way you study is also crucial. Although everyone is different, I prefer to study by thinking of possible test questions and trying to answer them to the best of my ability. I also like to create mnemonic devices in order to remember more information.

When you actually take a test, I suggest you write down what you know on the paper if you think you may forget it. Also, I would do the easy questions first, and if you come across a difficult one, mark it and then return to it later.

What will help me in the workplace:

While attending university I learned many things both inside and outside the classroom that will benefit me in the workplace. In classes, I learned fundamental skills and subject-specific knowledge. The fundamental skills included strong study habits, how to take good notes, and much more. Outside of my classes, I learned some valuable lessons about building strong relationships, working with others, and adapting to new environments. Many of these lessons were learned on the basketball team, and I know they will be useful in my future workplace.

Kelcy McNally. University of Prince Edward Island, Charlottetown, PEI. Reprinted by permission.

and finals week and see if you can postpone social activities, reduce your work schedule or take days off, and bow out of less-important meetings and gatherings.[12] Downgrade any nonessential activity to lower priority until final exams are over.

Make sure that high-priority assignments due near the end of the term are turned in on time so that they do not interfere with your studying for finals. Also, if you have courses for which the final is a project rather than a timed test, getting such projects finished up before reading period is a great way to open up study time in your schedule.[13]

A final word: Tests reflect your ability to *show* what you know. They do not necessarily indicate what you know, and certainly they do not define who you are. Understand the limitations of tests. Learn from them and take from them what reward you can as you move into the greater test of life in the 21st century.

revisit RISK AND REWARD

What happened to Suzanne? To her surprise, Suzanne returned to the newsroom after her nerve-wracking live TV debut to a standing ovation from her colleagues. The next day, the producer sent Suzanne on another live assignment, and she was rock solid. "The second time I went out there it was like I had been doing it for years," she recalls. "A calmness washed over me."

Two decades later, the reward for Suzanne's risk taking and persistence is a sterling reputation in broadcast journalism. She is a national correspondent for CNN. Previously, she covered Presidents Bill Clinton, George W. Bush, and Barack Obama during her ten years as CNN White House correspondent. In 2011, Suzanne was embedded with U.S. troops in Afghanistan and led breaking news coverage of the terrorist attack on the U.S. embassy.

Suzanne has earned an Emmy Award for her coverage of the revolution in Egypt. She was named one of "America's Most Powerful Players Under 40" by *Black Enterprise* magazine and *Essence* magazine's 2009 Journalist of the Year. Recently, the Columbia University Graduate School of Journalism recognized her coverage of the 2008 Obama campaign as "One of the Top 50 Stories of the Century."

What does this mean for you? Suzanne has had plenty of pressure to excel in her career. Her story of risk and reward is valuable no matter your academic or career path. "Are you going to make a mistake or excel in that moment when everybody is watching? That's when you have to dig deeper and find that faith and courage and confidence in yourself," Suzanne says. "At some point in your life, you have to be fearless, and that's when you turn the corner." Describe a moment when you struggled with a test—academic or otherwise—but risked action and ultimately were rewarded with success. What got you through? How can you put that experience to use with future tests in and out of the classroom?

What risk may bring reward beyond your world? Much of Suzanne's work at CNN involves using the power of knowledge and discourse to spark change. You too can seize the opportunity, to understand and affect what's happening. Vote in elections: municipal, provincial, and federal. Read about issues and discuss them with friends and family. See how you can change the world by getting involved in your community.

Courtesy of Suzanne Malveaux

Test Taking

GLOBAL RISK AND REWARD

Vinzenz Weidenhofer/123RF

PaylessImages/123RF

In the late 1990s, the new country of Estonia had just won its independence from Russia, and Estonian citizens felt energy and possibility. Empowered by this sense of potential, a group of Estonians highly trained in computer technology took the risk to develop the platform for Skype, creating a new way to communicate over the internet at little or no cost using video or microphone. While the world enjoys the reward of connecting via Skype, the company earned significant reward for its risk as well when it was bought by Microsoft for $8.5 billion.[14]

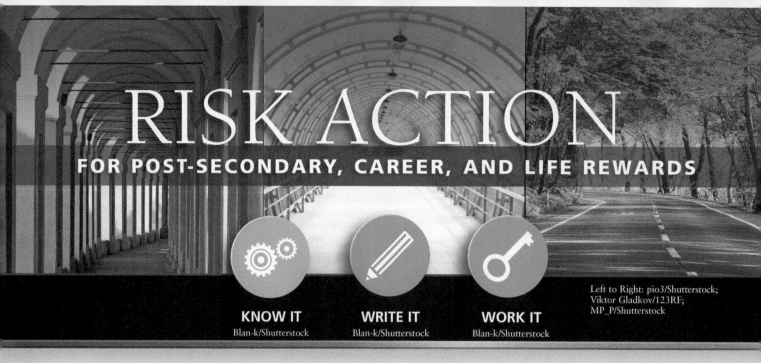

Left to Right: pio3/Shutterstock; Viktor Gladkov/123RF; MP_P/Shutterstock

RISK ACTION
FOR POST-SECONDARY, CAREER, AND LIFE REWARDS

KNOW IT
Blan-k/Shutterstock

WRITE IT
Blan-k/Shutterstock

WORK IT
Blan-k/Shutterstock

Complete the following on paper or in digital format.

KNOW IT *Think Critically*

Effectively Prepare for Tests

Take a careful look at your performance on and preparation for a test you took recently.

Build basic skills. Think about how you did on the test. Were you pleased or disappointed with your performance and grade? Explain your answer.

List any of the problems below that you feel you experienced in this exam. If you experienced one or more problems not listed here, include them in your document. For each problem you identified, think about why you made mistakes.

- Incomplete preparation
- Fatigue
- Feeling rushed during the test
- Shaky understanding of concepts

- Poor guessing techniques
- Feeling confused about directions
- Test anxiety
- Poor essay organization or writing

Take it to the next level. Be creative about test-preparation strategies.

1. If you had all the time and materials you needed, how would you have prepared for this test? Describe briefly what your plan would be and how it would address your problem(s).
2. Now think back to your actual test preparation—the techniques you used and amount of time you spent. Describe the difference between the ideal study plan you just described and what you actually did.

Move toward mastery. Improve your chances for success on the next exam by coming up with specific changes in your preparation.

1. Actions I took this time, but do *not* intend to take next time.
2. Actions I did *not* take this time, but do intend to take next time.

WRITE IT *Communicate*

Emotional intelligence journal: Test types. What type of test do you feel most comfortable with, and what type brings up more negative feelings? Thinking of a particular situation involving the test type that challenges you, describe how it made you feel and how that feeling affected your performance. Discuss ways in which you might be able to shift your mindset in order to feel more confident about this type of test.

Real-life writing: Ask your instructor for help studying for a test. Focus on a course that has a challenging test coming up. Take advantage of your instructor's time, knowledge, and advice. Check your syllabus to see when and where you instructor holds office hours, and note his or her email address. Then compose a polite email that first asks for a meeting during office hours and, second, asks for information about what the test or final exam will cover. Proofread and send it. After you meet, compose and send one more short and respectful email thanking your instructor for his or her time.

WORK IT *Build Your Brand*

On-the-Job Testing

You may encounter different tests throughout your career. For example, if you are studying to be a nurse, you are now tested on subjects like anatomy and pharmacology. After you graduate you will be required to take certification and recertification exams that gauge your mastery of the latest information in various aspects of nursing.

Some post-graduate tests are for entry into the field; some test proficiency on particular equipment; some move you to the next level of employment. Choose one career you are thinking about and investigate what tests are involved as you advance through different career stages.

Create a document with your chosen career area as the title. On your document, create a grid that has several rows and the following five headers:

- Test name
- When taken
- What it covers
- How to prepare
- Web resources

Finally, search for the information you need to fill in the grid. Use one row for every test that you find.

Answers to Get $mart quiz:

1. I
2. C
3. J
4. G
5. B
6. A
7. H
8. D
9. E
10. F

Courtesy of Georgina Arreola

What your post-secondary education has to offer incorporates, but goes far beyond, what you learn in the classroom. Learn about your school's resources and opportunities—and then, most importantly, take the risk to try them.

People, Resources, and Opportunities

HOW CAN YOU MAKE THE MOST OF POST-SECONDARY LIFE?

What Would You Risk? *Georgina Arreola*

THINK ABOUT THIS SITUATION AS YOU READ, AND CONSIDER WHAT ACTION YOU WOULD TAKE. THE POST-SECONDARY EXPERIENCE GOES BEYOND COURSEWORK. THIS CHAPTER GIVES YOU A "TASTING MENU" OF THE SOURCES OF HELP AND OPPORTUNITY THAT AWAIT YOUR INITIATIVE THROUGHOUT COLLEGE OR UNIVERSITY.

Georgina and her two sisters aimed to be the first of their family to go to post-secondary school. Growing up, her parents demanded that Georgina succeed in school, and with hard work she lived up to their expectations. "I was very studious as a high school kid," she remembers. "My parents were very protective of us. Studying was the only thing that we absolutely had to do."

Georgina excelled in high school, earning a ticket to university. Her older sister had enrolled in a school close to home. But Georgina took the risk to study six hours away from her parents—and from parental restrictions. "I found myself with a lot of freedom, and there were a lot of things I wanted to do besides study," she says. "I spent so much time enjoying my freedom and not managing my time very well."

She struggled too with the competition on campus. In high school, she was an elite academic performer. Just one quarter into her academic adventure, Georgina was placed on academic probation for poor grades. She cringed when she got the letter, and had to break the news to her parents. "If I didn't improve my grades in the next quarter, I could potentially be out of school," Georgina recalls. It was time to focus on what she wanted out of school and what she was willing to do to get it.

To be continued . . .

LIKE MANY, GEORGINA EXPECTED THE TRANSITION TO POST-SECONDARY LIFE TO BE SEAMLESS. BUT THE COURSEWORK WAS A MAJOR STEP UP, THE STUDY LOAD WAS HEAVY, AND THE LIFESTYLE OFFERED NUMEROUS DISTRACTIONS. WHAT COULD GET HER BACK ON TRACK? YOU'LL LEARN MORE ABOUT GEORGINA, AND THE REWARD RESULTING FROM HER ACTIONS, WITHIN THE CHAPTER.

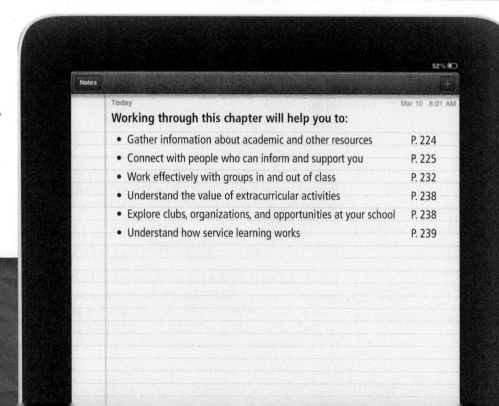

Today   Mar 10   8:01 AM

Working through this chapter will help you to:

statusCHECK

How Well-Informed Are You About Resources and Opportunities?

For each statement, fill in the number that feels right to you, from 1 for "not at all true for me" to 5 for "very true for me."

1. I know where to find my student handbook both in hard copy and online.	① ② ③ ④ ⑤
2. I am already considering activities that interest me outside of my coursework.	① ② ③ ④ ⑤
3. I do not hesitate to contact a person or office when I need information or support.	① ② ③ ④ ⑤
4. In high school and/or the workplace, I have experienced working in teams.	① ② ③ ④ ⑤
5. I am an effective team player and work hard to fulfill my responsibilities.	① ② ③ ④ ⑤
6. I understand how working with a study group can help me learn and remember.	① ② ③ ④ ⑤
7. I have an idea of the range of activities available to me at my school.	① ② ③ ④ ⑤
8. I welcome the opportunity to meet new people through extracurricular activities.	① ② ③ ④ ⑤
9. I feel confident that I will be able to manage my time so that participation in activities does not compromise my ability to manage my coursework.	① ② ③ ④ ⑤
10. I know what service learning is and whether it is offered at my school.	① ② ③ ④ ⑤

Each of the topics in these statements is covered in this chapter. Note those statements for which you filled in a 3 or lower. Skim the chapter to see where those topics appear, and pay special attention to them as you read, learn, and apply new strategies.

REMEMBER: NO MATTER HOW WELL YOU UNDERSTAND WHAT'S AVAILABLE TO YOU, YOU CAN IMPROVE WITH EFFORT AND PRACTICE.

HOW CAN YOU CREATE A WELL-ROUNDED
post-secondary experience?

By now you are aware that what college or university has to offer you incorporates, but goes far beyond, what you learn in the classroom. Post-secondary school is an opportunity for change and growth in every aspect of your life—intellectual, social, physical, emotional, psychological, and experiential. Even within each of those realms there are diverse ways to develop. For example, social development can mean increased acceptance of diversity, more skill in managing friendships, and growing confidence in leading a group.

As you read this chapter, remember that you have two important responsibilities: One, *learn about your school*. Two, *take risks*. In other words:

Learn the unique details of your school's resources. Because *Keys to Success* is used in a variety of schools, this chapter can only offer general information. Your job is to understand the specific details of what your school offers—where services are located, who can help and how to reach those people, when activities or meetings take place, how you can gather information, and so on. Your student handbook, whether in hard copy or online, is an essential tool for this purpose. Don't let it sit unread and unused. Keep it handy, or bookmark it, and make it your go-to resource for anything you need to know as you navigate your first year and beyond.

Take risks that can bring you rewards. You are now the architect of your experience, the head of "team you." Parents and guardians will not be signing you up for clubs, checking your schedule for conflicts when you have an activity planned, and swooping in to help you when they see you looking worried while studying. Your own risks will bring those rewards. When you want to branch out, check the list of clubs and organizations and contact one that looks interesting. When you need help, call or email the counselling centre, an academic centre, residence life, or whatever resource you think can best help you. Getting rewards from these resources depends on your willingness to risk moving out of your comfort zone.

Read through the rest of the chapter with a focus on these responsibilities. You may want to keep your student handbook available while you read, so you can refer to school specifics.

WHAT RESOURCES AND PEOPLE
can provide support?

Most colleges and universities introduce resources to new students. You may have an in-person or online orientation, materials to read, and perhaps activities through this course that connect you with resources around campus. After that time, the onus is on you to stay aware of what's available.

Resource offerings may change as you progress through school. Resolve to connect with people and resources periodically throughout your academic career. Your school will probably help you with that resolution—most schools for example, require students to meet with their advisors at least once per term as well as in connection with declaring a major.

Instructors and Teaching Assistants

Faculty and staff are among the most valuable, but underused, sources of help. A recent survey of first year post-secondary students indicated that only 25% of students asked a teacher for advice after class throughout the term.[1] That means that 75% did not ask an instructor for help, and it's likely that at least some of those students could have used it.

Your coursework brings you into constant contact with instructors and teaching assistants who see your work and, in small classes, may get to know you well. Consult them to:

- Clarify material presented in class
- Get homework help
- Find out how to prepare for a test
- Ask about a paper you are working on
- Find out why you received a particular grade on a test or assignment
- Get advice about the department—courses, majoring—or related career areas

If you have a quick question, it's best to grab a moment with your instructor before or after class. When you want to speak for longer than a minute or two, make an appointment during office hours, send an email, or leave a voicemail message.

Office hours. You can find instructors' regular office hours on your syllabus, on office doors, and online at the course site or department web page. Face-to-face conferences are best for working through problems or soliciting advice. Always make an appointment for a conference.

Estudi M6/Fotolia

Email. Instructors' email addresses are generally posted on the first day of class and on your syllabus. Use email to clarify assignments and assignment deadlines, to ask questions about lectures or readings, and to clarify what will be covered on a test.

Voicemail. If something comes up at the last minute, leave a short and specific message on your instructor's voicemail. Do not call instructors at home unless they give you permission to do so.

Keep in mind that *adjunct faculty* (temporary or part-time instructors) may not have offices or voicemail connected with the school. If you need to meet with an adjunct instructor, get in touch using the contact information from your syllabus, and the instructor will arrange a specific meeting location.

Academic Advising

Most schools have an advising office or centre that oversees academic advising. Academic advisors help students navigate coursework, registration, majors, and more. At some schools, every student is assigned an advisor; at others, students select their advisors. Either way, you will have an advisor who serves as your personal connection with the school.

Your advisor will help you select and register for courses every term, plan your overall academic program, and understand academic regulations, including graduation requirements. You may be required to meet with your advisor once each term. However, once may not be enough, and many advisors report that their services are underused for most of the term until registration and final grade time roll around.

As with any relationship, the more time and effort you risk, the more rewarding the connection will be. Don't hesitate to schedule additional meetings with your advisor beyond the minimum requirements. If your advisor teaches one or more courses, consider adding one to your schedule so that you can experience your advisor in a classroom setting.

Academic Centres and Tutoring

Tutors can give you valuable and detailed help on specific academic subjects. Most campuses have private tutoring available, and many schools offer free peer tutoring. If you feel you could benefit from one-on-one support, ask an instructor or academic advisor to recommend a tutor.

If your school has one or more *academic centres*, you may be able to find a tutor there. Academic centres, including reading, writing, math, and study-skills, help students improve skills at all levels. Another type of academic centre is linked with a specific department or academic focus, such as technology or environmental studies. They have extensive programs and support services that help students majoring in that area connect with internships, investigate graduate programs, collaborate on research projects, and more.

Need-Specific Offices

Colleges and universities serve students with a staggering range of needs, and have developed specific offices and programs to address them. What your school offers depends on the characteristics of the student body. For example, a school with commuter students will have a transportation office, and a diverse student body may be served by an office of diversity or multicultural affairs. Think about who you are and what you need, and explore your school's specific offerings. Key 9.1 has details about some general offices found at almost any school.

Need-specific offices

Residence life. Handles issues for students living in school housing. Resident assistants (RAs) live with students.

Transportation. Help with parking, public transportation options, and involvement (for commuters who feel disconnected from the campus community).

International student services. Help with documentation and federal regulations; support for adjusting to a new environment.

Campus computing and information technology (IT) services. Help working in a computer centre or assistance with your own personal computer.

Transfer student services. Support with integrating into the school community, transferring credits, and declaring majors.

Career services. Help with job searches for current students as well as career planning and placement for after graduation.

Services for students with disabilities. Helps students with disabilities navigate campus and receive accommodations necessary to facilitate learning.

Services for ethnic or cultural populations. Offerings depend on the student body. Examples include support for indigenous, international, and LGBTQ students.

Administration

Out of all of the offices that comprise a school's administration, the *office of student affairs* is one of the most important for students. In many schools, the office of student affairs is the centre for student services, overseeing all kinds of organizations, student support offices, and activities. Staff members there can answer your questions or direct you to others who can help.

Deans are administrators who are in charge of various areas at your university or college. Although each school has its own administrative structure, every school has the following.

A dean of students. The dean of students and his or her staff oversee the non-academic part of your experience—programs pertaining to diversity, wellness, living arrangements, commuting, and any other student life issues. Call on the dean of students for help with legal and judicial services, emergencies, conflict resolution, help with particular needs (working students, students with families, transfers, and so on), support for students with disabilities, safety issues, and any other concern.

Academic deans. These deans oversee everything pertaining to your academic life. There may be one dean with a supporting staff of associate or assistant deans, or there may be deans of different divisions of the school. Your academic dean may be assigned to you according to your major or the person who acts as your advisor. Consult your academic dean for issues related to courses, majors (selecting, changing, or designing), instructors, internships, study abroad, graduate programs, or anything else academic.

You will also interact with the registrar's office and the bursar's office. The *registrar's office* is the part of your school's administration that handles course registration, sends grade reports, and compiles your official transcript (a comprehensive record of your courses, grades, and status). Graduate school admissions offices require a copy of your transcript, as do many prospective employers. The *bursar's office* is the home of the school's accounting system, issuing bills for tuition and room and board and collecting payments from students and financial aid sources.

Finally, schools with students who live on campus have an *office of residence life*. The people who work there address needs that arise with students living in campus housing, from key requests and laundry questions to conflicts with roommates, suitemates, or hallmates. Residence life supervises the RAs (resident assistants) who live in campus housing with students and provide the most immediate and accessible support.

Student Health

Your school has a student health office that provides medical services. Most colleges and universities offer a health insurance plan to students. If you're still covered by your parent's insurance plan or have your own, most colleges and universities offer a way to opt out of their student insurance plans.

On-campus health centres generally offer a combination of both preventative and diagnostic care, as well as emergency services and opportunities to receive immunizations such as the meningococcal meningitis vaccine. You will need to make and keep your own appointments and manage your own medications and other therapies as needed. Many student health centres are linked to the school's counselling centres, which is helpful if your medical needs have a psychological component. In addition, if you need specialized care not available at your student health centre, someone will refer you to a care provider in the area.

Counselling

Counselling is confidential, focused on your particular needs, and directed toward helping you handle what is bothering you. Whatever type of personal problem you encounter, a counsellor can help you get through it. In most cases, your counselling sessions will end when you achieve the goals you and your counsellor have defined.

Most colleges and universities have a counselling centre with several counsellors and support staff. Contact them over the phone or through email to set up an initial appointment. As with faculty office hours and academic advising, counselling services are underused by students. If you have a problem, get help from a counsellor who can make a difference for you. If you feel unwilling to risk opening up to someone, weigh the potential reward against the potential negative result of keeping your feelings to yourself.

Peer Leaders and Mentors

Recognizing the value of connecting new students to ones who have been there for a while, many schools have instituted *peer leadership programs*. Peer leaders go through training and then connect with new students in various ways—including orientation programs, first-year experience courses, and advising services—depending on how the school structures its program. Peer leaders often become mentors to new students and build friendships that extend beyond their official duties.

Some universities and colleges have formal mentoring programs that connect students—usually new students—with an on-campus mentor who can guide them as they integrate into the school community. This type of structured mentoring program may have an academic focus, a student life focus, or both, and may involve instructors as well as other campus employees. Mentors can also come into your life informally. If you develop a strong bond with an instructor or administrator, for example, you may find that he or she has become a mentor to you.

Lisa F. Young/Fotolia

Counselling can benefit anyone, not just students who are in a crisis or who have a diagnosed mental health issue. Take advantage of a counsellor's training and wisdom for any stumbling block you encounter as a student.

MENTOR
A trusted counsellor or guide who takes a special interest in helping you reach your goals.

Financial Aid Office

The importance of this resource has grown as the challenge of paying for your post-secondary has intensified. Your school's financial aid office handles all sources of monetary aid, including loans and grants (federal and provincial) and scholarships. The staff can help you determine your eligibility, search for aid sources, apply for aid, and manage your costs by putting together aid "packages" that may include a mix of grants, loans, and on-campus jobs or work–study programs.

The details and forms involved can be overwhelming, and the array of scholarships, grants, and loans available is far too large for any one student to navigate alone. The financial aid staff members know what's out there and understand the specific eligibility requirements. With their expertise, they can help you narrow the field of possibilities, as well as identify opportunities that you may not have uncovered. Call on them, especially if you are worried you will not be able to continue financing your education.

Safety Resources

Every school has its particular issues—problematic areas of the campus, celebrations that get out of control, and students propping open security doors, among other safety issues. Here are ways that many schools keep students safe and build awareness.

Campus security. Your school's security services are available to you 24 hours a day, 7 days a week. Before you set foot on campus, program the campus security number into your phone. Contact security to report a medical emergency, assault or other crime, issues with substances, security concerns, suspicious activity, or any other situation that threatens your safety.

get analytical

Darren Baker/
Shutterstock

EXPLORE WHAT YOU NEED NOW

Dario Sabljak/Shutterstock

Complete the following on paper or in digital format.

Consider this list of different aspects of the post-secondary experience.

Student status   Culture and ethnicity   Fears or insecurities

Academic challenges   Living situation   Work obligations

Physical or learning disabilities   Being a transfer student   Being a first-generation student

1. Analyzing the list, choose two with which you could use support. Write each choice on your document.
2. For each choice, describe the details specific to your situation (for example, if you chose "living situation," you might write "challenges with my roommate;" or, if you chose "culture and ethnicity," you might write "connecting with others who share my culture"). Be as specific as you can.
3. Thinking about what you have read in the chapter so far and examining your school's specific resources, identify a person or office that can help you with each one of your choices. Include a contact phone number or email.
4. Finally, describe the next step you plan to take to access each of these resources, and when you will take it.

Student walking services. Many schools provide on-foot or vehicle services to students, particularly at night, when you have to get from place to place after dark and don't have someone to walk with, or if you find yourself in an uncomfortable situation and need to find a different way home than you had planned. These services are free to students, staff, and faculty, and are often underused, so you shouldn't have much of a wait.

Support for online issues. Students may experience compromised credit cards, identity theft, or cyberbullying. Some schools have specific offices geared toward online safety; others provide support through offices such as student affairs. Be wary of sharing personal information and photos online, and get help as soon as you suspect a problem.

Off-Campus Resources

Your sources of support are not limited to campus. Help can also come from the following sources.

Online. Countless websites and online organizations provide information and assistance to post-secondary students on any imaginable topic. Use your critical thinking and information literacy to choose sites that have reputable, updated information. Links provided on your school's website are a good bet, since they have been explored and approved by campus employees. A word of caution: For serious psychological issues such as an eating disorder, suicidal thoughts, or any desire to cause yourself or someone else harm, talking to a counsellor or therapist in person is generally more effective than looking online for help.

multiple intelligence strategies

FOR STRESS MANAGEMENT

Name a stressful university or college life issue you want to address: _____. In the right-hand column, record specific ideas for how MI strategies can help you manage it.

INTELLIGENCE	USE MI STRATEGIES TO MANAGE STRESS	IDENTIFY MI STRESS-MANAGEMENT STRATEGIES THAT CAN HELP YOU MANAGE
Verbal-Linguistic	• Keep a journal of what situations, people, or events cause stress. • Write letters or email friends about your problems.	
Logical-Mathematical	• Think through problems using a problem-solving process, and devise a detailed plan. • Analyze the negative and positive effects that may result from a stressful situation.	
Bodily-Kinesthetic	• Choose a physical activity that helps you release tension—running, yoga, team sports—and do it regularly. • Plan physical activities during free time—go for a hike, take a bike ride, go dancing with friends.	
Visual-Spatial	• Enjoy things that appeal to you visually—visit an exhibit, see an art film, shoot photos with your camera. • Use a visual organizer to plan out a solution to a stressful problem.	
Interpersonal	• Talk with people who care about you and are supportive. • Shift your focus by being a good listener to others who need to talk about their stresses.	
Intrapersonal	• Schedule downtime when you can think through what is causing stress. • Allow yourself five minutes a day of meditation where you visualize a positive way in which you want a stressful situation to resolve.	
Musical	• Listen to music that relaxes, inspires, and/or energizes you. • Write a song about what is bothering you.	
Naturalistic	• See whether the things that cause you stress fall into categories that can give you helpful ideas about how to handle situations. • If nature is calming for you, interact with it—spend time outdoors, watch nature-focused TV, read books or articles on nature or science.	

Old friends. Modern technology allows students to keep in touch with friends from home more easily than ever. However, it can be problematic to stay so connected that you don't become a part of your new community. Remember that while you can benefit from the support of those who know you well and have a shared history with you, it is good to get to know new people at your school. As the saying goes, "Make new friends, but keep the old."

Family. Post-secondary life is a crucial time to grow more independent and relax your family ties somewhat. However, that doesn't mean you shouldn't reach out for help and advice when you need it. Just think before you act, and avoid contacting family for things you can and should handle on your own.

All of these resources can be part of your quest to stay focused and reduce stress. The Multiple Intelligence Strategies for Stress Management table on page 231 shows how students might use MI-based strategies to manage issues that come up in post-secondary life.

HOW CAN YOU WORK WITH
others in and out of class?

In today's workplace, almost everything is accomplished by a *team*. The Conference Board of Canada identifies teamwork skills as "the skills and attributes needed to contribute productively."[2] Aware of the importance of working with others, academic institutions have increased the teamwork component of many courses, and students work together to create documents, presentations, and projects. The prime advantage to working in teams is the ability to combine skills and talents. An academic or work team benefits from a wide array of skills that no single student or employee could possess alone. Working with others has its challenges, too. See Key 9.2 for the pros and cons of teamwork.

Teamwork Basics

Every team needs collaboration and process to get things done. *Collaboration*—working together toward a common goal—demands honesty, openness, consistency, and respect.

1. *Honesty* means that team members tell one another the truth, not just what each wants to hear. They disclose problems so that other members can join in the problem-solving process.

KEY 9.2 Consider the advantages and disadvantages of teamwork.

ADVANTAGES	DISADVANTAGES
Generates multiple ideas for solving problems, making it easier to resolve issues.	Slows down the problem-solving process because of discussion and disagreements. This is particularly true when teams grow larger. As a result, deadlines may be compromised.
Provides wide pool of talents, letting members work together to complete tasks.	Potentially challenging for individuals who prefer working alone or are not comfortable working with people with widely divergent skills and backgrounds.
Strengthens bonds between team members and improves job satisfaction.	May allow some team members to do less work than others and not participate as much.

2. *Openness* means that team members do not fear repercussions for communicating their thoughts. They share information and are confident that others won't make fun of their ideas.

3. *Consistency* means that each team member works, and interacts, in a consistent manner. This allows members of the team to know what to expect from one another.

4. *Respect* means that team members speak and behave respectfully toward one another. They listen to everyone's ideas without judgment, and offer constructive criticism.

Following a process helps things get done step by step and assures that nothing will be missed (that is, if everyone does his or her job). The process below has five stages.

1. Before anything else, identify the desired goal so the team starts working with the end in mind.

2. Once team members know the goal, define roles and expectations. Who is going to do what and how does it need to be done? As part of this stage, identify a leader who will define a plan and delegate tasks.

3. Then it's time for planning and scheduling. Certain tasks may depend on others, so the team leader needs to set a realistic schedule and communicate it clearly to everyone.

4. Throughout the process, the team must monitor its performance to see if deadlines are being met and teammates are performing their tasks to the best of their abilities.

5. Finally, the team needs to evaluate its performance. What went well? What didn't? What might team members change next time, either with this same team or another?

Project Teams

Although every team project has elements unique to the course and the assignment, team projects usually follow a standard course of action.

Instructor assigns the project. Group presentations may be described in the class syllabus and can be a significant portion of your grade. Your instructor will spell out what is expected.

Instructor may create groups or allow students to create their own. Most of the time, instructors assign groups. If you can choose your own team, look for conscientious classmates.

Have your first team meeting. Discuss the project and outline the parts, making sure that everyone understands the goal and responsibilities. At this meeting, define:

- A comprehensive vision of the goal
- A clear definition of each member's roles and responsibilities
- A schedule of interim and final deadlines linked to future meetings
- Contact information for all team members

Whether or not there is an official team leader, it is likely that at least one person will take on this role. A team member and a team leader both work with the team and share a common goal. The primary difference is that the *team member* is responsible for his or her contributions to the team, while the *team leader* is responsible for his or

Tips for Participation

- Be clear on your skills and talents so you know how to best contribute.
- Listen to others without interrupting.
- Concentrate on the task at hand.
- Take notes so that you do not forget what is said.
- Communicate clearly, especially when giving instructions or documenting something.
- Set goals for yourself so that you know what to do and when.
- Manage your own time so that you complete tasks on time.
- Follow through—finish what you start.

Tips for Team Leadership

- Set an example of integrity and positive attitude.
- Communicate the goal clearly so that your team understands it.
- Motivate your team members as they work toward the goal.
- Set group goals and goals for individual team members.
- Delegate tasks so that each team member knows what he or she is responsible for.
- Set up a system to communicate progress.
- Create schedules so that the team knows what must be completed and when.
- Monitor schedules and adjust if necessary.
- Don't value your contribution over that of others.

her contributions as well as the success of the entire team. See Key 9.3 for tips for both team leaders and team members.

Start individual work. As you complete your part of the project, keep the end result in mind. If the group is presenting the project in front of the class, think also of the presentation.

Gather for a second meeting (or more if necessary). When team members are finished with individual work, gather to share and combine it. If possible, send drafts or visuals via email before the meeting, so people will have time to review them. Expect that your work—and everyone else's—will need adjustment, so don't be discouraged by the need for more work. This give and take is an essential part of how this process creates an effective result.

Have a final group meeting. At this final stage, focus on:

- Putting project pieces together
- Polishing writing or visual elements
- Planning your delivery, if your team is required to present the project to the class

Study Groups

Study groups differ from project teams in that they don't always have a specific goal. Sometimes a study group will meet throughout the term, focused on a general goal of enhancing understanding of the material. Other study groups may be more goal oriented, such as a group that meets several times over a two-week period to prepare for a midterm or final.

Working with a study group holds enormous benefits for all involved, and many that go beyond the obvious benefit of greater communication and teamwork skills. See Key 9.4 for many great reasons to get involved in a study group.

Instructors sometimes initiate student study groups, commonly for math or science courses, known as *peer-assisted study sessions* or *supplemental instruction*. However, don't wait for your instructor—or for exam crunch time—to benefit from studying with others. As you get to know students in your classes, start to exchange phone numbers and emails, form groups, and schedule meetings. Here are some strategies for study group success:

- *Limit group size.* Groups of five or less tend to experience the most success.
- *Set long-term and short-term goals.* At your first meeting, determine what the group wants to accomplish, and set mini-goals at the start of each meeting.
- *Determine a regular schedule and leadership rotation.* Determine what your group needs and what the members' schedules can handle. Try to meet weekly or, at the least, every other week. Rotate leadership among members willing to lead.
- *Create study materials for one another.* Give each person a task of finding a piece of information to compile and share with the group. Teach material to one another.

KEY 9.4 Studying in groups has many benefits.

Studying in groups . . .

- Gets you to say what you know out loud, which anchors information in memory
- Introduces you to different note-taking and study skills
- Exposes you to the ideas of others and gets you thinking in different ways
- Helps you fill in gaps in your notes
- Increases the chance that all of the important information will be covered
- Breaks the monotony of solo studying
- Motivates you to study because others are counting on you
- Subjects you to questions that make you clarify and build on your thinking

Diego Cervo/Fotolia

Source: Petress, Kenneth C. "The Benefits of Group Study." *Education*, 124. 2008; and Desmond, Nate. "6 Benefits of Study Groups." Debt-Free Scholar, 2012. From www.debtfreescholar.com/2010/02/6-benefits-of-study-groups

- *Be prepared, every time.* If everyone is given a piece of the puzzle, the only way to complete the puzzle is for everyone to come with ideas and materials in hand.
- *Share the workload and pool note-taking resources.* The most important factor is a willingness to work, not knowledge level. Compare notes and fill in missing information.
- *Set your phone aside.* Texting, talking, and surfing Facebook during your study group meeting distracts you as well as others, and without paying attention you won't benefit from the interaction. Unless it is an emergency, get back to your contacts later.

Getting your study group together in person is preferable, but when schedules are tough or you are taking an online course, coordinate a virtual meeting using online conferencing technology (Skype, Vyew, Mikogo) or document collaboration technology (NoteMesh, Wikidot, Google Docs). To make a virtual meeting manageable, keep your group small and focused, log on from someplace quiet, and stay off your email until after the meeting.[3] Some learning management systems (LMS) facilitate or link to online meeting technology; if your course uses an LMS, check it to see what's possible.

Roommate Relationships

For those of you sharing living quarters with a roommate, the ability to interact effectively with others takes on even greater importance. The experience is an adjustment for everyone, even if you have shared a room with a sibling in the past or have chosen to room with a friend (an option at some schools). Even the best of friends may find that sharing a room brings up conflicts they never imagined in high school. Education expert Kelci Lynn Lucier offers some ways to manage roommate relations.[4] These suggestions can apply to suitemates, hallmates, or housemates as well.

Be clear at the start about needs and habits. Maybe you like to study in a quiet room, or have stuffed animals you don't want to be teased about, or keep your things extremely neat. If you communicate what you need right away, you may prevent later problems.

Address issues when they are minor. Calmly bring up small annoyances—too much borrowing of hair products, or too much noise—before they make you so crazy that you are unable to control your emotions.

Treat your roommate's stuff with respect. Ask first before borrowing or using anything—you would want your roommate to do the same with your stuff. And lock the door and windows when you go out—you aren't just protecting your own belongings, but your roommate's as well.

Be friendly and control your expectations. You and your roommate may become the best of friends—or not. You may just be acquaintances. You may not get along very well. Whatever your connection, friendly and respectful behaviour will contribute to the best possible experience.

Be open minded. Your roommate may introduce you to a new culture, religion, lifestyle, music, food, or ideas. Take in what's new and use it to learn and to broaden your horizons.

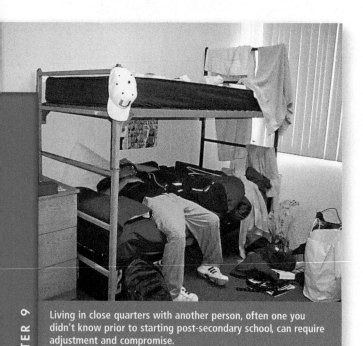

Living in close quarters with another person, often one you didn't know prior to starting post-secondary school, can require adjustment and compromise.

Sunshine Photos/Fotolia

get creative

REWRITE AN EXPERIENCE OF CONFLICT

Astroid/123RF

Complete the following on paper or in digital format.

Think of a time when you had a conflict with someone, either one on one or in a group setting, and there were negative effects for you and perhaps for others as well.

1. Briefly describe what happened.
2. Thinking about what you've read, and what you know now, ponder what you could have done differently, and generate two or three ideas about how the situation could have unfolded.
3. Of the ones you've written, choose the one that you think would have been most helpful and describe it in more detail, including information about how all parties would benefit.
4. Finally, in one sentence, describe the essence of the lesson you learned from this interaction.

Not every roommate relationship is sunny, of course. Some roommates will have minor problems, and some major conflicts. When you have a problem with a roommate, consider talking with him or her directly at first. If that doesn't work, or if you don't feel comfortable going to your roommate, have a conversation with your RA. He or she may then want to facilitate a conversation involving the roommate as well. If you can't resolve the conflict to anyone's satisfaction, consult with your RA about how to switch rooms. This may take some time and create negative feelings, so use it as a last resort.

Courtesy of Georgina Arreola

talk risk and reward . . .

Risk asking tough questions to be rewarded with new insights. Use the following to inspire discussion with classmates, in person or online.

- How inclined are you to risk reaching out to people when you need help with academics, health issues, or personal problems? Give yourself a percentage ("I am inclined to seek help 30% of the time."). Would you like to increase your percentage? Why or why not? What is the risk of *not* seeking help?

- Do you feel that getting involved in nonacademic organizations and activities helps or hinders students? Or maybe both? Give specific examples to back up your opinion. How should students get involved so that it won't get in the way of academic achievement?

CONSIDER THE CASE: When students begin university or college, many react against their upbringing or home environment, as Georgina did when she experienced increased freedom and independence. What defined your upbringing and home environment during high school? What might you be reacting against now, and what is the result of your action? What might you want to retain, and for what reward?

get $mart

ACQUIRING FINANCIAL INFORMATION

Creativenv/Shutterstock

Racorn/123.RF

Complete the following on paper or in digital format.

When you set yourself up to effectively access financial information, you will be more able to make the most of money-oriented resources on campus. Explore how you prefer to acquire financial information.

1. Which style of reading is most comfortable to you—print or electronic?
2. Rewrite this list of information sources according to how you would rank them, from 1 (I respond best to this) to 7 (I respond least to this).

   a. In-person conversations
   b. Magazines/newspapers
   c. Books
   d. Websites

   e. YouTube
   f. Blog posts
   g. Twitter feeds

3. Given these preferences, identify three specific sources that will best help you stay informed. Name each source and give a brief description of what it offers. *Note:* Use the library and internet to locate the sources.
4. What are two of your most pressing questions about personal finances right now?
5. Using one or more of your three top sources, find and write answers to these questions.

WHICH ACTIVITIES CAN
enrich your experience?

Activities and organizations provide more than just fun and a break from your studies. They give you a chance to meet people who share your interests, and an opportunity to develop teamwork, leadership, and emotional intelligence skills, along with skills specific to the activity. Furthermore, studies continue to show that students who join organizations tend to persist in their educational goals more than those who don't branch out.[5]

Following are some general activities offered by many colleges and universities. As with student services, consult your school's student handbook and website, or contact the student activities office, to find specific activities and organizations. If you want to do an activity or join a group that doesn't exist on your campus, you may be able to start an organization yourself, with some initiative and the help and support of your student affairs office.

Academic and Professional Organizations

Organizations support students in a wide variety of academic interests. What your school offers will depend on school size and course offerings. Some clubs are geared toward students in a particular major, such as an Economics Club or Philosophy Students Reading Group. Others have a professional focus, such as Future Civic Leaders or Pre-Veterinary Society. Still other organizations will combine an academic orientation with a cultural, ethnic, or lifestyle focus such as the Society of Asian Scientists and Engineers, Queer MD, or the Islamic Finance Association.

Academic and professional organizations welcome interested students, and usually have few requirements—check individual organizations for details. Chances are good that, whatever your interests or professional plans, an organization on your campus will support and enrich your studies. If you can't find one in your student handbook or on the school's website, ask an advisor or RA. You may also want to search online to see if it exists anywhere. If an organization has no chapter at your school, risk exploring how to start one.

Zurijeta/Shutterstock

Student Government and Judicial System

Most colleges and universities, in addition to the system of governance run by their employees, have a *student government* and perhaps even a *student judicial system*. The student government acts as a liaison between the student body and the administration and faculty. Consisting of representatives from the student body, a student government operates much in the way that any representative body does—bringing up issues, considering different actions, and making recommendations on behalf of those represented.

Every college and university has a judicial system that handles violations of the school's code of conduct. At some schools, students participate in the system. Students may serve on juries, as judges, or as "attorneys" representing other students accused of misconduct. The student judicial system may be of particular interest if you are considering a career in the legal system.

Print and Electronic Media

All kinds of media and reporting thrive on campuses. Your school may have print media, electronic media, one or more radio stations, and perhaps even televised journalism.

Newspapers can be campus-wide general news publications appearing weekly or more often, or focused on a specific interest or topic and less frequently published. Magazines, in print or online, may publish student poetry and prose, artworks, political essays, or writings on a particular topic. Academic journals are magazines with a more serious academic focus, and are usually focused on one academic area such as medicine or business. Literary journals publish fiction and poetry and sometimes art and photography as well.

Volunteering and Service Learning

Volunteering. Helping others in need can introduce you to careers and increase your experience, as Kelly discovered. Many schools establish committees to organize volunteering opportunities or sponsor their own groups. You may even be able to find opportunities that mesh with an area of interest. For example, if you are studying accounting, donating your time as a part-time bookkeeper in a shelter will increase your skills while you help those less fortunate than you. Many employers look favourably on volunteering. Check out Volunteer Canada (volunteer.ca) or Canada World Youth (canadaworldyouth.org/).

Service learning. The goal of service learning is to integrate the community with learning activities.[6] Students in service learning programs often enrol in for-credit courses in which volunteer service and related assignments are required. Taking the risk of service

Service learning differs from volunteering and community service.

VOLUNTEERING AND COMMUNITY SERVICE	SERVICE LEARNING
Donating emergency kits to a local Red Cross organization and helping to educate local citizens about how to use them.	As part of an emergency management course, working with a number of local nonprofit agencies to develop emergency management plans and, the end of the term, presenting plans to agency representatives along with emergency kits.
Helping a local Habitat for Humanity chapter restore some local homes that had fallen into disrepair.	As part of a survey design class, creating and administering surveys within several neighbourhoods, and giving the data to a local organization that plans to use it to make improvements to residential properties.

learning can reward you with a sense of civic responsibility, opportunity to apply what you learn in the classroom, and personal growth. If you are interested, talk to your advisor about whether your school offers service learning programs. The Canadian Alliance for Community Service Learning has more information at www.communityservicelearning.ca.

Intramural Athletics

All students can play, enjoy, and benefit from sports. Many colleges and universities have an intramural program that provides opportunities for students not competing at the level of intercollegiate athletics. Games and competitions are restricted to groups of students within the school (*intramural* is Latin for "within [the] wall") and are voluntary and open to all.

Different sports and teams function independently, although there is usually a director who oversees all intramural sports. Participation is not restricted to playing the sport itself. You could also coach or officiate or help out in some other capacity. Furthermore, even if your school does not have an official intramural program, other opportunities exist. Explore your school's list of clubs to see if there are any club sports that interest you.

Visual and Performing Arts Groups

You don't have to be an art, music, theatre, or dance major to participate in an art form that you enjoy. Most arts groups will welcome students whether they are majors or not, although particular groups may hold auditions or require you to meet other selection criteria.

You may find groups offering different types of vocal or instrumental music, dance styles, and improv or other acting opportunities. A cappella (vocals without instrumental accompaniment) groups have become extremely popular in recent years, and some campuses feature several groups. Visual arts groups may focus on all kinds of art media, including graphic arts. Some groups may produce performances or have opportunities for competition, and some may simply provide a chance for people with similar interests to develop their talents.

Chuck Rausin/Shutterstock

get practical

FIND INTERESTING CLUBS

binkski/123RF

Diego Cervo/
Shutterstock

Complete the following on paper or in digital format.

Read through your student handbook and school website about all of the clubs offered at your school and note what catches your attention. The following are just some of the possible categories, to get you thinking:

Religion	Instrumental/vocal music	Volunteering and service
Politics	Cultures	Print and electronic media
Sports	Ethnicities	Academic organizations
Fitness/wellness	Foods	Professional organizations
Visual art	Students with disabilities	Student government
Dance and theatre	Countries and languages	

List two specific groups that you will explore in the next month. Find contact information for them using school publications or online resources. Then contact them and have a real-time conversation with an officer or member of each club or group. Ask questions like:

- What is the time commitment?
- What are the people like who participate in this group?
- Are there costs involved in participating?
- Are there any requirements for members?

With your increased understanding of what membership in these two groups is like, make an informed decision about whether to get involved.

Taking the risk to perform on stage can be a challenge. However, you may enjoy the reward of bringing a new experience to an audience. Increased confidence is another potential reward, one that can help you take productive risks in other areas of your life.

Clubs of Every Type

Larger schools have hundreds of clubs and organizations, and even small schools will have a myriad of opportunities. Different clubs focus on areas such as:

- Religious ideals or practice
- Political parties or groups
- Physical or learning disabilities
- Sports and physical fitness
- Creative interests
- Ethnic groups and cultures
- Countries and languages
- Foods
- Games and gaming

student PROFILE

Olivia Daub

UNIVERSITY OF WATERLOO, WATERLOO, ONTARIO

Courtesy of Olivia Daub

About me:

I am a second-year university student at the University of Waterloo, double majoring in Psychology and English. I love working with kids, and my (current) goal for after I complete my bachelor's is to get my master's in Speech Pathology. I love to change my mind though, so who knows where I'll end up after university!

What I focus on:

I try to focus on the end of the four years, as a motivation to continue at Waterloo in my particular program. First year was frustrating because the courses were so general, and I had to take a number of breadth courses that weren't specialized. Around the mid-term point of first semester, I was wondering whether university was right for me, and whether I should transfer into something more specific, such as an Early Childhood Education program at a community college. I managed to pull through, and I chose to stay at Waterloo because I know at the end of it all my B.A. will give me more options and lead to many different career or education paths. College might be a path I explore down the road.

What will help me in the workplace:

My advice for future students is to learn time management. Know when things are due and how long you'll need to complete the assignments or study for a test. First term, I missed a lot of fun things because of either school work or my part-time job. Second term, I planned to give myself enough time for assignments, while still having a flexible enough schedule that if something came up with friends, I wouldn't miss out. This ability to balance life and work is a skill everyone will need to master.

Olivia Daub. University of Waterloo, Waterloo, Ontario.
Reprinted by permission.

A final point to ponder as you explore everything your school has to offer: Use your critical thinking skills to find the balance between work and play that suits you. Some students become so overloaded with activities that it takes a toll on their academic performance. Others avoid activities and feel disconnected from people and from the broader post-secondary experience. Pace yourself the first year, trying a couple of activities that interest you and monitoring how well you are managing your time. Evaluate periodically and reduce your involvement if you find your studies are suffering. The right balance will enrich your life without overloading it.

revisit RISK AND REWARD

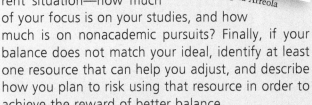

What happened to Georgina? Georgina learned that her university offered a tutoring and mentoring program called Bridge, geared to students from disadvantaged backgrounds as well as first-generation students. Many of the mentors were third- or fourth-year undergraduates. "It was all about time management and figuring out when I could take the time out of my schedule to do fun things," Georgina says. With help from Bridge and hard work, Georgina was taken off academic probation and thrived in her last two years, graduating with honours from the management science program. She moved on to earn her masters degree in public policy. She now works for an organization that specializes in the adoption of renewable energy and energy efficiency technologies.

What does this mean for you? On her path from struggling student to part-time master's-level instructor, Georgina learned a lot about what it takes to succeed academically while making the most of her new-found post-secondary "freedom." "Get to know your professors," she advises students, especially those who know they need to engage more in their coursework. "If they generally feel you are interested, they will put in the extra effort."

Think about your mix of work and play at school. First, describe what you perceive as an ideal balance of how you want to spend your time, using percentages (e.g., 70% coursework related and 30% school life related). Next, describe your current situation—how much of your focus is on your studies, and how much is on nonacademic pursuits? Finally, if your balance does not match your ideal, identify at least one resource that can help you adjust, and describe how you plan to risk using that resource in order to achieve the reward of better balance.

Courtesy of Georgina Arreola

What risk may bring reward beyond your world? Georgina is an inspiration to students, especially women, in math and science. Women are underrepresented in science, technology, engineering, and math (STEM) fields, and currently hold only 27% of all computer science jobs. Pursuing a STEM-related career can bring satisfaction beyond good earnings, and Georgina has travelled the globe making a difference. She worked with Engineers Without Borders—installing solar photovoltaic systems in low-income households in rural Mexico, and has joined forces with local leaders in Honduras to improve access to clean water. Whether you're male or female, you may find a STEM field career that both interests you and can change the world. Check out www.womeninscience.org and/or www.stemcareer.com to find out more about what's possible.

GLOBAL RISK AND REWARD

Vinzenz Weidenhofer/123RF

tamarindarts/123RF

Hepatitis B infects millions of Indian citizens and kills over 100 000 per year. In the 1980s, the vaccine was unaffordable, costing 23 times more than most Indian families earned in a day. Dr. K.I. Varaprasad Reddy was compelled to risk solving this problem despite having no funding or biotech experience. He founded Shantha, which, after years of fundraising and research, developed a vaccine that cost one U.S. dollar per dose and has protected millions of Indian citizens from the disease. Bought by a major pharmaceutical company for hundreds of millions of dollars, Shantha continues to bring reward to the average citizen in the form of medical innovations.[7]

People, Resources, and Opportunities

RISK ACTION

FOR POST-SECONDARY, CAREER, AND LIFE REWARDS

KNOW IT
Blan-k/Shutterstock

WRITE IT
Blan-k/Shutterstock

WORK IT
Blan-k/Shutterstock

Complete the following on paper or in digital format.

KNOW IT *Think Critically*

Improve How You Relate to Others

Build basic skills. Effective teamwork in study groups and project teams depends in part on team members knowing themselves well and contributing in ways that best suit them. Answer the following questions to define yourself as a team member:

1. What are your natural talents and abilities?
2. What skills have you worked hard to build and maintain?
3. What are your teamwork "likes"—what you like to do when working with others?
4. What are your teamwork "dislikes"—what you do *not* like to do when working with others?

Take it to the next level. Now consider past experience with pair or group work. Continuing your written or typed work, describe:

- Types of people or situations that boost your productivity and attitude, including an example of this from your life
- Types of people or situations that make you less productive and positive, including an example of this from your life

Move toward mastery. Considering your self-knowledge and experience, design your involvement for maximum benefit in both a project team and a study group. Ideally, you will write plans for a specific study group that you are in for a course, and a specific project team that you are in or will need to participate in this term for one of your classes (search your syllabi for possibilities). If you are not in a study group and/or have no project this term that requires teamwork, create imaginary groups with specific goals and projects. Describe, as specifically as you can:

- Your most productive role in an actual or imagined study group
- Your most productive role in an actual or imagined project team

WRITE IT *Communicate*

Emotional intelligence journal: Where can you give back? As a new student, you may feel overwhelmed with responsibilities. However, looking beyond your own needs to help someone else can lend balance and perspective to your life. Imagining you have no time issues, write about what types of volunteer or community service work would be meaningful to you, and why. Then, considering your current schedule and what's available in your school community, describe one or more specific ways you might make this possibility a reality.

Real-life writing: Connect with your advisor. Few students make use of everything academic advisors can offer. Think of a question you have regarding a specific course, major, or academic situation that your advisor might help you answer. Craft an email in appropriate language to your advisor, and send it. Then, to stretch your communication skills, rewrite the same email twice more: once in a format you would send to an instructor, and once in a format appropriate for a friend. Send either or both of these if you think the response would be valuable to you.

DO IT *Build Your Brand*

Learn More about Career Success

Investigate what brings success in the workplace.

1. Choose and list three career areas that interest you.
2. Next, visit a website, such as YouTube, that hosts user-loaded videos. Search for an interview with someone working in one of your listed career areas. Try search terms like "marketing interview," "what's it like to be a dental technician?" or "what does a movie producer do?" Once you find a usable video (one with credible, realistic information), take notes on the interview using a note-taking technique you have learned in this course.

   a. Watch the video all the way through, concentrating on main points and overall themes.
   b. Watch it again to fill in gaps, understand key terms and concepts, and gather interesting additional facts and ideas.
   c. After you watch the video twice and have thorough notes, write a one-page summary of the career for your portfolio. Include important information discussed in the video, such as what training is required, salary expectations, daily duties, challenges, and rewards. Keep the summary in your portfolio for future career searches.

CHAPTER

10

Post-secondary education provides an extraordinary opportunity to explore yourself and the knowledge available to you. The earlier you risk thinking about career goals, the greater reward you can receive from your education, which can prepare you for work in both job-specific and general ways.

Plan for Career Success

WHAT IS YOUR PURPOSE AND YOUR PASSION?

What Would You Risk? *Dan Oltersdorf*

THINK ABOUT THIS SITUATION AS YOU READ, AND CONSIDER WHAT ACTION YOU WOULD TAKE. THIS CHAPTER HELPS YOU FIRST TO EXPLORE YOUR ACADEMIC FOCUS WHILE IN SCHOOL. THEN IT EXAMINES THE VARIOUS WAYS YOU CAN PREPARE FOR A SUCCESSFUL CAREER WHILE YOU ARE IN SCHOOL.

For a small minority of people, the career road map is clear from an early age. Dan Oltersdorf was not one of those people.

Dan grew up in a modest household. His parents did not attend post-secondary school and did not think it made sense for him to go either, unless he could specify an occupational target. Dan planned to attend trade school instead, honing his skills during high school with a 30-hour-per-week job working with machines. That experience taught him that he preferred working with people. Dan decided to become a chiropractor.

He took part-time jobs to pay expenses, working in marketing at the student union and as an orientation leader and a resident assistant (RA). Although he mainly became an RA to save on room and board, Dan discovered something more. "I loved working in that environment, loved working with college students," he says.

Halfway through his undergraduate education, Dan faced a dilemma. He had invested two years in coursework and didn't want to disappoint his parents, who urged him to stick to the path he had laid out. But Dan was most fulfilled as a resident assistant, serving as a confidant, mentor, advisor, and friend, someone who could defuse a crisis, prevent substance abuse, offer encouragement, and foster a sense of community. Were there any career opportunities for someone who majored in "resident assistance"? He could not see what viable reward could come from this risk, and he hesitated to make another detour.

To be continued . . .

MANY STUDENTS STRUGGLE WITH THE DECISION TO CHANGE MAJORS. DAN TOOK A RISK AND FOLLOWED HIS PASSION, NOT SURE WHETHER HE WOULD FIND A REWARDING CAREER FURTHER ALONG DOWN THE PATH. YOU'LL LEARN MORE ABOUT DAN, AND THE REWARD RESULTING FROM HIS ACTIONS, WITHIN THE CHAPTER.

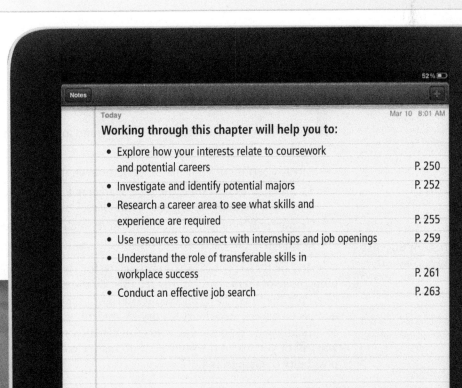

Notes   52% 🔋 ＋

Today   Mar 10 8:01 AM

Working through this chapter will help you to:

- Explore how your interests relate to coursework and potential careers .... P. 250
- Investigate and identify potential majors .... P. 252
- Research a career area to see what skills and experience are required .... P. 255
- Use resources to connect with internships and job openings .... P. 259
- Understand the role of transferable skills in workplace success .... P. 261
- Conduct an effective job search .... P. 263

statusCHECK

Left to Right: Luis Santos/Shutterstock; Antonio Guillem/Shutterstock; antoniodiaz/Shutterstock; mimagephotography/Shutterstock; Djomas/ Shutterstock; WAYHOME studio/Shutterstock

How Prepared Are You for Workplace Success?

For each statement, fill in the number that best describes how often it applies to you.

1 = never   2 = seldom   3 = sometimes   4 = often   5 = always

1. I have thought about careers that may suit my interests and abilities.   ① ② ③ ④ ⑤

2. I have looked into majors that match up with my career interests.   ① ② ③ ④ ⑤

3. I have, or intend to get, hands-on experience through an internship, job, or volunteer work.   ① ② ③ ④ ⑤

4. I understand the value of emotional intelligence in today's workplace.   ① ② ③ ④ ⑤

5. I am aware of unconventional options for majoring at my school.   ① ② ③ ④ ⑤

6. I am familiar with online job search, social networking, and career planning sites.   ① ② ③ ④ ⑤

7. I know how to write an effective cover letter.   ① ② ③ ④ ⑤

8. I have a current résumé to send out to prospective employers.   ① ② ③ ④ ⑤

9. I am prepared to give a good impression during interviews.   ① ② ③ ④ ⑤

10. I plan to stay open to possibilities, and will be flexible if I decide I want to change my major.   ① ② ③ ④ ⑤

Each of the topics in these statements is covered in this chapter. Note those statements for which you filled in a 3 or lower. Skim the chapter to see where those topics appear, and pay special attention to them as you read, learn, and apply new strategies.

REMEMBER: NO MATTER HOW PREPARED YOU ARE TO SUCCEED IN THE WORKPLACE, YOU CAN IMPROVE WITH EFFORT AND PRACTICE.

HOW CAN YOU DETERMINE
your academic focus?

Think for a moment about where you stand in the process of choosing a major. Are you:

- Already certain of your major, perhaps even in the process of making it official?
- Thinking of two or three areas of academic focus, and planning to test how you feel about them by taking particular classes over your first two years?
- Certain only of a general academic area, such as engineering or the humanities?
- Completely unsure of what you will choose to major in?

Any of these positions is appropriate for the beginning of your career. Furthermore, none of them is necessarily reliable. By the end of this term, a student determined to go pre-med may have rejected it outright because of an intense dislike of a course, and become interested in art history. A student with no idea at all may have connected so strongly with a particular course that it becomes the inspiration for a major. In a way, all of you are in the same boat no matter your status, all able to benefit from the possibility of change and discovery.

MyLab Student Success
(www.mystudentsuccesslab.com) is an online solution designed to help you "Start Strong, Finish Stronger" by building skills for ongoing personal and professional development.

Your work this term on self-exploration and goal setting has set the stage for you to explore majors. This chapter goes into more detail about the process of focusing your academic work on one or more majors.

Majors and Concentrations

At some point during the first year or two of college or university, nearly all students are required to declare a *major*—an intention to focus your studies in a particular academic subject area, requiring a specific course of study. You may or may not need to declare a *concentration* (a subset of your major) or a *specialization* (an even more specific area of application). See Key 10.1 for some examples that illustrate how majors, concentrations, and specializations relate to one another.

Declaring a major largely determines the courses you take, what you learn, and with whom you spend your school time. Your major may also have a significant influence on your future career. Money expert Michelle Singletary strongly recommends that students think about how their majors will translate into income post-graduation, and that they plan ahead by weighing potential earnings against the debt they will incur through their college or university years.[1] Although she doesn't discourage students from following their passions, she feels that productive risks should be made with future rewards in mind:

> An education is not an investment in your future if you are taking out loans just for the experience. It's not an investment if you're not coupling your education with training. It's not an investment if you aren't researching which fields are creating good-paying jobs now and 30 years from now.[2]

KEY 10.1   You may need a concentration or specialization within your major.

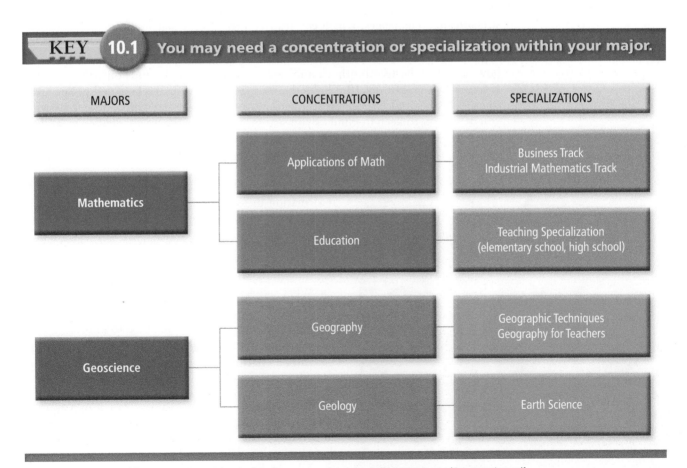

MAJORS	CONCENTRATIONS	SPECIALIZATIONS
Mathematics	Applications of Math	Business Track / Industrial Mathematics Track
	Education	Teaching Specialization (elementary school, high school)
Geoscience	Geography	Geographic Techniques / Geography for Teachers
	Geology	Earth Science

Source: Examples from Middle Tennessee State University, http://www.mtsu.edu/admissn/pdf/MTSUMajorsAndConcentrations.pdf

No one would suggest that you declare a major that you can't stand simply to increase your chances of making a living—a reward that may not be worth it in the long run. What's important is to make career potential one of several significant factors in your decision-making process.

Taking a practical approach to declaring a major can help you avoid feeling overwhelmed. Think of it as a long-term goal made up of multiple actions or steps (short-term goals) that begin with knowing yourself, exploring academic options, and establishing your academic schedule. Start the process now, even if you don't need to declare right away, so that you can give this life-changing decision the time it deserves.

Examine Strengths, Interests, and Talents

Considering what you like and what you do well can lead to a fulfilling area of study. In addition, when you focus on an area that involves your interests and talents, you are likely to have a positive attitude and perform at your highest level, both at school and in the workplace.

Like Dan, many students initially don't know what feels right, and often discover their majors—and/or careers—through chance and risk-taking. Multi-millionaire author J.K. Rowling, for example, earned a degree in French and worked in research as well as at several other jobs. Raising her daughter alone after a divorce and struggling to make ends meet, she risked working on a book idea she had come up with several years before. Her books about student wizard Harry Potter became the best-selling book series in history. The reward was, and continues to be, significant.

Because who you are as a learner relates closely to who you are as a worker, results from learning assessments provide clues in the search for the right career. For example, the Multiple Intelligences assessment points to information about your natural strengths and challenges, which can lead you to careers that involve these strengths. Look at Key 10.2 to see how those intelligences may link up with various careers.

The Personality Spectrum assessment is equally significant, because it focuses on how you work best with others, and career success often depends on your ability to function in a team. Key 10.3 links the four dimensions of the Personality Spectrum to career ideas and job search strategies. Look for your strengths and decide what you may want to keep in mind as you search. Look also at areas of challenge, and try to identify ways to boost your abilities in those areas. Every job will involve some tasks outside of your comfort zone.

Use your self-assessment results, along with the information in Keys 10.2 and 10.3, as a starting point for thinking about majors and careers. Consider questions like these:

- What courses did I enjoy the most in high school? What do these courses have in common?
- What subjects am I drawn to in my personal reading?
- What activities do I look forward to most?
- In what skills or academic areas do I perform best? Am I a "natural" in any area?
- What do people say I do well?

Finally, one other way to investigate how your personality and strengths may inform career choice is to take an inventory based on the Holland Theory. Theorizing that personality was related to career choice, psychologist John Holland came up with six different types that

Courtesy of Sarah Lyman Kravits

Taking courses in an area of interest can help you see how well a major or a career in this area might suit you. These students get hands-on experience in respiratory therapy as well as advice from an experienced instructor.

KEY 10.2 Multiple intelligences may open doors to careers.

MULTIPLE INTELLIGENCE	LOOK INTO A CAREER AS...
Bodily-kinesthetic	• Carpenter or draftsman • Physical therapist • Mechanical engineer • Dancer or actor • Exercise physiologist
Intrapersonal	• Research scientist • Computer engineer • Psychologist • Economist • Author
Interpersonal	• Social worker • PR or HR rep • Sociologist • Teacher • Nurse
Naturalistic	• Biochemical engineer • Natural scientist (geologist, ecologist, entymologist) • Paleontologist • Position with environmental group • Farmer or farm management
Musical	• Singer or voice coach • Music teacher • Record executive • Musician or conductor • Radio DJ or sound engineer
Logical-mathematical	• Doctor or dentist • Accountant • Attorney • Chemist • Investment banker
Verbal-linguistic	• Author or journalist • TV/radio producer • Literature or language teacher • Business executive • Copywriter or editor
Visual-spatial	• Graphic artist or illustrator • Photographer • Architect or interior designer • Art museum curator • Art teacher • Set or retail stylist

Top to Bottom: Alexander Raths/Shutterstock; focal point/Shutterstock; Helder Almeida/123RF; Ambient Ideas/Shutterstock; Simeon Donov/123RF; kak2s/Shutterstock; TatsianaTur/Shutterstock; Neelsky/123RF.

identify both personality and career areas: **R**ealistic, **I**nvestigative, **A**rtistic, **S**ocial, **E**nterprising, and **C**onventional (together known as **RIASEC**).[3] Holland developed two interest surveys that allow people to identify their order of preference for the six types and help them link their stronger types to career areas. Ask your career centre about these surveys: the Vocational Preference Inventory (VPI®) or Self-Directed Search (SDS®).

KEY 10.3 Personality Spectrum dimension indicates strengths and challenges.

DIMENSION	JOB STRENGTH	JOB CHALLENGES	WHAT TO LOOK FOR IN JOBS/ CAREERS
Thinker	• Problem solving • Developing ideas • Keen analysis of situations • Fairness to others • Working efficiently through tasks • Innovating plans and systems • Ability to look strategically at the future	• A need for private time to think and work • A need, at times, to move away from established rules • A dislike of sameness—systems that don't change, repetitive tasks • Not always being open to expressing thoughts and feelings to others	• Some level of solo work/think time • Problem solving • Opportunity for innovation • Freedom to think creatively and to bend the rules • Technical work • Big picture strategic planning
Organizer	• High level of responsibility • Enthusiastic support of social structures • Order and reliability • Loyalty • Following through on tasks • Detailed planning skills with competent follow-through • Neatness and efficiency	• A need for tasks to be clearly, concretely defined • A need for structure and stability • A preference for less rapid change • A need for frequent feedback • A need for tangible appreciation • Low tolerance for people who don't conform to rules and regulations	• Clear, well-laid-out tasks and plans • Stable environment with consistent, repeated tasks • Organized supervisors • Clear structure of how employees interact and report to one another • Value of, and reward for, loyalty
Giver	• Honesty and integrity • Commitment to putting energy toward close relationships with others • Finding ways to bring out the best in self and others • Peacemaker and mediator • Ability to listen well, respect opinions, and prioritize the needs of co-workers	• Difficulty handling conflict, either personal or between others in the work environment • Strong need for appreciation and praise • Low tolerance for perceived dishonesty or deception • Avoidance of people perceived as hostile, cold, or indifferent	• Emphasis on teamwork and relationship building • Indications of strong and open lines of communication among workers • Encouragement of personal expression in the workplace (arrangement of personal space, tolerance of personal celebrations, and so on)
Adventurer	• Skilfulness in many different areas • Willingness to try new things • Ability to take action • Hands-on problem-solving skills • Initiative and energy • Ability to negotiate • Spontaneity and creativity	• Intolerance of being kept waiting • Lack of detail focus • Impulsiveness • Dislike of sameness and authority • Need for freedom, constant change, and constant action • Tendency not to consider consequences of actions	• A spontaneous atmosphere • Less structure, more freedom • Adventuresome tasks • Situations involving change • Encouragement of hands-on problem solving • Travel and physical activity • Support of creative ideas and endeavours

Top to Bottom: onilmilk/Shutterstock; PHENPHAYOM/Shutterstock; Tatiana Popova/123RF; James Steidl/123 RF.

Determine Academic Options

Next, find out about the academic choices available at your school.

Learn what's possible. Consult your school's calendar for guidelines on declaring (and changing) your major. Find answers to these questions:

- When do I have to declare a major? (Generally at the end of the second year; earlier for programs that have a heavier load of required courses.)
- What are my options in majoring (double majors, minors, interdisciplinary majors)?
- What majors are offered at my school?

If a major looks interesting, explore it further:

- What minimum grade point average, if any, does the department require before it will accept me as a major?
- What GPA must I maintain in the courses included in the major?
- What preparatory courses (prerequisites) are required?
- What courses will I be required to take and in what sequence? How many credits do I need to graduate in the major?
- Will I have to write a thesis to graduate in this major?
- If I plan to go to graduate school, is this major appropriate for the kind of graduate school that interests me?

Work closely with your advisor. Early on, begin discussing your major with your advisor; he or she can help you evaluate different options.

Visit the department. When considering a major, analyze your comfort with the academic department as well as with the material. Find the department office during weekday hours and ask the department secretary for information. Sit in on several classes to get a feel for the instructors and the work. Consider asking an instructor for an appointment to discuss the major. Check out the department website if there is one.

Speak to people with experience in the major. Ask students who are a year or two ahead of you to describe their experiences with the courses, the workload, and the instructors.

Risk creative choices. Consider the rewards that may lie beyond the traditional path and investigate the possibilities at your school. One or more of the following may be open to you:

- *A variety of concentrations and specializations.* Many schools offer you the chance to focus closely on a small aspect of a larger area. For example, an education major might concentrate in special education and specialize in either elementary or high school students.
- *Double majors.* You may want to major in two distinct areas. Because double majoring means significantly more required courses, students who double major should consider declaring early to avoid having to extend your education (and payments) past four years.
- *Interdisciplinary majors.* If your preferred major isn't in the calendar, consult your advisor. Some schools allow students to design interdisciplinary majors (combining aspects of two or more academic focus areas) with guidance.
- *Minors.* A minor involves a concentration of departmental courses, but has fewer requirements than a major. Many students choose a minor that links effectively with a major and/or enhances career prospects. For example, a sociology major who wants to work in a hospital in Quebec might minor in French.

Manage Your Academic Schedule

Effective time management will enable you to fulfill the requirements of your major and complete all additional credits.

Look at your time frame. Do you intend to finish your requirements in four years? Be honest with yourself about what you can reasonably expect to accomplish, considering all your responsibilities. If you're working 20 to 30 hours a week *and* attending school, it may be very difficult to graduate on schedule. Do you plan to attend graduate school? If so, do you plan to go there directly after graduation or take time off?

get analytical

INVESTIGATE WHERE PASSION AND JOB PROSPECTS INTERSECT

Dario Sabljak/Shutterstock

Darren Baker/Shutterstock

Use the Venn diagram in this exercise to find majors that take your interests and abilities into account while offering as much employment potential as possible. In the left-hand circle, list 5 or more interests and abilities. In the right-hand circle, list 5 or more areas that show steady or growing employment (do some research to find the most recent statistics).

Then turn to the middle section of the diagram where the two circles intersect. Referring to your school's list of majors/concentrations/specializations for ideas, list in that middle section at least two majors (with concentrations or specializations if applicable) that in some way combine what you like and do well with where you can expect good job prospects.

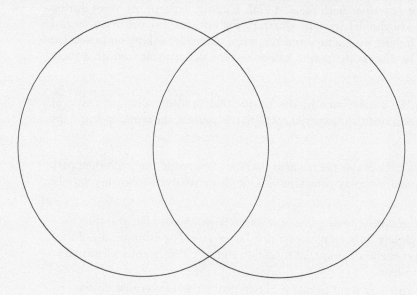

Set timing for short-term goals. Within your time frame, pinpoint when to accomplish the short-term goals that lead to graduation. What are the deadlines for completing core requirements, declaring a major, writing a thesis? Drafting a tentative *curriculum*—the set of courses required for a degree, both within and outside your major—can help clarify where you are heading.

Identify dates connected to your goal fulfillment. Pay attention to academic dates (you will find important academic dates and deadlines in each year's calendar and on the website). Such dates include registration dates, final date to declare a major, final date to drop a course, and so forth. Plan ahead so you don't miss a deadline.

When You Want to Change Your Major

As Dan did, many students change their minds as they consider majors; some declare a major and then change it one or more times before finding a good fit. When you take a course in an area you think you will like, you might discover that something central to

CHAPTER 10

that subject doesn't work for you—writing papers (in a history course), for example, or working in the lab (for a biology course). This is a sign that you should consider alternatives.

Discuss any change with your advisor, and perhaps a faculty member, before you make your decision. If you decide that the risk will be worthwhile, take action as soon as possible. Work with your advisor to complete any required paperwork and redesign your schedule to reflect the change. If you have already taken a semester or a year of courses in one major, fulfilling the requirements in your new major may mean putting off graduation. Consider that possibility as you weigh the pros and cons of the change.

HOW CAN YOU LAY THE GROUNDWORK
for a rewarding career?

Every student has a unique career preparation status. Some already have a work history, and others none; some have known for a while exactly what they want to do, others have no idea at all; and still others are in the middle, with some thoughts but no focus yet. Keep in mind that your starting point is not better or worse than anyone else's. Knowing exactly what you want is not "better" than having no clue—it's just different. Different starting points mean different courses of action. Someone who is driven to pursue engineering, for example, will follow a different path than someone who has not yet pinpointed an area of academic interest. Know where you are now so that you can choose the best path for you. Keep the following in mind:

The modern workplace is defined by change. The working world is changing more rapidly than in any other time in history, responding to technological developments, global competition, economic change, and other factors. Although this brings a risk of frequent job changes, it also offers the reward of a myriad of opportunities to learn and reinvent yourself throughout your career. This is why the Conference Board of Canada says that employees need to be adaptable and "be open and respond constructively to change" in its Employability Skills 2000+ Profile.[4] Furthermore, it increases the importance of strong transferable skills such as thinking, teamwork, writing, and goal setting.

Now is the time to start thinking about careers. University and college provide a once-in-a-lifetime opportunity to explore yourself and the knowledge available to you. The earlier you take the risk to consider career goals, the greater reward you can receive from your education and your school's resources, which can prepare you for work in both job-specific and general ways.

Ideally, your career will reflect your values and talents and reward you with the income you need. The "right" career means something different to everyone. Read on about more career preparation strategies.

Connect Major to Career

Many sources of career advice say that pursuing a passion is a key element of career success. This doesn't mean that you'll love every aspect or every day of your job—no one does. However, you improve your chances of thriving if you spend the bulk of your job doing work that interests you and taps into your strengths.

As you begin to implement what you worked on in the Get Analytical exercise, ask for advice. An academic advisor can help you define which careers need specific majors and which are accessible from a broader range of educational backgrounds. For example, students going into medical professions usually need to major in a science or premed area, while students aiming to work in business might major in anything from technology to liberal arts. Business owners are becoming more aware of how liberal arts majors bring value to the workplace through skills such as problem solving and writing.[5]

Investigate Career Paths

Career possibilities extend far beyond what you can imagine. Talk to instructors, relatives, mentors, and fellow students about careers. Explore job listings, occupation lists, assessments, and other information at your school's career centre. Check your library for books on careers or biographies of people who worked in fields that interest you. Visit websites such as Workopolis that provide information about education and skills required for particular occupations, on-the-job tasks, possible salaries, and more. You should also read magazines such as *Maclean's* and *Canadian Business* that often publish issues about jobs that are hot or not. Look at Key 10.4 for the questions you might ask yourself as you conduct your research.

Keep the following in mind as your investigate careers.

A wide array of job possibilities exists for most career fields. For example, the medical world consists of more than doctors and nurses. Administrators run hospitals, researchers test drugs, pharmacists prepare prescriptions, security experts ensure patient and visitor safety, and so on.

Within each job, there is a variety of tasks. You know that an instructor teaches, but you may not think about the fact that instructors may also write, research, study, design courses, give presentations, counsel, and coach. Take your career exploration beyond first impressions to get a broader picture of what's possible in the careers that interest you.

Some career areas are growing more than others. If you have an interest in a growing career area, statistically you will have a better chance of finding a job. For the latest data, check www.jobbank.gc.ca for the latest occupational forecasts. You'll be able to refine your search to include your province/territory or city.

Expand Knowledge and Build Experience

Even after investigation, it's hard to choose the right path without knowledge or experience. Courses, volunteering, service learning, clubs, and travel are risks that promote those rewards.

KEY 10.4 Ask questions like these to analyze how a career area or job may fit you.

What can I do in this area that I like and do well?	Do I respect the company or the industry? The product or service?
What are the educational requirements (certificates or degrees, courses)?	Does this company or industry accommodate special needs (child care, sick days, flex time)?
What skills are necessary?	Do I need to belong to a union? What does union membership involve?
What wage or salary and benefits can I expect?	Are there opportunities near where I live (or want to live)?
What personality types are best suited to this kind of work?	What other expectations exist (travel, overtime, and so on)?
What are the prospects for moving up to higher-level positions?	Do I prefer the service or production end of this industry?

Courses. Take a course or two in your areas of interest to determine if you like the material and excel in it. Find out what courses are required for a major in those areas. Check out your school's course catalogue for detailed information. Also, consider talking with the department chair, or an older student who has taken some of the courses, to gain more insight into the field.

Volunteering. Helping others in need offers rewards including an introduction to careers, experience, new contacts, and a positive impression on potential employers. Many schools sponsor volunteer groups or have committees that organize volunteering opportunities. Many employers look favourably on applicants who have volunteered their time while in school. For more information, check out Volunteer Canada (volunteer.ca) or Canada World Youth (canadaworldyouth.org).

Service learning. The goal of service learning is to provide the community with service and give students knowledge gained from hands-on experience.[6] Taking the risk of service learning can reward you with a sense of civic responsibility, opportunity to apply what you learn in the classroom, and personal growth.

Clubs and organizations. Getting involved in activities has several career benefits. You increase knowledge in the area of the club's focus, and may also learn about career possibilities from people you meet through club activities. You build experience both in the club's focus area as well as in transferable skills areas such as teamwork, communication, and self-management.

Travel. Whether your travel is part of a study-abroad program or independent of your coursework, the ways in which travel broadens your perspectives can help you generate career ideas. You may meet people who have particular jobs, observe career possibilities in the area where you are visiting, learn about international divisions of Canadian companies that have outposts in other countries, or even come up with career ideas related to the act of travelling itself.

Consult Your School's Career Services

Every university and college has a career-focused office, perhaps referred to as the *career centre* or *office of career planning and placement*, staffed with well-informed people and stocked with a wide array of resources. Your career office can help you both in your exploration period as well as when you need more specific guidance for job applications and interviews. Do not hesitate to visit early and often. Generally, most career offices can help you with the following tasks.

Exploration through self-assessment. Ask about what self-assessment tools your office has available for you—perhaps one involving the aforementioned Holland Theory, or one looking at your Myers-Briggs Type Indicator code, or a host of others. Tools like these will help you look at your interests and abilities and see what majors and career may make the most of them.

Information on specific careers and the general job market. Whatever career interests you, the office will have information on it, as well as ideas about other places online and at the library to research further. Staffers will also be informed about trends such as which industries are growing and which are suffering, and where the jobs are projected to be as you enter the workforce.

LifeBound, LLC

get creative

YOUR STRATEGIC TIMELINE

Complete the following on paper or in digital format.

Considering your self-knowledge, experience, possible career paths, and understanding of the workplace, create a practical five-year timeline as a strategic plan to achieve a career goal. First, describe where you do want to be in five years. For each of the following time frames, write in the steps you think you will need to take toward that five-year goal. Include anything you envision in your path toward a career, such as steps related to declaring a major or a transfer to another school to pursue additional degrees.

- One month from now. . .
- Three months from now. . .
- Six months from now. . .
- One year from now. . .
- Two years from now. . .
- Three years from now. . .
- Four years from now. . .

Finally, create a timeline version of your plan, using a visual format you like and adding smaller goals as necessary. Keep your timeline where you can refer to it and revise it, since changes in the world and in your knowledge and experience may require adjustments in your plan.

Preparing important materials. Creating a résumé and cover letter can be daunting. The career centre staff can guide you with choosing a format and selecting information to include. They may review your materials for you and offer suggestions. They may also have electronic templates that you can use to create documents more easily.

Bart Ah You/Modesto Bee/
ZUMA Press Inc/Alamy Stock Photo

Take advantage of career fairs sponsored by your school or town. These career fair attendees pick up useful information and applications from a variety of employers.

Interviews and placement. Career offices often sponsor job fairs where you can connect with a variety of employers, and they have updated job listings available. They may coach you one-on-one before your interview, and may also have interview workshops available to students.

Along with your future planning, you may want or need to work now, during your post-secondary career. Even the most basic job has benefits in both the short term and long term.

WHAT CAN WORKING NOW
do for you later?

Combine recent economic challenges with the rise in tuition costs over the last generation, and you have a recipe for financial challenge that nearly every post-secondary student has to reckon with. It's not unusual for a Canadian post-secondary student to graduate with roughly $25 000 in student loan debt.[7] Outstanding student loans in have passed $28 billion dollars in Canada.[8]

To improve this grim picture, the number of students combining coursework with one or more jobs has grown. The most recently tabulated data from Statistics Canada (2010) showed that almost half of traditional-aged undergraduates held jobs of some kind while in school, with the average student logging 16 hours a week working part time.[9] Given the economic challenges that have hit since that time, these numbers have probably increased.

If you have to work or choose to work, take heart. Whatever you risk in devoting time and energy to your work, you will take away a reward that will serve you in the future.

Working On and Off Campus

Students have a range of job options, although many factors affect which jobs suit a given student and how likely the student is to be hired. Remember that any job, no matter what area or what tasks it requires, may in some way connect to future career success. Someone who takes a legal proofreading job to make extra cash might discover an interest in law. Someone who answers phones for a newspaper company might be drawn into journalism. A seemingly random job might lead you down a major life path.

On-Campus Jobs

Jobs on campus may or may not be part of a (work–study) program (such as the Canadian Student Employment Program).

On-campus jobs can help you forward your career goals in several ways. One, if you work in an area of academic or career interest, you are building knowledge and perhaps experience as well. Two, because they are close by, often flexible and part time, and may even allow for you to study while at work (depending on the nature of the job), on-campus jobs can help you stay on track with your studies while earning extra cash. Three, as with any job, on-campus jobs will build transferable skills.

WORK–STUDY
A program providing employment to college and university students to help pay school expenses. Work-study jobs can be federally funded or independent and are usually related to students' area of study or focused on community service.

Off-Campus Jobs

Students who work off campus may do so because they want to do a particular type of work not available on campus, want to work longer hours than on-campus jobs offer, have an existing connection with an employer, are ineligible for on-campus jobs, or were unable to get an on-campus job due to overwhelming demand.

Off-campus jobs build transferable skills just as on-campus jobs do. Because they may demand more of your time, though, you may want to prioritize working in an area of interest if you are going to go to the trouble of working off campus. One additional benefit is that if your job is in a career area that you want to continue to explore, you may be building networking contacts and a reputation that will serve you well after graduation.

Internships

An (internship) gives you a chance to work in a field to see how you like it. Internships are usually unpaid, although some carry a small salary or stipend. They generally happen over a limited period of time, for example, over the summer, or for three to six months.

INTERNSHIP
A temporary work program in which a student can gain supervised practical experience in a particular professional field.

Pros and Cons

Internships have grown in potential significance as the job market has tightened in recent years. Trudy Steinfeld, a career development expert, reports that internships "have never been more closely tied to permanent hiring than they are today," because of how they provide "a way to test-drive potential employees."[10] With stakes ever higher for employers, and companies less willing to take a chance, knowing what to expect out of a potential employee can be a significant factor in the hiring decision. Plus, the test-drive goes both ways—an intern can evaluate the experience and decide if the company's culture works for him or her.[11]

What potential downsides do internships hold? First of all, just as there is more competition for jobs, more students and graduates are competing for internships. Second, not every internship holds value, and interns sometimes end up doing menial work unrelated to the company's specific goals. In Canada, each province has its own set of guidelines regarding internships. For more information on the rules and regulations in your province, and to download a copy of The Canadian Intern Rights Guide, go to internassociation.ca.

Finding and Making the Most of Internships

Being able to take initiative will serve you here. Call a company you are interested in, recommends Lauren Berger of Internqueen.com, and ask if it would consider having an intern. She notes, "If the employer tells you they've never had an intern before, ask them if you can be the first." She also advises students to list 10 companies they like and search online for the names of people who coordinate internships for those companies.[12] As the saying goes, "If you don't ask, the answer is always no."

How can you make the most of an internship experience? First of all, during the interview, ask for specifics about the tasks you will be performing. Second, if you take the internship, understand that you may spend some time in menial tasks or with nothing to do at all, and that handling it pleasantly can build transferable skills (diligence, patience, finishing a task) as well as make a positive impression on employees that may lead to a paid position down the road. Third, if you feel that you are learning nothing valuable, consider politely speaking up to see if your tasks can be adjusted.

Practical Tools for the Job Search

Whether you are looking for a job now or planning ahead for a search closer to graduation, you can increase your success by using the resources available to you, following a strategic plan, and knowing the basics about résumés, formal interviews, and informational interviews.

NETWORKING
The exchange of information or services among individuals, groups, or institutions.

Use Available Resources

Use your school's career office, your networking skills, classified ads, and online services to help you explore possibilities for career areas or specific jobs.

The career office. Look for job listings, interview sign-up sheets, and company contact information. Go to informational workshops and job fairs. Meet with a staff member to explore work–study offerings on campus or other opportunities.

Networking in person. The most basic type of networking—talking to people about fields and jobs that interest you—is one of the most important job-hunting strategies. Networking contacts can answer questions regarding job hunting, job responsibilities and challenges, and salary expectations. Risk reaching out to friends and family members, instructors, administrators, counsellors, alumni, employers, coworkers, and others for the reward of the help they can offer you.

Networking online. Tools like LinkedIn, Facebook, and Twitter allow members to connect with other individuals through groups, fan pages, and similar interests. During a job search, these sites can be used to meet people who work at companies you are interested in and showcase portfolio pieces. A word of caution: Your online presence is public.

If you wouldn't want a potential employer (or your parents, instructor, or religious leader) to see something, don't post it. In fact, many employers review Facebook pages of applicants before inviting them for interviews.

Online services and classified ads. Although classified ads are still helpful for local possibilities, the internet—with its enormous information storage capabilities and low cost—is a better location for job postings. Many employers post job openings through online boards. In addition to a job description and salary information, most online postings will contain company information and a link to where you can submit an application. To get the most out of your virtual resources:

- Join a business-focused social networking site, like LinkedIn, and look at jobs posted there. Network with your contacts to find out about upcoming and existing openings.
- Check the web pages of individual associations and companies, which may post job listings and descriptions.
- Look up career-focused and job listing websites such as monster.ca, Canadajobs.com, or ca.indeed.com. *Note:* Competition is fierce on these large sites and you may not hear anything from them. Target companies where you think there is a fit, and try to find a specific person at that company to whom to submit your résumé.
- If you see several jobs posted for a company, but none that you are qualified for, contact someone at the company and ask if there may be openings in your area of expertise in the near future. Consider sending your résumé with a cover letter, to increase the chances that your name will come up when a position does become available.

If nothing happens right away, follow up with a short email, or mail a hard copy version of your résumé with a note that you are still interested, or call and ask the status of the application process. Keep in mind that statistically, networking results in far more hires than online posting. Some experts recommend you spend no more than 10 to 20% of your time responding to online job sites.[13] You don't risk much with this activity, but your chances for reward are similarly low.

Use an Organized, Consistent Strategy

Organize your approach according to what you need to do and when you have to do it. Do you plan to make three phone calls per day? Will you fill out one job application each week? Keep a record—on 3 by 5 cards, in a computer file or smartphone, or in a notebook—of the following:

- People you contact plus contact information and method of contact (email, snail mail, phone)
- Companies to which you apply
- Jobs for which you apply, including ones you rule out or that become unavailable
- Responses to communications (phone calls, interviews, written communications), information about who contacted you (name, title), and the time and dates of contact

Keeping accurate records allows you to both chart your progress and maintain a clear picture of the process. Your records help you follow up and stay in touch. Key 10.5 shows you what part of a typical contact list might look like. If you don't get a job now but another opens up later at the same company, well-kept records will enable you to contact key personnel efficiently.

Your Résumé and Cover Letter

Cover letters and résumés allow you to introduce yourself to prospective employers. Here are a few basic tips on giving yourself the best possible chance at employment.

KEY 10.5 Keep accurate records to follow up and stay in touch.

CONTACT AND COMPANY	INITIAL PHONE CALL	LETTER/RÉSUMÉ	FOLLOW-UP	INTERVIEW
Out Signals Jackson Fortnet PR Director 312-505-0400 jfortnet@outsignals.com	SEPT. 13 Called and spoke briefly	SEPT. 14 Sent email to Jackson, along with resume and job description.	SEPT. 21 Made follow-up call to find out if graphics design manager would be available for an informational interview. No such luck. Very unfriendly.	NO
Carto Net Scott de Frey scott.defrey@cartonet.com	SEPT. 15 Called Scott re: info. interview. He suggested sending in a résumé . . . but I don't know.	SEPT 19 Emailed Scott my letter and résumé.	SEPT. 22 Called Scott to set up info interview. Need to come up with list of questions	SEPT. 27 at 10:00 AM Informational interview with Scott by phone
Map Communication, Inc. Rachael and David Jacobson 203-0101 rjacobson@mapcomm.com	—	SEPT. 19 Responded to ad with résumé and cover letter	SEPT. 26 Called to check if my info. was received. Rachael said she liked what she saw and talked to me some more. She wants to interview me!	**SEPT. 28** **At 3:30 PM** Interview at Map Communication

Cover letter and résumés. The purpose of the cover letter is to get the reader to look at your résumé. Keep your cover letter short, but attention getting. Make sure it is focused on the job and company you are interested in. A good cover letter usually covers four main points:

1. The position you are applying for and how you learned about it
2. Why you are the best person for the job (your abilities)
3. Why you want to work for the employer
4. A call to action (how you plan to follow up)

Résumé. The purpose of your résumé is to get the reader to call you in for an interview. Design your résumé neatly, using a current and acceptable format (books or your career office can show you some standard formats). Make sure the information is accurate and truthful. Check it for errors and have someone else proofread it as well. Type or print it on high-quality paper (a heavier bond paper than is used for ordinary copies). Key 10.6 shows an example of a professional résumé. Here are general tips for writing a résumé:

- Always put your name and contact information at the top. Make it stand out.
- State an objective whenever possible. If your focus is narrow or you are designing this résumé for a particular interview or career area, keep your objective specific; otherwise, keep the objective more general.
- Provide a "core competencies" section that lists your key skills.
- List your post-secondary education, starting from the latest and working backward. This may include summer school, seminars, and accreditations.
- List jobs in reverse chronological order (most recent job first). Include all types of work experience (full time, part time, volunteer, internship, and so on).
- When describing work experience, use action verbs and focus on what you have accomplished. Try the P + A = R formula when writing job tasks—identify a

Désirée Williams

237 Custer Street, San Francisco, CA 94101   (415) 555-5252 (W)   (415) 555-7865 (H)

email: desiree@comcast.net   website: www.DesireeCulture.com

OBJECTIVE

To use my language, cross-cultural, and web skills to help children in an educational or corporate setting.

EDUCATION

2012 to present	San Francisco State University, San Francisco, CA
	Pursuing a B.A. in the Spanish BCLAD (Bilingual, Cross-Cultural Language Acquisition Development)
	Education and Multiple Subject Credential Program
	Expected graduation: June 2016

SKILLS SUMMARY

Languages:	Fluent in Spanish and English.
	Proficient in Italian and Shona (majority language of Zimbabwe).
Computer:	Programming ability in HTML, PHP, Javascript, .Net, and Silverlight.
	Multimedia design expertise in Adobe Photoshop, Netobjects Fusion, Adobe Premiere, Macromedia Flash, and other visual design programs.
Personal:	Perform professionally in Mary Schmary, a women's a cappela quartet.
	Climbed Mt. Kilimanjaro.

PROFESSIONAL EMPLOYMENT

Sept. 2013 to present	**Research Assistant, Knowledge Media Lab**
	San Francisco State University, San Francisco, CA
	Develop ways for teachers to share their teaching practices online, in a collaborative, multimedia environment.
June 2013 to present	**Webmaster/Web Designer**
	Quake Net, San Mateo, CA (internet service provider and web commerce)
	Designed several sites for the University of California, Berkeley, Graduate School of Education, as well as private clients, such as A Body of Work and Yoga Forever
Sept. 2012 to June 2013	**Literacy Coordinator (internship)**
	Prescott School, Oakland, CA
	Coordinated, advised, and created literacy curriculum for an America Reads literacy project.
	Worked with nonreader 4th graders on writing and publishing, incorporating digital photography, internet resources, and graphic design.
June 2012 to August 2012	**Bilingual Educational Consultant (volunteer)**
	Children's Television Workshop, San Francisco, CA
	Field-tested bilingual materials. With a research team, designed bilingual educational materials for an ecotourism project run by an Indigenous rain forest community in Ecuador.
June 2009 to Sept. 2009	**Children's Recreation Director: After-School Program**
	San Francisco Recreation and Parks Department
	Performed playground supervision, taught arts and cultural activities, provided homework assistance, and managed summer reading program.
	Worked primarily with low-income, Hispanic children, grades 1 to 5.

References and Portfolio of Work

Available upon request

get $mart

Creativenv/Shutterstock

Racorn/123RF

FIND WORK THAT COMBINES EARNINGS AND FULFILLMENT

Complete the following on paper or in digital format.

Investigate which jobs in your areas of interest can earn you what you need. Answer the following questions:

1. What are your most significant interests and skills?
2. What are three possible careers you feel would suit your interests and skills?
3. Identify three people you could talk to who work in, or know about, any of these careers. For each, write down the name, career, and contact information.
4. Contact an individual from the list to set up an informational interview. *Note:* Refer to "Informational Interviews and the Hidden Job Market" in this chapter for assistance.
5. Develop a list of questions to ask the individual about his or her job, making sure to focus on the question of how to balance passion and earnings. Save the list on a computer and print it.
6. Attend the informational interview, taking notes on your printed list. Send a follow-up thank you note. If you can, repeat the informational interview process with the other two people.

problem, the action taken to solve it, and the results. For example: "Organized randomly filed client records in alphabetical and date order, reducing the time to access them by 80%."

- Always make sure the descriptions in your job history demonstrate the skills listed as your core competencies section and that they relate to the job for which you are applying.
- Include keywords that are linked to jobs for which you will be applying.
- List references on a separate sheet (names, titles, companies, and contact information). Put "References upon request" at the bottom of your résumé.
- Use professional formatting and bullets to emphasize important information. Stick with one font family for the body of the résumé and one for the headings (usually larger and bolded). Use italics sparingly because they are hard to read.
- Get several people to look at your résumé before you send it out. Other readers will have ideas you haven't thought of and may find errors that you have missed.

Prospective employers often use a computer to scan résumés, selecting the ones that contain *keywords* relating to the job opening or industry. Résumés without enough keywords probably won't even make it to the human resources desk. When you construct your résumé, make sure to include relevant keywords. For example, if you are seeking a computer-related job, list computer programs you use and other specific technical proficiencies. To figure out what keywords you need, look at job descriptions and job postings and search online for examples of keywords related to your career interest.[13]

get practical

FIND USEFUL KEYWORDS

binkski/123RF

Complete the following on paper or in digital format.

Name two career fields you would consider pursuing. Then, research résumé keywords that employers in these fields look for. To do so, enter the words "keyword," "resume," and a word or phrase related to the field ("chemical engineering," "criminal justice," and so on) into your favourite search engine. List at least five keywords for each field. Keep them on hand for tailoring your résumé to a job in either one of these fields.

Interview

Be clean, neat, and appropriately dressed. Avoid tight or baggy clothing, extreme hairstyles, and flashy jewelry. Choose a nice pair of shoes—people notice (avoid spiky heels if you are a woman). You want interviewers to focus on you and your achievements, not your appearance.

Bring an extra copy of your résumé and any other materials that you want to show the interviewer, even if you sent a copy ahead of time. Avoid chewing gum and fidgeting. Don't text or check your Instagram—as a matter of fact, put all electronic devices away completely so you are not tempted to use them. Offer a confident handshake. Make eye contact. Show your integrity by speaking honestly about yourself. After the interview, no matter what the outcome, follow up right away with a formal but pleasant thank-you note.

Being on time to your interview makes a positive impression—and being late will almost certainly be held against you. If you do not consider being late a sign of disrespect, remember that your interviewer may not agree.

Informational Interviews and the Hidden Job Market

When you find someone who is doing the job you want to do, teaching in your field of interest, or responsible for hiring in that field, try to set up an *informational interview* with this person—an opportunity for you to ask questions about what they do, how they got into the job, what they like or don't like, and who they know. Since you are asking the questions and there is less at stake than in a traditional interview, you are likely to feel less nervous. Despite the lower risk, there is still potential for reward in the form of information and networking contacts.

To set up an interview, call or email the person. Introduce yourself and make it clear you are not looking for a job, just advice and support. Ask for 30 minutes of the person's time—find out when he or she is are available and then suggest a meeting by phone, in the office, or at a coffee shop, whatever is most convenient. Ahead of time, prepare a set of questions about things that matter to you. See Key 10.7 for a good list of informational interview questions.

On the day of the informational interview, dress professionally and arrive early. Have a copy of your résumé in case the person you are interviewing wants to see it. Take notes during the interview, and consider writing by hand so you do not distract the interviewee by typing. When you finish, express appreciation and ask if you can keep in touch. Provide your contact information (or a business card, if you have one) and ask for his or her card. Follow up with a personal thank you note and send it by

1.	How did you find out about the job you are now in?
2.	What skills do you have that are useful on the job?
3.	Did you have those skills when you first started?
4.	What are you good at?
5.	Tell me about your typical day—what you do and who you work with.
6.	What are your manager and co-workers like?
7.	What's the communication style at your workplace?
8.	What do you like about your job?
9.	What makes your job difficult?
10.	What is your educational and job background? Have you found it useful on the job?
11.	What kind of education or experience do you recommend to get a job like the one you have?
12.	What are the most important abilities you think someone needs to do your job well?
13.	What is the starting salary range in your field?
14.	About how many hours a week do you work?
15.	Does your job have any benefits?
16.	What do you think would prepare someone for your type of work?
17.	Is there anything else you would like to share with me about your job?
18.	Can you think of anyone else I should talk to?

mail—handwritten notes get remembered. Then type up your notes and think about what they tell you about the job or career area you are investigating.

Through informational interviewing, you tap the "hidden job market"—unadvertised jobs that are filled through networking. More than 80% of new jobs are unadvertised.[14] Most companies would rather find a qualified person through word of mouth or a referral, and one of the best ways to get referred is to meet some of those employees through informational interviewing.

Emotional Intelligence

Emotional intelligence is one of the strongest draws for today's employers, and something that you can build in any job that brings you into contact with other people. As he gained experience as an RA, Dan built an extraordinary amount of emotional intelligence.

Consider this scenario: You arrive at work distracted by a personal problem and tired from studying late the night before. Your supervisor is overloaded with a major project due that day. The person you work most closely with is coming in late due to a car problem. Everyone is stressed out. What does an emotionally intelligent person do?

- *Tune in to everyone's emotions first.* You: Tired and distracted. Your co-worker: Worried about the car and about being late. Your supervisor: Agitated about the project.
- *Pinpoint the thoughts that arise from these emotions.* People are likely to think that the deadline is in jeopardy.
- *Understand what the emotions are telling you.* Thinking that the deadline may not be met means that everyone is going to need an extra-focused and positive state of mind to get through the day and set aside distracted, negative thinking.
- *Manage the emotion with action.* You come up with several things you can do:

  - Prioritize your task list so that you can concentrate on what is most pressing.
  - Call your co-worker on his cell phone while he settles the car problem and let him know what's happening so he can prioritize tasks and support the supervisor when he arrives.
  - Ask another co-worker to bring in a favourite mid-morning snack to keep everyone going during the long day ahead.

The current emphasis on teamwork has highlighted emotional intelligence in the workplace. The more adept you are at working with others, the more likely you are to succeed.

As you ponder the ideas that you've explored in this chapter, keep in mind the "near-universal view" from a research project involving interviews with over 1000 older individuals: "The most important thing is to be involved in a profession that you absolutely love," said an 83-year-old research subject, "and that you look forward to going to work every day."[16]

talk risk and reward . . .

Courtesy of Dan Oltersdorf

Risk asking tough questions to be rewarded with new insights. Use the following questions to inspire discussion with classmates, either in person or online.

- As one saying goes, "Do what you love and the money will follow." Do you agree that this risk will bring financial reward, or disagree? Support your opinion with examples.
- Freelance workers make their own schedules but need to be careful money managers in order to save, pay for extra health insurance, and pay taxes. People who are employed by companies may have less freedom but are more likely to enjoy benefits such as life insurance, savings plans, and having taxes deducted. Which suits you better?
- Have you had a job application rejected, failed to get a job after an interview, or been fired from a job? How did you cope? What reward resulted from your risk taking?

CONSIDER THE CASE: While in school, Dan could not perceive a way to both fulfill his passion and earn a good living. For him, at that time, a Venn diagram of those two items seemed to have no overlap in the centre. What do you love to do that you can't imagine could translate into a career? Once everyone in the group has named a passion, see if another student has an idea for you, and offer ideas to others about their passions.

student PROFILE

Patrick Belliveau

SHERIDAN COLLEGE, TORONTO, ONTARIO

Courtesy of Patrick Belliveau

About me:

I am a third-year business student who has changed his mind about careers and educational paths numerous times. I started in an honours psychology program at a prominent university, but after a year and a half I decided it was not right for me. The electrical field seemed to be my dream career, so I completed a one-year pre-apprentice program and began working. After one year of working as an electrical apprentice, I was laid off during the turbulent economic time of 2008. That was the motivation I needed to go back to school and complete a degree that I now know was the one I should have chosen from the start. However, without trying different programs, I would have never been sure of the right path for me.

What I focus on:

My biggest focus, other than academic work, is networking. I try to create meaningful relationships with individuals who have already completed a business career in my field of interest.

Asking questions about how they succeeded or how they approach decision making helps me build my own decision-making model. The biggest lesson I've learned in networking is that a person will form an initial opinion of you starting from your opening sentence. Therefore, you want to make sure you have a well-thought-out opening sentence that will intrigue or at least generate some interest in who you are and what you have to say.

Remember: if the individual is successful in business, you are neither the first nor the last to speak to him or her about their career. This means it is crucial to captivate the person's attention and make him or her remember you!

What will help me in the workplace:

In the business world, any worthy opponent will likely have a fairly similar degree to yours, or perhaps even the same one. Therefore, experience will be what sets you apart from the competition. Try to join as many different clubs as you can without interfering with your schoolwork. However, I suggest waiting until the second semester to join any club, as adjusting to post-secondary school will be hard enough without any added stress.

Patrick Belliveau. Sheridan College, Toronto, Ontario. Reprinted by permission.

revisit RISK AND REWARD

Courtesy of Dan Oltersdorf

Plan for Career Success

What happened to Dan? Dan took the risk to change from a pre-med major to human development and family studies. Energized by the vision of working with young people, Dan started the website ResidentAssistant.com, an online sourcebook for RAs. This risk paid off, as the website soon became the go-to resource for RAs nationally. "The key is to be passionate but willing to change direction. It was scary to change my major as a junior, but these experiences have led me to places I never thought I would be." Dan earned a master's degree in higher education at Florida State University and was named Graduate Student of the Year in the Southeast. He now has a rewarding role as vice president, resident life for Campus Advantage, a national student housing and services leader. "I'm still an RA," he says, "I just have 26 000 residents."

What does this mean for you? One experience led Dan to discover that he could, indeed, forge a nontraditional career in higher education. Perhaps risking an unfamiliar experience will reward you with career possibilities. Visit your school's student activities website. Explore the offerings and make contact with a club that interests you. If you have an interest for which no club exists on campus, meet with an administrator who can help you start one.

What risk may bring reward beyond your world? Dan took advantage of his post-secondary education far beyond textbooks and lectures. "Utilize the college experience to grow, build yourself up and explore, and also to network," he advises. Remember that in any network, you have as much opportunity to help another as you do to receive help. Investigate your school's website for opportunities to be a helpful part of someone's network through tutoring or peer mentoring. If you are already a member of a club or organization, consider mentoring a new recruit. Reach out to others and see where your reach might lead you.

GLOBAL RISK AND REWARD

Vinzenz Weidenhofer/123RF

zloyel/123RF

Understanding the role of reading in knowledge growth, Rana Dajani took the risk to promote reading for pleasure in her country of Jordan, where the practice is uncommon, especially for girls and women. Her program, We Love Reading, brings storytelling sessions and books to communities all over Jordan. A significant part of the reward for these efforts is that 80 libraries have been established that are helping thousands of children build knowledge through reading.[17]

RISK ACTION

FOR POST-SECONDARY, CAREER, AND LIFE REWARDS

KNOW IT
Blan-k/Shutterstock

WRITE IT
Blan-k/Shutterstock

WORK IT
Blan-k/Shutterstock

Left to Right: pio3/Shutterstock;
Viktor Gladkov/123RF;
MP_P/Shutterstock

Complete the following on paper or in digital format.

KNOW IT *Think Critically*

Become a Better Interviewee

Build basic skills. Make a list of questions that a job applicant would typically hear in an entry-level interview. Recall questions from job interviews you've had, look up questions using online sources, or consult books on job interviews. List 15 to 20 questions.

Take it to the next level. Imagine yourself as the interviewer. Thinking about learning preferences, life experiences, learning from failure, role models, and more as you ponder, write five additional questions.

Move toward mastery. Pair up with a student in your class and interview each other. Person A interviews Person B for 5 to 10 minutes and takes notes. Then switch roles: Person B interviews Person A and takes notes. Each person uses the set of questions developed in the first and second parts of the exercise.

When you are done, share with each other what interesting ideas stand out from the interviews. If you have suggestions, offer constructive criticism to each other about interview skills.

Finally, to sum up, write a brief analysis and summary of your experience, including what you learned and would keep in mind for a real interview—both the good and the bad.

WRITE IT *Communicate*

Emotional intelligence journal: Compare your vision with others. Dan's vision of the future ended up differing from how his parents envisioned his career. First, describe your current vision for how you might pursue your passions in the working world. Then describe what your parents or other family members have in mind for you. Compare these two visions. How are they similar, and how are they different? How do the differences make you feel, and how do they affect your family members emotionally? Finally, discuss how you plan to manage the situation if what you envision is significantly different from what others want for you.

Real-life writing: Create a résumé. On one electronic page or sheet of paper, list information about your education (where and when you've studied, degrees or certificates you've earned) and your skills (what you know how to do, such as use a computer program or operate a type of equipment). On another, list job experience. For each job, record job title (if you had one), dates of employment, and tasks performed. Include tasks that demonstrate skills. Be as detailed as possible. When you compile your résumé, you will make this material more concise. Keep this list and update it periodically as you gain experience and accomplishments.

Using the information you have gathered and Key 10.6 as your guide, draft a résumé. There are many ways to construct a résumé. Consult resources for different styles (your library or bookstore will have multiple resources, or look online at sources such as resumehelp.com or Monster.com). You may want to format your résumé according to a style that your career counsellor or instructor recommends. Also, certain career areas may favour a particular style of résumé (check with your career counsellor or an instructor in that area).

Keep this résumé draft in hard copy and on a computer hard drive or disk. When you need to submit a résumé with a job application, update the draft and print it out on high-quality paper. For electronic submission, convert your résumé file to PDF format.

WORK IT *Build Your Brand*

Write a Job Interview Cover Letter

To secure a job interview, you will have to create a cover letter to accompany your résumé. With this key communication tool, you can pull out your best selling points from your résumé and highlight them to a potential employer so the employer wants to read your résumé.

Write a one-page, three-paragraph cover letter to a prospective employer, describing your background and explaining your value to the company. Be creative—you may use fictitious names, but select a career and industry that interest you. Use the format shown in Key 10.8.

- *Introductory paragraph.* Start with a statement that convinces the employer to read on. You might name a person the employer knows who suggested you write, or refer to something positive about the company that you read in the newspaper or on the internet. Identify the position for which you are applying, and tell the employer why you are interested in working for the company.

First name Last name
1234 Your Street
City, Province, Postal Code

November 1, 2018

Ms. Prospective Employer
Prospective Company
5432 Their Street
City, Province, Postal Code

Dear Ms. Employer:

On the advice of Mr. X, career centre advisor at Y College, I am writing to inquire about the position of production assistant at your radio station. I read the description of the job and your company on the career centre's employment-opportunity bulletin board, and I would like to apply for the position.

I am a fourth-year student at Y College and will graduate this spring with a degree in communications. Since my third year when I declared my major, I have wanted to pursue a career in radio. For the last year I have worked as a production intern at the college's station, and have occasionally filled in as a disc jockey on the evening news show. I enjoy being on the air, but my primary interest is production and programming. My enclosed résumé will tell you more about my background and experience.

I would be pleased to talk with you in person about the position. You can reach me anytime at 555/555–5555 or by e-mail at xxxx@xx.com. Thank you for your consideration, and I look forward to meeting you.

Sincerely,

Sign Your Name Here

First name Last name

Enclosure(s) *(use this notation if you have included a résumé or other item with your letter)*

- *Middle paragraph*. Sell your value. Try to convince the employer that hiring you will help the company in some way. Centre your "sales effort" on your experience in school and the workplace. If possible, tie your qualifications to the needs of the company. Refer indirectly to your enclosed résumé.
- *Final paragraph*. Close with a call to action. Ask the employer to call you or tell the employer to expect your call to arrange an interview.

Exchange your first draft of the cover letter with a classmate. Read each other's letters and make marginal notes to improve impact and persuasiveness, writing style, grammar, punctuation, and spelling. Discuss and then make corrections. Create a final draft for your portfolio.

statusCHECK

Left to Right: Luis Santos/Shutterstock; Antonio Guillem/Shutterstock; antoniodiaz/Shutterstock; mimagephotography/Shutterstock; Djomas/Shutterstock; WAYHOME studio/Shutterstock

How Effectively Do You Manage Money?

For each statement, fill in the number that best describes how often it applies to you.

1 = never   2 = seldom   3 = sometimes   4 = often   5 = always

1. I am aware of my personal views on spending and saving money.   ① ② ③ ④ ⑤

2. I know how much money I can spend each month.   ① ② ③ ④ ⑤

3. I know the difference between things that I want and things that I need, and I shop accordingly.   ① ② ③ ④ ⑤

4. I control my spending by using a monthly budget.   ① ② ③ ④ ⑤

5. I successfully balance my responsibilities at work and at school.   ① ② ③ ④ ⑤

6. I understand the benefits and responsibilities of financial aid.   ① ② ③ ④ ⑤

7. I know the current interest rate, late fees, and balances on my credit cards.   ① ② ③ ④ ⑤

8. I know my credit rating and its potential effect on my finances in the future.   ① ② ③ ④ ⑤

9. I add to a savings account or TFSA regularly.   ① ② ③ ④ ⑤

10. I plan to start saving for my retirement while I am in completing my studies.   ① ② ③ ④ ⑤

Each of the topics in these statements is covered in this chapter. Note those statements for which you filled in a 3 or lower. Skim the chapter to see where those topics appear, and pay special attention to them as you read, learn, and apply new strategies.

REMEMBER: NO MATTER HOW EFFECTIVELY YOU MANAGE YOUR MONEY, YOU CAN IMPROVE WITH EFFORT AND PRACTICE.

WHAT CAN MATH
do for you?

MyLab Student Success
(www.mystudentsuccesslab.com) is an online solution designed to help you "Start Strong, Finish Stronger" by building skills for ongoing personal and professional development.

If you already gravitate toward math and science and related subjects you don't need any prodding to understand why math is important. You know that math is an essential tool with which to learn and build your career in whatever STEM (science, technology, engineering, and mathematics) field you pursue. Literature and language buffs, history and communications majors, students with no idea of a major but who don't plan to go anywhere near a STEM field—many of you may not see the reward of taking the math classes your school requires. However, there are reasons to believe that your efforts will pay off. Here are some of them.

Math Is a Life Tool

You use aspects of quantitative thinking—thinking with numbers—every day, including arithmetic calculations for your chequing account, geometrical thinking for how to pack items into the trunk of your car, figuring ratios for allowable deductions on a tax return, and so on. When you are comfortable with basic quantitative skills such as the following, you can face any numerical life challenge that comes your way. The Conference Board of Canada states that the ability to use numbers is also an employability skill.[1]

Maxim_Kazmin/Fotolia

Arithmetic. Many everyday tasks, especially those involving money, require arithmetic (numerical computations such as addition, subtraction, multiplication, and division, plus the use of fractions and percentages). You are using arithmetic when you calculate how much tuition you can cover in a semester or figure out what to tip in a restaurant. You also use arithmetic when you examine ingredient percentages on food labels in the effort to improve your health.

Algebra. A knowledge of *algebra*—a generalization of arithmetic in which letters representing unknown quantities are combined, often with other numbers, into equations according to mathematical rules—is needed almost as frequently as arithmetic. Algebra involves determining an unknown value using known values. You use algebra when you figure the interest on a loan or compute what an item costs when the store offers 20% off the price.

Geometry. The most common uses of *geometry*—the mathematics of the properties, measurement, and relationships of points, lines, angles, surfaces, and solids—occur in determining areas and volumes. Figuring out how much flooring, carpet, or wallpaper you need for a room requires the ability to calculate the size of the area being covered. You also use geometric principles without even thinking about it when, for example, you determine how to pass a car or pack a suitcase so that it can close.

Probability and statistics. A knowledge of basic *probability* (the study of the chance that a given event will occur) and *statistics* (collection, analysis, and interpretation of numerical data) is needed for understanding the relevance and importance of the overwhelming amount of statistical information you encounter. For example, a woman's knowledge of probability can help her determine her risk of getting breast cancer; a student's understanding of statistics can help him analyze his chances of getting accepted at a particular graduate school.

Sciences. Biology, anatomy, and other sciences directly related to the human body can help you to better manage your health through a greater understanding of how your body works. Chemistry can help you figure out how to substitute ingredients in a recipe or become aware of possible interactions between medications you are taking.

Math Is a Problem-Solving Training Ground

Math and science are relevant to any academic subject because they promote problem-solving and thinking skills. When your brain moves from mathematical questions to solutions, you build the kind of critical thinking necessary to think through any type of problem, from reconciling different perspectives in a philosophy course to examining the causes of a historical event.

Statistics is one particularly useful area when it comes to building universally applicable problem-solving and decision-making abilities. "Statistical reasoning supports decision making under conditions of uncertainty, an inescapable condition of modern life. This is math that will help . . . students understand the world around them, and it's math they can use right now," says the president and senior partner of the Carnegie Foundation.[2]

As you contemplate math and problem solving in your life, remember that humans have invented mathematical language to describe and use mathematical principles that have always existed as properties of the universe. There is math behind the weather patterns that shape your days and involved in how what you eat affects your health. Math drives how effectively your car uses gas and determines the likelihood of getting a good turnout at an event. Understanding how numbers work increases your understanding of—and your ability to manage—your world.

Money Is Math

Speaking of management, having basic math skills makes money manageable, because money is real-life math. Every time you pay for a meal, check your bank balance online, apply for a student loan, think about whether you can afford a big purchase, contemplate what you want to earn in the workplace, or in any way use or think about money, your brain is working with numbers. Of all of the ways that you interact with numbers, money is the most unavoidable. Make the unavoidable more comfortable with basic math skills as well as savvy management strategies.

HOW CAN YOU
W *manage your money?*

e all worry about money. A study by Sun Life Financial suggests that 72% of Canadians experience "excessive levels of anxiety" over their financial situation.[3] Tuition and books and other school expenses take a toll on bank accounts. Self-supporting students pay for living and family expenses. It's easy to understand the concern over financial well being. According to the Canadian Federation of Students, the average student graduates with a debt of $37 000.[4] It adds up to challenging financial situations for the vast majority of students.

Who You Are As a Money Manager

Thinking analytically, creatively, and practically about money management can help you take calculated risks that reward you with increased control over your finances. First, analyze who you are as a money manager. How you interact with money is unique. Are you more of a spender or a saver? Of the rewards you seek, which are measured in dollar amounts and which in nonmaterial terms? Your spending and saving behaviours tend to reflect your values and goals. Consider these influences in Key 11.1.

Improving how you handle money requires that you analyze your attitudes and behaviours. Says money coach Connie Kilmark, "If managing money was just about math and the numbers, everyone would know how to manage their finances sometime around the fifth grade."[5] Students on their own for the first time may have not yet had a reason to define their money management style. If this describes you, now is the time to investigate, as you begin your life as a money-managing adult. Start by looking at needs versus wants.

Needs versus Wants

People often confuse what they *need* with what they *want*. True needs are absolutely essential for your survival: food, water, air, shelter, and some mode of transportation. Everything else is technically a want—something you would like but could live without. When people spend too much on wants, they may not have enough cash for needs.

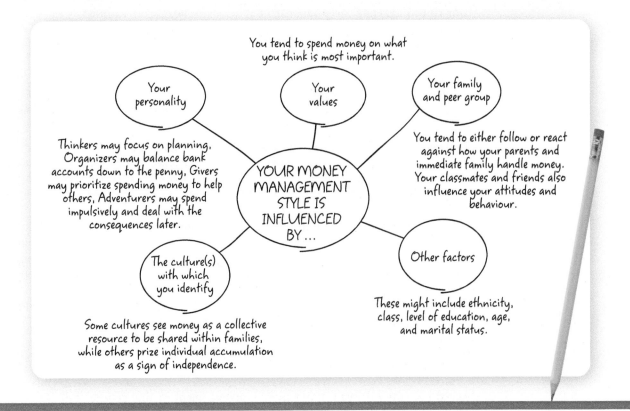

You might want to buy a $1000 flat-screen TV, but might regret the purchase if your car broke down and needed a $1000 repair.

Check your spending for purpose. What do you buy with your money? Are the items you purchase necessary? When you do spend on a want rather than a need, do you plan the expense into your budget with an eye toward a specific reward, or buy on the spur of the moment? With a clear idea of what you want and what you need, you can think through spending decisions more effectively. This is not to say that you should never spend money on wants. Just take calculated risks that satisfy your needs first, and then decide what to do with what is left over.

How Your Time Relates to Money

When you spend money from your paycheque, you exchange the time you spent earning that money for a product or service. For example, let's say you are thinking about spending $200 on a cell phone upgrade. If you have a part-time job that pays you $10 an hour after taxes, you need to work a full 20-hour week just to buy the phone ($200). Ask yourself: Does the risk of the expense justify the reward? If the answer is no, put the money away and use it for something you value more. Exchange the risk of your work hours for rewards that matter most to you.

The relationship between time and money becomes clear when you compare how long it takes to earn money to what you spend on a day-to-day basis. Key 11.2 shows how reducing regular expenses can make a difference.

Getting a post-secondary education is a risk that costs many hours of work, and student debt continues to rise. However, as Tererai's choices demonstrate, tuition and

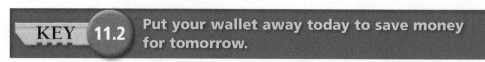

DAY-TO-DAY EXPENSE	APPROXIMATE COST	POTENTIAL SAVINGS
Gourmet coffee	$4 per day, 5 days a week, totals $20 per week	$80 per month; $960 for the year. Invested in a 5% interest account for a year, would amount to over $1000.
Alcohol	Two drinks plus tip total about $20 per night, two nights per week amounts to $40 per week	$160 per month; $1920 for the year. Invested in a 5% interest account for a year, would amount to over $2000.
Ordering in meals	$15 per meal, twice per week, totals $30 per week	$120 per month; $1440 for the year. Invested in a 5% interest account for a year, would amount to nearly $1550.

time spent reward you with improved chances of long-term financial success. Take this opportunity to review Key 1.1 in the first chapter of the textbook. Look at what the benefits a post-secondary education in Canada mean in terms of income. *Opportunity cost* refers to what you give up to get something. For most students, the opportunity cost of going to post-secondary school is worth it.

With more of an idea of what values and perspectives lie behind the financial decisions you make, you will be more able to choose and take productive risks that move you toward meaningful financial goals. Start with creating a budget.

Personal Budgeting

Everything you will read about money management in this chapter falls under the "umbrella" of one central concept: Live below your means, or in other words, spend less than you earn—whenever possible. When money in is more than money out, you will have extra to save or spend. To find out the difference between what you spend and what you earn, track spending and earning and create a budget that balances both. Because many expenses are billed monthly, most people use a month as a unit of time. Creating a budget involves several steps:

BUDGET
A plan to coordinate resources and expenditures; a set of goals regarding money.

1. Gather information about what you earn (money flowing in).
2. Figure out your expenditures (money flowing out).
3. Analyze the difference between earnings and expenditures.
4. Come up with creative ideas about how you can make changes.
5. Take practical action to adjust spending or earning so you come out even or ahead.

Your biggest expense right now is probably the cost of your education, including tuition and perhaps room and board. However, your family may be covering part of this cost, and your responsibility may not kick in until after you graduate and begin to repay any student loans you may have taken out. (Financial aid will be explored later in the chapter.) For now, as you consider your budget, include only what you are paying for now, while you are in school.

Figure out what you earn

To determine what is available to you on a monthly basis, start with the money you earn in a month's time on the job, if you have one. Then, if you have savings set aside for your education or receive spending money from your parents, determine how much of it you can spend each month and add that amount. For example, if you have a grant for the entire year, divide it by 12 (or by how many months you are in school over the course of a year).

multiple intelligence strategies

FOR FINANCIAL MANAGEMENT

Name a significant upcoming expense: _____.

In the right-hand column, record specific ideas for how MI strategies can help you afford it.

INTELLIGENCE	USE MI STRATEGIES TO MANAGE YOUR MONEY	APPLY MI STRATEGIES THAT CAN HELP YOU MAKE A PURCHASE
Verbal-Linguistic	• Talk over your financial situation with someone you trust. • Write out a detailed budget outline. If you can, store it on a computer file so you can update it regularly.	
Logical-Mathematical	• Focus on the numbers; with a calculator and amounts that are as exact as possible, determine your income and spending. • Calculate how much you'll have in 10 years if you start now to put $2000 in a 5% interest-bearing RRSP account each year.	
Bodily-Kinesthetic	• Create a set of envelopes, each for a different budget item—rent, dining out, phone, and so on. Each month, put money, or a slip with a dollar amount, in each envelope to represent what you can spend. When the envelope is empty or the number on the paper is reduced to zero, stop spending.	
Visual-Spatial	• Set up a budgeting system that includes colour-coded folders and coloured charts. • Create colour-coded folders for papers related to financial and retirement goals—investments, accounts, and so on.	
Interpersonal	• Whenever money problems come up, discuss them right away with a family member, partner, or roommate. • Brainstorm a five-year financial plan with one of your friends.	
Intrapersonal	• Schedule quiet time to plan how to develop, follow, and update your budget. Consider using financial management software, such as Quicken. • Think through where your money should go to best achieve your long-term financial goals.	
Musical	• Include a category of music-related purchases in your budget—going to concerts, buying CDs—but keep an eye on it to make sure you don't go overboard.	
Naturalistic	• Analyze your spending by using a system of categories. Your system may be based on time (when payments are due), priority (must-pay bills versus extras), or spending type (monthly bills, education, family expenses).	

Mathematical and Financial Literacy

Figure out what you spend

First, note regular monthly expenses. Students in dorms or school-owned apartments may have few monthly bills, whereas students in off-campus housing may have expenses such as rent, phone, and cable (look at cancelled cheques and electronic debits to estimate what the month's bills will be). For expenses like automobile insurance that are billed only once or twice a year, divide the yearly cost by 12 to see how much you spend every month. Then, over a month's time, keep a spending log in a small notebook to record each day's cash or debit card expenditures. Be sure to count smaller purchases if they are frequent (for example, one or two pricey coffees a day add up over time). By the end of the month, you will have a good idea of where your dollars go.

Key 11.3 lists common sources of income and expenses for students. Use the total of all your monthly expenses as a baseline for other months, realizing that spending will vary depending on factors such as life events or seasons.

Personal finance software programs, such as Quicken, can help you track spending and saving and categorize expenses—for example, you can create reports about how much you spend on food in a one-month period or how much you earned from work in a year's time. Also, if you manage bank and credit accounts online, you can access information about earning and spending.

Evaluate the difference

Once you know what you earn and what you spend, calculate the difference: Subtract your monthly expenses from your monthly income. Ideally, you have money left over

---

KEY 11.3 Where money comes from, and where it goes.

Common Sources of Income

ppart/Shutterstock

- Take-home pay from a full-time or part-time job
- Take-home pay from summer and holiday employment
- Money earned from work–study or paid internship
- Money from parents or other relatives
- Scholarships
- Grants
- Loans

Adela Lia Rusu/Shutterstock

Common Expenses

- Tuition you are paying now
- Books and other course materials
- Room and board (if living at college)
- Rent or mortgage (if living off campus)
- Utilities (if living off campus—electric, gas, oil, water)
- Telephone (cell phone and/or landline)
- Food
- Clothing, toiletries, household supplies
- Transportation and auto expenses (gas, maintenance, service)
- Credit cards and other payments (car payment)
- Entertainment (cable TV, movies, eating out, books and magazines, music downloads)
- Computer-related expenses, including online service costs
- Insurance (health, auto, homeowner's or renter's)

to save or spend. However, if you are spending more than you take in, examine these areas of your budget.

- *Expenses.* Did you forget to budget for recurring expenses such as the cost of maintaining your car? Or was your budget derailed by an emergency expense?
- *Spending patterns and priorities.* Were you careful, or did you overspend on wants?
- *Income.* Do you bring in enough money? Do you need another income source or better job?

Adjust spending or earning

If you spend more than you are earning, you can earn more, spend less, or better yet, do both. There are many ways to decrease spending. Perhaps the most important one is thinking before you buy: Do I really need this? Is the expense worth it? Just answering those questions will reduce unnecessary purchases. Other ways to manage spending include the following.

Set up automatic payments. If you set up electronic monthly payments for bills and schedule regular automatic transfers of small amounts into your savings, you will take care of your needs first without thinking about it. Then, you can decide what to do with what is left over.

Comparison shop. Again, think before you buy. If you are in the market for an expensive item such as a cell phone, a computer, or a car, research prices at stores and online. Shopbot, Pricebat, or Price Finder allow you to compare prices in Canadian dollars on items you wish to purchase. You can also find coupons with WagJag. Consider buying used items at Value Village or any local second hand shops. Local online bargains can be found on Kijiji.

Show your student ID. Your student identification card is your ticket to savings for a variety of items such as movies, shows, concerts, restaurant meals and take out, book and clothing stores, travel services, electronics, and much more.

Finally, work to save money on a day-to-day basis. The effort of saving small amounts regularly can eventually bring significant reward. Key 11.4 has some suggestions.

Call on your dominant multiple intelligences when planning your budget. For example, visual learners may want to create a budget chart, and bodily-kinesthetic

KEY 11.4 Look for ways to spend less.

- Shop in grocery stores for food you can keep around for snacks and small meals.
- Cut back on take-out orders and eating in restaurants.
- If you live off campus, share living space and cook at home more often.
- Fill a water bottle with tap water instead of buying bottles.
- Keep your student ID on you at all times for discounts.
- Walk, bike, carpool, rollerblade, or use public transportation.
- Watch your spending when you are out socializing.
- Shop in secondhand or consignment stores or swap clothing with friends.
- Use cheap or free methods of communicating (choose online and cell phone services carefully).
- Take advantage of student discounts when purchasing computers and software.
- Look for free fun on campus and in your local area.
- Use on-campus exercise facilities and services.

get practical

Diego Cervo/
Shutterstock

binkski/123RF

MAP OUT YOUR BUDGET

Use this exercise to see what you take in and what you spend. Then decide what adjustments you need to make. Consider using an online calculator for this task, such as Calculatorweb.com.

Before You Begin. Keep a spending log for one week or one month, whatever you have time for (if you use one week, multiply it by four to determine estimated monthly expenses in Step 1). Note purchases made by cash, cheque, debit card, and credit card.

Step 1: Expenses. Based on your spending log, estimate your current expenses in dollars per month, using the following table. The grand total is your total monthly expenses. If any expense comes only once a year, enter it in the "Annual Expenses" column and divide by 12 to get your "Monthly Expenses" figure for that item.

EXPENSES	MONTHLY EXPENSES	ANNUAL EXPENSES
School supplies including books and technology		
Tuition and fees		
Housing: Dorms, rent, or mortgage		
Phone (cell and/or landline)		
Cable TV, internet		
Gas and electric, water		
Car costs—monthly payment, auto insurance, maintenance, repairs, registration, inspections		
Travel costs—gas, public transportation, parking permits, toll		
Vacations, trips home		
Food: Groceries, meal plan cafeteria, eating out, snacks		
Added health insurance		
Health maintenance costs—gym, equipment, sports fees, classes		
Medical costs—dentist visits, vision, prescriptions, counselling		
Entertainment—movies, music purchases, socializing		
Laundry costs—supplies, service		
Clothing purchases		
Household supplies		
Payments on credit card debt		
Student loan or other loan repayment		
Donations to charitable organizations		
Childcare		
Other: emergencies, hobbies, gifts		
TOTAL EXPECTED EXPENSES		

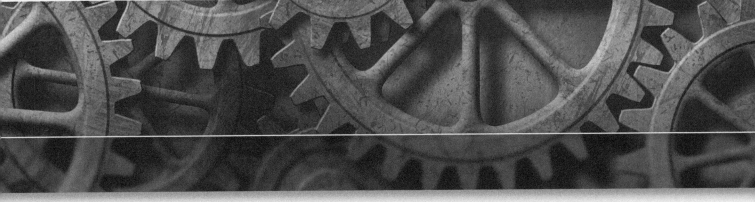

Step 2: Gross Income. Calculate your average monthly income. As with expenses, if any source of income arrives only once a year, enter it in the annual column and divide by 12 to get the monthly figure. For example, if you have a $6000 scholarship for the year, your monthly income would be $500 ($6000 divided by 12).

INCOME/RESOURCES	MONTHLY INCOME	ANNUAL
Employment (after federal/provincial/territorial taxes)		
Family contribution		
Financial assistance: grants, provincial/territorial and other loans		
Scholarships		
Interest and dividends		
Other gifts, income, and contributions		
TOTAL EXPECTED INCOME		

Step 3: Net Income (Cash Flow). Subtract the grand total of your monthly expenses from the grand total of your monthly income.

INCOME PER MONTH	
Total expected expenses	
Total expected income	
NET INCOME (INCOME MINUS EXPENSES)	

Source: Adapted from Julie Stein, California State University, East Bay. Reprinted with permission.

Step 4: Adjustments. If you have a negative cash flow, what would you change? Examine your budget and spending log to look for problem areas. Remember, you can increase income, decrease spending, or do both. Describe two ideas about how to get your cash flow back in the black.

learners may want to dump receipts into a jar and tally them at the end of the month. Personal finance software can accommodate different types of learners with features such as written reports (verbal-linguistic) and graphical reports (visual). Consider using online tools such as mint.com/canada or quicken.com/canada. You can also use the personal budget templates on Google Docs to get you started. See the Multiple Intelligence Strategies for Financial Management (page 281) for more MI-based ideas on how to manage your money.

Mathematical and Financial Literacy

HOW CAN YOU INCREASE INCOME
through work and financial aid?

If you reduce your spending and still come up short, as Tererai did repeatedly and as countless people do, you may need to look at ways to increase your income. The rising cost of education leads most students to seek additional dollars through work, financial aid, or both.

- According to a 2007 survey, nearly 50% of first-year post-secondary students add a job to their scheduled weekly responsibilities to earn money for tuition.[6]
- Statistics Canada's *The Daily* reports that 43% of college students and 50% of university students needed student loans to help them pay for their education.[7]

If you regularly spend more money than you have available, as countless students do, read on to find ways to get as much help as possible from these income sources.

Work–Study and Part-Time Jobs

How about a job? Working while in school has both positive and negative effects. Consider the following as you think about whether working is right for you:

PROS OF WORKING WHILE IN SCHOOL	CONS OF WORKING WHILE IN SCHOOL
• Gain general and career-specific experience.	• Have less time to study due to time commitment for your job.
• Develop contacts.	• Have less time for nonacademic activities.
• Can become more focused and motivated to use time wisely.	• Must shift gears mentally from work to classroom.
• Earn money.	• Can stretch yourself too thin, becoming fatigued and anxious.

Balancing a job with your academic work and goals can be challenging. For most students, a part-time local job is the best choice. In fact, research indicates that students who work on campus earn better grades than those working elsewhere, and students working 10 to 15 hours a week are more likely to stay in school than those working

talk risk and reward . . .

Risk asking tough questions to be rewarded with new insights. Use the following to inspire discussion with classmates, in person or online.

- What obstacles, reasonable or not, have kept you from applying for financial aid? Identify a risk you can take today to earn the reward of overcoming one or more of them.

- How good are you at differentiating between needs and wants? At prioritizing needs?

- Everyone has coping strategies that involve spending: some people like new clothes, others like expensive restaurants. What can you do to make the reward of saving money seem worth the risk of feeling deprived?

CONSIDER THE CASE: Tererai's financial situation was made even more challenging with her husband's illness. Are you prepared to handle a sudden drain on your bank account or loss of financial support from your family? What could you do to be ready? If you have experienced a financial crisis, how did you get through it?

Heifer International

more—or even than those working less.[8] If you decide that the reward of a job is worth risking time and effort, ask questions like these to define your needs:

- How much money do I need to make—weekly, per term, per year?
- What time of day is best for me? Should I consider night or weekend work?
- Do I want hands-on experience in a particular field?
- Where do I want to work, and how would I get to and from my job?

With the information you have gathered and analyzed, look at what is available on and off campus, and apply for jobs that best suit your needs. Work–study programs are a good place to start because they tend to be flexible and nearby. Federal work–study programs such as the CSEP (Canada Student Employment Program) are need based.

Continue to evaluate whether the reward of your job is worth the risk. Are you staying on top of your schoolwork? Are you making enough money? Are you getting enough sleep? If the job doesn't benefit you as much as you anticipated, perhaps you can renegotiate your job duties and schedule, or maybe you need to change jobs. Make careful, well-considered choices that bring you the rewards you need most.

Loans, Grants, and Scholarships

Financing your education—alone or with the help of your family—involves gathering financial information and making decisions about what you can afford and how much help you need. First, become informed about what is available to you. Then be proactive and go out and get it.

Explore and Apply for Financial Aid

Let's face it: post-secondary education in Canada is not cheap. As a result, many students need some sort of financial help. Most sources of financial aid don't seek out recipients. It is up to you to learn how you (or you and your parents, if they currently help to support you) can finance your education. Visit your school's financial aid office, research what is available, weigh the pros and cons of each option, decide what works best, and then apply early. Above all, think critically. Never assume that you are not eligible for aid. The types of aid available are student loans, grants, and scholarships.

Student loans

As the recipient of a student loan, you are responsible for paying back the amount you borrow, plus interest, according to a predetermined payment schedule that may stretch over a number of years. The amount you borrow is known as the loan *principal*, and *interest* is the fee that you pay for the privilege of using money that belongs to someone else.

The federal government administers or oversees most student loans. To receive aid from any federal program, you must be a citizen or eligible noncitizen and be enrolled in a program that meets government requirements. The federal government recently took over control of the Canada Student Loans Program. Applying for assistance, no matter what province or territory you live in, is done with a single application form. Your application is evaluated for eligibility for several programs, including the Canada Millennium Scholarship Program, provincial loans, plus any bursaries and grants you may be entitled to. For information regarding student loans in Canada, get an application form from your school. You can also contact the Canada Student Loans Program,

Many students are able to fit part-time work into their schedules if they stay local. Look for jobs at nearby businesses such as restaurants and retailers.

Paul Vasarhelyi/Shutterstock

get creative

GENERATE DAY-TO-DAY WAYS TO SAVE MONEY

Astroid/123RF

Complete the following on paper or in digital format.

Think about all the ways you spend money in a month's time. Where can you trim a bit? What expense can you do without? Where can you look for savings or discounts? Can you barter a product or service with a friend? Give yourself a day or two to come up with a list of ideas on a sheet of paper or computer. Create a list of five to ten workable ideas.

Then, give some of your ideas a try and see how they can help you save. Describe a plan for how you will use three to five ideas right away.

Consider making the experiment tangible by putting cash into a jar daily or weekly in the amounts that these changes are saving you. See what you have accumulated at the end of one month—and bank it.

administered through Human Resources and Skills Development Canada, by calling 1-800-O CANADA (1-800-622-6232), or you can find the latest information available by going to www.canlearn.ca. There are many helpful online references for student loans, some of which even enable you to apply online. Be sure to apply early. Get your application completed at least two to three months prior to the start of your studies to ensure it will have time to be processed.

Grants and scholarships

Unlike student loans, neither grants nor scholarships require repayment. *Grants*, funded by governments as well as private organizations, are awarded to students who show financial need. *Scholarships* may be financed by government or private organizations, schools, or individuals, and are awarded to students who show talent or ability in specified areas.

Even if you did not receive a grant or scholarship in your first year, you may be eligible for opportunities in other years of study. These opportunities are often based on grades and campus leadership and may be given by individual departments.

If you are receiving aid from your school, follow all the rules and regulations, including meeting application deadlines and remaining in good academic standing. In most cases, you will be required to reapply for aid every year.

- *Scholarships.* Scholarships are given for various abilities and talents. They may reward academic achievement, exceptional abilities in sports or the arts, citizenship, or leadership. Certain scholarships are sponsored by government agencies. If you display exceptional ability and are disabled, female, of an ethnic background classified as a minority, or a child of someone who draws government benefits, you might find federal scholarship opportunities geared toward you.

  All kinds of organizations offer scholarships. You may receive scholarships from individual departments at your school or from your school's independent scholarship funds, local organizations such as the Rotary Club, or privately operated aid foundations. Labour unions and companies may offer scholarships for children of employees. Membership groups, such as Scouting organizations or the YMCA/YWCA, might offer scholarships, and religious organizations are another source of money.

- *Researching grants and scholarships.* It can take work to locate scholarships and work-study programs because many are not widely advertised. Start digging at your financial aid office and visit your library, bookstore, and the internet. Two good places to start looking are www.studentawards.com and www.scholarships-canada.com/.

WHAT MONEY ISSUES REQUIRE
W*particular caution?*

ith your new independence comes increased responsibility. However, not everyone sees or accepts that responsibility right away. Without the boundaries imposed by family, many students go overboard with eating, don't sleep enough, and—you guessed it—pay little attention to their finances. To avoid the problems that befall many students, take charge of the following issues.

Managing and Paying Loans

In response to rising education costs, students are borrowing ever-larger amounts of money. Stats Canada's *The Daily* says that on average, student debt for college graduates is $14 900; for university grads it was closer to $26 000.[9]

Debt is a costly burden, and can drain your finances for years to come, costing you an enormous amount of money in interest charges. In addition, the consequences for defaulting on a loan are severe and include credit trouble, money taken from your salary, and more. Look at your needs year by year and make sure you are only taking out what is absolutely necessary.

Credit Card Use and Abuse

Credit cards are a handy alternative to cash and can reward you with a strong credit history if used with a reasonable level of risk. But they also can plunge you into debt. Students are acquiring cards in droves. Credit cards are a particular danger for students, because so many lack knowledge about how credit works. Too much focus on *what* they can purchase with credit cards (rather than *how much* it will really cost them) leads students to spend more than they can afford. Many students charge expenses like clothes, food, and school costs. Before they know it, they are deeply in debt.

How credit cards work

To charge means to create a debt that must be repaid. The credit card issuer earns money by charging interest, often 18% or higher, on unpaid balances. Basically, if you carry an unpaid balance, you are using someone else's money and paying extra cash (the interest) for the privilege. Credit card companies are in the business to make money from card owners like you. Focusing on what's best for your finances is *your* job, and the first step is to know as much as you can about credit cards. Start with the concepts presented in Key 11.5, read the fine print about any card you are considering, and stay focused on productive rewards that are worth the risk of spending on credit.

Watch out for these policies and problems, both when seeking a new card and when looking at existing card statements:[10]

- *New fees.* In addition to annual fees, a card may charge fees for reward programs, paying your bill by phone, or even checking your balance. Find out what the fees are, and switch cards if you feel they are excessive.

KEY 11.5 Learn to use credit carefully.

WHAT TO KNOW ABOUT . . .	AND HOW TO USE WHAT YOU KNOW
Account balance. A dollar amount that includes any unpaid balance, new purchases and cash advances, finance charges, and fees. Updated monthly.	Charge only what you can afford to pay at the end of the month. Keep track of your balance. Hold on to receipts and call customer service if you have questions.
Annual fee. The yearly cost that some companies charge for owning a card.	Look for cards without an annual fee or, if you've paid your bills on time, ask your current company to waive the fee.
Annual percentage rate (APR). The amount of interest charged yearly on your unpaid balance. This is the cost of credit if you carry a balance in any given month. The higher the APR, the more you pay in finance charges.	Shop around for the best rate available for students. Also, watch out for low, but temporary, introductory rates that skyrocket to over 20% after a few months. Always ask what the long-term interest rate is and look for fixed rates (guaranteed not to change).
Available credit. The unused portion of your credit line, updated monthly on your bill.	It is important to have credit available for emergencies, so avoid charging to the limit.
Cash advance. An immediate loan, in the form of cash, from the credit card company. You are charged interest immediately and may also pay a separate transaction fee.	Use a cash advance only in extreme emergencies because the finance charges start as soon as you complete the transaction and interest rates are greater than the regular APR. It is a very expensive way to borrow money.
Credit limit. The debt ceiling the card company places on your account (e.g., $1500). The total owed, including purchases, cash advances, finance charges, and fees, cannot exceed this limit.	Credit card companies generally set low credit limits for students. Owning more than one card increases the credit available, but most likely increases problems as well. Try to use only one card.
Delinquent account. An account that is not paid on time or one where the minimum payment has not been met.	Always pay on time, even if it is only the minimum payment. If you do not pay on time, you will you be charged substantial late fees and will risk losing your good credit rating, which affects your ability to borrow in the future. Delinquent accounts remain part of your credit records for years.
Due date. The date your payment must be received and after which you will be charged a late fee.	Avoid late fees and finance charges by paying at least a week in advance.
Finance charges. The total cost of credit, including interest, service fees, and transaction fees.	The only way to avoid finance charges is to pay your balance in full by the due date. If you keep your balance low, you will be more able to pay it off.
Minimum payment. The smallest amount you can pay by the statement due date. The amount is set by the credit card company.	Making only the minimum payment each month can result in disaster if you charge more than you can afford. When you make a purchase, think in terms of total cost.
Outstanding balance. The total amount you owe on your card.	If you carry a balance over several months, additional purchases are hit with finance charges. Pay cash for new purchases until your balance is under control.
Past due. Your account is considered "past due" when you fail to pay the minimum required payment on schedule.	Look for past due accounts on your credit history by getting a credit report from one of the credit bureaus (TransUnion and Equifax) or Credit Karma.

- *Reward program changes.* A reward program you've enjoyed for a while, such as airline miles or cash back, may change. Cards may charge for reward programs or may change or remove them if you are late with a payment.
- *The universal default clause.* This increasingly common policy allows a creditor to increase your interest rates if you make a late payment to *any* account, not just the accounts you have with those creditors. This means that if you are late on your payment for an unrelated loan, your creditors can increase your credit card interest rate.
- *Phishing emails.* Phishing is a technique for obtaining private information illegally. An email appearing to come from a legitimate business such as your credit

card company asks you to verify information such as your social insurance number or PIN. If you click on the link in the email, you are taken to a fraudulent website where any personal information you enter can be stolen. To avoid phishing scams, do not respond to any email that asks you to enter personal financial information. Your real bank and credit card companies would never ask you for it via email.

■ *Identity theft.* The downside of technology is that identity theft makes a mess of hundreds of thousands of people's finances each year. Do your best to prevent it by holding onto receipts, shredding documents when you are done with them, making sure no one sees you enter a PIN, only using secure sites when shopping with your credit card online (they begin with an "https" instead of "http"), and avoiding giving out your social insurance number (SIN) or other personal data unless absolutely necessary.[11]

To maintain an accurate perspective on where your money goes, keep credit card receipts and include those purchases as you track expenses.

Courtesy of Sarah Lyman Kravits

The best way to avoid problems is to read the fine print, pay attention to your balances, and pay your bills on time. Using a *debit card* is a smart alternative to paying on credit, because purchases are deducted directly from your chequing account and appear on your bank statement. Paying by debit assures that you will only spend money you have available.

Manage credit card debt

Even if you limit your card use to needs, you can still get into trouble. Debt can escalate quickly and can even lead to personal bankruptcy—a major blot on your credit that can last for years, and one to avoid at all costs. A few basics will help you stay in control.

■ *Choose your card wisely.* Carefully sort through all of the offers you receive. Look for cards with low interest rate cards, no annual fee, and a rewards program.

■ *Ask questions before charging.* Would you buy that item if you had to pay cash? Can you pay the balance at the end of the billing cycle?

■ *Pay bills regularly and on time, and try to make more than the minimim payment.* Set up a reminder system by creating an email alert through your card account, making a note in your datebook, or setting an alarm on your electronic planner.

■ *If you get into trouble, call the credit company and ask to set up a payment plan.* You may even be able to make partial payments or get a reduced interest rate. Contact your school's counselling centre for information on free or low-cost credit counselling agencies in your area.

■ *Shred credit cards when you close an account* or if you feel you have too many cards. Remember, even though you've destroyed the card, the debt remains until you've paid it in full and sent a written statement to the company asking to close the account.

■ *Stay aware of your credit score.* Your credit score is a prediction of your ability to pay back debt. If you've ever bought a car or signed up for a credit card, the deal you got was related to your credit score. If you rent an apartment, sign up for a cell phone plan, or apply for a job where you are required to handle money, someone will examine your credit score. Most credit scores fall on a credit-scoring scale running from 300 to 850. Your number gives creditors an idea of how reliable you are. In general, a higher score is more favourable.

> **CREDIT SCORE**
> A measure of how likely you are to pay your bills, calculated from a credit report using a standarized formula.

> **CREDITOR**
> A person or company to whom a debt, usually money, is owed.

get analytical

EXAMINE CREDIT CARD USE

Dario Sabljak/Shutterstock

Darren Baker/Shutterstock

Complete the following on paper or in digital format.

Take a careful look at who you are as a credit consumer. Gather your most recent credit card statements to prepare for this exercise. Answer questions 1 through 5.

1. How many credit cards do you have? For each, list the following:
   - Name of card and who issued it (for example, VISA from a national bank or credit union)
   - Current interest rate
   - Current balance
   - Late fee if you do not pay on time
   - Approximate due date for card payment each month

2. Add your balances together. This total is your current credit debt.

3. How much did you pay last month in finance charges? Total your finance charges from the most recent statements of all cards.

4. Do you pay on time, do you tend to pay late, or does it vary?

5. Estimate how many times a year you pay a late fee. Looking at how much your cards charge for late fees, estimate how much money you spent in the last year in late fees.

When you've gathered all your information, analyze how effectively you currently use credit. If you are satisfied with your habits, keep up the good work. If not, identify your bad habits and write specific plans about how to change those habits.

- *Keep an eye on your credit history.* Building, maintaining, and repairing credit is an ongoing challenge. Two credit bureaus in Canada note past-due accounts on your credit history: TransUnion and Equifax. You can contact them for a copy of your credit report to make sure there are no errors.

Overreliance on Family Support

The majority of students are considered dependents of their parents or guardians throughout their post-secondary careers. For many of these students, it's easy to fall back on family support when money gets tight or runs out. When you are used to your family providing for you, you may be comfortable with that arrangement and not want to take the reins.

However, there are drawbacks to continuing to depend financially on your family the way you have until you entered university or college. For one, money management, like so many other skills, is learned through practice. If you have no experience managing your money while at school, you will be unprepared for living on your own after graduation. Your family may also expect to stop providing financial support after you graduate. If you gradually wean yourself from that support over the course of your academic career, you will be more ready for financial independence than if you stay dependent and have to handle being cut off suddenly.

Now is the time to begin owning both your money mistakes and your smart money plans. If you overspend, decide on your own to be more careful until you build up your cash flow. If you want to make a big purchase, set a goal to save for it and work toward that goal on your own. Feel both the pain and the pride of your choices and take future risks based on the rewards you need most, and you will build skills that will serve you for life.

HOW CAN YOU PLAN FOR A
stable financial future?

Being able to achieve long-term financial goals such as buying a car or house or saving for the future requires that you think critically about short-term risks that will bring long-term financial reward. The strategies you've examined so far contribute to your long-term goals because they help you spend wisely and establish good habits that will help you stay in control moving forward. Similar to the situation with time, you can't always control how much money comes in, but you *can* control how you use what you have. Working to stash away as much as possible now will give you more freedom in the future. How can you do it?

Put Your Money to Work

When you live below your means, the money left over can go into savings accounts and investments, which can help you with regular expenses, long-term financial plans, and emergencies (financial advisors recommend a cash "emergency fund" that will cover at least three months worth of expenses). Savings accounts, GICs, and money market accounts can help your money grow.

Savings accounts. Most savings accounts have a fixed rate of *interest* (a sum paid for the use of your money while it is in the bank). Money in those accounts earns compound interest. Here's how it works: If you put $1000 in an account that carries 5% interest, you will earn $50 over the course of the first year. Your account then holds $1050. From that point on, interest is calculated on that $1050, not just on the original $1000. Imagine this: If you invested that $1000 at the age of 22 and put a mere $50 in the account each month, by the time you turned 62 you would have over $100 000.

Since 2009, Canadians have had the option of opening a Tax-Free Savings Account (TFSA). Any money you put into a TFSA is still subject to income tax; however, any interest you earn on the account, plus any money you withdraw from the account, is tax-free.

Chequing accounts. Most banks offer more than one chequing plan. Some accounts include cheque-writing fees, a small charge on every cheque you write or on any cheques above a certain number per month. Some accounts have free chequing, meaning unlimited cheque writing without extra fees—but you often have to maintain a minimum balance in your account to qualify. Some accounts charge a monthly fee that is standard or varies according to your balance. Chequing accounts pay you a low rate of interest, although you may have to keep a certain balance or have a savings account at the same bank.

Consider Saving for Retirement

With so many workers switching jobs frequently and working freelance, fewer people are retiring with guaranteed income other than the Canada Pension Plan (CPP). As more and more large and small employers eliminate pension benefits, it's up to you to put away some money for retirement. Starting your Registered Retirement Savings Plan (RRSP) as early as possible and making yearly contributions, gives you the benefit of growth over time. Key 11.6 shows the earning potential of an RRSP.

COMPOUND INTEREST Interest calculated on the principal (original investment) as well as the interest already added to the account.

Mathematical and Financial Literacy

Shutterstock

get $mart

YOUR FINANCIAL LIFESTYLE

Creativenv/Shutterstock

Examine your current financial lifestyle. Circle your answers to the following questions:

1. Which do you typically spend money on first?
   a. Needs
   b. Wants

2. Where do you tend to find yourself at the end of the month?
   a. With a little bit of spending money
   b. Down to zero

3. How do you typically use credit cards?
   a. Only when I know I can pay off the balance at the end of the month
   b. Frequently, and I pay the minimum each month

4. How aware are you of money coming in and going out?
   a. I check my finances regularly and stay aware
   b. I don't pay much attention to my finances

5. Where do you keep money that you've saved?
   a. In a chequing or savings account
   b. I don't have savings

Add up the number of a and b answers: a_____ b_____

More a answers than b answers indicates *more* financial stability. More b answers than a answers indicates *less* financial stability. Whether you tend to be more or less stable is not a judgment on you, but an opportunity to assess the effects of your financial lifestyle and decide if you want to adjust it in order to increase your stability. What is your reaction to this small look at your habits? Describe your reaction in a short paragraph on a sheet of paper or digital file.

KEY 11.6 Use an RRSP to grow your retirement investment.

Initial investment and contributions	Investment growth, based on 10% return, after . . .		
	10 years	25 years	40 years
$5000 one-time investment	$12 969	$54 174	$226 296
$2000 investment plus $2000 annual contribution	$37 062	$218 364	$975 704

Note: Calculations based on 10-percent average annual S & P Index growth from 1926 to present, as per "Investment Intelligence," Legg Mason Investor Services, 2007 (http://investorservices.leggmason.com/doc_library/1730.pdf?seq=11).

student PROFILE

Christian Gaumont

SPROTT-SHAW COMMUNITY COLLEGE, BRITISH COLUMBIA

About me:

I'm a single dad of French Canadian descent on the cusp of turning 40. My shoes are worn thin from walking many, many avenues of life. I live with passion, lead by example, and cultivate compromise rather than despise it. Every day, for me, is a privilege and an adventure.

What I focus on:

For me, managing money starts with managing myself. It's about attitudes and emotions, self-control and priorities. If I am to dress for success, the fabric of my suit must be tightly woven with all these threads. Once the self is well managed, it becomes much easier to apply and properly execute a financial plan, or any plans for that matter; that's my way of doing. I entered this current academic year with just enough money to cover tuition fees and a few groceries. From the very beginning, the order was tall: coordinate studies, work, and family. I can say that hardship builds character and hunger prompts action. I know what the phrase "starving student" means now; my only food comes from what my children leave on their plates after each meal. Money is that tight, but my motto is to not complain.

I find my present lifestyle resembling in many ways the lifestyle of those who faced great adversity during the Great Depression. Just like them, I am developing a strong aversion to waste and unnecessary luxuries. Yes, hardship builds character.

What will help me in the workplace:

This school year I have learned more than textbook material. I have learned to strengthen myself and humble my soul, while also learning the real value of money. Essentially, I will carry these things with me forever in all my future quests for success.

Christian Gaumont. Sprott-Shaw Community College, British Columbia. Reprinted by permission.

If you're feeling a bit overwhelmed about finances at this point in your life, you're not alone. Many students, especially those for whom financial responsibility is a new experience, have similar feelings. However, as one university study reported, "the benefits of financial knowledge extend beyond having money into realms of physical and psychological well-being."[12] Keep learning about money management and making thoughtful decisions, and your actions will contribute to success for life.

Mathematical and Financial Literacy

revisit RISK AND REWARD

Heifer International

What happened to Tererai? Feeling the pull of family obligation, Tererai worked to support her family and care for her husband. Adjusting but not abandoning her risk-taking, she slowed her progress toward her master's degree but still completed it. After her husband's death, she began doctoral work on AIDS prevention in Africa. Tererai checked off the last goal on the worn piece of paper when she received her Ph.D. Now enjoying the rewards of financial stability and career satisfaction as a program evaluator for Heifer, she continues to "work for the causes of women and girls in poverty" (as she wrote on the piece of paper that contained her original four goals).

What does this mean for you? You don't have to have begun your life in poverty in another country or have had five children by your early twenties to feel that you have a long road ahead to achieve financial stability. Let Tererai Trent's story inspire you to take the calculated risks of focusing strongly on your needs and living beneath your means. Describe the financial status you want to achieve—how much you will earn and save each month—by this time five years from now. List three wants you can spend less on, or stop purchasing entirely, as a start toward that reward.

What risk may bring reward beyond your world? The more financially secure you become, the more able you will be to put a few of your dollars toward rewarding those in need. Go to www.heifer.org and click on Our Work, then on Our Initiatives. There you will see seven areas where Heifer International intends to make a difference. Choose one that you find important and read about what Heifer is doing. In addition, consider contributing in other ways by clicking on the Get Involved button.

GLOBAL RISK AND REWARD

Vinz89/Shutterstock

petch one/Shutterstock

Precede Technologies, an Israeli firm, takes financial risks on ideas that it believes will bring both problem-solving and financial rewards. Pondering the worldwide and growing problem of energy use and sourcing, Precede teamed up with a physicist to develop Pythagoras Solar, a way of embedding solar cells in building windows. An office building with these windows installed could literally provide its own electrical supply.[13] Pythagoras Solar won the GE Ecomagination Challenge in 2011 along with a $100 000 prize, and is making the green building a reality.

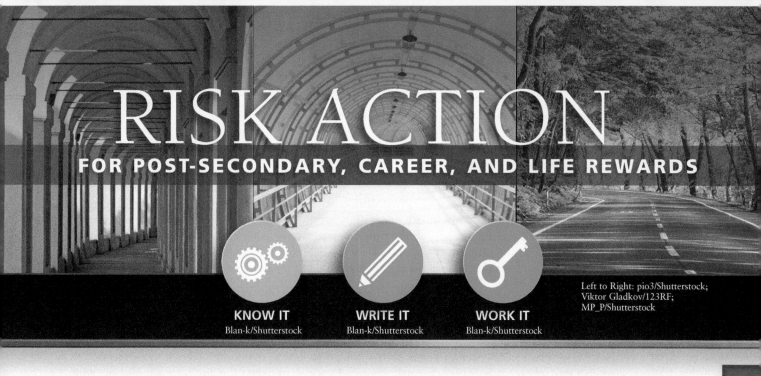

RISK ACTION
FOR POST-SECONDARY, CAREER, AND LIFE REWARDS

KNOW IT
Blan-k/Shutterstock

WRITE IT
Blan-k/Shutterstock

WORK IT
Blan-k/Shutterstock

Complete the following on paper or in digital format.

KNOW IT *Think Critically*

Your Relationship with Money

Getting a handle on money anxiety starts with an honest examination of how you relate to money.

Build basic skills. Analyze yourself as a money manager. Look back at page 279 for a description of what influences the way people handle money. Make some notes about your personal specifics in the following areas.

1. What do you most value spending money on?
2. How do you manage money?
3. How does your culture tend to view money?
4. How do your family and friends tend to handle money?

Take it to the next level. Generate ideas about what you want to do with your money. If you had enough money for your expenses and then some, what would you do with the extra? Would you save it, spend it, do a little of both? Describe what you would do if you had an extra $10 000 to spend this year.

Move toward mastery. Look for practical ways to move toward the scenario you imagined. Realistically, how can you make that $10 000 a reality over time? You may need to change how you operate as a money manager. You may need to make some sacrifices in the short term. Describe two specific plans involving changes and sacrifices that will move you toward your goal.

Mathematical and Financial Literacy

297

WRITE IT *Communicate*

Emotional intelligence journal: You and credit. First, describe yourself as a credit card user. Do you pay in full or run up a balance? Pay on time or pay late? Restrict use to emergencies or use your credit card (or cards) all the time? Describe how using credit cards makes you feel. Examine those feelings and their affect on how you use credit. Then describe a change in your thinking you could make that would help you handle money more wisely.

Real-life writing: Apply for aid. Use internet or library resources to find two scholarships that are not federally funded, available at your school, and for which you are eligible. They can be linked to academic areas of interest, associated with particular talents you have, or offered by a group to which you or members of your family belong. Get applications for each and fill them out. Write a one-page cover letter for each application, telling the committee why you should receive this scholarship. Have someone proofread your work, *send the applications*, and see what happens.

WORK IT *Build Your Brand*

Be Specific About Your Job Needs

As you consider specific job directions and opportunities, look at a variety of job-related factors that may affect your job experience and personal life. These factors include the following:

- Benefits, including supplemental health insurance, vacation, pension
- Integrity of company (its reputation)
- How the company deals with employees
- Promotion prospects (your chances for advancement)
- Job stability
- Training and educational opportunities (Does the company offer training or fund job-related coursework?)
- Starting salary
- Quality of employees and physical environment
- Quality of management
- Nature of the work you will be doing (Will you be required to travel extensively? Will you be expected to work long hours? Will you be working in an office or in the field?)
- Your relationship with the company (Will you be full time or part time? An independent contractor?)
- Job title
- Location of your primary workplace
- Company size
- Company's financial performance over time

Think about how important each factor is in your job choice. Then list them separately, giving each a rating each on a scale of 1 to 10, with 1 being the least important and 10 being the most important. Keep in mind that even if you consider something very important, you may not get it right away if you are just beginning your career.

Finally, consider the results of a survey of students conducted by the National Association of Colleges and Employers. According to students, their top two reasons for choosing an employer are *integrity of organization in its dealings with employees* as number one and *job stability* as number two. How do these top choices compare to your own?[14]

CHAPTER

12

Courtesy of Lauren Ward Larsen

With successful intelligence, a growth mindset, and learned optimism, you will always have an opportunity to grow as a person and make a difference as a citizen of the world.

Thriving in a Diverse Global Community

HOW CAN YOU COMMUNICATE EFFECTIVELY AND MAKE A DIFFERENCE?

What Would You Risk? *Lauren Ward Larsen*

THINK ABOUT THIS SITUATION AS YOU READ, AND CONSIDER WHAT ACTION YOU WOULD TAKE. THIS CHAPTER EXPLORES HOW TO MAKE A DIFFERENCE IN THE WORLD BY RELATING EFFECTIVELY TO DIVERSE PEOPLE, TAKING ACTION AS A GLOBAL CITIZEN, AND FINDING YOUR OWN RECIPE FOR LEADERSHIP.

Despite the sudden death of her father when she was six years old, Lauren Ward Larsen had a fulfilling childhood and did well in school, earning an undergraduate degree and a master's of business administration. She held management positions with companies such as Pepsi-Cola, Simon & Schuster, and 3DO, a video game company.

In her mid-thirties she married, and several years later was pregnant with her first and only child. Her workplace savvy, she thought, had prepared her well: "I had a hard-core success mentality from the business world that I planned to simply transfer to motherhood." In hindsight, and due to a major life detour, Lauren came to understand the saying: "We plan, God laughs."

Her unforeseen risk came in the spring of 2000, when a pregnancy-related disorder, preeclampsia, nearly took her life and that of her daughter. Baby Clare recovered quickly, but Lauren spent six weeks in intensive care with multiple organ failure, seizures, and in a coma, during which time she required 203 pints of blood, all given by volunteer donors she didn't know. Finally, the transfusions and surgeries proved successful, and Lauren was able to leave the hospital. However, she needed to learn to walk again, rebuild her ravaged body, and get to know her baby—who, at six days old, had been sent to live with Lauren's brother's family 600 km away. She could not imagine any reward coming from this challenge. "I felt like this carefully constructed life my husband and I had built together had crumbled into a big pile of rubble before our eyes," Lauren says.

To be continued . . .

A NEAR-FATAL ILLNESS MADE LAUREN AND HER HUSBAND REALIZE THE PRECARIOUS NATURE OF LIFE AND THE PRECIOUSNESS OF TIME. SIMILARLY, AN UNEXPECTED DETOUR COULD TAKE YOU PLACES YOU NEVER IMAGINED. YOU'LL LEARN MORE ABOUT LAUREN, AND THE REWARD RESULTING FROM HER ACTIONS, WITHIN THE CHAPTER.

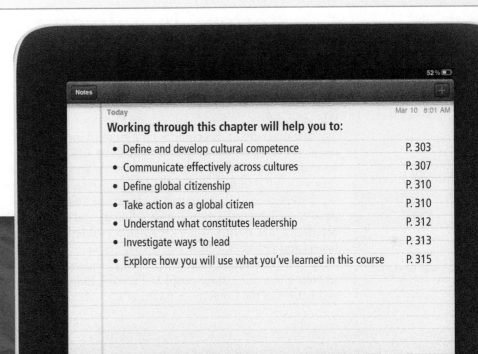

Notes

Today   Mar 10 8:01 AM

Working through this chapter will help you to:

- Define and develop cultural competence — P. 303
- Communicate effectively across cultures — P. 307
- Define global citizenship — P. 310
- Take action as a global citizen — P. 310
- Understand what constitutes leadership — P. 312
- Investigate ways to lead — P. 313
- Explore how you will use what you've learned in this course — P. 315

status CHECK

Left to Right: Luis Santos/Shutterstock; Antonio Guillem/Shutterstock; antoniodiaz/Shutterstock; mimagephotography/Shutterstock; Djomas/Shutterstock; WAYHOME studio/Shutterstock

How Effectively Do You Communicate and Contribute as a Global Citizen?

For each statement, fill in the number that best describes how often it applies to you.

1 = never   2 = seldom   3 = sometimes   4 = often   5 = always

1. I consistently work to develop cultural competence. ① ② ③ ④ ⑤

2. I seek exposure to new and different people, ideas, and experiences. ① ② ③ ④ ⑤

3. I can adjust how I communicate to more effectively connect with others. ① ② ③ ④ ⑤

4. I am able to receive constructive criticism and use it to improve. ① ② ③ ④ ⑤

5. I understand what it means to be a "global citizen." ① ② ③ ④ ⑤

6. I am aware that there is a variety of ways to be a leader. ① ② ③ ④ ⑤

7. I am able to motivate people toward a common goal. ① ② ③ ④ ⑤

8. When I have a vision of what is possible, I convey it effectively to others. ① ② ③ ④ ⑤

9. I keep the needs of others in mind as I make personal choices. ① ② ③ ④ ⑤

10. I feel responsible for making things better in my corner of the world. ① ② ③ ④ ⑤

Each of the topics in these statements is covered in this chapter. Note those statements for which you filled in a 3 or lower. Skim the chapter to see where those topics appear, and pay special attention to them as you read, learn, and apply new strategies.

REMEMBER: NO MATTER HOW WELL YOU COMMUNICATE AND CONSIDER THE NEEDS OF OTHERS, YOU CAN IMPROVE WITH EFFORT AND PRACTICE.

HOW CAN YOU GET ALONG WITH
others in a diverse world?

A century ago it was possible to live an entire lifetime surrounded only by people from your own culture. Not so today. Canadian society consists of people from a multitude of countries and cultural backgrounds. As of 2016, there are over 35 million people who call Canada home.[1] One out of every five Canadians is a member of a visible minority.[2]

The diversity of this country continues to increase. You may encounter all kinds of people in class, at work, and in your daily life. You may experience diversity within your own family. Even if friends or family members share your ethnic background, they may differ in ways such as values, lifestyle, or sexual orientation.

Diversity exists both within each person and among all people. Differences *among* people, such as gender, skin colour, ethnicity and national origin, age, and physical characteristics, are most visible. Other less visible factors include cultural and religious beliefs and practices, education, sexual orientation, socioeconomic status, family background, marital status, even health status (evidenced by Lauren's experience). Being able to "recognize and respect people's diversity, individual experiences and perspectives" is highlighted in the Conference Board of Canada's Employability Skills 2000+ report.[3]

MyLab Student Success
(www.mystudentsuccesslab.com) is an online solution designed to help you "Start Strong, Finish Stronger" by building skills for ongoing personal and professional development.

Furthermore, the Canadian Charter of Rights and Freedoms guarantee everyone "freedom of thought, belief and expression." Diversity isn't just part of your academic experience, it's part of every Canadian's life.

Differences *within* people refer to the set of factors defining your personal diversity, such as personality traits, learning style, strengths and weaknesses, and natural talents and interests. No one else has been or ever will be exactly like you.

Taking the risk to embrace diversity carries significant rewards. Recent research indicates that first-year post-secondary students who befriend people from other races and are exposed to different ideas (religious or political, for example) actually demonstrate larger gains in critical thinking skills.[4] Major life transitions, such as the first year of college or university, bring an uncertainty that spurs brain development. Basically, when you encounter the unfamiliar, your brain needs to make sense of it, and actively looks for information.[5] Combine this with the fact that the years from 18 to 25 are a time when the brain is most primed to form personal and social identity, and you have a recipe for enormous congnitive development.[6]

Almost every student enters a more diverse environment in the first year of their post-secondary career along with the unfamiliar cultures and ideas that go with it.[7] If you give in to the human tendency to avoid the risk of exposure to differences, you can actually lose out on brain development, not to mention a connection with people who could change your life. You can choose what to believe and how to live. Risk opening your mind to people and ideas without fearing that your autonomy will be undermined. In fact, when you explore other ways of being, any beliefs you retain may be enriched and strengthened from the challenge.

Courtesy of Sarah Lyman Kravits

Cultural Competence

Along with the general population, universities and colleges in Canada have grown more diverse in recent years. Even if your student body seems more homogenous on first glance, it is still a group of unfamiliar people, with all kinds of diverse characteristics that lie beneath what's immediately visible.

Interacting successfully with all kinds of people is the goal of *cultural competence*—the ability to understand and appreciate differences among people and adjust your behaviour in ways that enhance relationships and communication. According to the National Center for Cultural Competence, developing cultural competence requires five actions (see Key 12.1). These actions help you develop practical skills that connect you to others, bridging the gap between who you are and who they are.[8]

An important note: Developing cultural competence is about more than just passively being *tolerant* of the world around you. It moves further than that, toward *acceptance*—the practice of actively working toward teamwork and friendship—not just recognizing the differences between cultures but celebrating them as an enriching part of life.[9]

Action #1: Value diversity

Every time you encounter someone new, you choose how to interact. You won't like everyone you meet, but if you value diversity, you will choose to treat people with respect, avoiding assumptions about them and granting them the right to think and believe without being judged. This attitude helps you to take emotionally intelligent actions, as shown in Key 12.2.

Action #2: Identify and evaluate personal perceptions and attitudes

Bringing emotional intelligence into play, you identify perceptions and attitudes by first noticing your feelings about others, and then evaluating these attitudes by looking at the effect they have on you and others. Many who value the *concept* of diversity

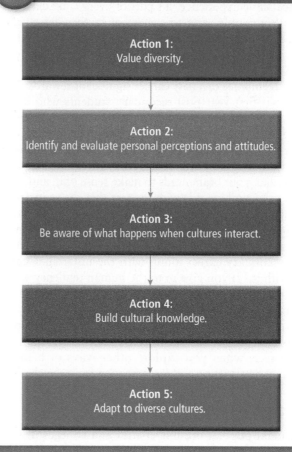

KEY 12.1 Actions move you toward cultural competence.

Action 1:
Value diversity.

Action 2:
Identify and evaluate personal perceptions and attitudes.

Action 3:
Be aware of what happens when cultures interact.

Action 4:
Build cultural knowledge.

Action 5:
Adapt to diverse cultures.

KEY 12.2 Approach diversity with emotional intelligence.

YOUR ROLE	SITUATION	CLOSED-MINDED RESPONSE	EMOTIONALLY INTELLIGENT RESPONSE
Fellow student	For an assignment, you are paired with a student old enough to be your mother.	You assume the student will be clueless about the modern world. You get ready to react against her preaching about how to do the assignment.	You acknowledge your feelings but try to get to know the student as an individual. You stay open to what you can learn from her experiences and realize you have things to offer as well.
Friend	You are invited to dinner at a friend's house. When he introduces you to his partner, you realize that he is gay.	Uncomfortable with the idea of two men in a relationship, you pretend you have a cell phone call and make an excuse to leave early. You avoid your friend after that.	You have dinner with the two men and make an effort to get to know more about them, individually and as a couple. You compare your immediate assumptions to what you learned about them at dinner.
Employee	Your new boss is of a different racial and cultural background than yours.	You assume that you and your new boss don't have much in common. Thinking he will be distant and uninterested in you, you already don't like him.	You acknowledge your stereotypes but set them aside to build a relationship with your boss. You adapt to his style and make an effort to get to know him better.

experience negative feelings about the *reality* of diversity in their own lives. This disconnect reveals prejudices and stereotypes.

Almost everyone has some level of (prejudice,) usually on the basis of gender, race, sexual orientation, disability, and religion. People judge others without knowing anything about them because of factors like the following:

- *Influence of family and culture.* Children learn attitudes—including intolerance, superiority, and hate—from their parents, peers, and community.
- *Fear of differences.* It is human to fear the unfamiliar and to make assumptions about it.
- *Experience.* One bad experience with a person of a particular age, race, or religion may lead someone to condemn all people with the same characteristic.

Prejudice is usually based on (stereotypes)—assumptions made without proof or critical thinking about the characteristics of a person or group, based on factors such as the following:

- *Desire for patterns and logic.* People often try to make sense of the world by using the labels, categories, and generalizations that stereotypes provide.
- *Media influences.* The more people see stereotypical images—the airhead beautiful blonde, the jolly fat man—the easier it is to believe that stereotypes are universal.
- *Laziness.* Labelling group members according to a characteristic they seem to have in common takes less energy than asking questions that illuminate the qualities of individuals.

Stereotypes derail personal connections and block effective communication, because pasting a label on a person makes it hard for you to see the real person underneath. Even stereotypes that seem "positive" may not be true and may get in the way of perceiving uniqueness. Key 12.3 lists some "positive" and "negative" stereotypes.

Action #3: Be aware of what happens when cultures interact

Interaction among people from different cultures can promote learning, build mutual respect, and broaden perspectives. However, as history shows, such interaction can also produce problems. At their mildest, these problems obstruct relationships and communication. At their worst, they set the stage for acts of discrimination and hate crimes.

According to the Canadian Human Rights Commission, based on the Charter of Rights and Freedoms, you cannot be discriminated against because of race, national or ethnic origin, colour, religion, age, sex, sexual orientation, gender identity or expression, marital status, family status, genetic characteristics, disability, or a conviction for

PREJUDICE
A preconceived judgment or opinion formed without just grounds or sufficient knowledge.

STEREOTYPE
A standardized mental picture that represents an oversimplified opinion or uncritical judgment.

KEY 12.3 Both positive and negative stereotypes mask uniqueness.

POSITIVE STEREOTYPE	NEGATIVE STEREOTYPE
Women are nurturing.	Women are too emotional for business.
White people are successful in business.	White people are cold and power hungry.
Gay men have a great sense of style.	Gay men are overly effeminate.
People with disabilities have strength of will.	People with disabilities are bitter.
Older people are wise.	Older people are set in their ways.
Asians are good at math and science.	Asians are poor leaders.

Thriving in a Diverse Global Community

which a pardon has been granted or a record suspended.[10] http://www.chrc-ccdp.gc.ca/eng/content/what-discrimination. Despite these legal protections, discrimination is common and often appears on campuses. Students may not want to work with students of other races, members of campus clubs may reject prospective members because of religious differences, and so on.

When prejudice turns violent, it often manifests itself in *hate crimes*—crimes motivated by a hatred of a specific characteristic thought to be possessed by the victim—usually directed at people based on their race, ethnicity, or religious or sexual orientation.

Action #4: Build cultural knowledge

Focusing on the positive aspect of intercultural interaction prepares you to push past negative possibilities and open your mind to positive ones. Taking the risk to learn about people who are different from you, especially those you are likely to meet on campus or on the job, sets you up for productive relationships. How can you begin?

- Read newspapers, books, magazines, and websites that feature a variety of perspectives.
- Ask questions of all kinds of people, about themselves and their traditions.
- Observe people—how they behave, what they eat and wear, how they interact with others.
- Travel internationally and locally where you can experience different ways of living.
- Build friendships with fellow students or coworkers you would not ordinarily approach.

Building knowledge also means exploring yourself. Talk with family, read, and seek experiences that educate you about your own cultural heritage. Then share what you know with others.

Action #5: Adapt to diverse cultures

Now put what you've learned to work with practical actions. Taking the risk to open your mind can bring the reward of extraordinary relationships and new understanding. Let the following suggestions inspire more ideas about what you can do to improve how you relate to others.

Look past external characteristics. If you meet a woman with a disability, get to know her. She may be an accounting major, a guitar player, a baseball fan. These characteristics—not just her physical person—are part of the big picture of who she is.

Risk putting yourself in other people's shoes. Ask questions about what other people feel, especially if there's a conflict. Offer friendship to someone new to your class. Seek the reward of mutual understanding.

Adjust to cultural differences. When you understand someone's way of being and put it into practice, you show respect and encourage communication. For example, if a study group member takes offence at a particular kind of language, avoid it when you meet.

Stand up against prejudice, discrimination, and hate. When you hear a prejudiced remark or notice discrimination taking place, you may choose to make a comment or to approach an authority such as an instructor or dean. Sound the alarm on hate crimes—let authorities know if you suspect that a crime is about to occur, and support organizations that encourage tolerance. The reward of keeping someone safe is worth the risk.

Recognize that people everywhere have the same basic needs. Everyone loves, thinks, hurts, hopes, fears, and plans. When you are trying to find common ground with diverse people, remember that you are united first through your essential humanity.

Just as there is diversity in skin colour and ethnicity, there is diversity in the way people communicate. Effective communication enables people of all cultures to connect.

Effective Communication

Like many other skills covered in this course, communication is a tool to use toward achieving an important goal. When you communicate with a person, thinking about your specific goal in that moment—improving your experience in the classroom, strengthening a friendship, avoiding a conflict, and so on—will help you communicate in the most effective way possible.

Communicating across cultural lines is often a challenge, and several types of barriers tend to get in the way. Taking the risk to jump these barriers will bring the reward of more effective communication in personal, academic, and professional situations.

Ethnocentrism. This "my way or the highway" attitude demeans anyone outside that culture. Ethnocentrism practically guarantees anger and misunderstanding on a person-to-person level. *To jump this barrier:* Understand that no culture is superior to another. Even if some ways of thinking and acting work for you, they may not be right for all people. Refrain from putting your attitudes and practices ahead of those of other cultures. Also, learn about other ways of thinking, being, and doing. The more you know, the less ethnocentric you are likely to be.

ETHNOCENTRISM
The belief that your own culture is superior to all others, and that the beliefs and values held by that culture are correct.

Assumptions and stereotypes. A student whose study partner fails to show up for work sessions, for example, might assume that all students from the same race, gender, ethnic group, and so on are irresponsible. However, the assumption would be dead wrong. Assumptions have a negative impact on relationships and communication and are often born out of stereotypes. *To jump this barrier:* Be aware of your thoughts when you encounter someone from another culture. Observe what assumptions come to mind and set those thoughts aside. Work to get to know each individual without resorting to stereotypes.

Closed mindedness. Not being open to different perspectives and choices is related to ethnocentrism. Closed mindedness short circuits communication with people outside your culture. Without a willingness to explore other cultures, you can't respectfully exchange ideas with anyone from those cultures. You are less likely to make new friends, eat new foods, and seek out new experiences—and the boundaries you set up around yourself can sharply limit your potential. *To jump this barrier:* Choose to open your mind to new ideas and experiences. Depending on the person, this is easier said than done. Try putting an unfamiliar experience on your schedule—a restaurant, arts performance, book, visit to the home of someone from a different culture, and so on. Exposure to differences tends to open your mind bit by bit.

Lack of knowledge. If you don't understand a culture's values and customs, you may unknowingly behave in disrespectful ways. If an North American woman tries to shake hands with a man from a culture where unrelated men and women don't make contact in public, for example, she will be embarrassed at the least, and at the worst may shut down the interaction. *To jump this barrier:* The cure is education. Be informed. If you do something that makes a bad impression on someone from another culture, politely ask for information on the acceptable way to behave, and keep it in mind for next time. If you know you will encounter people from a particular culture either at school, at work, or while travelling for business or pleasure, read up on how to dress, greet people, and behave in public—and what to avoid doing or saying.

Mangostock /Fotolia

Thriving in a Diverse Global Community

get creative

EXPAND YOUR PERCEPTION OF DIVERSITY

Astroid/123RF

Complete the following on paper or in digital format.

The ability to respond to people as individuals requires you to become more aware of diversity that is not always on the surface. Start by examining your own uniqueness. Write 10 words or phrases that describe you. The challenge: Minimize references to ethnicity or appearance (brunette, Caribbean Canadian, wheelchair dependent, and so on), and fill the list with characteristics not visible at a glance (visual learner, only child, drummer, marathoner, and so on).

Next, pair up with a classmate whom you do not know well. First, list any characteristics you think you know about him or her—chances are most of them will be visible. Then talk together for a few minutes, each taking a turn to introduce yourself. As you talk, fill out and correct your lists about each other from discoveries made during the conversation. Finally, answer three questions.

1. What stands out to you about what you learned about your classmate, and why?
2. What would you like people to focus on more often about you, and why?
3. Name a communication strategy you used in this conversation. How was it effective?

Fear. It is human to fear people and ideas that are unfamiliar to you. It is also problematic. Fear of differences can make you uncomfortable around others, leading you to avoid them. Inaccurate judgments and prejudices arise, making it impossible to communicate or work together successfully. Trying to listen through your fear is like trying to have a conversation with loud music blaring. Emotions can block comprehension just as loud music makes it tough to hear. *To jump this barrier*: The main antidotes to fear are education and experience. As you learn more and have positive experiences with different people, you become more comfortable with them, and fear lessens over time. Have you ever been the "different" one wanting to be understood and accepted? How did it make you feel? Even if you have never been that in position, imagine what it would be like and how it would affect your interaction with others.

Finally, because you are a full participant in the communication experience, self-knowledge will help you understand what role you play and how you can play it better. The Multiple Intelligence Strategies grid for Communication on page 309 provides ideas about communication strategies that align with strength in different intelligences.

In the modern world, people cross real and virtual paths with individuals from other cultures more and more every day. With the cultural competence and communication strategies you have explored, you will be as prepared as possible to receive your passport as a global citizen.

Riccardo Piccinini/Fotolia

Communication with others is essential to every school and work goal, from team projects to study groups to on-the-job collaborations.

multiple intelligences strategies

Describe an upcoming study group meeting or team project (course, topic): _____. In the right-hand column, record specific ideas for how MI strategies can help you make the most of it.

INTELLIGENCE	USE MI STRATEGIES TO IMPROVE COMMUNICATION	IDENTIFY MI COMMUNICATION STRATEGIES THAT CAN HELP YOU WORK WELL WITH OTHERS
Verbal-Linguistic	• Find opportunities to express your thoughts and feelings to others—either in writing or in person. • Keep in mind that listening to words is at least as important as speaking them.	
Logical-Mathematical	• Allow yourself time to think through a problem before discussing it. Write out an argument on paper and rehearse it. • When communicating with others whose styles are not as logic-focused, ask specific questions to learn the facts you need.	
Bodily-Kinesthetic	• Have an important talk while walking, running, or performing a task that does not involve concentration. • Work out to burn off excess energy before having an important discussion.	
Visual-Spatial	• Make a drawing or diagram of points you want to communicate during an important discussion. • If you are in a formal classroom or work setting, use visual aids to explain your main points.	
Interpersonal	• If you tend to dominate group conversation, focus more on listening. • If you tend to prioritize listening to others, work on becoming more assertive about expressing your opinion.	
Intrapersonal	• Be as clear as possible when expressing what you know about yourself, and recognize that not all communicators may be self-aware. • When you have a difficult encounter, take time alone to decide how to communicate more effectively next time.	
Musical	• Before communicating difficult thoughts or feelings, work through them by writing a poem or song. • Be sensitive to the rhythms of a conversation. Sense when to voice your opinion and when to hang back.	
Naturalistic	• Use your ability to recognize patterns to evaluate communication situations. Employ patterns that work well and avoid those that do not. • When appropriate, make an analogy from the natural world of plants or animals to clarify a point in a conversation.	

Thriving in a Diverse Global Community

WHY BE A
global citizen?

A message sent over digital phone systems, email, or Facebook goes from Singapore to Germany in seconds—or even milliseconds. A work team made up of people living in New York, Calgary, Hamilton, and St. John's has meetings over the phone and on Skype. Businesses based in one country hire and manage employees who live and work in other countries and time zones. These changes and others like them have forged new connections among people from around the globe, effectively creating a *global community*.

Consider the Global Community Earth Government's definition of a global community: "All that exists or occurs at any location at any time between the Ozone layer above and the core of the planet below." By this definition, everything that lives in the air, on the earth, and below the earth's surface is part of the global community, and all of these living things are connected one to the other.[11] Because of these connections, your actions affect people and things all around you. A negative effect: Throwing cell phone batteries away can put them into a landfill where acids can cause damage to plant and animal life. A positive effect: 203 strangers took action to donate blood, which saved Lauren's life.

Global Citizenship Defined

To define global citizenship, first note the two components of (citizenship:)

1. What you *receive*, that is, rights and privileges
2. What you *give*, that is, your duties and obligations to others

CITIZENSHIP
Having the rights, privileges, and duties associated with membership in a particular society or community.

Global citizenship, therefore, is being a member of the global community, and having both the benefits (rights and privileges) and the obligations (duties) that come with that membership (see Key 12.4). You will notice that many of these are also reflected in Canada's Charter of Rights and Freedoms. The scope of global citizenship goes beyond individual people. Each school, company, organization, and nation can be seen as a global citizen, enjoying the privileges of the global community while being obligated to consider the needs of other people, schools, companies, organizations, and nations when choosing actions.

Taking Action as a Global Citizen

With every action, you have a choice. It is human, and has been common, to make choices with one's own needs as the primary consideration. However, that self-centred

KEY 12.4	Being a global citizen carries both rights and obligations.

RIGHTS AND PRIVILEGES INCLUDE. . .	DUTIES AND OBLIGATIONS INCLUDE. . .
Equal status as a person before the law	To consider the needs of others when making decisions
Right to move freely	To act in ways that do not harm others
Freedom of opinion and expression	To choose actions that have a positive effect on other members
Freedom of peaceful assembly and association	To choose actions that protect the environment
Freedom to work	To respect other members of the global community
Right to an education	To build multicultural knowledge

get practical

Diego Cervo/Shutterstock

binkski/123RF

ACT AS A RESPONSIBLE CITIZEN OF A COMMUNITY

Complete the following on paper or in digital format.

First, generate a list of communities to which you belong. This includes but is not limited to your family, cultural, neighbourhood, religious, spiritual, educational, organizational, and social communities.

Next, if there are any ways in which you have already helped any of these communities through volunteer service, service-learning, internship, or employment, list them.

Finally, plan to carry out your obligation as a local and global citizen—to *make* things better in some way—in one community from your list. You may plan to continue service you have performed in the past, or you may decide to do something totally new.

1. Name the community you will focus on.

2. Describe your goal for how to make things better.

3. Next, identify:

   a. A specific action or set of actions

   b. A date on which, or by which, you intend to accomplish action(s)

   c. A person with whom you can partner to check on you to make sure you have taken action

   d. A list of potential issues requiring cultural awareness and competence that could arise from this experience (differences in values or ethics, gender roles, family interactions, and so on)

4. Take practical action. Write down your goal and action(s) in a calendar. Communicate with the person who will check on you. Then carry out your plan.

5. Evaluate the experience afterward. Write a paragraph or two that answers the following questions: Did you accomplish your goals? How did you feel? Would you take action again in a similar way? Would you do something different? How will you make a difference in the future?

focus is becoming more and more problematic as the connections among all living things grow stronger and more visible. Although global citizens should not ignore their own needs, they should broaden their decision-making processes to consider the needs of others in the global community. The benefit of this consideration will be shared across the board.

When you risk your time and energy and act with an awareness of the needs of others, your actions can bring rewards for the community. For example:

- Reusing water bottles means fewer plastic bottles in bodies of water all over the globe, resulting in less money spent on cleanup and greater survival of marine life

- Tutoring a foreign student in English helps improve his chances for success at school and at work, making it more likely that he will earn a steady income, which can in turn improve the lives of his family members

- Donating to an organization working to prevent HIV infection in southern Africa helps to improves the health of citizens there, allowing those countries to allocate more resources for the growth and development of industry and education

Consider this partial list of actions as you ponder what your global citizenship means to you.

Communicate with cultural awareness. You show respect when you keep culture in mind as you communicate. Listen actively to understand expressions and dialects from languages and cultures that are unfamiliar to you. Note customs and behaviours. Ask when you need clarification.

Be an environmental steward. Do your part to protect the health and safety of living things and the environment through your actions. Reduce, reuse, and recycle. Minimize your environmental footprint by using less energy and leaving less trash.

ENVIRONMENTAL FOOTPRINT
The impact that the actions of one person or company (what is consumed and what is thrown away) have on the world's resources, based on a measure of the amount of carbon dioxide produced.

Take action with your wallet. Determine who makes the products and provides the services you use regularly, and investigate whether those companies act responsibly toward the environment and promote sustainable growth and development. Consider prioritizing responsible companies when spending your money. Also, support local goods and services—the less travel involved in connecting you with your needs, the fewer resources used in transport.

Consume responsibly. The "more is better, bigger is better" way of being in North America was born of a more prosperous, more ignorant time. Question your purchases: Do I really need this, or more of this? What are the pros and cons? Generally, the more stuff you own, the more time and resources you spend storing it, cleaning it, caring for it, fuelling it. For example, a second car means more gas, more servicing, more inspections, and more insurance.

This is just the tip of the iceberg. You can trace nearly any action back many steps and find its effects, good and bad, on people and environments. Each person's actions have consequences that ripple across the globe. Make your ripples ones that you can point to with pride.

HOW CAN YOU
be a leader?

When you hear the word *leader*, your first thought may be of someone in a highly visible and powerful position—the Prime Minister of Canada or the Chancellor of Germany, the CEO of Microsoft or the Royal Bank of Canada, the Dalai Lama, or the Pope. However, there are many ways to lead, and not all leaders carry such a high profile.

Think of your community. You may know of leaders such as deans, senior professors, business managers, and people in local government positions. You probably can also think of people who you consider leaders even though they hold no official position—they just seem to motivate people, or set an example that others want to follow.

Leadership Defined

There are two ways to define leadership:

1. The ability and process of motivating people to move toward a common goal
2. The ability and process of affecting thoughts and behaviours of others[12]

The first definition refers to a more visible, typical kind of leadership. It is the job of the CEO of a company, for example, to motivate people employed by the company to create and sell the company's products; likewise, it is the job of a quarterback to motivate his team to move the ball downfield. However, a person—CEO, quarterback, or anyone else—can also lead in the second way, by setting an example that inspires others to positive thought and productive action.

Think of leaders who have inspired you. Do you look up to humanitarian heroes such as Mahatma Ghandi or Nelson Mandela? Perhaps you admire agents of social change such as Martin Luther King, Jr. or Aung San Suu Kyi. Maybe you are motivated by the leadership of influential politicians, writers, scientists, artists, athletes, and businesspeople. Consider whether these people embody just one or both of the definitions of leadership. When you read the last part of Lauren's story at the end of the chapter, think about what kind of leadership she demonstrates.

Being comfortable speaking in front of a group is an essential skill for the modern workplace. Take advantage of opportunities, in class as well as with campus activities, to hone your speaking skills.

Components of Leadership

There are several components that make up the experience of leadership. They are as follows:[13]

1. Leadership is a process, not a state of being. A leader can't just be a leader when given a title—a leader *does*. Leadership demands action, following a process toward a goal.
2. Leadership means influencing the thoughts, feelings, and actions of others, whether by example or by directive (see Key 12.5 for the ways that effective leaders set an example).
3. Leadership happens in the context of a group. A leader working alone is not a leader—there must be followers involved.
4. Leadership involves reaching a goal together with efforts from others in the group.
5. Leadership demands that the group and the leader share the same goal.

These components show that a leader is able to generate motion and energy, moving currents of action and communication throughout a group and propelling them toward a common goal. Being a leader is a risk, but the reward is that effective leaders of any scope—from the head of the United Nations to the chairperson of a community board—get things done.

Making a Difference as a Student Leader

Students can and should find opportunities to lead, either by action or by example. Leadership now gives you opportunities to make a difference for others within and

KEY 12.5	Effective leaders set an example through . . .			
BEHAVIOUR	**FOLLOW-THROUGH**	**POSITIVE SELF-IDENTITY**	**VALUES**	**VISION**
Leaders model most effective, positive behaviours. When they ask others to behave in a certain way, they do the same. They take responsibility for their actions.	Leaders do what they say they will do. They meet deadlines and deliver on their promises.	Leaders are aware of both their strengths and weaknesses. They believe in themselves and work to grow and improve.	Leaders demonstrate values that inspire team members as well as support team goals.	Leaders have a vision of what is possible and know how to convey it. They maintain their vision in the face of obstacles.

without your academic community. It also builds leadership skills that will serve you in the workplace and in life.

What risks can you take now to lead in ways that can bring rewards for you and others?

Help to lead organizations that interest you. Once you have joined an organization and learned more about how it works, consider pursuing a leadership position in the club. Find out more about what these positions involve (duties, time commitment) and see what might suit you best. To make the most of your experience, find a group that holds meaning for you.

Form study groups. Take the lead on getting fellow students together in person or online for a study group. When the group is formed, take a turn leading a meeting, or come up with a plan for preparing for a test. Use leadership and participation strategies.

Express yourself in front of others. When an opportunity to speak in front of others comes up, take it. Present in front of a class; post a message to your class online; speak to members of a club at a meeting. Communicate your message while building your confidence.

Volunteer in or outside your academic community. Making a difference for others around you can build leadership skills. If you have a strong interest in an organization, you may even consider pursuing a specific leadership position with the organization, or heading up a project.

Take initiative at work. If you have a job, speak out respectfully about systems, teams, or situations that aren't working well and need to be adjusted. Talk to a supervisor about ideas you have that you might be able to implement. Set an example for others with whom you work.

Start a club. If your school doesn't have a particular type of club that interests you, communicate with others to see who else might share your interest. Have an initial conversation or meeting and come up with some specific goals. If your group takes root, see if the school will recognize it as an official club.

Tutor or mentor others. Helping other students with academic development, career planning, or personal needs builds all kinds of leadership skills.

Courtesy of Lauren Ward Larsen

talk risk and reward . . .

Risk asking tough questions to be rewarded with new insights. Use the following questions to inspire discussion with classmates, either in person or online.

- Has a point of difference ever kept you from connecting with someone? What makes you hesitate? What reward might you gain from the risk of connection?

- In which communities do you feel like you belong? What communities do you come into contact with that make you uncomfortable? Discuss why and offer ideas of rewards that could come from leaving your comfort zone.

CONSIDER THE CASE: Imagine you had gone through a life-or-death medical trial as Lauren did. In the wake of that experience, how do you think you would feel? Would you be able to see any potential for growth, or do you think you would be overwhelmed with the struggle?

get $mart

Racorn/123RF

YOUR PERSONAL RELATIONSHIP WITH MONEY

Creativenv/
Shutterstock

Complete the following on paper or in digital format.

Think about how you relate to money and why. Answer the following questions.

1. Do members of your family discuss finances? If they do, what do they talk about? If they do not discuss finances, why do you think that is?
2. Do you spend money on things you want but do not need? If and when you do, how do you feel before, during, and after the purchase? One week later?
3. How does the topic of money make you feel?
4. How often, and how regularly, do you actively manage your money?
5. What do you feel are your biggest problems with money?
6. Do you borrow money from friends or family? If so, how do you pay it back—on time or not, all at once or in smaller amounts, not at all?
7. Do you talk with friends and family about money problems? Why or why not?
8. Based on your answers, how would you summarize your relationship with money in a short paragraph?

HOW WILL YOUR WORK
in this course serve you?

You leave this course with far more than a final grade and credit hours on your transcript. You leave with a set of skills and attitudes that open the door to success throughout life.

Continue to Grow as a Risk-Taker and Thinker

Finishing this course is the beginning of your career as a calculated risk taker and a successfully intelligent learner. How can you stay motivated to keep thinking and risking? Earlier in this text, you may have completed a self-assessment to examine your levels of development in 20 characteristics that promote action and productive risks. According to Sternberg, successfully intelligent people:[14]

1. *Motivate themselves.* They make things happen, spurred on by a desire to succeed and a love of what they are doing. They rarely need others to tell them what to do.
2. *Learn to control their impulses.* Instead of going with their first quick response, they sit with a question or problem. They take time to let ideas surface before making a decision.
3. *Know when to persevere.* When the reward is worth the effort, they push past frustration and stay on course. They also recognize when they've hit a dead end and shift gears in response.
4. *Know how to make the most of their abilities.* They understand what they do well and capitalize on those skills and abilities in school and work.
5. *Translate thought into action.* Not only do they have good ideas, but they are also able to turn those ideas into practical actions that bring ideas to fruition.

Thriving in a Diverse Global Community

6. *Have a product orientation.* They want results. They focus on the reward they are aiming for first, then figure out what risks will get them there.

7. *Complete tasks and follow through.* With determination, they finish what they start. They also follow through to make sure loose ends are tied and the goal has been achieved.

8. *Are initiators.* They commit to people, projects, and ideas. They risk action rather than sitting back and waiting for things to happen to them.

9. *Are not afraid to fail.* Because their risks don't always bring the reward they seek, they often learn from mistakes, build brain power, and enjoy greater success down the road.

10. *Don't procrastinate.* They are aware of the negative effects of putting things off, and they avoid it. They create schedules that allow them to accomplish what's important on time.

11. *Accept fair blame.* They strike a balance between never accepting blame and taking the blame for everything. If something is their fault, they accept responsibility.

12. *Reject self-pity.* When something goes wrong, they find a way to solve the problem. They don't get caught in the energy drain of feeling sorry for themselves.

13. *Are independent.* They can work on their own and think for themselves. They take responsibility for their own schedule and tasks.

14. *Seek to surmount personal difficulties.* They keep things in perspective, looking for ways to remedy personal problems and separate them from their professional lives.

15. *Focus and concentrate to achieve their goals.* They create an environment in which they can best avoid distraction and they focus steadily on their work.

16. *Spread themselves neither too thin nor too thick.* They do neither too much, resulting in little progress on any, nor too little, which can reduce the level of accomplishment.

17. *Have the ability to delay gratification.* They risk effort in the present for the reward of gratifying goal achievement in the future.

18. *Have the ability to see the forest and the trees.* They are able to see the big picture and get a sense of the specifics, without getting bogged down in each and every tiny detail.

19. *Have a reasonable level of self-confidence.* They believe in themselves enough to keep moving, while avoiding the kind of overconfidence that stalls growth and learning.

20. *Balance analytical, creative, and practical thinking.* They sense what to use and when to use it. When problems arise, they combine all three skills to arrive at solutions.

These "self-activators" are your personal motivational tools. Consult them when you need a way to get moving. You may even want to post them on a bulletin board, in the front of a notebook, or as a note in your smartphone. Use the "Get Analytical" exercise on page 317 to see where you are now in terms of your development of these self-activators.

Although you certainly used analytical, creative, and practical skills before, your work this term has built and strengthened new neural pathways in your brain, allowing you to engage them more consciously and effectively. Every day of your post-secondary career and beyond, you will analyze something, come up with an idea, or take a practical action on your way to a meaningful goal. Every time you solve a problem or make a decision, you take a risk. Successful intelligent thinking and risk taking will bring you rewards throughout your life.

get analytical

Darren Baker/
Shutterstock

EVALUATE YOUR SELF-ACTIVATORS

Dario Sabljak/Shutterstock

To see how you use successful intelligence in your daily life, assess your perceived development on Sternberg's activators. Circle the number that best represents your answer, with 1 being "not at all like me" and 5 being "definitely like me."

1. I motivate myself well.	1 2 3 4 5
2. I can control my impulses.	1 2 3 4 5
3. I know when to persevere and when to change gears.	1 2 3 4 5
4. I make the most of what I do well.	1 2 3 4 5
5. I can successfully translate my ideas into action.	1 2 3 4 5
6. I can focus effectively on my goal.	1 2 3 4 5
7. I complete tasks and have good follow through.	1 2 3 4 5
8. I initiate action—I move people and projects ahead.	1 2 3 4 5
9. I have the courage to risk failure.	1 2 3 4 5
10. I avoid procrastination.	1 2 3 4 5
11. I accept responsibility when I make a mistake.	1 2 3 4 5
12. I don't waste time feeling sorry for myself.	1 2 3 4 5
13. I independently take responsibility for tasks.	1 2 3 4 5
14. I work hard to overcome personal difficulties.	1 2 3 4 5
15. I create an environment that helps me concentrate on my goals.	1 2 3 4 5
16. I don't take on too much or too little work.	1 2 3 4 5
17. I can delay gratification in order to receive the benefits.	1 2 3 4 5
18. I can see both the big picture and the details in a situation.	1 2 3 4 5
19. I am able to maintain confidence in myself.	1 2 3 4 5
20. I balance my analytical, creative, and practical thinking skills.	1 2 3 4 5

If you completed this self-assessment at the beginning of the course, look back at your original scores. On a piece of paper or digital file, describe three changes over the course of the term that feel significant to you.

Finally, choose one self-activator that you feel still needs work. Analyze the specific reasons why it remains a challenge. For example, if you are still taking on too much work, is it because you want to please others? Write a one-paragraph analysis, and let this analysis guide you as you work to build your strength in this area.

Use Your Tools of Success

This course has introduced you to a collection of powerful tools that you have explored and built throughout the text. They make your risk taking more likely to result in rewards both now and in the future. You will make the most of your hard work if you use (and don't lose) the following.

Transferable skills. Outside of the specific subject knowledge and skills you build in your coursework, everything else you learn is transferable to any class and any career. Your liberal arts education provides you with many opportunities to build these skills.

317

Emotional intelligence. Teamwork is important now, in school, and will continue to feature prominently in your working and personal life. Tuning into yourself and others in an emotionally intelligent way is at the heart of effective, goal-achieving communication.

Growth mindset. With the attitude that you can always grow and learn, you are as ready to achieve the goals you set today as you are to achieve future goals you cannot yet anticipate.

Integrity. Risking day-to-day choices that display academic integrity rewards you with a habit of personal integrity for life. The neural pathways those habits forge in your brain will benefit you, leading you to consistently make honest and moral choices.

Self-sufficiency. Having gotten through your first term you are likely to have tackled several challenges on your own. If you handle problems with initiative and action and solicit experienced advisors when you need backup, you will be both self-advocate and first responder.

Responsibility and planning. Taking the risk to be self-sufficient and responsible rewards you with increased ability to manage your life. Every life and study skill you've built this term increases your ability to plan.

Self-control and willpower. Your most important goals demand energy and time that the temptations of modern life can drain away. Managing your exposure to technology and systematizing your schedule are risks calculated to help you minimize decision fatigue and conserve your resources.

As you continue in school remind yourself that you are creating tools that will benefit you in everything you do. You don't stop learning because you graduate. Lifelong learning is the master key that unlocks the doors you encounter on your journey. With it firmly in your hand, you will discover worlds of knowledge—and a place for yourself within them.

Face Change and Challenges with Risk-Taking

As a citizen of the 21st century, you will experience exciting changes as well as troubling ones. Changes and challenges such as failed or incomplete courses, job offers or job losses, scholarship offers or financial struggles may arise. Your ability to respond to change with risk-taking aimed at a positive reward, especially if the change is unexpected and difficult, is crucial to your future success. The ability to "make lemonade from lemons" is the hallmark of people who know how to hang on to hope.

Use your optimistic explanatory style to analyze situations, generate solutions, and take practical action. With this skill you can:

- *See adversity as temporary.* Consider losing a job, for example, as a step along the way to a better one.
- *See the limited scope of your problems.* One issue does not make your entire life a disaster.
- *Avoid the personal.* If you look for explanation in the details of a situation instead of seeing yourself as incompetent, you can keep your self-esteem and creative energy alive.

With successful intelligence, a growth mindset, and learned optimism, you will always have a new direction in which to grow. Your willingness to take calculated, productive risks will allow you to put these valuable

leungchopan/Shutterstock

student PROFILE

Dion Redgun
CDI COLLEGE, CALGARY, ALBERTA

Courtesy of Dion Redgun

About me:

I am a First Nation's member from Siksika. I am the head of a family with ten grandchildren—one granddaughter and nine grandsons. My studies are in Business Administration and Management.

What I focus on:

I own and operate a small business on Siksika Nation lands. I give back to the community by hosting youth camps and providing river floats and cultural excursions. My goal is to graduate in order to take all the teachings and knowledge back to Siksika Nation to help it utilize its natural resource, the Bow River, to promote First Nations culture through tourism. Being a mature student has provided me with many challenges. I have suffered and lived with arthritis for over 12 years and have recently had four surgeries. Using modern technology has helped me cope with the hardship and obstacles that I have faced as a student. I am truly a product of modern technology; joint replacements, a power chair, a voice recorder, and an iPad have allowed me to continue with my journey to wellness through education.

What will help me in the workplace:

My advice to any future generations and entrepreneurs venturing out into the business industry and into new life experiences in general is don't give up. Stay focused. With discipline, courage, and education, your outlook on life will change, whether or not you have a disability.

Dion Redgun. CDI College, Calgary, Alberta. Reprinted by permission.

tools to work and reward you with the achievement of your most-valued goals. Risk being true to yourself, a respectful friend and family member, a focused student who believes in the power of learning, a productive employee, and a contributing member of society. These risks will earn you the ultimate reward of a meaningful life—a life that can change the world.

Thriving in a Diverse Global Community

revisit RISK AND REWARD

What happened to Lauren? Nearly dying actually brought Lauren—and her husband, Jeff—the reward of understanding how to live. "We asked ourselves, 'Do we want to rebuild the same life? Or something more authentic to who we have become?' Knowing the role that blood transfusions played in her survival, Lauren began travelling to give speeches in hopes of inspiring others to become blood donors.

Lauren earned the 2006 Outstanding Achievement Award from the American Association of Blood Banks, and was named one of the "100 Most Inspiring Alumni" in the 75-year history of the UCLA Anderson Graduate School of Management, all from her desire to thank the quiet heroes who had helped save her life with their blood.

What does this mean for you? As Lauren sought to express gratitude to countless blood donors, nurses, doctors, rehab specialists, family, and friends, she rediscovered her true passion—storytelling. One tangible result was her memoir, *Zuzu's Petals: A True Story of Second Chances*, but the broader result was a new career direction, focused on telling "true stories that touch people's hearts to inspire action in whatever way is meaningful to them." Reflect on your long-term life goals. Write them down. Why have you chosen these paths? Are they authentic to who you are as a person? Will they bring rewards that reflect your values?

What risk may bring reward beyond your world? Lauren took advantage of her second chance by becoming a driving force behind several humanitarian efforts. In 2006 and again in 2011, she chaired the two largest fundraisers to date for the Preeclampsia Foundation. In 2007, Jeff and Lauren launched a grassroots initiative to drill water wells in war-torn areas of South Sudan. Go to www.thefabc.org to learn how vital blood donations are to human health.

GLOBAL RISK AND REWARD

Vinz89/Shutterstock

Peter Etchells/123RF

Living in a high-risk area for seismic activity prompted several Chilean scientists to consider how to protect buildings from earthquake damage. Together they developed a U-shaped metal device that is integrated into strategic locations in the building's support structure. In the event of an earthquake, the devices absorb the seismic force by bending, and then renew structural support when they regain their original shape. The risk these scientists took will offer reward to people living wherever their technology is installed, in earthquake zones all over the world.[15]

RISK ACTION

FOR POST-SECONDARY, CAREER, AND LIFE REWARDS

KNOW IT
Blan-k/Shutterstock

WRITE IT
Blan-k/Shutterstock

WORK IT
Blan-k/Shutterstock

Left to Right: pio3/Shutterstock; Viktor Gladkov/123RF; MP_P/Shutterstock

Complete the following on paper or in digital format.

KNOW IT *Think Critically*

Take the Lead

Build basic skills. Create an image of yourself as a leader. Referring to the coverage in the chapter, generate a list of five leadership traits or skills you commonly demonstrate. Thinking about these traits, describe a situation in your life—personal, academic, or workplace—where you could take a leadership role.

Take it to the next level. Keeping in mind the components of leadership from this chapter on page 313, answer the following questions:

1. Leadership demands action. What would be your action as a leader in this situation?
2. Leadership means influencing others. Would you lead by example or directive? How would you like to influence the thoughts, feelings, or actions of those in your group?
3. Leadership happens in the context of a group. Who are the people with whom you would be working?
4. Leadership involves reaching a goal together. What is your goal for the group?
5. Leadership demands that the group and the leader share a goal. How would you get the rest of your group on board with this goal?

Move toward mastery. Identify the specific steps you will take in the next three months to lead in this situation. Put them in your calendar and treat them as tasks to be completed. If possible, evaluate your experience after three months. How well did you follow your plan? Did you and your group achieve a goal? How did your actions move the group forward?

Thriving in a Diverse Global Community

WRITE IT *Communicate*

Emotional intelligence journal: Consider prejudice and stereotypes. As human as it is to prejudge and stereotype, it is possible to set these tendencies aside. Describe an experience of holding a prejudiced or stereotypical thought that was proven wrong. What did you think? What effects did it have on you and on others? What happened to prove your perspective inaccurate? Discuss what you have learned from the experience and how it informs your life now. Finally, if anyone has had a thought about you that was wrong, describe the situation. What did the person think? How did it make you feel? What other effects did it have?

Real-life writing: Global citizenship in your career. You are likely to have thought about your career in terms of what it can do for you, and perhaps even what it can do for others (deliver products, provide services, and so on). Now think about how you could act as a global citizen in the context of your career, or how a company in your career area might take on global citizenship. Choose someone who can give you perspective on a career area that interests you—an instructor or professional. Draft a polite inquiry to this person, asking for information about how you can be a responsible global citizen in this career. Ask about jobs to look for, companies focused on making a difference, and actions to take on the job no matter where you work. Send your letter over email or regular mail. If you receive a response, keep it in mind as you make decisions about how you will pursue your career.

WORK IT *Build Your Brand*

If you have been completing portfolio items throughout the term, read through your entire career portfolio. You have gathered a lot of information to turn to on your path to a fulfilling, successful career.

Without looking at any previously completed versions of these assessments or the wheel on page 25, chapter 1, analyze where you are after completing this course by taking the three assessments.

Assess Your Analytical Thinking Skills

For each statement, circle the number that feels right to you, from 1 for "not at all true for me" to 5 for "very true for me."

1. I recognize and define problems effectively.	1 2 3 4 5
2. I see myself as a thinker and as analytical and studious.	1 2 3 4 5
3. When working on a problem in a group setting, I like to break down the problem into its components and evaluate them.	1 2 3 4 5
4. I need to see convincing evidence before accepting information as fact.	1 2 3 4 5
5. I weigh the pros and cons of plans and ideas before taking action.	1 2 3 4 5
6. I tend to make connections among pieces of information by categorizing them.	1 2 3 4 5

7. Impulsive, spontaneous decision making worries me.   1 2 3 4 5

8. I like to analyze causes and effects when making a decision.   1 2 3 4 5

9. I monitor my progress toward goals.   1 2 3 4 5

10. Once I reach a goal, I evaluate the process to see how effective it was.   1 2 3 4 5

Total your answers here: _____

Assess Your Creative Thinking Skills

For each statement, circle the number that feels right to you, from 1 for "not at all true for me" to 5 for "very true for me."

1. I tend to question rules and regulations.   1 2 3 4 5

2. I see myself as unique, full of ideas, and innovative.   1 2 3 4 5

3. When working on a problem in a group setting, I generate a lot of ideas.   1 2 3 4 5

4. I am energized when I have a brand-new experience.   1 2 3 4 5

5. If you say something is too risky, I'm ready to give it a shot.   1 2 3 4 5

6. I often wonder if there is a different way to do or see something.   1 2 3 4 5

7. Too much routine in my work or schedule drains my energy.   1 2 3 4 5

8. I tend to see connections among ideas that others do not.   1 2 3 4 5

9. I feel comfortable allowing myself to make mistakes as I test out ideas.   1 2 3 4 5

10. I'm willing to champion an idea even when others disagree with me.   1 2 3 4 5

Total your answers here: _____

Assess Your Practical Thinking Skills

For each statement, circle the number that feels right to you, from 1 for "not at all true for me" to 5 for "very true for me."

1. I can find a way around any obstacle.   1 2 3 4 5

2. I see myself as a doer and the go-to person; I make things happen.   1 2 3 4 5

3. When working on a problem in a group setting, I like to figure out who will do what and when it should be done.   1 2 3 4 5

4. I apply what I learn from experience to improve my response to similar situations.   1 2 3 4 5

5. I finish what I start and don't leave loose ends hanging.   1 2 3 4 5

6. I note my emotions about academic and social situations and use what they tell me to move toward a goal.   1 2 3 4 5

7. I can sense how people feel and use that knowledge to interact with others effectively.   1 2 3 4 5

8. I manage my time effectively.   1 2 3 4 5

9. I adjust to the teaching styles of my instructors and the communication styles of my peers.   1 2 3 4 5

10. When involved in a problem-solving process, I can shift gears as needed.   1 2 3 4 5

Total your answers here: _____

With your new scores in hand, create the most updated representation of your thinking skills. In each of the three areas of the wheel, draw a curved line approximately at the level of your number score and fill in the wedge below that line. Compare this wheel to your previous wheel and note any change and development.

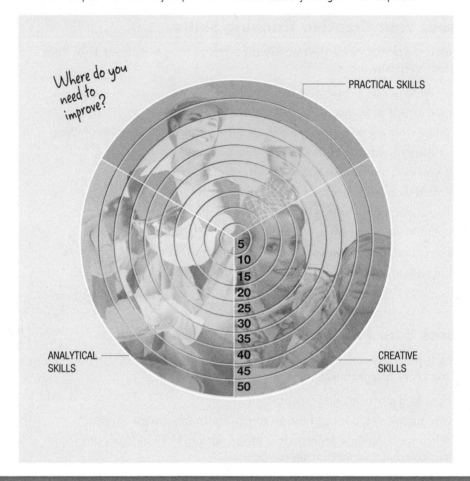

Source: Based on "The Wheel of Life" model developed by the Coaches Training Institute. © Co-Active Space 2000.

After you finish, fill in your new scores in the blank Wheel of Successful Intelligence in Key 12.6. If you completed a wheel at the beginning of the term, compare it to this wheel and look at the changes. Complete the following on a sheet of paper or digital file:

- Note the areas where you see the most change. Where have you grown, and how has your self-perception evolved?
- Note three *creative ideas* you came up with over the term that aided your exploration or development.
- Note three *practical actions* that you took that moved you toward your goals.

Let what you learn from this new wheel inform you about what you have accomplished and what you plan to accomplish. Continue to grow your thinking skills and use them to manage the changes that await you in the future.

ENDNOTES

QUICK START

1. Sternberg, Robert J. *Successful Intelligence: How Practical and Creative Intelligence Determine Success in Life*. New York: Plume, 1997, p. 24.

CHAPTER 1

1. Matheson, Kathy. "College Freshmen Troubled But Optimistic: Study." Huff Post College, January 27, 2011. From http://www .huffingtonpost.com/2011/01/27/college-freshmen-troubled_n_814686.html

2. Dictionary.com, "global community." Retrieved July 8, 2013 from http://dictionary.reference.com/browse/global+community

3. Statistics Canada, "Labour Force Statistics," http://www.statcan.gc.ca/tables-tableaux/sum-som/l01/cst01/lfss01a-eng.htm

4. Human Resources and Skills Development Canada, *Special Reports: What Difference Does Learning Make to Financial Security?* January 2008, www4.hrsdc.gc.ca/.3ndic.1t.4r@-eng.jsp?iid=54

5. Statistics Canada, "The Long Term Labour Market Premiums Associated with a Postsecondary Education." http://www.statcan.gc.ca/daily-quotidien/140227/dq140227c-eng.htm.

6. Thomas Friedman, *The World Is Flat*, New York: Farrar, Straus & Giroux, 2006, p. 8.

7. Daniel Pink, "Revenge of the Right Brain," *Wired Magazine*, February 2005, www.wired.com/wired/archive/13.02/brain.html?pg=1&topic=brain&topic_set=.

8. Conference Board of Canada, "Employability Skills 2000+," www.conferenceboard.ca/topics/education/learning-tools/employability-skills.aspx

9. Council of Ministers of Education Canada, *Learn Canada 2020*, April 15, 2008, www.cmec.ca/Publications/Lists/Publications/Attachments/187/CMEC-2020-DECLARATION.en.pdf.

10. Adecco College Graduate Survey.

11. Sternberg, Robert J. *Successful Intelligence: How Practical and Creative Intelligence Determine Success in Life*. New York: Plume, 1997, pp. 85–90; Dweck, Carol S. *Mindset: The New Psychology of Success*. New York: Random House, 2006, p. 5;

Jaeggi, Susanne, Martin Buschkuehl, John Jonides, and Walter J. Perrig. "Improving Fluid Intelligence with Training on Working Memory." 2008, Proceedings of the National Acadamy of Sciences USA 105, pp. 6829–6833.

12. Sternberg, p. 11.

13. Dweck, pp. 3–4.

14. The Society for Neuroscience. *Brain Facts: A Primer on the Brain and Neurosystem*, Washington, DC: The Society for Neuroscience, 2008, pp. 34–35.

15. Sternberg, p. 12.

16. Ibid., p. 127.

17. Ibid., p. 11.

18. Ibid., pp. 127–128.

19. Mayer, John D., Peter Salovey, and David R. Caruso. "Emotional Intelligence: New Ability or Eclectic Traits?" *American Psychologist,* vol. 63, no. 6, p. 503. September 2008.

20. Lehrer, Johah. "Hearts & Minds." *The Boston Globe,* April 29, 2007. From http://www.boston.com/news/globe/ideas/articles/2007/04/29/hearts__minds/?page=full

21. Caruso, David R. "Zero In on Knowledge: A Practical Guide to the MSCEIT." North Tonawonda, NY: Multi-Health Systems Inc., 2008, p. 3.

22. Blakeslee, Sandra. "Cells That Read Minds." *The New York Times,* January 10, 2006. From http://www.nytimes.com/2006/01/10/science/10mirr.html

23. Mayer, Salovey, and Caruso, pp. 510–512.

24. Tough, Paul. "What if the Secret to Success Is Failure?" *New York Times*, September 14, 2011. From http://www.nytimes.com/2011/09/18/magazine/what-if-the-secret-to-success-is-failure.html?pagewanted=all

25. Material in this section from Seligman, Martin E. P. *Learned Optimism: How to Change Your Mind and Your Life*. New York: Vintage Books, 2006, pp. 45–53, 207–222.

26. Dweck, Carol. "The Mindsets." 2006. From http://www.mindsetonline.com/whatisit/themindsets/index.html

27. Dweck, *Mindset*, p. 16.

28. *The Fundamental Values of Academic Integrity*, The Center for Academic Integrity, Rutland Institute for Ethics, Clemson University, October 1999. From http://www.academicintegrity.org/ fundamental_values_project/index.php

29. Taylor, William M. "Academic Integrity: A Letter to My Students." Oakton Community College, Des Plaines, IL. From http://www.academicintegrity. org/educational_resources/pdf/LetterToMyStudents Rev2010.pdf

30. Ibid.

31. Babcock, Philip, and Mindy Marks. "Leisure College, USA: The Decline in Student Study Time." Education Outlook, American Enterprise Institute for Public Policy Research, August 2010, no. 7, p. 1.

32. Tierney, John. "Do You Suffer From Decision Fatigue?" *New York Times*, August 17, 2011. From http://www.nytimes.com/2011/08/21/ magazine/do-you-suffer-from-decision-fatigue. html?_r=1&ref=johntierney

33. Ibid.

34. Tough.

35. PBSC Urban Solutions. 2010. From http://www. publicbikesystem.com

36. List and descriptions based on Sternberg, pp. 251–268.

CHAPTER 2

1. LiveScience. "College Students Value Self-Esteem Over Sex." FoxNews.com, January 10, 2011. From http://www.foxnews.com/health/2011/ 01/10/college-students-value-self-esteem-sex

2. Conference Board of Canada, "Employability Skills 2000+," www.conferenceboard.ca/topics/ education/learning-tools/employability-skills.aspx

3. Pavlina, Steve. "10 Tips for College Students." stevepavlina.com, May 8, 2006. From http:// www.stevepavlina.com/blog/2006/05/10-tips-for- college-students

4. Covey, Stephen. *The Seven Habits of Highly Effective People*. New York: Simon & Schuster, 1989, pp. 70–144, 309–318.

5. Pavlina.

6. Brody, Jane E. "At Every Age, Feeling the Effects of Too Little Sleep." *New York Times*, October 23, 2007. From http://www.nytimes.com/2007/10/23/ health/23brod.html

7. Burka, Jane B., and Lenora M. Yuen. *Procrastination: Why You Do It, What to Do*

About It. Reading, MA: Perseus Books, 1983, pp. 21–22.

8. Sheridan, Richard, and Lisamarie Babik. "Breaking Down Walls, Building Bridges, and Taking Out the Trash." InfoQ, December 22, 2010. From http://www.infoq.com/articles/ agile-team-spaces

9. Schwarz, Tony. "Four Destructive Myths Most Companies Still Live By." *Harvard Business Review*, November 1, 2011. From http://blogs. hbr.org/schwartz/2011/11/four-destructive-myths- most-co.html

10. "Takeaways and Quotes from Dr. John Medina's Brain Rules." Slideshare presentation, Slide 79. From http://www.presentationzen.com/ presentationzen/2008/05/brain-rules-for.html

11. mtvU and Associated Press College Stress and Mental Health Poll Executive Summary. Spring 2008. From http://www.halfofus.com/_media/_pr/ mtvU_AP_College_Stress_and_Mental_Health_ Poll_Executive_Summary.pdf

12. Sparks, Sarah D. "Study Reveals Brain Biology Behind Self-Control." *Education Week*, January 31, 2012. From http://www.edweek.org/ew/articles/ 2011/09/21/04selfcontrol_ep.h31.html?tkn=MYY FqQfiSJulpkZPARGNdmV6MpM7mcZJsHb1&c mp=clp-edweek

13. Ibid.

14. Mariotte, Benjamin. "Sergio Castro—Portrait of a Healer." *Optimist Stories*, January 20, 2012. From http://optimistworld.com/Sergio-Castro- Healer

CHAPTER 3

1. Patty Winsa, "National Survey of Post-Secondary Students in Canada Show Stress and Anxiety Are Major Forces in Mental Health," *Toronto Star*, June 17, 2013. From https://www.thestar.com/ news/gta/2013/06/17/national_survey_of_ postsecondary_students_in_canada_shows_stress_ and_anxiety_are_major_factors_in_mental_health .html.

2. Conference Board of Canada, "Employability Skills 2000+," www.conferenceboard.ca/topics/ education/learning-tools/employability-skills. aspx

3. Begley, Sharon. "The New Science of Stress." *The Saturday Evening Post*, November/December 2011. From http://www.saturdayeveningpost. com/2011/11/04/in-the-magazine/health-in-the- magazine/stress.html

4. Ibid.

5. Kolata, Gina. "A Surprising Secret to a Long Life: Stay In School." *New York Times*, January 3, 2007, pp. A1 and A16.

6. Information based in this section based on materials from Dr. Marlene Schwartz of the Rudd Center for Food Policy and Obesity at Yale University.

7. Strauss, Valerie. "'Freshman 15' Weight Gain a Myth, Study Says." *The Washington Post*, November 1, 2011. From http://www.washingtonpost.com/blogs/answer-sheet/post/freshman-15-weight-gain-a-myth-study-says/2011/11/01/gIQATa4RdM_blog.html?wpisrc=nl_cuzheads

8. Stats Can Daily, "Canadian Community Health Survey, 2014," June 17, 2015.

9. CMAJ, Current and Predicted Prevalence of Obesity in Canada: A Trend Analysis," http://cmajopen.ca/content/2/1/E18.full

10. Stats Can Daily, "Canadian Community Health Survey, 2014," June 17, 2015.

11. Rudd Center for Food Policy and Obesity. "Employment." 2005. From http://www.yaleruddcenter.org/what_we_do.aspx?id=203

12. Mayo Clinic. "Aerobic Exercise: Top 10 Reasons to Get Physical." Mayoclinic.com, 2012. From http://www.mayoclinic.com/health/aerobic-exercise/EP00002/NSECTIONGROUP=2

13. Centers for Disease Control and Prevention. "How Much Physical Activity Do Adults Need?" CDC website, March 30, 2011. From http://www.cdc.gov/physicalactivity/everyone/guidelines/adults.html

14. Evans, Mike. "23½ hours." *YouTube*, December 2, 2011. From http://www.youtube.com/watch?v=aUaInS6HIGo

15. CBS News. "Help for Sleep-Deprived Students." April 19, 2004. From www.cbsnews.com/stories/2004/04/19/health/main612476.shtml

16. "College Students Sleep Habits Harmful to Health, Study Finds." *The Daily Orange—Feature Issue,* September 25, 2002. From http://www.dailyorange.com/2.8656/college-students-sleep-habits-harmful-to-health-study-finds-1.1251402#.TsSALHLNRww

17. Benson, Herbert, and Eileen M. Stuart, et al. *The Wellness Book.* New York: Simon & Schuster, 1992, p. 292; Jacobs, Gregg. "Life Style Practices That Can Improve Sleep (Parts 1 and 2)." *Talk About Sleep,* 2004. From http://www.talkaboutsleep.com/sleep-disorders/archives/insomnia_drjacobs_lifestyle_part1.htm and http://www.talkaboutsleep.com/sleep-disorders/archives/insomnia_drjacobs_lifestyle_practices_part2.htm

18. Sapolsky, Robert. *On Stress: An Interview.* Retrieved from http://boingboing.net/2011/11/23/robert-sapolsky-on-stress-an.html.

19. Statistics Canada, "Canadian Community Heath Survey: Mental Health 2012," http://www.statcan.gc.ca/daily-quotidien/130918/dq130918a-eng.htm

20. Centre for Addiction and Mental Health (CAMH), "Depression," www.camh.ca/en/hospital/about_camh/newsroom/understanding/Pages/depression.aspx

21. American Psychological Association. "College Students Exhibiting More Severe Mental Illness, Study Finds." August 12, 2010. From http://www.apa.org/news/press/releases/2010/08/students-mental-illness.aspx

22. SAVE (Suicide Awareness Voices of Education). "Symptoms of Major Depression." 2010. From http://www.save.org/index.cfm?fuseaction=home.viewPage&page_id=A806E240-95E6-44BB-C2D6C47399E9EFDB)

23. Gustafson, Timi. "Anxiety Disorders Are Sharply on the Rise." SeattlePi.com, October 23, 2011. From http://blog.seattlepi.com/timigustafsonrd/2011/10/23/anxiety-disorders-are-sharply-on-the-rise

24. National Eating Disorders Association. "Learning Basic Terms and Information on a Variety of Eating Disorder Topics." 2010. From http://www.nationaleatingdisorders.org/information-resources/general-information.php#facts-statistics

25. Solomon.

26. Knox, Richard. "The Teen Brain: It's Just Not Grown Up Yet." NPR.org, March 1, 2010. From http://www.npr.org/templates/story/story.php?storyId=124119468

27. Foster, Linda. "Teen Alcoholism and Drug Addiction." EverydayHealth.com, April 20, 2009. From http://www.everydayhealth.com/addiction/addiction-in-adolescence.aspx

28. Centers for Disease Control and Prevention. "Alcohol and Public Health: Frequently Asked Questions—How Does Alcohol Effect a Person?" October 28, 2011. From http://www.cdc.gov/alcohol/faqs.htm#howAlcoholAffect

29. Substance Abuse and Mental Health Services Administration. *Results from the 2010 National Survey on Drug Use and Health: Summary of National Findings.* NSDUH Series H-41, HHS Publication No. (SMA) 11-4658. Rockville, MD: Substance Abuse and Mental Health Services Administration, 2011. From http://www.samhsa.gov/data/NSDUH/2k10NSDUH/2k10Results.htm#Fig3-3

30. Seguine, Joel. "Students Report Negative Consequences of Binge Drinking in New Surey." The University Record, University of Michigan, October 25, 1999. From http://www.umich.edu/~urecord/9900/Oct25_99/7.htm

31. Statistics Canada, "Canadian Community Heath Survey: Mental Health 2012," http://www.statcan.gc.ca/daily-quotidien/130918/dq130918a-eng.htm

32. Encyclopedia of Drugs and Addictive Substances. "Nicotine—What Kind of a Drug is it?" Gale Cengage, 2006. From http://www.enotes.com/drugs-substances-encyclopedia/nicotine

33. Health Canada, "Dangers of Second Hand Smoke," www.canada.ca/en/health-canada/services/smoking-tobacco/avoid-second-hand-smoke/second-hand-smoke/dangers-second-hand-smoke.html#a2

34. Smith, Hilary. "Excerpts from: The High Cost of Smoking." Ash.org, November 11, 2005. From http://ash.org/no-smoking/nov05/11-21-05-2.html

35. National Cancer Institute at the National Institutes of Health. "Cigarette Smoking: Health Risks and How to Quit." From http://www.cancer.gov/cancertopics/pdq/prevention/control-of-tobaccouse/Patient.

36. Substance Abuse and Mental Health Services Administration. From http://www.samhsa.gov/data/NSDUH/2k10NSDUH/2k10Results.htm#2.9

37. Nettleton, Steve. "Invented in China." Aljazeera.com, February 9, 2010. From http://www.aljazeera.com/programmes/witness/2009/10/2009101165910611337.html

38. Rape Abuse and Incest National Network. "Statistics." From http://www.rainn.org/statistics

CHAPTER 4

1. Conference Board of Canada, "Employability Skills 2000+," www.conferenceboard.ca/topics/education/learning-tools/employability-skills.aspx

2. Gardner, Howard. Multiple Intelligences: New Horizons. New York: Basic Books, 2006, p. 180.

3. Gardner, Howard. Multiple Intelligences: The Theory in Practice. New York: HarperCollins, 1993, pp. 5–49.

4. Gardner, Multiple Intelligences: New Horizons, p. 8.

5. Gardner, Multiple Intelligences: The Theory in Practice, p. 7.

6. Boeree, C. George. "Carl Jung." George Boeree personal website, 2006. Accessed on November 5, 2013 at http://webspace.ship.edu/cgboer/perscontents.html

7. Waters, John K. "Broadband, Social Networks, and Mobility Have Spawned a New Kind of Learner." The Journal, December 13, 2011 Chatsworth, CA: 1105 Media, Inc. From http://thejournal.com/Articles/2011/12/13/Broadband-Social-Networks-and-Mobility.aspx?Page=1

8. Learning Disabilities Association of Canada, "Official Definition of Learning Disabilities," http://www.ldac-acta.ca/learn-more/ld-defined

9. Ibid.

10. "LD Advocates Guide" (no date). National Center for Learning Disabilities. From www.ncld.org/index.php?option=content&task=view&id=291

11. Learning Disabilities Association of Ontario, "Educational Implications of Recent Supreme Court Ruling," http://www.ldao.ca/educational-implications-of-recent-supreme-court-ruling/.

12. Hippo Water Roller Project. "About Us." February 7, 2013. From http://www.hipporoller.org/project/about-us

CHAPTER 5

1. Willis, Judy. "Understanding How the Brain Thinks." Edutopia.org, June 13, 2011. From http://www.edutopia.org/blog/understanding-how-the-brain-thinks-judy-willis-md

2. Dobbs, David. "Beautiful Brains." National Geographic, October 2011. From http://ngm.nationalgeographic.com/print/2011/10/teenage-brains/dobbs-text

3. Ibid.

4. Ibid.

5. Ibid.

6. Ruggiero, Vincent. Beyond Feelings: A Guide to Critical Thinking, 9th ed. New York: McGraw-Hill, 2012, p. 19.

7. Paul, Richard. "The Role of Questions in Thinking, Teaching, and Learning." 1995. Accessed April 2004 from http://www.criticalthinking.org/resources/articles/the-role-of-questions.shtml

8. "The Best Innovations Are Those That Come from Smart Questions." Wall Street Journal, April 12, 2004, p. B1.

9. Begley, Sharon. "Critical Thinking: Part Skill, Part Mindset and Totally Up to You." Wall Street Journal, October 20, 2006, p. B1.

10. Hyerle, David. "Thinking Maps: Visual Tools for Activating Habits of Mind." Learning and Leading with Habits of Mind, Arthur L. Costa and Bena Kallicks, eds. Alexandria, VA: Association

for Supervision and Curriculum Development, 2008, p. 153.

11. Ibid.

12. Conference Board of Canada, "Employability Skills 2000+," www.conferenceboard.ca/topics/education/learning-tools/employability-skills.aspx

13. Thomas, Matt. "What Is Higher-Order Thinking and Critical/Creative/Constructive Thinking?" (no date) Center for Studies in Higher-Order Literacy. From http://a-s.clayton.edu/tparks/What%20is%20Higher%20Order%20Thinking.doc

14. Lehrer, Jonah. *Imagine: How Creativity Works.* New York: Houghton Mifflin Harcourt, 2012, p. xx.

15. Ibid., pp. 7–8, 56.

16. Ibid., p. 69.

17. Kaufman, Scott Barry. "How Convergent and Divergent Thinking Foster Creativity." *Psychology Today*, February 9, 2012. From http://www.psychologytoday.com/blog/beautiful-minds/201202/both-convergent-and-divergent-thinking-are-necessary-creativity

18. Gibson, Jennifer. "The Art of Medicine." *Brain Blogger*, October 31, 2010. From http://brainblogger.com/2010/10/31/the-art-of-medicine

19. Adapted from Tardif, T. Z., and R. J. Sternberg. "What Do We Know About Creativity?" *The Nature of Creativity*, R. J. Sternberg, ed. London: Cambridge University Press, 1988.

20. Lehrer, pp. 175–212.

21. Cain, Susan. "The Rise of the New Groupthink." *New York Times*, January 13, 2012. From http://www.nytimes.com/2012/01/15/opinion/sunday/the-rise-of-the-new-groupthink.html?pagewanted=1&_r=1&smid=fb-nytimes

22. Ibid.

23. Michalko, Michael. "Twelve Things You Were Not Taught in School About Creative Thinking." *Psychology Today*, December 2, 2011. From http://www.psychologytoday.com/blog/creative-thinkering/201112/twelve-things-you-were-not-taught-in-school-about-creative-thinking

24. Ibid.

25. Lehrer, Jonah. "Groupthink." *The New Yorker*, January 30, 2012. From http://www.newyorker.com/reporting/2012/01/30/120130fa_fact_lehrer?currentPage=3

26. Ibid.

27. Sarah Lyman Kravits, 2012.

28. Lehrer, *Imagine*, pp. 163–164.

29. Gertner, John. "True Innovation." *New York Times*, February 25, 2012. From http://www.nytimes.com/2012/02/26/opinion/sunday/innovation-and-the-bell-labs-miracle.html?pagewanted=all

30. Lehrer, Jonah. "Five Tips for Reaching Your Creative Potential," Greater Good, April 11, 2012. From http://greatergood.berkeley.edu/article/item/five_tips_for_reaching_your_creative_potential

31. Lehrer, *Imagine*, pp. 123–130.

32. Lehrer, "Five Tips for Reaching Your Creative Potential."

33. Hayes, J.R. *Cognitive Psychology: Thinking and Creating.* Homewood, IL: Dorsey, 1978.

34. Sternberg, Robert J., and Elena L. Grigorenko. "Practical Intelligence and the Principal." Yale University: Publication Series No. 2, 2001, p. 5.

35. Rosenthal, Normal. "10 Ways to Enhance Your Emotional Intelligence." *Psychology Today*, January 5, 2012. From http://www.psychologytoday.com/blog/your-mind-your-body/201201/10-ways-enhance-your-emotional-intelligence

36. Sternberg, Robert. *Successful Intelligence.* New York: Plume, 1996, pp. 251–269.

37. Schwartz, Barry. TED talk. February 1, 2009. From http://www.ted.com/talks/barry_schwartz_on_our_loss_of_wisdom.html

38. Sternberg, *Successful Intelligence*, p. 241.

39. Willis, "Understanding How the Brain Works."

40. Nalewicki, Jennifer. "Bold Stroke: New Font Helps Dyslexics Read." *Scientific American*, October 26, 2011. From http://www.scientificamerican.com/article.cfm?id=new-font-helps-dyslexics-read

CHAPTER 6

1. Conference Board of Canada, "Employability Skills 2000+," www.conferenceboard.ca/topics/education/learning-tools/employability-skills.aspx

2. Robinson, Francis P. *Effective Behavior.* New York: Harper & Row, 1941.

3. Faragher, John Mack, Mari Jo Buhle, Daniel Czitrom, and Susan H. Armitage. *Out of Many: A History of the American People*, 5th ed. Upper Saddle River, NJ: Prentice Hall, 2005, p. xxxvii.

4. Bloom, Benjamin S. *Taxonomy of Educational Objectives, Handbook I: The Cognitive Domain.* New York: McKay, 1956.

5. Robinson, Adam. *What Smart Students Know.* New York: Three Rivers Press, 1993, p. 82.

6. National Council for the Social Studies. "The Themes of Social Studies." From http://www.socialstudies.org/standards/strands

7. Kessler, Sarah. "38% of College Students Can't Go 10 Minutes Without Tech." Mashable.com, May 31, 2011. From http://mashable.com/2011/05/31/college-tech-device-stats

8. Bauerlein, Mark. "Online Literacy is a Lesser Kind." The Chronicle of Higher Education, September 19, 2008. From http://chronicle.com/article/Online-Literacy-Is-a-Lesser/28307

9. Ibid.

10. Hertz, Mary Beth. "The Right Technology May Be a Pencil." Edutopia.com, November 29, 2011. From http://www.edutopia.org/blog/technology-integration-classroom-mary-beth-hertz?utm_source=facebook&utm_medium=post&utm_content=blog&utm_campaign=techisapencil

11. Information in this section based on materials from Office of Learning Resources. "Guide to Reading Primary Sources." University of Pennsylvania. From http://www.vpul.upenn.edu/lrc/lr/PDF/primary%20sources%20(W).pdf; Walbert, Kathryn. "Reading Primary Sources: An introduction for Students," LearnNC.org, 2004. From http://www.learnnc.org/lp/pdf/reading-primary-sources-p745.pdf; Wisconsin Historical Society. "How to Read Primary Sources." 2012. From http://www.wisconsinhistory.org/turningpoints/primarysources.asp

12. Schrag, Zachary M. "How To Read a Primary Source." Historyprofessor.org, 2011. From http://historyprofessor.org/research/how-to-read-a-primary-source

13. Leibovich, Lori. "Choosing Quick Hits over the Card Catalog." New York Times, August 10, 2001, p. 1.

14. Troyka, Lynn Quitman. Simon & Schuster Handbook for Writers. Upper Saddle River, NJ: Prentice Hall, 1996, pp. 22–23.

15. Cutler, Kim-Mai. "Whill, The Electric Wheelchair Add-on, Takes Home TechCrunch Tokyo's Grand Prize." TechCrunch.com, November 15, 2012. From http://techcrunch.com/2012/11/15/whill-techcrunch-tokyo

16. Macionis, John J. Sociology, 6th ed. Upper Saddle River, NJ: Prentice Hall, 1997, p. 174.

CHAPTER 7

1. Conference Board of Canada, "Employability Skills 2000+," www.conferenceboard.ca/topics/education/learning-tools/employability-skills.aspx

2. System developed by Cornell professor Walter Pauk. See Pauk, Walter. How to Study in College, 10th ed. Boston: Houghton Mifflin, 2011, pp. 236–241.

3. Miller, Greg. "How Our Brains Make Memories." Smithsonian Magazine, May 2010. From http://www.smithsonianmag.com/science-nature/How-Our-Brains-Make-Memories.html?c=y&page=2

4. Mohs, Richard C. "How Human Memory Works." howstuffworks.com, 2012. From http://science.howstuffworks.com/environmental/life/human-biology/human-memory1.htm

5. University of California–Irvine. "Short-term Stress Can Affect Learning And Memory." ScienceDaily, March 13, 2008. From http://www.sciencedaily.com/releases/2008/03/080311182434.htm

6. Ebbinghaus, Herman. Memory: A Contribution to Experimental Psychology, trans. H. A. Ruger and C. E. Bussenius. New York: Teachers College, Columbia University, 1885.

7. Miller.

8. Academic Skills Center. "How to Avoid Cramming for Tests." Dartmouth College, 2001. From http://www.dartmouth.edu/~acskills/handouts.html

9. Robinson, Adam. What Smart Students Know: Maximum Grades, Optimum Learning, Minimum Time. New York: Three Rivers Press, 1993, p. 118.

10. Dambeck, Holger. "New Zealand's Shweeb: Google Invests in Cycle-Powered Monorail." Spiegel Online International, October 6, 2010. From http://www.spiegel.de/international/zeitgeist/new-zealand-s-shweeb-google-invests-in-cycle-powered-monorail-a-721448.html

CHAPTER 8

1. Conference Board of Canada, "Employability Skills 2000+," www.conferenceboard.ca/topics/education/learning-tools/employability-skills.aspx

2. "The Role of Sleep in Memory." Mempowered, January, 2012. From http://www.memory-key.com/improving/lifestyle/activity/sleep

3. Speidel, Barbara J. "Overcoming Test Anxiety." Academic Success Center of Southwestern College. From http://www.swccd.edu/~asc/lrnglinks/test_anxiety.html

4. "Anxiety Management." Michigan Technological University. From http://www.counseling.mtu.edu/anxiety_management.html

5. Gwynne, Peter. "The Write Way to Reduce Test Anxiety." Inside Science News Service, January 14, 2011. From http://www.usnews.com/science/articles/2011/01/14/the-write-way-to-reduce-test-anxiety

6. From Nolting, Paul D. *Math Study Skills Workbook, Your Guide to Reducing Test Anxiety and Improving Study Strategies.* Boston: Houghton Mifflin Company, 2000. Cited in "Test Anxiety." West Virginia University at Parkersburg. From http://www.wvup.edu/Academics/more_test_anxiety_tips.htm

7. Duffy, Jill. "How Students Use Technology to Cheat and How Their Teachers Catch Them." PCMag.com, March 25, 2011. From http://www.pcmag.com/slideshow/story/262232/how-students-use-technology-to-cheat

8. Vogeler, Ingolf. "How to Prepare for an Essay Exam." Center for Teaching Excellence at the University of Wisconsin at Eau Claire, 2008. From http://www.uwec.edu/geography/ivogeler/essay.htm

9. Gose, Ben. "Notes from Academe: Living It Upon the Dead Days." The Chronicle of Higher Education, June 78, 2002. From http://chronicle.com/article/Living-It-Up-on-the-Dead-Days/8983

10. Talbert, Robert. "How to Prepare for Final Exams." Casting Out Nines, December 5, 2007. From http://castingoutnines.wordpress.com/2007/12/05/how-to-prepare-for-final-exams

11. Ibid.

12. Hyman, Jeremy S., and Lynn F. Jacobs. "Top 15 Hot Tips for Finals." Professors' Guide by *U.S. News and World Report*, December 10, 2010. From http://www.usnews.com/education/blogs/professors-guide/2010/12/10/top-15-hot-tips-for-finals

13. Ibid.

14. de Pommereau, Isabelle. "Skype's Journey from Tiny Estonian Start-Up to $8.5 Billion Microsoft Buy." *The Christian Science Monitor*, May 11, 2011. From http://www.csmonitor.com/World/Europe/2011/0511/Skype-s-journey-from-tiny-Estonian-start-up-to-8.5-billion-Microsoft-buy

CHAPTER 9

1. "Attitudes and Characteristics of Freshmen at 4-year Colleges, Fall 2007." *The Chronicle of Higher Education: 2008–9 Almanac*, vol. 55, issue 1, p.18. Data from "The American Freshman: National Norms for Fall 2007." University of California at Los Angeles Higher Education Research Institute.

2. Conference Board of Canada, "Employability Skills 2000+," www.conferenceboard.ca/topics/education/learning-tools/employability-skills.aspx

3. Moran, Joseph. "Channeling Jeff Winger: Create Your Own 'Community' Online Study Group." Schools.com, June 2, 2011. From http://www.schools.com/articles/create-your-own-community-online-study-group.html

4. Lucier, Kelci Lynn. "Living with a Roomate: 10 Tips for a Good Roommate Relationship." About.com, 2012. From http://collegelife.about.com/od/beforeyouarrive/qt/roommatetips.htm

5. Astin, Alexander W. *Preventing Students from Dropping Out.* San Francisco: Jossey-Bass, 1976.

6. http://communityservicelearning.ca/what-is-csl/

7. Chakma, Justin, Hassan Masum, Kumar Perampaladas, Jennifer Heys, and Peter Singer. "Indian Vaccine Innovation: The Case of Shantha Biotechnics." Globalization and Health, April 20, 2011. From http://www.globalizationandhealth.com/content/7/1/9

CHAPTER 10

1. Singletary, Michelle. "Not All College Majors Are Created Equal." *The Washington Post*, January 14, 2012. From http://www.washingtonpost.com/business/not-all-college-majors-are-created-equal/2012/01/12/gIQAfz4XzP_story.html

2. Ibid.

3. Self-Directed Search, http://www.self-directed-search.com

4. Conference Board of Canada, "Employability Skills 2000+," www.conferenceboard.ca/topics/education/learning-tools/employability-skills.aspx

5. "The Hot Jobs with High Pay." Career Prospects in Virginia, February 2007. From http://www.careerprospects.org/Trends/salary-high.html

6. National Service Learning Clearinghouse. "Service Learning Is … " May 2004. From http://www.servicelearning.org/article/archive/35

7. Sagan, Aleksandra. "As Student Debt Climbs to an Average Past 25K, Schools Invest in Battling the Mental Health Issues It Causes." *National Post*, May 30, 2016.

8. Masse, Bryson. "Here's the State of Student Debt in Canada." *Vice Money*, January 27, 2017.

9. Statistics Canada. "Employment Patterns of Postsecondary Students," *The Daily*, September 29,

2010, http://www.statcan.gc.ca/daily-quotidien/ 100929/dq100929c-eng.htm

10. Korkki, Phyllis. "The Internship as Inside Track." *New York Times*, March 25, 2011. From http:// www.nytimes.com/2011/03/27/jobs/27searches .html

11. Ibid.

12. Ibid.

13. Adams, Susan. "Get a Job Using the Hidden Job Market." *Forbes,* July 5, 2011. Accessed on October 1, 2011, from http://www.forbes.com/ sites/susanadams/2011/07/05/get-a-job-using-the-hidden-job-market

14. Job Interview and Career Guide. "Resume:Keywords for Resumes—Keywords List." December 8, 2009. From http://www.job-interview-site.com/resume-keywords-for-resumes-keywords-list.html

15. Dickler, Jessica. CNN Money, June 10, 2009. Accessed on October 1, 2011, from http://money .cnn.com/2009/06/09/news/economy/hidden_jobs

16. Brody, Jane E. "Advice From Life's Graying Edge on Finishing With No Regrets." *New York Times,* January 9, 2012. From http://www.nytimes.com/ 2012/01/10/health/elderly-experts-share-life-advice-in-cornell-project.html?_ r=3&pagewanted=1&smid=fb-nytimes

17. Synergos. "Rana Dajani, Jordan." From http:// www.synergos.org/bios/ranadajani.htm

CHAPTER 11

1. Conference Board of Canada, "Employability Skills 2000+," www.conferenceboard.ca/topics/ education/learning-tools/employability-skills.aspx

2. Bryk, Anthony S., and Uri Treisman. "Make Math a Gateway, Not a Gatekeeper." *New York Times,* April 18, 2010. From http://chronicle.com/ article/Make-Math-a-Gateway-Not-a/65056/#top

3. www.theglobeandmail.com/globe-investor/ personal-finance/household-finances/money-stress-catches-up-with-canadians/article5221810/

4. http://cfsontario.ca/en/section/182

5. Hanson, Jim. "Your Money Personality: It's All In Your Head." University Credit Union, December 25, 2006. From http://hffo.cuna.org/012433/ article/1440/html

6. "Attitudes and Characteristics of Freshmen at 4-Year Colleges, Fall 2007." Chronicle of Higher Education.

7. Statistics Canada, "Graduating in Canada: Profile, Labour Market Outcomes and Student Debt of the Class of 2009/2010, 2013," *The Daily*, November 11, 2014, http://www.statcan .gc.ca/daily-quotidien/141114/dq141114b-eng.htm

8. Perna, Laura. "Understanding the Working College Student." Academe Online, July/August 2010. From http://www.aaup.org/AAUP/pubsres/ academe/2010/JA/feat/pern.htm

9. Statistics Canada, "Graduating in Canada: Profile, Labour Market Outcomes and Student Debt of the Class of 2009/2010, 2013," *The Daily*, November 11, 2014, http://www.statcan .gc.ca/daily-quotidien/141114/dq141114b-eng .htm

10. Most items in bullet list based on Bowler, Michael. "Watch Out for Credit Card Traps." The Lucrative Investor, 2009. From http://www .thelucrativeinvestor.com/watch-credit-card-traps, and Arnold, Chris. "Credit Card Companies Abuse the Unwitting." NPR, November 6, 2007. From http://www.npr.org/templates/story/story .php?storyId=16035323

11. Arthur, Dani. "15 Must-Know Tips for Protecting Your Identity." Bankrate.com, August 5, 2004. From http://www.bankrate.com/brm/news/ cc/20020612a.asp

12. The University of Arizona. "Young Adults Financial Capability: APLUS Arizona Pathways to Life Success for University Students Wave 2." September 2011, p. 29. From http://aplus.arizona .edu/Wave-2-Report.pdf

13. Pythagoras Solar, http://www.pythagoras-solar .com

14. Porter, Eduardo, and Greg Winter. "'04 Graduates Learned Lesson in Practicality." *New York Times,* May 30, 2004, pp. A1 and A24.

CHAPTER 12

1. Statistics Canada, "Population Size and Growth in Canada: Key Results from the 2016 Census," *The Daily*, February 8, 2017, http://www.statcan .gc.ca/daily-quotidien/170208/dq170208a-eng .htm

2. Statistics Canada, "Immigration and Ethnic Diversity in Canada," http://www12.statcan.gc.ca/ nhs-enm/2011/as-sa/99-010-x/99-010-x2011001-eng.cfm

3. Conference Board of Canada, "Employability Skills 2000+," www.conferenceboard.ca/topics/

education/learning-tools/employability-skills
.aspx

4. Berrett, Dan. "What Spurs Students to Stay in College and Learn? Good Teaching Practices and Diversity." The Chronicle of Higher Education, November 6, 2011. From http://chronicle.com/article/What-Spurs-Students-to-Stay-in/129670/#top

5. Dey, Eric L., Gerald Gurin, Patricia Gurin, and Sylvia Hurtado. "Diversity and Higher Education: Theory and Impact on Educational Outcomes." *Harvard Educational Review,* vol. 72, no. 3, Fall 2002. From http://www.temple.edu/tlc/resources/handouts/diversity/Gurin_and_Hurtado.pdf

6. Ibid.

7. Ibid.

8. "Conceptual Frameworks/Models, Guiding Values and Principles." National Center for Cultural Competence, 2002. From http://gucchd.georgetown.edu//nccc/framework.html

9. Information in the sections on the five stages of building competency is based on King, Mark A., Anthony Sims, and David Osher. "How Is Cultural Competence Integrated in Education?" Cultural Competence. From www.air.org/cecp/cultural/Q_integrated.htm#def

10. http://www.chrc-ccdp.gc.ca/eng/content/what-discrimination.

11. Global Community WebNet Ltd. "The Global Community Concept and the Global Governments Federation." February 6, 2006. From http://globalcommunitywebnet.com/gceg/Act2006.htm#chapter4draft

12. Carter, Carol. *Keys to Business Communication: Success in College, Career, & Life*, Upper Saddle River, NJ: Pearson Education, 2012, p. 51.

13. Rowe, W. Glenn, ed. *Cases in Leadership*. 2007. From http://www.corwin.com/upm-data/15104_Rowe_Chapter_01.pdf

14. List and descriptions based on Sternberg, Robert J. *Successful Intelligence*. New York: Plume, 1997, pp. 251–269.

15. Hurtado, Maria Elena. "Chile Invention Protects Tall Buildings from Earthquakes." SciDev.Net, October 22, 2010. From http://www.scidev.net/en/news/chile-invention-protects-tall-buildings-from-earthquakes.html

NAME INDEX

Note: *n* indicates material in a note.

Note: **Bold** page numbers indicate definitions.